The Ecology and Semiotics of Language Learning
A Sociocultural Perspective

Educational Linguistics

Volume 3

General Editor:
Leo van Lier
Monterey Institute of International Studies, U.S.A.

Editorial Board:

Marilda C. Cavalcanti
Universidade Estadual de Campinas, Brazil

Hilary Janks
University of the Witwatersrand, South Africa

Claire Kramsch
University of California, Berkeley, U.S.A.

Alastair Pennycook
University of Technology, Sydney, Australia

The *Educational Linguistics* book series focuses on work that is: innovative, trans-disciplinary, contextualized and critical.

In our compartmentalized world of diverse academic fields and disciplines there is a constant tendency to specialize more and more. In academic institutions, at conferences, in journals, and in publications the crossing of disciplinary boundaries is often discouraged.

This series is based on the idea that there is a need for studies that break barriers. It is dedicated to innovative studies of language use and language learning in educational settings worldwide. It provides a forum for work that crosses traditional boundaries between theory and practice, between micro and macro, and between native, second and foreign language education. The series also promotes critical work that aims to challenge current practices and offers practical, substantive improvements.

The titles published in this series are listed at the end of this volume.

The Ecology and Semiotics of Language Learning
A Sociocultural Perspective

by

Leo van Lier
Monterey Institute of International Studies, U.S.A.

KLUWER ACADEMIC PUBLISHERS
Boston / Dordrecht / New York / London

Distributors for North, Central and South America:
Kluwer Academic Publishers
101 Philip Drive
Assinippi Park
Norwell, Massachusetts 02061 USA
Telephone (781) 871-6600
Fax (781) 681-9045
E-Mail: kluwer@wkap.com

Distributors for all other countries:
Kluwer Academic Publishers Group
Post Office Box 322
3300 AH Dordrecht, THE NETHERLANDS
Telephone 31 786 576 000
Fax 31 786 576 254
E-Mail: services@wkap.nl

Electronic Services < http://www.wkap.nl >

Library of Congress Cataloging-in-Publication Data

Van Lier, Leo
 The ecology and semiotics of language learning: a sociocultural perspective / by Leo van Lier.
  p. cm. – (Educational linguistics ; v.3)
 Includes bibliographical references and index.
ISBN HB: 1-4020-7904-4   PB: 1-4020-7993-1   ISBN E-book: 1-4020-7912-5
 1. Language and languages—Study and teaching—Social aspects. 2. Ecolinguistics. 3. Semiotics. I. Title. II Series.

P53.8.V36 2004
306.44—dc22   2004046572

Copyright © 2004 by Kluwer Academic Publishers

All rights reserved. No part of this work may be reproduced, stored in a retrieval system, or transmitted in any form or by any means, electronic, mechanical, photocopying, microfilming, recording, or otherwise, without the written permission from the Publisher, with the exception of any material supplied specifically for the purpose of being entered and executed on a computer system, for exclusive use by the purchaser of the work.

Permission for books published in Europe: permissions@wkap.nl
Permission for books published in the United States of America: permissions@wkap.com

Printed on acid-free paper.   Printed in the United States of America.

CONTENTS

Preface	vii
Acknowledgements	ix
1. Introduction: Why ecology	1
2. Theories of language	23
3. Semiotics: The making of meaning	55
4. Emergence and affordance	79
5. The self and language learning	107
6. Language learning pathways	133
7. Critical ecological linguistics	165
8. Ecological research	193
Epilogue for language teachers	221
References	225
Index	239

PREFACE

In this book I try to give a coherent and consistent overview of what an ecological approach to language learning might look like. This is not a fully fledged grand theory that aims to provide an explanation of everything, but an attempt to provide a rationale for taking an ecological world view and applying it to language education, which I regard as one of the most important of all human activities.

Goethe once said that everything has been thought of before, but that the difficulty is to think of it again. The same certainly is true of the present effort. If it has any innovative ideas to offer, these lie in a novel combination of thoughts and ideas that have been around for a long, long time. The reader will encounter influences that range from Spinoza to Bakhtin and from Vygotsky to Halliday.

The scope of the work is intentionally broad, covering all major themes that are part of the language learning process and the language teaching profession. These themes include language, perception and action, self, learning, critical pedagogy and research. At the same time I have attempted to look at both the macro and the micro sides of the ecological coin, and address issues from both a theoretical and a practical perspective. This, then, aims to be a book that can be read by practitioners and theoreticians alike, and the main idea is that it should be readable and challenging at the same time.

One of the things this ecological approach promises to do is to give coherence to a collection of ideas and practices that have been increasing in prominence and attraction for some time. Many of these ideas and practices come from different theoretical orientations, or just from good and well-informed practice, and it is assumed here that an ecological approach can lend consistency and methodological rigor to them. In other words, an ecological approach can act as a galvanizing force for many different – though sympathetic – initiatives. Let me briefly mention some of these initiatives. First among them is the current work in the area of sociocultural theory (SCT), which takes guidance from the work of Vygotsky and Bakhtin (as well as later work of Bruner, Mead, Rommetveit and others). In fact, ecology and SCT share many resemblances, as I point out in the first chapter. Yet, I argue here that an ecological foundation can give a theoretical strength and pedagogical focus to SCT that is otherwise not always evident. For example, a theory of language within a theory of semiotics is clearly needed for SCT, and I provide the groundwork for such a theory in chapters two and three.

There is an important and fascinating tradition of ecology in linguistics (sometimes called *ecolinguistics*, as in Fill & Mühlhäusler's recent collection of papers), but by and large this has focused on the macro aspects of the field, e.g. in terms of language contact, policy, linguistic rights, and so on. Vital though this work is (and I draw on it in chapters two and seven), it is worth pointing out that in ecological psychology the focus has been more on the micro side of things, e.g. in the work on developmental ecology of Bronfenbrenner and the work on visual perception of James and Eleanor Gibson. In chapters four and six I apply this more micro perspective to language learning, arguing for a focus on perception-in-action, and examining notions such as emergence, affordance, and scaffolding.

Arguably, one of the most significant developments of recent years is a focus on self and identity. The research in this area is still very tentative and exploratory, but I am convinced that this will be an extremely important aspect of language pedagogy in years to come. In chapter five I explore this concept, drawing on the work of Bakhtin, Neisser, Wiley and others, and trying to lay the foundation for an ecological perspective on the self as social, cultural and spatio-temporal. I realize this is just the foundation, the edifice will still need to be constructed over the years to come, in the face of many political, ideological and institutional battles .

This book is just an initial exploration of the value of an ecological world view for language education. There are many gaps, inaccuracies, and vague areas in the picture as it is drawn so far. It is a sketch rather than a polished work, but I hope it provides enough food for thought and action to set the stage for lively discussion and principled progress.

If I may twist Goethe's words a bit (assuming the bard would approve of the playfulness of it all), nothing has ever been finished before, the difficulty is to avoid thinking we can finish it now. I hope the reader may find some stimulation of thought and practice in these pages, whether this stems from agreement or from disagreement with what is actually said.

ACKNOWLEDGEMENTS

The ideas for this book have grown out of many years of study and teaching, and I must therefore thank all my students, teachers, friends as well as my family for the many years I have been privileged to know them. But I need to be a little more specific than that.

After a number of years of studying sociocultural theory, ecology and semiotics, I had the good fortune, in 2002, to teach two successive graduate seminars while writing the bulk of the book. Both seminars were called *The Ecology of Language Learning*, one took place at the University of Auckland between March and May, the other at Pennsylvania State University, State College, in July. These two classes were instrumental in helping me shape the book and translate vague ideas into some form of comprehensibility. To these students must therefore go my deepest appreciation for their participation, their discussion, their tough questions and doubts, and their – sometimes long-suffering – patience and kindness. In addition, many successive graduate classes in Second Language Acquisition at the Monterey Institute of International Studies have had to put up with my increasing obsession with things ecological and semiotic, perhaps wondering from time to time where I had lost my syllabus. My work as the Director of the Max Kade Language and Technology Center at MIIS allowed me to be involved in computer-assisted language classes applying innovative project-based curricula, under the inspired guidance and creative genius of Bob Cole and others.

I must also thank my colleague Steve Thorne who went through the entire manuscript in its half-baked state of development and who gave me many excellent suggestions and saved me from saying some of the most nonsensical things. My colleague at MIIS Kathi Bailey also commented on some of the early chapters and gave me very useful feedback. Thanks also to Leticia Pastrana who, in her capacity as my research assistant, straightened out chapters and references, looked for gaps and redundancies, gave me many substantive suggestions, and in general kept the work on track. And to Lee-Ellen Mascal and Sarah Springer for their assistance in the final editing and formatting stages. Finally I am extremely grateful for the generous advice and very useful suggestions of two colleagues who reviewed the entire manuscript for Kluwer Academic Publishers. Needless to say, without the help and inspiration of all of these people this book would not exist. However, I must also stress that it is not their fault that I couldn't make it better.

CHAPTER 1

INTRODUCTION

Why ecology?

LANGUAGE IN EDUCATION: MIXED EMOTIONS

Imagine a school without language. Classrooms without explanations, discussions, drills, or admonishments. No opinions from teachers or students. Silent hallways, no voices over loudspeakers, no talk in the front office or the principal's office. No phone calls to and from the district office. No email, no fax, no announcements. In such a language-less environment, hardly any of the activities we associate with education could get accomplished. In our educational systems, language does the educating, language organizes the educational activities, and language supervises, controls and evaluates the educational process. And language, in a significant sense, creates education, perpetuates it, and reproduces it.

Clearly, a school without language could not exist, and education could not take place. Not only is language the vehicle by which education is conducted in every classroom in every school, it is also the main tool by means of which the institution of education is organized. The student records, the database, the codes of conduct, the mission statement, the lunch menu, the evening performance of the theatre club – there is not a single aspect of school life that is not permeated by language.

That is not all, of course. Language is part of other message systems that are tied up with all our sensory systems, and all our memories, and all the stories we construct to create and nurture our identity. It is not possible to sever language from all those ties and yet have education make sense. This observation is the key to linking language to both ecology and semiotics.

What do we remember of school after we've been out of it for ten, twenty, or forty years? What do we remember as the successes and failures of that time, the good and bad moments? What do we answer if we are asked, "In the end, what did you learn?"

Each one of us will come up with moments, memorable occasions and random happenings that somehow stuck with us. Once again, the memories bring forth the language, and the language brings forth the memories. Our schooling becomes a remembered narrative, a narrated memory. This way of looking at education as a narrative or a story is a powerful counterweight to the prevailing view of schooling as an institution and a bureaucracy, enshrined in budgets and buildings, and defined by the collective struggles of administrators, teachers, students and parents. The ecology of schooling and of language learning takes into account both the narrative (or discursive) and the institutional structures of education.

LANGUAGE IN EDUCATION

This book is an introduction to the field of language education, seen from an ecological and sociocultural perspective. In this introductory chapter I will provide a rationale for taking such a perspective, explain what ecology means in this context, and why it provides a different outlook on the role of language in education. I hope to convince the reader that this is a fresh and different approach to the role of language in education in general, and to first and subsequent language education in particular.

The role of language in education is not limited to first, second or foreign language classes, it pervades all of education, in all subjects. In my account in this book I will often use examples of second or foreign language teaching since this is my primary area of experience, but most of the arguments are also relevant to all educational activity in all subject matter areas, whether they be science, language, mathematics, sports, painting, or whatever. All education is language education, since language is a defining quality of what it means to be human.

There is clearly a very tight relationship between language and education at the practical level, but at the theoretical and academic level the two disciplines, education and linguistics, appear to be poles apart. Academic compartmentalization, the *balkanization* that Hargreaves talks about (1994), makes it difficult to focus on the dynamic and central role that language plays, and in my ecological account I hope to show how a more integrated and holistic view of language and education can give a deeper understanding of the nature of education.

In earlier work (van Lier, 1994a), I argued for a new field of *educational linguistics*. If we define field as a socially, historically, and politically constituted and institutionalized area of human knowledge and activity which has its own discourse practices, its academic departments, its journals and conferences, and its entitled members and practitioners (cf. Bourdieu, 1991), then educational linguistics is not a field. However, there are many university departments that explicitly aim to combine an educational and linguistic focus or a focus on *language education* (see van Lier, 1994a; Brumfit, 1997; Hornberger, 2001). These include departments called *educational linguistics*, and also departments of applied linguistics, of ESL, of SLA, of language studies, modern languages, and so on.

The terms *ecology of language learning*, and *educational linguistics*, as used in this book are best seen not as a separate field or discipline but as a *transdisciplinary* endeavor (Halliday, 2001). As I have argued elsewhere (van Lier, 1994a; 1994c), this homeless, nomadic, academically disembodied, and non-franchised field of work (or dream of field) might fulfill a useful function for linguistics and for education in two ways:

a) for linguistics, it would inform the theoretical linguistics community of educational issues regarding language learning and language use (Firth & Wagner, 1997) that could improve the teaching of language in the schools, the relevance of linguistic theories in the real world, and the teaching of linguistics to undergraduates and graduates the world over;

b) for education, it would make the study of language a more central, relevant, and interesting part of the education of teachers, especially since they increasingly face linguistically heterogeneous classes of students (Trappes-Lomax & Ferguson, 2002).

The inseparable connection between language and education lies at the core of the ecological approach to language learning described in this book. In this book I will look at language from an educational perspective, and at education from a linguistic perspective. The connections require both a practical, pedagogical and a theoretical, philosophical perspective. The ecological approach developed here is neither a theory nor a method. It is a way of thinking and a way of acting. It draws, however, on specific theoretical positions in linguistics and in learning, and these will be outlined in the chapters to follow. The goal is not to provide readymade answers or prescriptions, but to provide food for thought, to encourage reflection about language and education, and to stimulate critical discussion.

ECOLOGY: DEEP AND SHALLOW

The earth has a skin and that skin has diseases; one of its diseases is called man.
- Friedrich Nietzsche (1844-1900)

Ecology[1] as a scientific discipline was established around the middle of the 19th century, when the term was invented by the German biologist Ernst Haeckel (Arndt & Janney, 1983) to refer to the totality of relationships of an organism with all other organisms with which it comes into contact. Originally, ecology was the study and management of the environment (ecosphere, or biosphere) or specific ecosystems. However, it is nowadays also used to denote a world view that is completely different from the scientific or rational one inherited from Descartes and some of his contemporaries, which assumes that it is the right and destiny of the human race to control and exploit the earth and all its inanimate and animate resources (the *anthropocentric* world view). The ecological worldview is, by contrast, *ecocentric* or *geocentric*, and it assumes that humans are part of a greater natural order, or even a great living system, Gaia (the living earth; see Capra, 1996; Goldsmith, 1998; Lovelock, 1979; as well as the indigenous peoples of North and South America and elsewhere). This view of ecology is called *deep ecology*[2] by the Norwegian philosopher Arne Naess, and is contrasted with *shallow ecology*, which studies ways of controlling ecosystems and managing them (Allen & Hoekstra, 1992).

Since ecology studies organisms in their relations with the environment, ecology is a contextualized or situated form of research. Traditional science controls the environment conceptually or experimentally, and selects from the complexity particular phenomena to be observed, manipulated and measured. The value of such

---

[1] The prefix *eco* (also in economics) is derived from a Greek word (oekos) meaning *household*.
[2] Related movements are eco-feminism and radical ecology.

procedures is not in doubt, given the enormous progress that has been made over the centuries in many areas of science and technology. However, there is also no doubt that this progress has been costly in terms of environmental problems and the deterioration of ecosystems worldwide. Corresponding to this reality, there are two basic approaches to ecological work. One is to use the methods of traditional science to prevent, solve or minimize the environmental impact of human activity and natural disasters, the management of the environment mentioned in the previous paragraph (*shallow* ecology). This includes such fields as environmental engineering, waste management, recycling, reforestation, pollution control, and so on. It involves the measurement of certain particles in the air and water, tracking and checking the presence of crucial species in ecosystems, studying the effects of urban water drainage on wetlands, and so on.

Another approach is to seek new methods of research that take account of the full complexity and interrelatedness of processes that combine to produce an environment. This approach (i.e., deep ecology) links up with systems theory and cybernetics, and in more recent years also with chaos and complexity theory (see Chapter 8).

Both perspectives can inform educational research and practice, in fact, they do not have to be mutually exclusive. Ecological engineering, management and repair are necessary in a world in which the environment is clearly under extreme stress. It is not too farfetched to say that the same is true of educational, social and economic systems. Ecological studies can help provide understanding and suggest treatment. However, the dominant dynamic can very easily be one of crisis management, a constant fixing of things gone awry. In addition, it can create the (probably false) impression that everything can be 'fixed,' and the status quo in terms of exploitation and contamination can be maintained. The second approach (*deep* ecology) proposes that 'fixing' is not enough, adds a sense of vision, purpose, and an overt ideology of transformation (a critical perspective), and is the one I will primarily focus on here for an ecological perspective on language education.

The ecological approach has a number of characteristics that will be addressed in many different ways in the pages that follow (see especially a further elaboration on deep and critical ecology in Chapter 7). These characteristics are not exclusive to the ecological approach in each and every case, but in their totality they amount to a new way of looking at language learning. As a signposting exercise and a statement of purpose, here are brief descriptions of the main characteristics, not in any particular order.

RELATIONS

Ecological linguistics (EL) focuses on language as relations between people and the world, and on language learning as ways of relating more effectively to people and the world. The crucial concept is that of *affordance*, which means a relationship between an organism (a learner, in our case) and the environment, that signals an opportunity for or inhibition of action.[3] The environment includes all physical,

---

[3] It may appear curious that an affordance may inhibit as well as instigate action. We will have more to say about this in Chapter 4, but for now, imagine a hot stove. It has a number of properties that can

social and symbolic affordances that provide grounds for activity. The notion of *relation* permeates all the topics discussed in the book: language, learning, action, curriculum. If we see language as a system of relations, rather than a collection of objects, a number of consequences follow in terms of how we define linguistics, and how we conceptualize learning. *See further: Halliday, 1993; Harris, 1996; Saussure, 1983.*

CONTEXT

EL regards context as not just something that surrounds language, but that in fact defines language, while at the same time being defined *by* it. A common piece of advice in research is "to take the context into account." Such advice raises questions like how, how much, what aspects of the context, and so on. It also suggests that contextual information is added on to whatever is investigated, in a supplementary sort of way. But in ecology, context is the heart of the matter. *See further: Drew & Heritage, 1992; Duranti & Goodwin, 1992.*

PATTERNS, SYSTEMS

EL sees language as patterns of patterns, and systems of systems. "Patterns that connect," as Bateson used to say. Words like *pattern* and *system* sidestep the notion of *rules* and *structures*. The latter terms are associated with predetermined and predictable states of affairs, situations that are more or less fixed and that remain the same over time and space. *See further: Bateson, 1979; Capra, 1996; see also Chapter 8.*

EMERGENCE

EL regards language learning not as gradual, linear acquisition, but as emergence. Emergence happens when relatively simple elements combine together to form a higher-order system. The whole is not only more than the sum of its parts, it is of a different nature than the parts. The new system is on a different scale, and has different meanings and patterns of functioning than the simpler ingredients had from which it emerged. In language, grammar emerges from lexis (Bates & Goodman, 1999), symbols emerge from tools (Vygotsky, 1978), learning emerges from participation (Lave & Wenger, 1991). Language proficiency emerges from all these transformations. *See further: Hopper, 1998; Johnson, 2001; MacWhinney, 1999.*

QUALITY

EL makes the notion of quality a central construct to be investigated. The quality of educational experience is seen to be crucially different from educational standards, though a valid ecological aim of education is to harmonize quality and standards, by investigating both how they are different and how they are related. Arne Naess pointed out long ago that quality of life is not the same as standard of living. Our

---

become affordances for the people around it. In terms of activity, it can promote culinary activity, conversation on a cold winter evening, warmth for the room, and so on. In terms of inhibiting action, it can burn you, so it inhibits touching.

standard of living may be so high that we have three shiny cars parked in front of the house. If everybody's standard of living is this high, our quality of life may be reduced because the air is polluted, the noise level increases, and we can't walk around the neighborhood any more. The same may be true (in different ways, of course) in education: there may be so much focus on higher standards that there are tougher and tougher tests all the time, and there is no more time for music, field trips, art, and just exploring knowledge and broadening one's mind. *See further: Naess, 1989; Capra, 1996; Goldsmith, 1998.*

VALUE

EL proclaims that all action, all research, all practice, is value-laden, value-driven, and value producing. It says that language education is, in addition to whatever else it is, always also a *science of values* (Reed, 1996). This goes against the traditional Cartesian ideal of science, which separated the *res cogitans* (the domain of theology) from the *res extensa* (the domain of science). The object of this enterprise was "to carve out a sphere of influence for science so that it would be freed from the shackles of theological control, and at the same time, to reassure the Church that science was not threatening to take over its territory" (Goldsmith 1998, p. 6). The resulting view of science is one that sets aside issues of morality and social concerns, and it is dominant to this day, with all the pernicious consequences that have followed therefrom. This explains why Chomsky separates his scientific work (generative linguistics) from his political activism, and cannot conceive that one might be relevant to the other. Instead, EL asserts that we can – and should – define science (and its processes of production and consumption) in a different way, as a critical and moral enterprise. *See further: Bowers, 1993; Capra, 1996; Goldsmith, 1998.*

CRITICAL

If we look at language learning from a contextual perspective, if we put quality before quantity, and if we focus on value and values rather than on so-called objective facts or the status quo, then it is inevitable that our approach will be a critical one. In other words, we will examine to what extent educational practices further the specific goals and ideals that we have articulated. If they do not, then we will elaborate practices that *do* further those goals and ideals. The critical perspective requires a constant evaluation of what is actually happening (what we are doing, in other words) with what we think (in line with our principles, moral values, and so on) *should* be happening. It is not an indoctrination into any particular way of thinking, but rather a call to critical thinking and critical acting, based on well-articulated principles and personal convictions. Notions of power and constraints on principled action (by bureaucratic and other forms of irrational control) will undoubtedly come to the fore in any critical approach to thought and action, and when that happens, critical ecology implies an activist stance. *See further: Bowers, 1993; Pennycook, 2001.*

VARIABILITY

A teacher might proudly announce: "I treat them all the same." But children – learners of all ages for that matter – are all different, so that equal treatment is surely a doubtful pedagogical practice. There are many differences among learners that are relevant to their educational opportunities in general, and their classroom learning opportunities in particular. A good teacher understands the learners, and this means taking the differences into account. However, there is also variability at a much more macro level: educational systems, far from being the equalizers that policy makers suggest they are,[4] actually manufacture inequalities across regional and socio-economic fault lines. Not all schools are created equal in any country, so that school systems both homogenize and select at the same time, however paradoxical this may seem. *See further: Bourdieu, 1991; Gardner, 1993; McLaren, 1998.*

DIVERSITY

Diversity relates to variability, but it is not the same. Whereas variability relates to the ways different learners learn, and what that means for the teacher, diversity addresses the value of having different learners and teachers in a class (or school), and in more general terms, different kinds of people in a society, rather than a homogeneous population, however defined. In biology, diversity is essential in an ecosystem,[5] and in the same way, a diverse society (in terms of language, ethnicity, religion, interests, etc.) may be healthier in the long run than a homogeneous one. In addition, the language to be learned (whether L1 or L2) is presented as one that is not one monolithic standardized code, but a collection of dialects, genres and registers. It is often tacitly assumed that learners would be confused by being presented with a diversity of dialects, cultures, social customs, but it can be argued that more confusion ultimately results from the presentation of a homogeneous language and a single speech community, generalizations that in fact do not exist. With appropriate language and learning awareness activities, learners should be perfectly capable of understanding diversity, since it will be easy to establish that it exists in the language all around them, at home, in the community, in school, and around the world. The reader be warned: this is a very tricky and loaded subject, one that raises passions rather than rational argument. *See further: Phelan & Davidson, 1993; Miramontes, Nadeau & Commins, 1997.*

ACTIVITY

Ecological linguistics studies language and language learning as areas of activity. Gone is the picture of a classroom with rows of empty heads passively soaking up knowledge issuing forth (in the form of pedagogical discourse) from the talking

---

[4] At the time of writing, the operative equalizing slogan of the George W. Bush administration in the USA is "No Child Left Behind," yet, given drastic reductions in funding, the only things that children are not left behind on, especially in the poorest schools, are standardized tests. As W. himself put it so eloquently, while addressing a schoolful of adolescents, "Taking tests aren't fun... too bad!" (TV News, 2002).

[5] More on this in Chapter 7. In ecological terms, more diversity is not necessarily always better. However, reducing diversity is almost always detrimental to an ecosystem. The crucial variable is *balance*.

head at the front of the room. Instead, we visualize a community of practice in which learners go about the business of learning by carrying out activities of various kinds, working together, side by side, or on their own. In this ecosystem, learners are autonomous, i.e., they are allowed to define the meaning of their own acts within their social context *(Shotter 1984, p. 147, cited in Oyama, 2000, p.189)*. Autonomy in an ecological approach does not mean independence or individualism, however. It means having the authorship of one's actions, having the voice that speaks one's words, and being emotionally connected to one's actions and speech (Damasio, 2003), within one's community of practice *(Wenger, 1998)*. This type of autonomy is dialogical in Bakhtin's sense (1981): socially produced, but appropriated and made one's own. *See further: Engeström, Miettinen & Punamäki, 1999; Wenger, 1998.*

All these characteristics form the basis for much more detailed examination later on in this book.

ECOLOGY IN THE SOCIAL SCIENCES

We can distinguish several broad strands of ecological work in the social sciences: anthropological, educational, psychological, and linguistic. All these strands have their separate trajectories, but they also intermingle in a number of ways and directions. Around and above these disciplinary approaches there are certain philosophical and ethical perspectives as well. Here I will focus on the classical, founding texts. Then, in subsequent chapters, I will explore in more detail how current work builds on these foundations.

In the opening pages of his book on chaos and complexity, Roger Lewin (1993) describes a trip to Chaco Canyon in New Mexico, and addresses the mysterious disappearance of the Anasazi culture. Apparently, this advanced society once flourished in the region, only to collapse suddenly and inexplicably almost a thousand years ago. There is no clear explanation for this, but chaos theory and complexity theory look at such phenomena as the evolution of complex adaptive systems, and of attractors that can suddenly bring about huge changes after periods of relative calm. Surface complexity arises out of deep simplicity, and big changes can come of small events (the butterfly effect – see Chapter 8).

Applying the notions of chaos and complexity to language learning (Larsen-Freeman, 1997, 2002) can have a number of consequences for the way in which we think about 'learning.' Within an ecosystem, including any social ecosystem (a family, a classroom, a school – see Bronfenbrenner, 1979) a large number of influences are present in a partially chaotic, that is, unpredictable and uncontrolled way, and somehow among all the movement and interaction a social system, a complex order emerges. This order, which is dynamic rather than static, provides affordances for active participants in the setting, and learning emerges as part of affordances being picked up and exploited for further action. This view of situated learning is quite different from the assumptions of scientific research in which every input has an output, and every effect has an identifiable cause preceding it. Investigating learning from this perspective cannot be done effectively by using the methods of traditional experimental science. New ways of doing scientific work are therefore needed.

For a long time there has been a struggle to put the social sciences (the human sciences, the humanities, etc.) on the scientific map. In many traditions, such as ancient Chinese philosophy, Indian philosophy, the narrative traditions of many African, American and European peoples, ancient Greek and Etruscan thought, and so on, such a split between 'scientific' and 'non-scientific' work does not exist. It is important that we remember such traditions, if only to avoid the temptation to regard scientific thought as the unquestionable pinnacle of all human endeavor.

In the Western tradition, science emerges as a dominant force in terms of prestige around the time of the Renaissance, with the work of Galileo, Bacon, Descartes, Newton, and others. Of course, the roots of science go much further back, to Pythagoras, Aristotle, Avicenna and so on. But the real split between scientific and 'other' work became canonized in the work of Descartes, who set up a dichotomy between the realms of religion and the realms of science (although William of Occam had already ventured to do so more than two centuries earlier). One reason to do so was presumably to avoid having his heretical head removed by the Papal authorities (Descartes was surely familiar with the fate of Bruno).

After Descartes and others separated the scientific enterprise from the rest (religion, mysticism, alchemy, magic, and art), the scientific revolution began in earnest. Enormous progress was made in a number of fields with truly astounding results: the proof that the earth was round, explanations of gravity, motion, magnetism, electricity – the list goes on and on. Add to this the rise of technology, starting with Galileo's makeshift telescope, and culminating in the almighty automobile barely three centuries later. It is easy to be captivated by the lure of science, illuminated by the glitter of technology, and understand why it would end up stealing the limelight from quiet religious pursuits such as piety and penance.

Physics has long been the science *par excellence*. To be sure, other fields such as medicine and biology produced interesting new ideas (nothing really dramatic, though, until Darwin's theory of evolution in the latter part of the 19th Century, and Pasteur's work in vaccination), but physics stole the show. As Lord Rutherford remarked, famously, "There is physics and there is stamp collecting." Nowadays, of course, physics has taken a turn towards uncertainty (e.g., in quantum theory), and biology appears to be the new science *par excellence* (Capra, 1996).

There have been many proposals to establish the social sciences on the basis of research methodologies and ways of theory construction that are different from the standard scientific models. Indeed, ecological approaches are not the only ones that examine scientific models in a critical light (e.g., Passmore, 1978), but ecology is what I will focus on here.

Scientific work requires at least three levels of reductionism: *context* reduction, *data* reduction, and *complexity* reduction (Checkland, 1981):

CONTEXT REDUCTION

In order to conduct coherent investigations it is necessary to simplify and select from the infinite variety of the real world. This means that potentially significant aspects of the environment or setting may simply be ignored, or that contextual variables are eliminated by setting up experiments in controlled settings. The problem is that learners may not behave in controlled experiments the way that they behave in natural learning environments.

DATA REDUCTION

In accordance with Occam's razor, the simplest explanations that minimally account for the data are to be preferred. This law of parsimony is designed to cut the fat from theorizing, but it presupposes that we already know how to distinguish fat from lean; in other words, it is based on prior assumptions about importance. The danger here is that we overlook things that may be important.

COMPLEXITY REDUCTION

Problems must be broken down into their component elements and these must be analyzed one by one. Language learning in classroom is undoubtedly a complex affair, so how are we going to document that learning occurs? One way to do so is to focus on one component that we assume is important, let's say correction of errors. If an error is corrected and replaced by a correct item, and then henceforth the learner doesn't make the error any more, then we have isolated one clear element of learning. We can then go on to other elements that we might tackle separately, and thus, over time, build a picture of learning based on all these pieces of the puzzle. A problem with this approach is that it may be difficult – or impossible – to establish how various learning elements are related.

Educational linguistics has not escaped the pressure exerted by the physical sciences (the "aristo-sciences" as Passmore called them – see Goldsmith, 1998) in terms of how scientific activity is defined, and what counts as legitimate research activity. Central to this legitimacy is the use of numbers. Galileo said: "That which cannot be measured and reduced to numbers is not real" (cited in Goldsmith, 1998, p. 61). Of course, we have to realize that he was referring to observing movements of planets and moons through a rickety home-made telescope, a task complicated by weak lenses and weakening eyesight. "I think it moved a bit to the right since yesterday" clearly does not sound very convincing, and it is understandable that careful numerical documentation of movement over a long period of time is required to achieve some consistency in patterns.

The need for numerical precision in the work of Galileo is entirely reasonable, but that does not mean that it can be or has to be applied to all other fields of enquiry. Yet, such has been the dominance of the physical sciences in terms of theories, methods, and not least prestige, that all incipient researchers and disciplines have sought (or have been coerced) to emulate them, whether the types of phenomena and data have been suitable for such an approach or not.

In recent years the respectability of qualitative (i.e., non-quantitative) approaches to EL has grown, along with a greater acceptance of such approaches across the social sciences in general. When issues of power and territory (and in some cases, invested egos) are stripped away, a few real issues remain that are common across both quantitative and qualitative ways of doing research. What are these issues? I suggest that they are often expressed as dichotomies, in an either/or fashion and here are a few of them:

theory	←--------------------------------→	*practice*
commonality	←--------------------------------→	*variation*
whole	←--------------------------------→	*parts*
linearity	←--------------------------------→	*emergence*
nature	←--------------------------------→	*nurture*
product	←--------------------------------→	*process*

How do dichotomies such as these influence language education? Even though all these dichotomies may well be false ones, they do produce common trains of thought in curriculum development, research and language policy. On the other hand, sometimes even common acceptance of a particular feature may not be enough to change educational practices. For example, I take it that pretty much everybody (including administrators and politicians) agrees that all learners are different, that they learn at different rates and in different ways. Yet, when the current US President George W. Bush emphatically proclaims that 'no child will be left behind,' meaning that all will be tested frequently in exactly the same way, the surface assumption is that they all *should* be the same, or perhaps *become* the same. Bureaucratic convenience and political expediency therefore easily override even the most commonly held beliefs, and the most firmly established research findings. In reality, the across the board testing system produces a failure/dropout rate of about 30% (especially among students for whom English is not the native language or dialect), something the politicians appear to find perfectly acceptable so long as it can be ignored.

The ecological approach looks at the entire situation and asks, what is it in this environment that makes things happen the way they do? How does learning come about? Ecology therefore involves the study of context (see Chapters 2, 8). In addition, things are happening all the time, in schools, classrooms, at desks and around computers. So, ecology is also the study of movement, process, and action. Most educational research tries to pinpoint the immediate, short-term, tangible effects of instruction. We teach a unit, then test the students to see if they 'learned' the material. We judge the success of education on the basis of its measurable products. Standards, national curricula, course materials, accountability, all these are premised upon short-term results, the products of instruction.

In this context, I'd like to quote a remark made by Ludwig Wittgenstein: "There are remarks that sow, and remarks that reap" (1980, p. 78e). Classrooms and schools are contexts designed to afford opportunities for learning, and they may be more or less successful at doing this. Learning opportunities can be of a sowing, or of a reaping kind. Which ones are more important, more valuable, deeper, more lasting, and more powerful? Furthermore, do we know (as teachers, as learners) when a learning opportunity is of a sowing or of a reaping kind? How can we tell? I take it that in the reaping scenario we can tell, because we hold something in our hand, we can see and point to a specific item, let's say a performance of some kind by the learner, or a number of bubbles correctly filled in on a test sheet. But in the sowing situation we may be unable to tell, the seeds lie hidden beneath the surface, and may or may not bear fruit, at some unspecified time in the future, in some unspecified way. That is too much uncertainty for learners, teachers, administrators, let alone politicians. For all practical purposes then, the sowing side of learning tends to be ignored, and the focus is on reaping, or at best on a souped-up crop cycle. If I sow a learning seed on Monday, I want to see a crop by Friday at the latest, because that's when we have the weekly achievement quiz. What good are the results of education that only appear at a distant time, and that cannot even be linked to specific teaching events? I, as a teacher, can neither be held accountable for them nor be rewarded for them.

The results of education that fall within the purview of standards, evaluations, performance reviews, accountability, and standardized tests are nothing but the shells that we find on the beach. They tell us that there is life in the ocean, but they do no more than give a hint of its nature and its variety.

Ecology wants to find a way to look deeper and further; it will address the notion of the *quality* of educational experience, as different from the documentation of educational *standards*. This is difficult, though I do not think that it is impossible. What is far more difficult is trying to convince educational policy makers that the pursuit of high standards, linked to mechanisms of accountability via high-stakes tests, does not promote educational quality.

ECOLOGY AND SOCIOCULTURAL THEORY (SCT)

SCT can be defined as a general approach to the human sciences whose goal it is "to explicate the relationships between mental functioning, on the one hand, and the cultural, institutional, and historical situations in which this functioning occurs, on the other" (Wertsch, Del Rio & Alvarez, 1995, p. 3). Michael Cole, in a similar vein, expands SCT into a *socio-cultural-historical* approach, one that is primarily concerned with the artifacts constructed over time in societies, and how these mediate in human activity (1995). Other terms used in relation to SCT include *sociohistorical* and *social constructionist* (Lantolf, 2000, p. 155), and *social interactionist* (Nystrand, 1992; van Lier, 1996).

The most central construct in SCT is *mediation*, in three ways: through tools and artifacts; through interaction; and through the use of signs (Ellis, 2003). More specifically, in second language learning, mediation involves (1) mediation by others in social interaction, (2) mediation by self through private speech and (3) mediation by artifacts (e.g. tasks and technology) (Ellis, q.v.; Lantolf, 2000). One might add to this, mediation by signs, by the native and other languages, and so on.

Mediation cuts across two major domains of study in Vygotsky's theory: the *phylogenetic* domain, which comprises both biological-evolutionary and social-cultural-historical development, yielding structures and institutions within which the child or learner is embedded; the *ontogenetic* domain, which includes the interactional processes in which social meanings become internalized, and the use of language and signs, linked with the development of higher mental functions (sometimes referred to as the *microgenetic* realm, see Wertsch, 1985). We thus have four interlinked planes (or scales, were we to use ecological terminology[6]): the biological-evolutionary, the social-cultural-historical, the interactional-dialogical, and the mental-symbolic.

In ecological research, analysis of one scale always needs to be conducted in the context of analysis of the scale above and the scale below. Taking the scale of mediated activity as the focal scale, the scale above is the social-cultural historical one, and the scale below is the mental-symbolic one (see the module - domain - field description in Chapter 8). This depth approach allowed Vygotsky to escape the limitations of the cross-sectional approach then predominant in psychology (Leontiev, 1997, p. 21). He followed here suggestions made by Kurt Lewin at the time, contrasting *phenotypic* (the study and description of actual objects and events, of external reality) and *genotypic* (explanation, including origin, development and essential features) analysis, and arguing that his developmental study (based on mediation) addressed both, but without confusing them.[7] The third scale, the one below the focal one, is the scale of mental processes that are of course not directly observable. However, the mediation process, especially in the differences between unmediated and mediated activity, allows the researcher a glimpse of where the developmental process is headed. Figure 1.1 below attempts to represent the various aspects of Vygotsky's developmental method graphically. Assuming this to be a fair representation of the core of SCT, now comes the question, how is this different from an ecological perspective? What does the latter add?

First, two caveats. It must be borne in mind that the term SCT itself is not clear-cut, homogeneous or uncontested. As partially signaled above, closely related designations include sociohistorical, activity-theoretical, social interactionist, and social constructionist (or social constructivist) approaches. All these names, and I'm sure there are several more, refer to very closely related perspectives, referring mostly to special emphases or foci, to mixed allegiances to different founding schools of thought, and to different traditions of schooling. Thus, we should expect there to be neither clear boundaries nor deep-seated disputes between these variants.

---

[6] In ecology, scales operate on separate spatial and temporal dimensions. The cultural-historical scale operates on a slower cycle and a larger terrain than the interactional-dialogical one, and this in turn on a slower time scale and a larger terrain than the mental-symbolic one. This means that changes in one scale may take time to effect changes in other scales, and studies of influences from scale to scale need to take temporal and spatial dimensions into account. In chaos theory this relates to phase transitions.

[7] As Steve Thorne points out (personal communication, 2003), in biology the terms genotypic and phenotypic have a different meaning from those employed by Vygotsky and Lewin. Genotype, in biology, refers to the propensity of the gene, whereas phenotype is the ecologically valid outcome (gene + context), that takes into account social-material conditions as co-evolutionary principles. Phenotype is thus the product of an interaction between the innate and the environment.

RESEARCH: GENOTYPIC

```
phylogenetic            | ontogenetic
                        | microgenetic
                        |
                        |      mental processes
                        |      mediation
                        |      activity
```

PHENOTYPIC

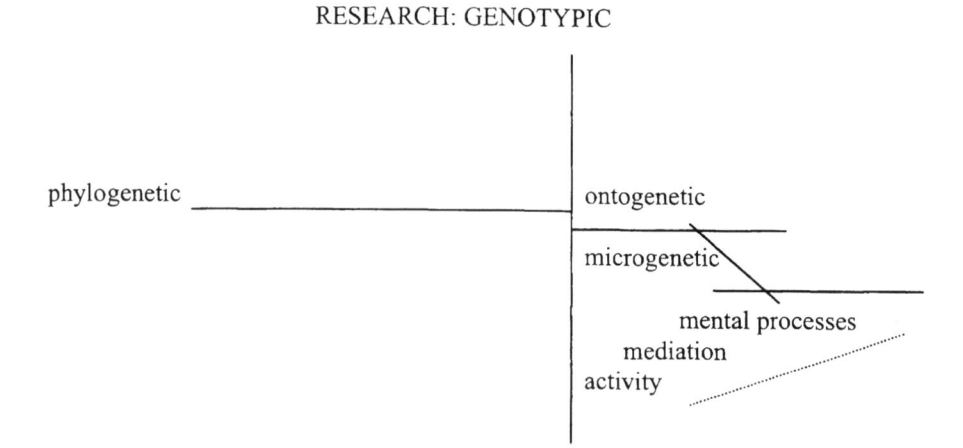

| the self: | me | - | I | - | you |

```
species              social   - individual -   social
PAST                 PRESENT                   FUTURE
  evolution...history...culture...   practices....projects...becoming...
```

Figure 1.1: Vygotsky's developmental method.

Second, ecological theories also come in various flavors. I have already mentioned the distinction between deep and shallow ecology (note that there are fundamental disputes between these two). Further, there is a clear distinction between macro perspectives that study language diversity, contact, imperialism, nationalism and related issues (see Chapter 7), and the micro perspective of affordances, perception, action and emergence (see Chapter 4). So far, to my knowledge, these perspectives remain largely disconnected, but over time this lack of connection can and must be overcome.

Here I will answer from the perspective in which I have formulated my own view of the *ecology of language learning*, the focus of which is primarily on the micro level, even though I will attempt to provide some links to macro issues (much more in this direction needs to be done).

SCT draws mainly on the work of Vygotsky, supplemented in most cases by the work of specific followers or interpreters, such as Leontiev, Luria, Wertsch (for an overview, see Wertsch, 1985), and in SLA, Lantolf, Kramsch, Donato (among others, for an overview, see Lantolf, 2000). Variously, the work of other, related scholars is drawn into the interpretive work: Bakhtin (1981) and his dialogical perspective on language (Rommetveit, 1974; Wells, 1999; Bakhurst, 1991); Dewey (1938) and his social behaviorism and democracy of education (Greeno, 1997; Kohonen, 2001); Mead (1934) and his symbolic interactionism (Wiley, 1994); Bateson (1973, 1979) and the ecology of mind (Bowers, 1993); Peirce (1992, 1998) and semiotics (Kramsch, 2000; van Lier, 2000); Wittgenstein and his meaning-as-use view of language (Bakhurst, 1991; van Lier, 1996); Gibson (1979) and the ecology of perception (Reed, 1996; Neisser, 1988; van Lier, 2000), and so on. Out of these mixes of various foundational sources new angles and slants emerge that do not necessarily revise or reject SCT, but envelop it in different global perspectives. And there are a number of other related key figures I have not even mentioned: Piaget, Bruner, Bronfenbrenner, Bernstein, Harris, Halliday, Hasan, and others – their voices will also sound in the chapters to follow. Many of the researchers and scholars who are relevant in our search for new approaches to language education do not refer to their work as SCT, but nevertheless it is relevant, related, and useful. The boundaries of SCT and ecology are highly permeable, as I believe they should be. Below, I shall elaborate briefly on SCT from past, current and future perspectives.

PAST

Vygotsky, whose work forms the core of SCT, did not present a finished or homogeneous body of work. Despite the undeniable fact that he produced an astonishing volume of work in both quantity and quality within a productive period of not much more than a dozen years, there are many unfinished and open-ended aspects to his work. This is not an indictment; it is an inevitable consequence of his untimely death at the age of 38, in 1934 (Vygodskaia, 1995). Vygotsky was increasingly interested, in the last few years of his life, in placing the word and its meaning (his basic unit of analysis) in the context of its use (we think of Wittgenstein here). This work remained unfinished, as did the notion of activity as a basic meaning-producing unit (his use of the unit *word*, has been a problem for many interpreters – see Lantolf [2000] on 'unit of analysis'). Further, the ZPD was extended by Vygotsky himself from a measurement context to a pedagogical context, while maintaining the asymmetry of the expert and the novice as a basic model (for more discussion, see Chapter 6; also, Wells, 1999). Even though the emphasis was on an inequality of skills and knowledge, and not on an inequality of power, the important notion of symmetry versus equality (van Lier, 1996) was itself not fully problematized. The other side of that coin, the emphasis on symmetry as *opposed* to inequality, an equal if not more serious muddle, was presented in the work of Piaget (1978) and Freire (1972), among others. It is clearly left to us to work out the consequences of this problematization (van Lier, 1996). The ambiguous status of the notion of ZPD, and the attendant pedagogizing of it in the processes of scaffolding, have led to a proliferation of interpretations and exemplifications, some more productive and justifiable than others. In some accounts any 'helping' or 'teaching' is called scaffolding or working in the ZPD, and the construct is in danger of becoming meaningless. See in this context Dunn and Lantolf's (1998) discussion of Krashen's $i+1$ (the idea that comprehensible input is all that is needed for L2 acquisition to take place, so long as it contains structures that are just a little bit ahead of the student's current level; see Krashen, 1985), and the ways in which this is incommensurable with the ZPD. The roles of pedagogy, engagement, activity, and co-construction can all too easily be ignored, turning the ZPD into a dangerously mechanical and asocial didactics.

A further historical issue is that of mediation. Here, the work of James Gibson throws an apparent spanner in the Vygotskyan works: Gibson says that perception is not primarily mediated, it is immediate, and the affordances that emerge in interaction are both *mediated* and *immediate*, in a dynamism that is not yet well understood, particularly as it relates to human social activity and language. Here a significant amount of work remains to be done, though it is foreshadowed, as so many other ideas, in the work of Vygotsky (see also Trevarthen, 1990).

CURRENT

We are now where we are, in the present time, over seven decades after Vygotsky's death, and the world is not the same as it was then. At the time of Vygotsky's death, his contemporary Jean Piaget still had more than four decades of intensive and very active work ahead of him. We have seen educational reform after educational reform, breaking like waves on the rocks of institutional inertia, opposing doctrines of democratization and centralized control, the rise of communication as a guiding metaphor for human activity and learning, and the explosion of new technologies in education and the world at large.

It would be unthinkable that Vygotsky's thought and work would be the same had it concluded in the year 2000 rather than in the year 1934. If he could have been informed by the philosophy of language of Wittgenstein, of the dialogical perspective of Bakhtin,[8] of the semiotics of C.S. Peirce, and other 20th century developments in language, psychology, philosophy and education, this no doubt would have enriched his work, in the same way that it was enriched by early Gestalt theory, his conversations with Kurt Lewin (Vygodskaia, 1995), Marxism, his studies of Piaget, Buhler, Kohler, Freud, and so on.

As I said, standing where we now stand, we clearly need to place the deep insights afforded by Vygotsky's theories in the context in which we live and work, taking account of all the influences that are available to inform us. This is currently being done by most of those who characterize their work as SCT, both in SLA and elsewhere, and hence I mentioned above that SCT is neither homogeneous nor uncontested. Starting from the ideas that have come down to our field from their Vygotskyan origins, or SCT in a narrow or 'orthodox' sense, I feel it is necessary for an educational linguist to re-contextualize and if necessary transform these original ideas into a present-day model for language education that takes account of all we have been able to learn to date from the best minds in the field.

---

[8] Although it is not clear that Vygotsky was directly familiar with the work of Bakhtin, he agreed with other leading intellectuals of the time that "dialogue is the most natural form of oral speech" (1987, p. 272). At the same time he considered written speech "the polar opposite of oral speech" (ibid.), a position Bakhtin would not have shared.

FUTURE

I don't pretend to be much of a futurologist, but there is no doubt that educational work must bear in mind both the desired future shape of educational activities and the lifelong careers and well-being of our students. It is part of the value system of educational work that it must be driven by what we regard as worthwhile and valuable outcomes in the future. We should put aside as immoral any views that consider students only or primarily as economic units (useful and productive citizens – in other words, fodder for a commercial and political machinery, or Foucault's *homo docilis*, 1977). Good teachers of course always see their students as whole persons, but at times they are almost forced into seeing their students as potential test scores, in the name of standards and accountability. An ecological and sociocultural perspective helps to provide a counter-balance and new arguments against the commercialization of schooling.

How does SCT assist us in achieving a critical stance, a practical ideology as to what a responsible and future-oriented language education should entail? This is not something that Vygotsky had a lot of time to focus on. Indeed, he considered the thinking of 'primitive' peasants as being of a quite significantly lower level than that of educated, literate humans. This is quite understandable within the time frame of his work. However, anthropological and linguistic studies during the 20th century have shown dramatically that the notion of primitiveness has very little if any stature in comparing so-called civilized and uncivilized (preliterate, perhaps) societies. The atrocities of WWII as well as many other conflicts before and after show that thought and civilization cannot be so easily divided into primitive and civilized.

SCT is not inherently critical, activist, political, or morally assertive (although some versions of activity theory are, e.g. Engeström [1999], and also Lantolf and Thorne's [forthcoming] interpretation of SCT). True, Vygotsky's work was all of those things in his time, but his ability to express them openly was increasingly curtailed in the rise of Stalinism. In any case, all these critical qualities must be re-articulated anew in every political conjunctural configuration, so here we can only rely on our own ideals and perceived options. SCT can be, and sometimes is, interpreted in a conformist way, assuming a benevolent teacher guiding a pliant student. This conformist stance is not possible in an ecological perspective, when the context is examined for its impact on learning. Vygotsky himself was by no means conformist, as the example of his rejection of mental testing practices shows (see next section). The future of SCT, as I see it, includes an activist, revolutionary ethic.

SCT AND ECOLOGY COMPARED

It is not farfetched to argue that SCT is in many ways an ecological approach to psychology. Indeed, van der Veer and Valsiner remark that Vygotsky's work in mental testing, which led to the development of the ZPD, was ecological, in that he rejected any results of such tests obtained in artificial situations (1991, p. 58). Furthermore, Vygotsky's insistence on studying the processes of development (rather than specific outcomes of tests), usually by offering various kinds of assistance to the subject in order to study the emergence of developmental patterns, are very much within the spirit of ecological inquiry.

Below I take the ten characteristics of an ecological perspective and comment on some of the similarities, differences and shared directions between SCT and ecology.

1. Relations – within language and with the world

The ecological perspective expands Vygotsky's view of language (informed by 19th century linguistics, and [arguably] the revolutionary work of Saussure, as well as Marxist doctrine). It does so by taking into account other semiotic traditions, notably Peirce and Halliday, and also Bakhtin's dialogical view of language. Vygotsky does not articulate an explicit theory of language. He refers to von Humboldt, Bühler, and Russian linguists of the time. Although he does not explicitly refer to Saussure, the latter's influence is almost palpable (see, e.g. Vygotsky's comments on the centrality of the phoneme as a sound linked with meaning, in *Thinking and Speech* [1987, p. 49]). In other places Vygotsky distinguishes pre-literate speech from academic language, and the comments here are very pertinent to today's debates on the development of academic language in L1 and L2 school contexts.

2. Context – meaning only emerges in a context

Vygotsky's context is a social-cultural-historical one. The focus is on tools, gradually transformed into signs. The ecological context is a physical as well as a social one. The growth of signs into signs (see Chapter 3) is a never-ending process. A further aspect of an ecological approach is the notion of *affordance*, which is dynamically related to mediation or tool/sign use. Affordance ties perception and attention to activity, and relates the agent to the environment in purposeful ways (see Chapter 4).

3. Patterns, Systems – not rules, but interrelated organizational forces

Vygotsky's language is a system of rules, particularly as regards foreign language, and the language of schooling. This gives important insights into the development of academic language, but ecological study examines in more detail the relation between natural and normative language systems.

4. Emergence – not accumulation of objects, but transformation, growth, reorganization

Vygotsky emphasized the notion of transformation, that is, new levels of learning cannot be directly derived from existing levels, thus his is an emergentist view of learning, even though he did not call it so. Recent studies in emergentism (MacWhinney, 1999) confirm the transformation notion, and provide strong evidence supporting Vygotsky's observations.

5. Quality – not just quantity; quality combines intellect and affect, and yields a higher level of consciousness

Vygotsky remarks, in the context of literacy – and referring to the work of Maria Montessori – that learning must be 'relevant to life'. It should be based on raising "intrinsic needs" in a context in which the educational activities are "necessary and relevant for life" (1978, p. 118). In this way SCT is an ecological approach to learning.

6. Value – overtly ethical and moral, embodying visions of self and identity

Ecology, especially if modeled on deep ecology (as in the work of Chet Bowers, e.g. 1993; Bowers & Flinders, 1990), examines in more detail the notions of moral purpose and the development of self and identity, not just as growing into an existing social-cultural-historical reality, but constructing such a reality.

7. Critical – oriented towards understanding and actively improving humanity in a healthy world

Continuing from the previous point, a critical perspective examines institutional structures involved in education and argues for change and improvement from a clearly articulated ideological perspective.

8. Variability – seeing variation not as a nuisance to be tied down and reduced, but as an indication of cultural and personal vitality

SCT in its original form does not question the hegemony of official language and mainstream culture, and could be used to maintain an elitist approach to education. Individual variation in learning as well as in cultural practices is not an integral part of SCT, although it is not denied by the theory either.

9. Diversity – under normal (non-colonial, non-imperialistic) conditions, languages are not threatened by contact with other languages, and are not improved by isolation or by purification efforts. Multilingualism offers cognitive and socio-economic advantages over monolingualism

Language contact, L1 and L2 influences in learning, and dialect variation are not a strong part of Vygotsky's sphere of discussion.

10. Activity – language is activity, not object. As a result it is in the world rather than in the head

Activity is central in Vygotsky's approach. However, it was left to followers such as Leontiev and Rubinstein to work out (opposing, it turns out) activity theories that were largely implicit in Vygotsky's work. Prominent current approaches include Engeström's activity model (see further Chapter 8). But this does not mean that these activity theories are automatic extensions of Vygotsky's work. He warned against approaches that would use activity at one and the same time as an explanatory principle AND as a subject for detailed study; such a procedure, he warned, would create a vicious circle (Kozulin, 1986, p. lii). This relates to the confusion between the genotypic and the phenotypic analyses mentioned above: both are necessary, but they must be kept separate. It is at this point not clear how current notions of activity theory such as Engeström's are able to escape the circularity and confusion signaled by Vygotsky.

To summarize, the ecological approach to language learning does exactly what all theorists and practitioners (except those who would wish to be strictly ortho-Vygotskyan) who engage in SCT do: extend the ideas of Vygotsky in the light of present-day needs and knowledge. However, it attempts to bring SCT into a motivated, well-articulated framework that accounts for language, semiosis, activity, affordance, self and critical action. Ecology offers a worldview that rejects the Cartesian dualist, anthropo-centric tradition (something that SCT does not do explicitly) and proposes an alternative quality-based pedagogy.

Further, the ecological perspective offers a theory of language integrated into a theory of semiotics, and a theory of learning as activity-in-the-world. Guidance of various kinds (Rogoff's [1995] troika of apprenticeship, guided appropriation, and participatory appropriation) is relevant, but secondary to, and attendant upon, the more central notion of perception/action/interpretation. The focus shifts from guidance to action.

CONCLUSION, AND A LOOK FORWARD

I have argued in this chapter that the ecological approach provides an alternative to traditional ways of doing educational theory, research and practice. Ecology is not just a handy (or trendy) descriptive metaphor for applied linguistics, it can also be a *prescriptive metaphor*, i.e., one that mandates specific ways of working and thinking: a new worldview that touches all aspects of how, why and what we educate may break through the perpetual stalemate of a system that never seems to change in permanently meaningful ways.

My main focus in this book is on how language learning can be studied from an ecological perspective. However, it should be clear already that I do not make a sharp distinction between language and other subjects. Language transcends subject matter and curricular boundaries, since it pervades all of education. This goes for first language as well as other language education (at least, in places where the latter is taken seriously – which is not necessarily the case in all countries).

The topic of this book is educational linguistics from an ecological perspective. This type of linguistics is *situated* or *contextualized*, that is, the roles of language in social activity are the core of the definition of language. This is different from most theories of language (exceptions include Halliday's social semiotic [1978], and Harris's integrationist linguistics [1996]) that in one way or another decontextualize, and abstract away from the everyday workings of language in the hope of getting at its essence. This essence is sometimes seen as a syntactic unit (the clause or the sentence), as a morphological or conceptual unit (the word), and so on. An ecological theory holds that if you take the context away there is no language left to be studied. It's like an onion. You can't peel away the layers and hope to get to the 'real' onion underneath: it's layers all the way down. So it is with language: it's context all the way down.

As language educators or applied linguists (or whatever we call ourselves – I happen to prefer the term educational linguist) we clearly need a theory of language. Equally clearly, this theory cannot be an idealized, abstract theory, because we work with language in an everyday setting. Education is a language-saturated enterprise. The ecological perspective acknowledges situated language as the central focus.

Ecology can be approached in a shallow or deep way. The shallow way just focuses on fixing problems without addressing the causes of those problems. The deep way addresses the underlying causes by examining them critically and advocating deep changes. It implies a new, 'ecocentric' worldview.

Ecology has a long tradition in the social sciences. It originated in biology, around the middle of the 19th century (Arndt & Janney, 1983). Vygotsky's psychology, and gestalt psychology, have strong ecological leanings. Ecological psychology in the US is pioneered in the work of Egon Brunswik, R. Barker, and Kurt Lewin. Other ecological theories in specific areas were developed by Jim Gibson (visual perception), Urie Bronfenbrenner (human development), and Ulric Neisser (memory, self).

In recent years the ecological perspective has received a strong push from the theories of chaos and complexity, as well as from systems theory. Another strong influence is Bateson's 'ecology of mind' perspective.

Ecology is the study of organisms and their relations with one another and their environment. Since it is contextual study, it rejects the usual scientific reductions or idealizations of context, data, and complexity. This means that different, non-traditional research methodologies have to be developed for doing ecological research. Requirements include ecological validity, intervention studies and other kinds of action research, case study, narrative and discursive research. This does not rule out regular quantitative or statistical models of various kinds, but these have to be motivated within specific contextual frameworks.

I have argued that ecology and sociocultural theory (SCT) share a number of important features. Indeed, Vygotsky's methods of investigation have been called ecological (van der Veer & Valsiner, 1991, p. 58). Yet, an ecological perspective or worldview can add significant direction and theoretical cohesion to SCT work. Some of the features are:

- A consistent theory of language within a theory of semiotics, clarifying the notion of *sign*, and emphasizing the dialogical nature of meaning.
- A view of context that includes the physical, the social, and the symbolic world.
- A focus on affordance as including both immediate and mediated action, perception and interpretation.
- A temporal and spatial interpretation of situated activity.
- A concern with the quality of learning environments, and a critical perspective on educational activity.
- An appreciation of variation and diversity.
- The integration of self and identity in the learning process.

Many of these features are shared in a variety of work under the present-day SCT umbrella (Lantolf, 2000), and it is suggested here that the ecological metaphor can provide a coherent conceptual and methodological worldview and frame of reference that can move SCT forward.

In the following chapters I will look at language from an ecological perspective (Chapter 2), discussing both the more common macro aspect (language diversity, linguistic human rights, etc.) and the less common micro aspect (emergence, language and perception, interaction). An interesting new connection is that between language and environmentalism, as discussed in a number of contributions to the recent book edited by Fill and Mühlhäusler (2001). Chapter 3 introduces semiotics, in its various versions, but specifically focusing on C.S. Peirce's triadic system of signs. Chapter 4 discusses the notions of emergence and affordance, taking a detailed look at how language growth comes about in situated action and perception. Chapter 5 is about self and identity, looking at various aspects including narrative, remembered, social, and conceptual selves. Chapter 6 elaborates a practical educational linguistics from an ecological world view, and Chapter 7 introduces critical perspectives. Chapter 8 discusses research-theoretical issues such as activity theory, chaos and complexity, and soft systems methodology.

CHAPTER 2

THEORIES OF LANGUAGE

INTRODUCTION

On my shelves I have a number of books entitled Introduction to Linguistics or other titles to that effect. Flipping through their pages we get a pretty good idea about how the profession looks at language. With very few exceptions (notably, Herbert Clark's *Using Language*, 1996), these introductory books divide the subject matter up into fairly standard elements: phonology, morphology, syntax, semantics, pragmatics, and then various other chapters as sort of extensions: animal communication, sociolinguistics, language acquisition, language and mind, and maybe a few more (perhaps the syllabus will say they are optional, or the instructor will cover them if there is time on the schedule).

So then, if we were to ask the question, 'What is language?' we will get an answer that includes a 'consists-of' portion (it consists of sounds, words, sentences, and so on), in addition to a more general functional statement such as 'a system for communicating.' How would you – the reader - define language? Can you come up with a definition that you are pretty sure is accurate and complete? If so, would you call dialects, baby talk, foreigner talk, dolphin sounds, the dancing of bees and the strutting of peacocks language? You probably agree that the question 'What is language?' is not so easily answered, and the more you think about it, the more difficult it gets. And if my quick survey of introductory textbooks (and theoretical treatises too, for that matter) is anything to go by, it is not much easier for professional linguists to come up with a definition that is definitive and agreeable to everybody up and down the city streets or the college corridor.

The subject of language is so enormous and varied that one single, all-encompassing theory of language is not to be to found anywhere. Instead we find theories of the origin of language, of language development, of language variation, of meaning, of grammar, and so on. Theories deal with aspects of language rather than the whole thing, and they tend to practice one or more forms of reductionism (see Chapter 1). Reductionism is the idea that complex things must be explained in terms of more elementary things. One reductionism is to bracket off the aspect to be studied (say, grammar), and purposely set aside the rest. Another is to combine aspects of language with other areas of study, e.g., cognitive or social science, so that relevant linguistic phenomena are selected and integrated with theories of thinking, social change, power, and so on. Sometimes such reductions or bracketing off of parts of the object under investigation are useful or even necessary. However, the study of the part should never be confused with the study of the whole, and at some point whatever is said about the part must be reconciled with the whole. And that is the difficulty.

An ecological theory of language does not purport to be a unified or total theory of language, but it tries to avoid the two forms of reductionism mentioned here, and to study language in a contextualized manner. In other words, the ecological perspective says that language cannot be 'boiled down' to grammar or meaning only, and it cannot be 'quarantined', or separated from the totality of ways of communicating and making sense of the world that we use. Gesture, expression and movement cannot be stripped away from the verbal message, and meaning making cannot be boiled down to syntax or lexical constructions. Language in its essence is both embodied and dialogical (McNeill, 2000; Ruthroff, 2000; Wells, 1999; McCafferty, 2002). This is an important point, because it sets ecological linguistics apart quite sharply from generative or other abstract theories of the Chomskyan kind.

The role of context in the definition of and theorizing about language has been quite controversial for a very long time. It is related to such notions as meaning, function, and communication. Remember that I gave some examples of the use of language in schools and classrooms in Chapter 1. Those are examples of language use in context. What would we be able to say about the language if we did not use information from the context at all? Let's take a short example to see how this works.

A. – Well, ask me some questions, Yuko.
B. – I'm totally lost – I don't even know what questions to ask.

We have here a request for some verbal action (asking questions), followed by a response that says that the request cannot be met, for a specific reason given, namely a state of 'lostness.' So far so good (for our analysis, not for Yuko of course). Notice that we already have a context: one of a dyadic interchange between two people. We are thus light-years away already from typical Chomskyan sentences such as 'John is too stubborn for anyone to talk to.' And even this last sentence, if we are to make sense of it, requires us to conjure up a context, so that we can think of a person, John, who is so pig-headed that he won't listen to anybody.

In our example we think of two people, A, probably a teacher, and B, probably a student. We imagine (i.e., create a plausible context) that A has explained or introduced some complex subject matter – maybe linguistics – and B, stressed, exasperated or despondent (we may imagine), indicates that she has been unable to keep up. We can continue, and imagine that there are 15 other people in the room who did manage to understand, thus further exacerbating Yuko's conundrum. We can weave a web of narrative where A finds a way, by applying magisterial skills, to help Yuko understand or make her feel less helpless.

Flights of the imagination or fancy are not language, but the point here is the question, can we, without using language, ever make sense of language at all?[1] And can we study language scientifically while ignoring the things that language is about?

As language education professionals (i.e., educational linguists) we all have theories about how to do our job. These include theories of teaching and of learning, and also some kind of theory of language. We do not always give the name 'theory' to these things, perhaps calling them belief systems, points of view, opinions, and the like. Nevertheless, these are the theories upon which our practical work is based, by which we justify our activities – unless we act entirely as robots.

As I wrote in an earlier book (van Lier, 1996), these theories are often implicit, that is, we do not sufficiently examine them or reflect on them (i.e., make them explicit). If we want to be in control of our own actions, we need to make our implicit theories explicit and ask ourselves, can I really stand behind these views, am I prepared and able to defend them against those who might disagree with the way I do things, and am I able to build on my prior, implicit theories, and make them more consistent, firmer, more in line with the sort of teacher I want to be? I argued in my book that we need to ask ourselves these questions, if we want to be in control of our own actions and be ourselves as teachers. That book documented my attempts, however imperfect, at doing these things in my own work.

A further consideration, noted by Lantolf and Thorne (forthcoming), is that implicit theories of language, specifically, may focus not just on language alone, but also on 'people as linguistically mediated beings,' i.e. linguistic notions are intertwined with views, value judgments, and beliefs about humanity in general.

SOME COMMON ASSUMPTIONS ABOUT LANGUAGE, LINGUISTIC THEORY, LEARNING AND TEACHING

I personally think we developed language because of our deep need to complain.

- Lily Tomlin

I entitled this chapter 'theories of language.' I will look in a moment at some 'official' theories, but before I do that I want to examine some of the most common assumptions that people (not specially teachers, but certainly including teachers as well as linguists and many educational policy makers) hold.[2]

In the table below I attempt to capture some of these implicit theories (middle column), suggest what linguistic or other theories they may relate to (left column) and, most importantly, what teaching practices are likely to derive from these assumptions and theories (right column).

---

[1] As Wittgenstein noted, "Language must speak for itself" (1974, p. 40).
[2] For a related discussion of assumptions, see Leather & van Dam (2003).

Table 2.1: Teachers' and learners' knowledge about language

UNDERLYING THEORY	←COMMON ASSUMPTIONS→	PRACTICES
The conduit metaphor; sender-receiver model; information processing; 'telementation' (Harris, 1996)	**1. COMPUTATIONAL assumption** Language use is information exchange, consisting of inputs and outputs	Information gap tasks; tasks where crucial information is hidden from one or more participants
Language as acquired habit; language as internal, mental competence (innate or learned); representation	**2. STORAGE assumption** Language learning means acquiring competence, i.e., internalizing knowledge and skills pertaining to a 'fixed code'	Memorizing lists of words, sentence practice, individual tests, building schemata and scripts
Structural, generative linguistics; speech act theory, functionalism	**3. EITHER-OR assumption** Language consists of two separate things: form (structure) and meaning (function)	Focus on form(s), input enhancement, consciousness-raising, content-based teaching, 'natural' approach
Descriptive linguistics; survey courses, e.g., 'Introduction to Linguistics' classes	**4. COMPONENTIAL assumption** Language consists of pronunciation, vocabulary, grammar and meaning (including discourse, pragmatics), as building blocks	Skill building exercises; practice in all skill areas; moving from small items (sounds) to larger items (texts), or vice versa
Normative, prescriptive linguistics. (Sociolinguistics, dialectology, etc. provide a critical focus)	**5. CORRECTNESS assumption** Language use can be correct or incorrect, standard or non-standard	Error correction; formal essay structure; accent reduction, standard tests
Early cognitive science; contrastive linguistics; behaviorism	**6. WARRING LANGUAGES assumption** Languages compete with one another in our brain, for our attention, or for storage space	Avoidance of use of L1 in L2 classes; arguments against bilingual education; amount of time on task
Universal Grammar or Generative Linguistics: Language as a 'mental organ,' something that just 'grows,' or even an 'instinct' (Pinker, 1994)	**7. SEPARATENESS assumption** Language is an autonomous system, quite separate from other aspects of our life or environment	One of two extremes: either just focus on exposure to comprehensible input (and the language will grow by itself), or explicit lecturing and drilling on language points

These are not the only unexamined assumptions, by any means. Others include the assumption that younger children always learn second languages faster than older children or grownups, and the assumption that written language is more grammatical than spoken language, both of which are quite untrue in many cases.

However, the seven assumptions listed in the table are enough to start with in order to make a case for an ecological linguistics.

To start with, let me emphasize that all of these assumptions[3] have more than a grain of truth in them. Far from dismissing them as crazy or dimwitted notions, I acknowledge that they make sense up to a point. But at the same time I argue that they generally emerge as half-truths that can easily lead to questionable teaching and learning practices. I will discuss them one by one, and use them to build a case for an ecological approach to language. In each case I will begin with the middle column, next examine the theoretical connections (left column), and then the practical consequences (right column).

1. THE COMPUTATIONAL ASSUMPTION

We all know the picture of two heads with arrows going in both directions between them, somewhat as follows:

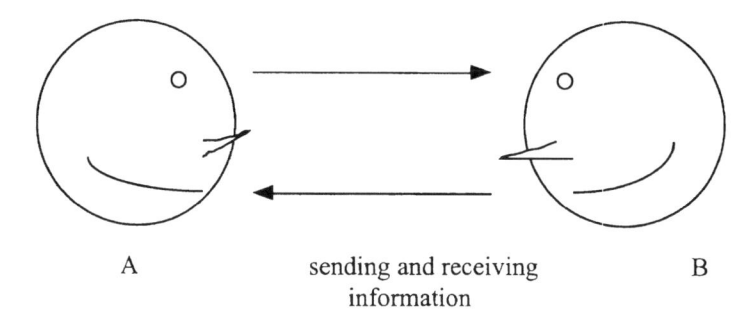

A   sending and receiving   B
information

This is the sender-receiver model of language. A sends a message, B receives it. Then B sends a reply message, and A receives it. The messages begin as thoughts, they are then encoded into language, and at the other end they are decoded again so that the thought A had is now conveyed to B. And so on.

Like a computer, the brain runs programs (rules, dictionaries, scripts of various kinds) to process incoming and outgoing data, connecting linguistic raw material to stored mental concepts and schemata, and vice versa.

The theories associated with this view are commonly known as information processing, and various versions of (early) cognitive science. The focus is primarily on what goes on in the brain, and much of this may be uncontrollable and perhaps impenetrable. A lot of what goes on may be innate, i.e. hardwired into the brain, just like the processors and chips in your computer.

Information-processing theories have been a dominant approach in cognitive science for several decades, and have led to a better understanding of mental processes, including language processing and production. But there have also been strong criticisms of the approach, both in terms of what was supposed to go on in the brain, and in terms of the nature of the messages were that were flying through

---

[3] I do not mean for the word "assumption" to carry a negative connotation here: assumptions can be true, false or partially true or false. They always need to be confirmed or disconfirmed by theoretical argument and empirical data.

the air from A to B and back again. Roy Harris, founder of integrationist linguistics (1996), calls information-processing the *telementation* view of language, arguing that it resembles 'the village post office,' with ready-made language packages that somehow allow the sharing of minds. Language is seen as a fixed code, and the brain as an independent, disembodied 'input cruncher' (Donato, 1994). The role of the environment, including the social aspects of people's activities, is neglected, if not ignored.

In the classroom, the computational assumption is related to practices based on promoting the exchange of messages, e.g. in pair work, where there is an information gap between learner A and learner B[4], thus necessitating lots of message sending and receiving, and therefore lots of processing in the respective brains.

2. THE STORAGE ASSUMPTION

The storage assumption is closely related to the previous one. Language is stored in the brain, and we access its various resources to send and receive our linguistic messages. Several theories are concerned mainly with the question "How does it get there?" and interestingly enough they include two arch-enemies: behaviorism and universal (or generative) grammar. Behaviorists have often assumed that the brain is a tabula rasa at birth, and everything gets stored in it as a result of experience, through imitation,[5] association, and rote learning. Universal grammar advocates, on the other hand, assume that the child is born with a sort of 'language organ' in the brain that will just 'grow' into a fully-fledged language merely as a result of exposure to language and it doesn't really matter how this exposure happens, just so long as it does happen.

In terms of language learning, practice, drilling and memorizing seem to be the way to get the language 'in there' for the behaviorist, but the universal grammar proponent might say that neither teaching nor learning is required at all, just exposure, being in the environment in which the language is spoken. A third way is the cognitive or psycholinguistic proposal to focus on schema building and advance organizing activities, that is, to set up expectations and activate interpretive structures to deal with new information. This continues to be an effective instructional strategy, supported in many studies of listening and reading comprehension.

3. THE EITHER-OR ASSUMPTION

There are two ways of looking at language: you either look at form (structure), or at function (meaning, use). As a result, there are theories of language that just look at structure (structuralism), and treat meaning as a separate thing (or don't discuss it at all). Apart from American structuralism (Bloomfield, 1933), early generative grammar also put meaning on the back burner while focusing squarely on the

---

[4] For a review of SLA research using information-gap activities, see Long, 1996.
[5] I do not wish to belittle the crucial role of imitation in human development, however, this is quite different from the mechanical rote drilling of the behaviorists. For some insightful studies on imitation, see Tomasello, 2001; Meltzoff & Prinz, 2002.

grammatical structure of language, as a separate and independent system. Chomsky's famous sentence "Beautiful green ideas sleep furiously" was effective because it forced us to distinguish meaning from grammaticality (the sentence is meaningless, yet clearly grammatical). Other theories (generative semantics, speech act theory, pragmatics) discussed meaning while making form secondary.

In language teaching we have all seen the pendulum swing from a focus on form to a focus on meaning, with various attempts at integrating the two over the years. This integration is not easy to achieve, in fact it tends to be quite elusive. I have seen teachers who attempted to integrate form and meaning teach as if they were two separate teachers in one person: communicatively during communicative parts of a lesson, and like a grammar driller during episodes that were set aside for formal practice.

Achieving integration, that is, teaching language as language (rather than now form, now meaning, now grammar, now sound) is not easily done when we are conditioned to look at language as a collection of different pieces that somehow must be fitted together. This leads to the next assumption.

4. THE COMPONENTIAL ASSUMPTION

As I mentioned at the beginning of the chapter, most linguistics courses and books divide the subject matter into the traditional parts of language: phonology, morphology, syntax, semantics and pragmatics. Language is built up from smaller pieces into bigger pieces, starting with sounds and ending up with texts. Sometimes second language courses are built up like that as well. I remember my first English classes started with learning the sounds (particularly the most difficult ones, such as th. Like Victor Borge (the famous Danish comedian), we had trouble with the t and the h, "especially when they were close together" (we knew we had to stick out our tongue, but we never knew how far), and then we had to learn words in lists. In this view, language knowledge is gradually accumulated, bit by bit, structure by structure, word by word. So, first the language is dismantled linguistically, and then it is presented piecemeal to the learners according to a sequence determined by syllabus writers. The diagram below (Figure 2.1; from van Lier, 1995) illustrates how language is built up in this perspective.

The componential view continues to exert a deadening effect on the real-life relevance of linguistics in many situations. For example, there is a brand-new test for English Language Learners in California, the CELDT (the California English Language Development Test), that includes a spoken portion. The first criterion refers to the need for learners to be able to recognize and/or pronounce all, most or some (depending on the level) initial, medial and final sounds. This refers to *phonemic awareness* (see http://ctb.com/state/CA/celdt/celdt_2001_tip_guide.pdf).

It seems that Latino students who pronounce *Spanish, study* and *speak* as *Espanish, estudy* and *espeak*, must be pounced on early on, regardless of the intelligibility and the content of their expressions. As a result, of course, more and more classroom time will have to be spent on drilling a myriad of such discrete bits of language, rather then on investigating, exploring and reporting on interesting and challenging issues. The psychometricians and test item writers who are charged with churning out such dehumanizing and oppressive pseudo-assessments for the prestigious (and profitable) test publishers, at the behest of local and national governments, are almost inescapably led towards the industrial production of tests that are linguistically flawed, morally indefensible, and pedagogically harmful.

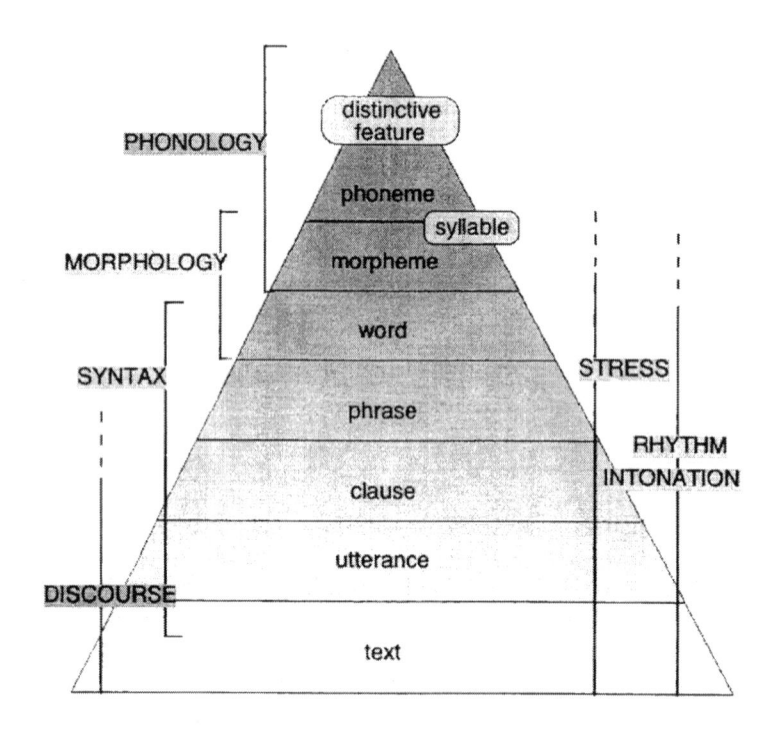

Figure 2.1: Units of language (van Lier, 1995)

This building-block approach is by no means an obsolete practice.

What are language teachers to do when faced with such reprehensible testing demands? A radical response would be for the teaching profession to boycott any tests that are deemed to be pedagogically harmful, as teachers in the UK have done successfully in the case of some tests mandated by the National Curriculum. Less radical, but possibly quite effective, would be to take a language awareness approach (van Lier, 1995) and examine, together with the students, the characteristics of tests and test items, along with their social, institutional and political motivations. When students know what is expected of them and why, they can make informed decisions on if and how to play the assessment game.

5. THE CORRECTNESS ASSUMPTION

A distinction is often made between fluency and accuracy, the former relating to a person's efficiency in getting meaning across, and the latter to the amount of error that is produced (this can apply to writing as well as speaking, and also relates to the meaning-form dichotomy discussed above). As in the other points, teaching approaches can veer towards one or the other end of this scale, or they can try to create a balance between them.

Traditionally, correctness has been considered a sine qua non of successful language learning. Errors are regarded as roadblocks to proficiency, and if we are not careful they might fossilize and then become virtually untreatable. It is therefore of crucial importance to either avoid or correct errors whenever they occur, especially if they are considered 'serious' ones, however seriousness happens to be defined (see the literature on error gravity, James, 1998). But how do we define an 'error'? It is clear that both native speakers and non-native speakers say and write things that grammar guides or dictionaries might disapprove of. "Cindy, we shoulda went to that party." "Hey, waddup dude, where's the concert at?" And so on. These are native speakers. Then, a non-native speaker comes along and greets a person with: "Sarah! Where are you always?" Or we see an ad in Japan that says: "I feel coke!" Now, where do we draw the line between the sorts of ungrammatical things a native speaker might say, and the errors that non-native speakers commit?

We all seem to know perfectly well what a native speaker is. Yet, this is a controversial issue nowadays, with a number of publications claiming that there is no such thing, and that in any case it is neither worthwhile nor realistic in most cases to (want to) strive for native speakership as a second language learner. Some fundamental considerations underlying this debate can be found in the discussion orchestrated by Tom Paikeday in his 1985 book, *The native speaker is dead!*, in which such notables as Noam Chomsky and Michael Halliday participated. That particular fight ended in an apparent stalemate, basically a recalcitrant Chomsky vs. the rest of the world (not an unusual scenario). But reading it does make you think.

So, at one end of the spectrum, the advice is to make sure all errors are corrected before it is too late. At the other end, there is the argument that correcting errors hampers language development (both first and subsequent), that it has never been shown to be effective, and that it puts a damper on the student's motivation.

A further consequence of the correctness assumption may be that there is one 'correct' version of the language, and all others are dialects, accents, foreign adaptations, and so on, and by default all these are 'incorrect' and should perhaps not be used as models or targets for our learners. As sociolinguistics and dialectology show us, the difference between an 'official' or 'standard' language and various dialects that might be spoken in its area of influence, is purely one of power and prestige – there is no such thing as linguistic superiority per se.

6. THE WARRING LANGUAGES ASSUMPTION

This is a particularly persistent assumption, that using one language while learning another, or using two languages in the same situation, is confusing and leads to cross-contamination. Many years ago psychologists made claims that bilingualism in early childhood caused everything from mental retardation to chronic bedwetting. Nothing of the sort is actually true, on the contrary, the evidence of research firmly points to bilingualism as an asset at any stage in life (Genesee,

2002). So, should we permit the use of two or more languages in one classroom? Would that not lead to a pidgin, to incorrect speech, to code-switching, to students avoiding making the effort to practice the target language? In actual fact, research shows that none of these dire effects actually need to take place, except code switching perhaps, but code switching is a normal occurrence in the social life of bilinguals. Interestingly, code switchers tend to have an impressive control over both languages. They do not just create a mush consisting of random bits of each language, they actually manipulate the codes with great skill and sensitivity to the context (Auer, 1998).

We often hear that second or foreign language students should be forced to use the second or foreign language, rather than being allowed to 'fall back' on their native language. In this way, they will get more practice, and they will also gradually learn to 'think in' the target language, and this is seen by many parents, teachers and students as one of the keys to becoming proficient or 'native-like.' It is in fact rather surprising to find that the research on this issue actually finds that the opposite is true. Under certain conditions, such as meaningful and interesting project work, use of the native language actually helps in the development of the target language, diminishing naturally as second language proficiency increases (Brooks, Donato & McGlone, 1997; Swain & Lapkin, 2000). I think using L1 and L2 is a bit like driving an automatic or a stick shift car. If you only experience one of these for several years, then suddenly switch to the other, then you will constantly be grabbing for that imaginary stick or pushing that nonexistent pedal. However, if you drove fifty different cars a day, half of them manual and the other half automatic (as a valet parking attendant might have to do), then neither the mechanics nor the size and shape of the car would cause you any trouble: you would instantly adjust to the car you happened to be in.

7. THE SEPARATENESS ASSUMPTION

Many linguistic theories operate on the assumption that language is an autonomous system, separate from the physical world, mental states, social activity, and so on. Or at least, they treat language *as if* it were separate and autonomous, for the purpose of theorizing. This is particularly the case in Chomskyan generative grammar, which I will come back to below. As I mentioned in the table, this assumption can lead to two different applications in teaching: if we believe, along with linguists such as Chomsky (2000) and Pinker (1994), that language is an 'organ' that just grows, or an 'instinct', then we believe also that language cannot be taught, but its growth can only be facilitated (as in Krashen's [1985] input approach, where all that is needed is to surround the learners with comprehensible input, in a pleasant environment). On the other hand, if we believe language is a separate system that must be learned (as e.g. behaviorists do), then explicit bits of the system must be systematically presented, studied, drilled, practiced and so on. If we don't buy into either one of these two beliefs, we have to come up with a whole new approach.

LINGUISTICS

Sweet is the lore which Nature brings;
Our meddling intellect
Misshapes the beauteous forms of things:
We murder to dissect.

- William Wordsworth, 1789, "The Tables Turned,"
quoted in Dennett, 1991, p. 21

My interest in linguistics has been fueled for more than twenty years by the work of Noam Chomsky. I am sure that it is the same for many other students of language. However, it has been fueled to the same degree by the work of Michael Halliday, and my problem is that these two linguists appear to be as opposite to one another as can be imagined. So I suppose I should say that my fascination for linguistics is fueled by the contradictions between the Chomskyan and the Hallidayan ways of doing linguistics. And this is not all. I am attracted to the integrationist approach of Roy Harris (1996), which tackles all the assumptions in the previous section, by the dialogical approach of linguists who are influenced by Mihael Bakhtin, and many others.

I find Halliday's functional perspective much more congenial to my philosophical beliefs and pedagogical ideals than Chomsky's, but I do not want to hide the fact that I find the latter's arguments very hard to counter, however many times I write words like 'rubbish' and 'nonsense' in the margins of his books and papers that I continue to eagerly read the moment they come out. I buy each one in the hope that this time, surely, I can finally tear the theory of generative and universal grammar to shreds by superior counter-arguments, drawing on various non- or anti-Chomskyan linguists. I also try to get ammunition from my favorite philosophers Wittgenstein, Peirce and Bakhtin.

However, I must confess that it is not easy. In any case, why do I object so much to the Chomskyan approach? Why do I believe that it has been detrimental to the academic discipline of linguistics in the US? Why do I think that it has been an obstacle for those of us who – as linguists – wish to improve the preparation of teachers and the education of language minority students? I do not pretend that the answers are easy at all, but let me try to give a few debating points.

The most important, and also the most complicated notion is that linguistics is a scientific enterprise. What is science? When you think of science, what sorts of people and theories are you thinking of? If you are like me, you think of Aristotle, Galileo, Newton, and Einstein, to name but a few. Theories of motion, gravity, relativity, and others. Ok, we probably all agree on these names. What about Darwin, Mendel, Pasteur, Konrad Lorenz, Freud, and Wundt? We will find some disagreement already. What about Peirce, Vygotsky, Jakobson, Sapir, Mead, Bruner and Bateson? The disagreement intensifies. I don't want to probe further and inquire about Montessori, Frankl, Maslow, and Kozol.

In one respect, science is the study of dead stuff. If it moves of its own volition, it can't be science. Or, paraphrasing Dave Barry (an American writer of comedy and satire), perhaps if we stomp on it until it stops moving it might become amenable to scientific investigation. We must look for mechanisms underneath the apparent chaos of the physical world. If it's not physics, it can't be more than stamp collecting, as the New Zealand physicist Lord Rutherford huffed many years ago (see also chapter 1).

How does this apply to language? Can there be a science of language, if so, do we have to stomp on it first to make it amenable? Do we have to "murder to dissect," to quote Wordsworth? There are several things the would-be linguistic scientist can do. One is to slice up language in such a way as to have one part that lives and moves about in crazy ways, and another that stays in one place and thus can be dissected to reveal its inner structure. This is essentially what Saussure did, when he distinguished *parole* (the unruly side) from *langue* (the quiet side). Parole refers to the actual language use of individual people in their everyday lives, and is too erratic to be studied, according to Saussure. Langue is the shared social structure of language, and is richly structured as a system of systems. The latter is what can be investigated scientifically. But we must bear in mind that Saussure's 'scientifically' is already miles removed from the traditional association of science with physics: he was guided by the notions of social science and social facts constructed by his contemporary Emile Durkheim (1964[1895]), who might be called the first sociologist. Durkheim was influenced by the pioneer of positivism Auguste Comte, for whom everything in the universe should, in principle, be measurable. So we are dealing with the status of social science as a science, itself a highly controversial topic, one that Chomsky dismisses out of hand.

Half a century after Saussure, Chomsky builds on Saussure's distinction to define the object of study in his own way, by distinguishing *competence* and *performance*. But Chomsky's competence and performance are not quite the same as Saussure's langue and parole. In fact, they are conceptually very distinct despite their superficial resemblance. In Saussure's scheme, langue is a common social good, whereas parole is a person's individual language use. In Chomsky, competence is individual and invariant, and performance is social and varying. Saussure therefore speaks of social constancy and individual variation, Chomsky of social variation and individual constancy. Presented graphically, the differences looks as in Figure 2.2 below.

As we saw above, Saussure took as his inspiration the work of sociologist Durkheim about *social facts*, whereas Chomsky's inspiration is Descartes' idealism. By refusing to study parole, Saussure emphasizes the social regularities and rules of language. Language as social semiotic, as Halliday would later call it. Saussure rejected the physical aspect of language as being irrelevant, and the psychological as only partially involved. Rather, langue was essentially a "social product ... a social bond ... a fund accumulated by the members of the community through the practice of speech" (1983, p.13). Langue is "social crystallization" (ibid).

What do these distinctions, and the differences between Saussure and Chomsky, mean for the educational linguist, and for the ecological perspective on language? For education, a Chomskyan perspective means that language development and second language acquisition are basically individual processes that are internally determined, though with some external exposure to relevant data (but the exact nature or amount of those data are a trivial matter). A Saussurian perspective, on the other hand, holds that engagement in social and cultural practices establishes the common social good of language. The crucial difference between Saussure and Chomsky, therefore, is the role of the social versus the role of the individual. As Saussure puts it: "The individual needs an apprenticeship in order to acquaint himself with [the language's] workings: as a child, he assimilates it only gradually" (1983, p.14). Chomsky, in contrast, holds that language acquisition is "much like the growth of organs ... it is something that happens to the child, not that the child does" (2000, p. 7).

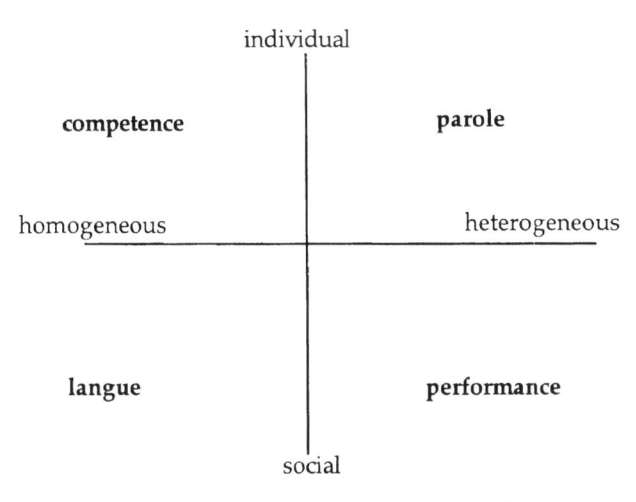

```
                          individual
                              |
          competence          |          parole
                              |
                              |
   homogeneous                |                heterogeneous
   _____|_____
                              |
                              |
             langue           |          performance
                              |
                              |
                            social
```

Figure 2.2: Saussure and Chomsky compared

Let us move on to the domain of schooling, where learners receive explicit instruction of various kinds in both the dominant language of the school system, and possibly in one or more foreign languages as well. For this domain neither Saussure nor Chomsky have much explicit advice. Do school language and foreign language learning proceed basically in the same way as childhood language acquisition? There was an assumption in the sixties and seventies that this was indeed the case. Basically, if one could just approach the learning of the second language (and possibly, of the academic genres of the first language as well, although there is very little explicit discussion of this possibility that I am aware of) in the same way that children approach the learning of their childhood languages at home, then the language learning in school would proceed in the same way as the learning at home. But for that to be possible, all kinds of conditions would have to change. First of all, according to Piaget's developmental stages, after age 12 or so people enter a 'formal operations' stage, where every problem they encounter is analyzed cognitively and analytically. That certainly is not the way children approach their language acquisition. Furthermore, since learners in school already have a language that they are perfectly able to express themselves in, there isn't really much of a natural urge to acquire the school languages, whether foreign languages or academic genres of the native language. There isn't an urgent need to communicate or construct a social, physical and symbolic reality in the new language or genre, since there already is one in place.

According to many researchers of language development, children have acquired the first language that they encounter, their mother tongue, by the age of five or so. Indeed, studies by child language acquisition researchers (Bowerman & Levinson, 2001) show that by that age children have a remarkably rich control of their grammar. That is certainly the case (and we must bear in mind that this represents five years of hard and full-time 'work'), but that is not the end of language development.

At all levels of the language pyramid (see page 31) there is still significant work to be done. Phonologically, some of the more complex sounds are not fully controlled until age 9 or so (in English, e.g. fricatives such as s, th, v, and f). Morphologically, word formation processes and inflections continue to develop; syntactically, complex subordination (such as conditional sentences) and nominalizations are examples of structures not yet available at age 5. At the textual (discoursal) and pragmatic levels even more work remains to be done, such as how to express opinions clearly and logically, debate ideas, tell stories effectively, engage in banter, tell jokes, and so on.

After age five there come six, nine, twelve or more years of instruction (for most children, though not in all areas of the world in the same way) in how to use language in academic subjects, how to appreciate literature, how to interpret a math problem, how to report on a scientific experiment, and so on. That is the situation so far as academic development is concerned. But I would argue that it is not all that different for non-academic children growing up through adolescence into adulthood. As Rampton (2002) illustrates, teenagers spend enormous effort in experimenting with and establishing language rituals that create and solidify their identities and sense of self. The articulate adult in any society, literate or not, educated or not, is judged on being a competent, creative, funny, captivating and charming language user, story teller, joker, and so on (among other possible qualifications). I don't think that the academic hoops are intrinsically any more difficult to jump through than the sociocultural hoops, there are just different access patterns and processes for different contexts.

What I am getting at is that the job of language competence is not done by age five, however much we may marvel at the complexity of the linguistic achievements by that time. This is so for a non-literate, non-instructional society, and of course it is even more true, and with considerable vengeance, in a society in which institutionalized education is a sine qua non, such as ours.

One of the more controversial elements of Chomsky's generative grammar is his claim that much of language is innate, i.e., that quite specific biological structures relating to language exist in the newborn child's brain. That some things related to language development are innate is not disputed by virtually anybody. However, the exact nature of the innate endowment, its specificity, and its role in language development are very much debated. Chomsky is about as far on the continuum towards biological specificity as anyone could be, as I mentioned above. Most child language researchers are a little more towards the middle. Many of them focus on the dynamic relationship between whatever is innate, and whatever happens during the first five years of life. So, in the age-old 'nature-nurture' debate, the dynamics of the interplay of inborn traits and experience are the focus of study. When Nobel laureate Peter Medawar was asked what in his view the ratio between nature and nurture is, he is reported to have replied that each contributes 100 percent (Bruner, 1986, p. 135). This is a very good answer: rather than arguing about the precise contribution of each, it is much more productive to look at how the child and the environment interact in the process of language development. This is in fact the essence of the approach by Lev Vygotsky. Development is not just the unfolding of innate properties, it is a gradual move towards control and self-regulation, through processes of participation and internalization. Learning is effective in these processes, in Vygotsky's view, when it is just ahead of development. Chomsky does not find the word 'learning' at all appropriate; he says language grows, just like any physical organ, it cannot be learned. There may be a semantic quibble in here, but there is no doubt that Vygotsky assigns a much larger role to environmental processes than Chomsky and his followers do. In particular, as I just mentioned, Vygotsky speaks of 'good learning' as that which is in advance of development. This is quite interesting, and I will return to the specifics of this relationship later in the book. But for now, we can note that the parents and the sociocultural community around the child project onto the child's actions a higher level of maturation than is actually manifested in the actions. So, when the baby points to a dog and says "Goh!", the caregiver will say, "Yes, isn't that a nice doggie?" or something similar. In other words, caregivers act as if children can do and say things that they actually cannot yet do and say, and this provides a conceptual and experiential 'space' for the child to grow into. Of course, the distance between what the child produces and what the caregiver pretends that the child produces must not be too great, or the resonance that drives the learning-development dynamic will not take place. For example, if in response to the baby's "Goh!" above the adult had responded: "Notice, small fellow, that this particular canine, which you have somewhat ambiguously referred to as 'Goh,' – presumably your immature approximation of the word 'dog' - is of the sub-species 'mutt,' characterized by crooked paws and lopsided ears, found originally in the foothills of Neasden, and recently promoted to the status of domestic companion in the Bavarian hinterland," the baby might not have made much headway linguistically, cognitively or socially, in spite of the vastly superior level of information provided. The close connection between the learners' actions and the adults' rejoinder relates to the notion of the ZPD, which we will examine further later on.

CONTEXT: A NOTE ON SCIENCE

Among scientists are collectors, classifiers, and compulsive tidiers-up; many are detectives by temperament and many are explorers; some are artists and others artisans. There are poet-scientists and philosopher-scientists and even a few mystics.

- Peter Brian Medawar, *The Art of the Soluble* (1967)

On several occasions I have mentioned or invoked the importance of context in the study and learning of language. Context is so important in ecological linguistics that it is necessary to devote a section to it. I will also return to it on several more occasions in later chapters, as a recurrent theme with variations.

As we have seen, in some prominent theories of language the context has been separated from language and regarded as not really an integral part of it, or at best as something to add on for additional illumination. On the other hand, many other theories of language do place context central, and I mentioned the work of Roy Harris and Michael Halliday as examples.[6] Such approaches might, from a rigid scientific perspective, be brushed aside as 'vacuous' theories of everything, unless they isolate subsystems and subject them to naturalistic inquiry, i.e. engage in scientific reductionism (Chomsky, 2000, p. 29).

The mainstream conception of scientific work includes, as I mentioned above, an abstraction of the object investigated from any contextual factors that might interfere in its behavior. Rats are put in mazes to study their drives and their memory of places, corn kernels are placed in glass cases to study the effect of light, moisture, and so on, and children are placed in rooms where strangers watch them put wooden blocks together.

According to Chomsky, if one wishes to study language scientifically, there is no choice but to engage in various levels of idealization, just the way physicists have done at least since Galileo. As Chomsky puts it, idealization is "the procedure we follow in attempting to discover reality, the real principles of nature" (2000, p. 123). He complains that if this is considered fine in all the established sciences, why should it be considered illegitimate in the study of mental phenomena (ibid)?

As mentioned in Chapter 1, traditional science practices three levels of idealization: context, data, and complexity reduction. In Chomsky's generative grammar, these are expressed as pretending a homogeneous community, an ideal native speaker, and a focus on internal language (that which is represented in the brain or mind) rather than language use in the world. The first and second clearly do not exist, but they are useful constructs for the purposes of rational theory development. The third is Indiana Jones's "X marks the spot," or the place where the real essence of language lies buried. The linguist attempts to uncover, untrammeled by all the weird and wonderful things people say and do in thousands of languages and tens of thousands of dialects, what the biological endowment called 'Language' really is. It is Chomsky's conviction that this endowment, which he calls I-language, holds the key to the real language, that which underlies Frisian, Quechua, Chinese, Scouse and Urdu alike (manifestations of E-language, see further below). These latter languages or dialects (what's the difference, anyway?[7]) are not real objects in the world, and are not amenable to scientific study, on this view. They can't even be defined.

---

[6] There are many other relevant contexualized approaches to language, in sociolinguistics, anthrolopogical linguistics, discourse analysis, and more. For representative anthologies, see Coupland & Jaworski, 1997; Jaworski & Coupland, 1999; see also Clark, 1996; Duranti & Goodwin, 1992; Hanks, 1995; Hymes, 1974.

[7] Since a linguistic definition of "dialect" is not possible, the distinction between language and dialect is a social, historical, cultural and political one. A famous quote, attributed to Max Weinreich, holds that a language is a "dialect with an army and a navy."

There are several comments to be made about this. First, one might propose that the idealizing, reductionist approach is not the only legitimate way to do scientific work. Or, if it turns out that those idealizations are what defines science, and thus other approaches should be called something else, then we might reply that the scientific approach is not the only way, or is not always the most appropriate way to arrive at useful knowledge. Both of these arguments and variations thereon have been made on numerous occasions, with considerable displays of passion, indignation, and disdain. It seems that here we are in the realm of legitimacy, power, control of resources, claims for recognition, and so on, i.e., social and political argument or hegemony, rather than scientific argument.

I could claim that if I just observe a person in natural interaction and make certain claims about the learning that goes on in that interaction, I am doing scientific work of equal or greater value than if I took that person into a psychological research lab, strapped a metal dome to her head, asked her to repeat words that flashed onto a screen, and mapped cerebral reactions during this activity. I might say that I am doing science, in spite of the complaints that might be made by old-fashioned idealizing experimental stick-in-the-muds. The reason is, there is no monopoly on what counts as scientific method, it is whatever works to advance knowledge. Anything goes, as Feyerabend used to say (1975).

In addition to this in-your-face challenge to the credentials of traditional science, it can be argued that many roads may lead to understanding. Already Aristotle said, "Follow the data wherever it leads ," and C.S. Peirce warned us "Do not block the way of inquiry" (Büchler, 1955). As I mentioned earlier, the model for true (hard, exact) science has long been physics, leading to such derogatory phrases as 'physics envy' for those who would emulate the methods of physics in their own, generally softer area of work. With physics, you know where you are, you focus on the facts, on their causes and effects.

Things are not quite that simple, however. From Galileo to Descartes to Newton to Einstein, and so on, views that were once considered rock-solid facts have been overthrown by undreamed-of new ways of constructing the physical world. And now, with such mind-boggling phenomena as double-slit experiments and quantum entanglement, particles (which could be waves, or other things – after all, Lewis Carroll's Snark "might be a Boojum, you see"[8]) seem to be influencing each other even when totally separated, and even seem to be influenced in their behavior by the observer just looking at them. I heard a Nobel Prize winner say on the radio that nobody understands quantum physics, it's just too crazy, you fool around and see what happens.

In recent years biology has emerged as a dominant force in science, with an enormous explosion of new ideas and possibilities, from the human genome to cellular structure to self-organizing systems, and with this growth have come a variety of new ways of doing research. These include a need to look at the whole as well as the parts, and to think of relations rather than objects (this is also increasingly the case in physics). A whole new science has sprung up called

---

[8] Lewis Carroll's poem *The Hunting of the Snark* can be read as a parody of the history of science. It is included in many editions of *Alice*, as well as reproduced on various websites.

complexity science (including chaos theory), which looks at physical, biological, mental and social phenomena in a completely new way. Like mathematics, it is some kind of 'suprascience,' that is, its ideas seem to be relevant to all domains of human knowledge and investigation. Chaos, strange attractors, emergence, holons, complex adaptive systems – these are relatively new phenomena that look, sound and behave quite differently from the old set of fact, proof, law and causality. Maybe the new distinction is not between hard and soft science, but between dry (physical) and wet (biological) science.

Language educators and language education students often complain in their more theoretical classes (Educational Theories, Second Language Acquisition) that there are so many theories that all seem to contradict each other, and so few answers that can anchor theory to practice. I have given a brief indication here that perhaps this is not just some flaw due to language and education being a field of woolly thinkers who fail to find the clarity that surely should be awaiting us right around the corner. In that case we would be like Wittgenstein's prisoner, who is "in a room with a door that is unlocked and opens inwards; as long as it does not occur to him to pull rather than push it" (1980, p. 42e). If he only realized that the door opens inwards he could be free in a second, but it doesn't occur to him to try. Finding that one single truth, the true answer, is like pushing a door that opens inwards. To open the door we must stop pushing and formulate questions that can enlighten our work in our own context. We don't expect to find universal answers, but with a bit of luck we may find better ways of dealing with the tasks before us. And perhaps the door just swings open, or perhaps we find that we can even push down the walls.

CONTEXT, LANGUAGE AND LINGUISTICS

In my 1988 book *The classroom and the language learner* I wrote that the context of language learning "extends like ever-widening concentric ripples, with the individual at the center" (1988, p. 83). I took a person's context to be a creation of the actions and interactions of that person. As Drew and Heritage put it, in conversation analysis (CA)[9] context "is treated as both the project and product of the participants' own actions and therefore as inherently locally produced and transformable at any moment" (1992, p.19). The context of learning is thus constructed by the learner and others in the settings in which the explicit, implicit and tacit pedagogical processes take place (Bernstein, 2000). It is also true however that we find ourselves in contexts that are created by others, including institutional systems, and that these contexts constrain or enable our own actions. There are thus interconnections between the contexts that we create by our own activity and the contexts that are created by others, in which we find ourselves, either by design or by accident.

It is clear that the neat concentric ripples I alluded to in my 1988 book are now criss-crossed by ripples coming from a number of different directions, so that the

---

[9] CA is the most well known manifestation of ethnomethodology, though not the only one. See Heritage, 1987.

picture I drew then is certainly only a partial and rather simplistic one. However, I still think that it is a reasonable position to hold to the ethnomethodological principle of only accepting as analytical constructs those phenomena that are manifested in the interaction itself. "If it's a phenomenon," Harvey Sacks used to say, "it must be in the interaction" (1963). Or, in other words, don't bring in ideas or concepts that are preconceived, or you will run the danger of skewing the analysis. The assumption in ethnomethodology is that, if you allow other constructs to enter the analytical picture from elsewhere, perhaps constructs such as 'role,' 'status,' 'power.' and so on, you are inevitably constructing theories that go beyond the empirical data given. That is, you are using your own ideas and assumptions to construct the context for you, and this may or may not be the context that the agents themselves are experiencing. In this light, conversation analysts make a serious methodological point when they reject the 'bucket' theory of context, "in which some pre-established social framework is viewed as 'containing' the participants' actions" (Drew & Heritage 1992, p. 19).

However, there are also arguments to be made for studying context on a larger scale, going beyond the actual actions and interactions that take place. In the case of language education, much of the interaction takes place within classrooms and schools in which numerous factors influence what is said and what is done. These things are not always visible and audible in the interaction, but they may nevertheless determine to a larger or lesser extent what happens. So, if we only studied the details of the interaction, we might never understand fully how the interaction relates to the various systems that impinge upon it. For example, in the following exchange there are a number of potential factors that can contribute to the meaning of what is said and done:

A: Aaaaw! you lost my picture!
B: Sorreeee- am I smart?

What do you make of this brief exchange?[10] However you interpreted it without additional information, it may take on additional meanings when I tell you that A is Anglo, B is Latina, they are both 4th graders, and B is classified as a special education student. They are teamed in heterogeneous groupings to do a semester long multimedia project. How do you interpret the exchange now, knowing these circumstances? One interpretation, plausible enough in my view, is that B has internalized her status as a special education student, and her response says, in effect, "sorry, what can you expect, I am stupid after all." Whether or not A shares this perception of B's status is not clear from this episode alone.

The contradictions hinted at here lead to two quite different approaches to the study of context, usually referred to as macro versus micro approaches. I will elaborate on this distinction in chapter 8, but meanwhile I will look at the relevance of the notion of context for language and linguistics.

As I indicated above, some traditions in linguistics assume that language is a self-contained system that can only be studied in depth by abstracting it away from

---

[10] See van Lier, 2003, for a more detailed discussion of this example

the situations in which language is actually used. Thus, Saussure came up with the abstract system of langue, and Chomsky with the underlying competence of the ideal native speaker. In recent years, Chomsky has replaced the notions of competence and performance with I-language and E-language respectively. I-language is the innately specified linguistic structure in the individual mind or brain. E-language is language as used in the world in all its thousands of varieties. Interestingly, Chomsky claims that only the former is real, and the latter doesn't exist in any scientifically relevant sense, being merely an "artificial construct" (1986, p. 31). It seems to me that Chomsky's insistence on brain-resident structures as the only things that are real, and his dismissal of external manifestations as unreal and unsuitable as data for basic linguistic study are wrong,[11] but this is not a debate I wish to take on in this book. Real and unreal, and scientifically useful or useless, are themselves notions that are open to investigation, there being no a priori reasons to declare this or that real, or useful or useless, on the basis of models of scientific procedures belonging to Galilean-Cartesian-Newtonian traditions. That would be just dogma. For example, a physicist might proclaim that there is no real stuff called 'water,' but just molecules with a certain precisely definable configuration of atoms combined in the shape of H_2O. After all, there are no clear boundaries between or definitions of rain, sleet, mist, fog, river, lake, creek, puddle, ocean, tears or perspiration. Yet, all sorts of perfectly legitimate fields of inquiry utilize water in all shapes and sizes for a large number of purposes. I certainly feel quite happy calling those field of inquiry examples of scientific work, even if they never find it relevant in a lifetime to make use of the information that there are two hydrogen atoms and one oxygen atom involved, however true and basic that is. I am confident that Chomsky himself would quite readily agree, even though he might draw the boundaries of what is called 'science' narrower than I would. After all, he has called sociolinguistics "a perfectly legitimate inquiry" (2000, p. 156). Anyway, much of present-day quantum work or chaos theory is not science in a narrow Cartesian definition either. Physics and mathematics have also broken that particular mould, and have to grapple with context and systems.

So, back to language. As an ecological/educational linguist I am studying language in context, not a hypothesized abstract mental endowment. I'm studying water, not H_2O – whether I'm a fisherman, a politician, a meteorologist, or a beer brewer.

As a contextualized linguist I study language as it occurs in the fields in which I am active. The molecular mental structure of language may be of interest possibly, at some point in the future (though I don't see much relevance now), but most of all its actual workings in the world are my field of study. This may be called applied linguistics, although the distinction applied - theoretical is a problematic one (see van Lier, 1996). It is educational linguistics in the sense that its focus is the pedagogical context, and it is ecological in the broader sense of a world view and

---

[11] I have a feeling that, even if the innate linguistic structure of language were to be explained in exactly the way Chomsky has hypothesized, all our current questions and problems relating to language and learning would remain unchanged, and the newly found knowledge would not help significantly in improving our understanding of the workings of language in the world.

an approach that states, as I indicated in chapter 1, that the focus of investigation is on the multiplicity of relations and activities in the context in which language is used.

ECOLOGICAL LINGUISTICS

The concentric circles depicted below (van Lier, 1995) suggest that there are many ways of interpreting linguistic action, and they cannot be limited to some inner formal core of words and sentence patterns. Indeed, verbal and non-verbal signs, as well as allusions to physical and social properties of the world, interface in intricate ways to create interpretations. And in most cases interpretations are interpretations-so-far, ready to be changed as soon as further information becomes available.

I like to present the concentric circles as layers of an onion – more layers, to be sure, than are shown here- rather than as parts of a machine or hierarchy (for comparison, see the triangle above). One cannot peel away the layers of an onion to eventually get to the 'real' onion within. It's layers all the way down. Any utterance carries multiple sources of potential information that are present all at once. Arriving at an interpretation requires that we 'scan' the utterance – and utterer – for particular meaning clues. It is as if we run our mental scanner across all the layers and 'read' a plausible interpretation. At any of the layers something can go awry- causing ambiguities or surprises. The interesting thing is that - in general – any problem that occurs at a particular layer (say, clause) will be resolved by looking at the next layer(s) up. Thus, the outer layers override the inner layers in cases of interpretive choice or conflict.[12]

If we look at interpretive work in this way (and assuming it is a joint construction between speaker and hearer), it becomes clear that the notion of 'core linguistics,' consisting of phonology, morphology and syntax (the three inner layers) is insufficient and in many ways artificial. Both from the perspective of the speaker and that of the hearer, information and affordances are brought to bear on the activity that do not just include core linguistic structures.

The term Ecological linguistics is generally credited to Einar Haugen (1972), though John Trim also used the term in a paper published in 1959. Further, linguists from Humboldt to Sapir and Whorf have studied the relationships between language and the environment, thus engaging in EL as far back as the 19th century and the first half of the 20th century (see further Chapter 7; see also Fill and Mühlhäusler, 2001, especially the Introduction).

---

[12] For example, the sentence "She won't go out with anyone" is ambiguous, and to resolve the ambiguity we need to get information from the next level up: intonation. If the word "anyone" is spoken with a rise-fall-rise intonation, then she will go out with someone – if that someone is special. If it is pronounced with a sharp falling intonation, then she will just not go out with anybody-period.

44   CHAPTER 2

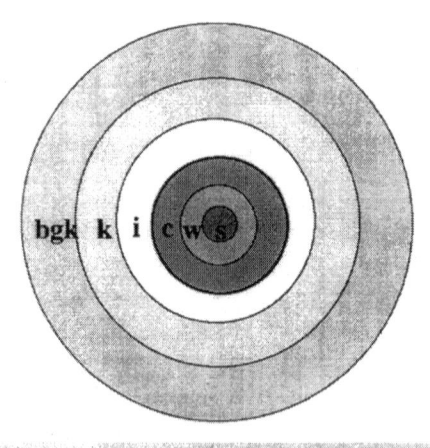

s (sound)   : pantyhose - patios
w (word)   : embarazada - embarrassed
c (clause)   : visiting aunts can be boring
i (intonation) : she won't go out with anyone / anyone?
k (kinesics)   : How interesting (roll eyes)
bgk (background knowledge) : "Let's buy a BMW". "Sure, we've got lots of money."

LAYERS OF MEANING, LEVELS OF INTERPRETATION

Figure 2.3: Layers of meaning, levels of interpretation

Ecological linguistics (EL) is the study of the relations between language use and the world within which language is used. This is a social world as well as a physical world. It can even be a private world and an imagined world. It includes Sartre's *Huis Clos*, the Little Prince's planet, Alice's looking-glass world, and James Joyce's Dublin. It also includes Kenya, Afghanistan, the White House, and Baghdad.

The relationships studied in EL can take various forms that are not mutually exclusive or neatly separable; for some of these, see table 2.2 below.

Table 2.2 Relationships

Relationships between language and the physical environment
- Iconicity, indexicality and deixis
- Eskimo vocabulary: Is it a hoax?
- The language of ecology (environmentalism, exploitation)

Relationships between language and the social/cultural environment
- The Sapir-Whorf hypothesis
- Sociolinguistics: dialects, language and power, discrimination

Relationships between and among languages, linguistic diversity
- Linguicism, linguistic imperialism, language death, language contact
- Bilingualism and multilingualism

Relationships between learner (child or second language learner) and the learningcontext
- Activity and perception, guidance and participation, emergence of language
- Physical, social and symbolic affordances
- Socialization

RELATIONSHIPS BETWEEN LANGUAGE AND THE PHYSICAL ENVIRONMENT

Language is tied in many ways to the physical world around us. Think of the following expressions:

1. Pow! Splat! Bam!
2. Look! What's that over there?
3. You and you and you, get some more chairs.

In 1, the words themselves indicate what they stand for, by virtue of imitating the sound. This is a simple example of iconicity, and similar words include *knock*, *cuckoo*, *shuffle*, and *flip-flop*. An example at the discourse level is order of mention and sequence of events: "The door opened. A stranger entered" (versus: "A stranger entered. The door opened" – which doesn't seem to make much sense). Saussure (1907/1983), among other linguists (e.g., Hockett, 1968), placed a heavy emphasis on the arbitrariness of language, meaning that the way a word relates to the object it stands for is purely arbitrary. There is nothing in the thing I'm looking at over there that says it should be called *chair*. It can also be called *silla*, *tuoli*, or *stoel*. That is true of course, but many linguists and semioticians feel that iconic aspects of language have been neglected.

In 2, we see that the words refer directly (point to, in a sense) to something in the environment. Words like *look*, *that*, and *there* have no fixed meaning, they basically just call attention to a particular thing in the physical environment. They are indexical expressions, fulfilling the function of pointing. The environmentally dependent nature of such language is dramatically illustrated by the old joke of the message in the bottle that washed up on the shore, which read: "Meet me here tomorrow with a stick about this big."

In 3, in a similar way, pronouns refer only on particular occasions to particular things or people. The word *you* doesn't mean the same thing every time. The functions expressed in 2 and 3 are also called deixis (meaning: pointing). In many cases they have to be accompanied by non-verbal gestures or gaze, so that we can locate the intended referent.

The next item, the Eskimo vocabulary phenomenon (or hoax), refers to a rather iconoclastic paper by Geoffrey Pullum of the University of Santa Cruz in California (Pullum, 1991). We have all heard how many words Eskimos have for snow (it varies from four dozen to four hundred). Presumably many more than Amazon Indians have, but they probably have many more words for shades of green. According to Pullum, such notions are largely hogwash. A *word* in an agglutinative language may be equivalent to a *sentence* in an analytical one, so that the Eskimo word for 'powdery snow that gathers in moving hills' might be the same as what people in Minnesota might call a 'snowdrift.'

In Quechua, a language of the high Andes, *wicharirpapun* means "he suddenly went up the hill to look for somebody else," and *qaraykurimullawankimanña* means "you may serve us now." The morphological investment[13] in these two expressions is quite different, and this difference is obviously culturally and environmentally motivated. There clearly are relationships between vocabulary choices (choices of expression) and the physical environment. For example, Quechua has many verbs for going up or down hill, while carrying light or heavy things of certain shapes, and so on. So, there might be one verb meaning: "He went up the hill slowly while carrying a heavy object on his back pretending that it was light." As with my example above, *wicharirpapun*, there wouldn't be much use for such hill-walking expressions in the streets of Amsterdam. And in New York, whatever you carry, you are simply *shlepping*. The physical world thus has a number of obvious and not so obvious connections with language use, and the ties between word and world are deep and numerous.

The next element (the language of ecology) is a less obvious extension of word-world correspondence, and also relates language with both the physical and the socio-political world. I refer to the way language is used to talk about the environment, often for the express purpose of either highlighting or downplaying environmental issues (problems, abuses, exploitation). This has in recent years received increasing attention, as can be seen in many of the papers in Fill &

---

[13] There is a possible iconic relationship between the importance ('cost' or 'imposition') of an expression and its linguistic elaboration: the more important (or potentially face-threatening) a speech act is, the more linguistic work tends to be done in producing it. As an analogy, if you lightly brush against someone in passing, you might just say "Sorry!" But if you spill hot coffee all over their expensive suit, you may find that your apology must be more elaborate.

Mühlhäusler (2001). I will not go into great detail here (see Chapter 7), but refer the reader to this collection. However, here are a few examples to give a flavor of the argumentation in this area of critical linguistics. How does the mainstream refer to people who show a concern for the environment? Here are a few of the things you might come across in the news:

- environmentalists
- environmental lobby
- greens
- tree huggers
- environmental activists
- ecoterrorists

Note that with just these few examples, there is a tendency towards identifying such people and groups as being somewhat on the fringe, outside of the mainstream, perhaps sentimental, unrealistic, or even dangerous.

For the non-environmentalists there appear to be no general terms. We don't hear words like pollutist (polluter would refer mostly to a single act or a time-bound accusation), log hugger, commercial activist, or corporate terrorist.[14] The opposite of Greenpeace is not Redwar, or Brownburn, or Smokechoke. It's probably closer to Free Trade, Growth, or Development.

The destruction of a forest is called clear cutting (nothing wrong with being 'clear,' is there? Logging and oil companies are really nice because they engage in reforestation. Recently (in 2002) President George W. Bush has defended logging in the interests of preventing forest fires. And so on. Words do not just reflect the world, they also create it.

Some ecolinguists (Fill & Mühlhäusler, 2001) propose that a conscious effort be made to change language so as to redress the balance that is currently strongly in favor of exploitation and that euphemizes destruction. For example, a proposed word for logging would be *Waldmord*, a German word that means 'wood murder,' but unfortunately it doesn't sound very catchy or effective in English. I personally don't see much hope for such an effort, mainly because the proponents are a group of people who, as indicated above, are not close to the centers of power, money or politics. More to the point may be a concerted effort to raise students' awareness of the ways in which language is used to reflect or influence policies and practices. In this way we can encourage learners to become critical readers and listeners, rather than just being passive consumers of biased language.

RELATIONSHIPS BETWEEN LANGUAGE AND THE SOCIAL/CULTURAL ENVIRONMENT

a) Sapir-Whorf and the Power of Discourse

---

[14] Although the environmentalist webzine 'Grist' has come up with the new name *pollutocrat* for a person who harms the environment.

> It becomes particularly important for anyone interested in the harmful effect of humans on the environment to consider what awareness-raising might be possible to change attitudes and to resist the environmentally hostile world-views represented and conferred by text and language (Goatly, 2001, p. 212).

In the pages above we have briefly looked at some of the ways language relates to the physical world. Language is also deeply connected to the social and cultural environment in which we live. One of the most well known discussions of this topic is the Sapir-Whorf hypothesis, named after Edward Sapir and his student Benjamin Whorf, American anthropological linguists of the first half of the 20th century. Since the days of their studies of a number of American Indian languages (most famously, Hopi), numerous other researchers have also commented for and against this hypothesis (Lee, 1996). Two major positions have emerged: linguistic determinism, and a more moderate linguistic relativism. The former argues that the language of a certain society or group determines the thought patterns and practices of that society, the latter merely maintains that culture and language influence one another.

I'll give an example of the kinds of thinking such views can inspire. I have very longstanding and strong connections with Latin America, and some years ago there was a TV series documenting the travels of a well-known British journalist. One of the ideas that he came up with on various occasions was what he called the "se me cayó" principle. This was based on an observation at a fiesta, where someone dropped a glass and said, "se me cayó," meaning, "it fell from me." According to the reporter, this showed the fatalism of the Latin American people, who don't have a strong sense of personal agency; instead, things just happen to them. So, they don't say, "I dropped it" like the stalwart Anglo-Saxon would, but "It fell from me." In the deterministic way of thinking, the use of this reflexive/passive construction (also common in Slavic languages) may be the result of a fatalistic disposition, or it may be a characteristic of language that encourages a fatalistic attitude, or it may be a bit of both, a reciprocal reinforcer of fatalism and lack of personal responsibility.

Examples such as these have, in my view, absolutely no basis in fact. They are utter nonsense, as becomes clear when patterns are examined over a range of languages and cultures, both current and historical. For example, the Spanish (with their "se me cayó" and all) conquered a huge chunk of the world, including Latin America, where (fatalistic?) people lived who spoke Guarani, Aguaruna, Quechua, Aymara, etc. Some of those languages have similar constructions, or perhaps they don't. Many languages have passive constructions of some sort, and they will be used especially frequently when the language also is of the *pro-drop* variety, meaning that the subject pronoun is often left out. Instead of saying "I'm going home," the speaker of Spanish will say, "Going home" ("voy a la casa"). English, French and German happen to be among the languages that require a subject pronoun, Spanish, Japanese and Turkish happen to be of the pro-drop variety. It would be silly to suggest that particular structural patterns somehow reflect a national character of some sort. However, such connections are often made, and they are usually the result of ignorance, stereotyping or – worse – racism.

However, that is not where the story ends. As the above quote from Andrew Goatly suggests, certain dominant views and purposes of powerful groups in society are encoded in various ways in language, including the 'official' language of politics, the media and economic policy. Therefore, unless students (and the public at large too, ideally) are made aware of these discursive practices of 'normalizing' and emphasizing dubious practices, they will be unable to push for meaningful change. Thus, Halliday and Martin (1993) examine the notion of grammatical metaphor, particularly nominalization, for its effect on the transparency of public discourse. They argue that nominalizations turn processes (actions, events, activities) into objects, things that assume a normalcy without attributing agency. Nominalizations give the message "That's just the way things are," rather than saying "So and so did this or that." An example of nominalization follows:

> 1. Protracted chemical runoff has resulted in a depletion of fish stocks in the Wazzoo River basin.
>
> or:
>
> 2. The runoff-related fish-depletion in the Wazzoo River basin has... etc. etc. ...
>
> This means the same as:
>
> 3. The Filth & Muck Mining Corporation has for years dumped toxic chemicals in the Wazzoo River, and as a result all the fish in the river have died.

Arguably, 1 and 2 are more abstract, more fait accompli, more neutral, less 'accusatory' or 'confrontational.' On the other hand, 3, by spelling out actions and results in detail, is more likely to cause indignation amongst citizens and hence to bring about opposition to such actions and their perpetrators.

Ecological linguistics, in this area of concern, lines up with critical language awareness and critical discourse analysis to expose linguistic practices that condone, whitewash or promote environmentally destructive policies, or that vilify, marginalize, or ridicule environmentally concerned citizens or groups. Through a focus on pedagogical processes of awareness raising and critical examination of texts, the ecological language educator makes learners aware of what is really being said about what is being done, and thus encourages the learners to take a critical stance.

b) Sociolinguistics: dialects, language and power, discrimination

Sociolinguistics studies the place, roles and uses of language in society. Its concerns range extremely broadly and widely, and it is closely interwoven with ecological linguistics, which attempts to give a sharper unifying focus and direction, as indicated by the features discussed in Chapter 1. It is not my intention to give a summary of the field of sociolinguistics, for this the reader can consult one of many excellent textbooks or anthologies (Coupland & Jaworski, 1997; McKay & Hornberger, 1996). But let us look briefly at some ways in which some of the concerns addressed by sociolinguists can be framed in a relational ecological way.

A central issue is that of speech diversity in a society. Every speech community includes dialectal variation along three dimensions (at least): space, social strata, and time. This means there will be regional variation (an Osaka versus a Tokyo dialect, for example), social variation (educated versus working-class speech), and age variation (teenage slang versus middle-aged speech). All these sources and manifestations of variation have been well documented and intensely studied. What is less well known is what the effect is of increased diversity versus increased homogeneity. How can the 'fitness' of a speech community be related to the variety of speech patterns in its domain? Is more diversity better, or is less diversity better for the 'health' of a community? It is tempting to relate linguistic diversity to biodiversity in an ecosystem. Clearly, a monocultural ecosystem (basically, this would be a cultivated field) is extremely fragile or barren. Left to its own devices such a system either explodes into diversity (as when the farmer abandons a field of cabbages) or else remains barren. A rich ecosystem on the other hand, one with many different species of flora and fauna, tends to maintain a balance and to flourish best when left alone. When you mess around with it, things tend to go spectacularly wrong. How far such metaphors can be stretched is unclear.

Within a social ecosystem, diversity can be seen to have a variety of effects. First of all, there is often a struggle to preserve or diminish the diversity. Very often one variety (one dialect) is set up by a dominant group as a 'standard' that carries more prestige than other dialects. This then creates a struggle between varieties, and this struggle is carried out in schools, in the media, in courtrooms, and in many public places. The standard variety is used by those who tend to it and nurse it as a marker of legitimacy and the exclusive semiotic inhabitant of domains that matter. Elsewhere the other varieties, often considered sub-standard or inadequate for use in important settings, can be used with impunity. The official dialect then is called 'language x,' and the other dialects are then called 'dialects of language x.' The official 'language x' can then be used as an exit mechanism for educational institutions and as an entry mechanism to jobs and positions that matter.

RELATIONSHIPS BETWEEN AND AMONG LANGUAGES, LINGUISTIC DIVERSITY

The argument here is in many ways quite similar to the previous one, except that here we are talking about different languages rather than dialects, and this creates quite a different landscape. Dialects, even though they may be despised, ridiculed, or even banned in some settings, are still recognized as being part of 'the language.' But other languages, even though they may exist within the boundaries of the state, are alien, foreign, incomprehensible. Given that they are usually also accompanied by different cultural practices, they have often been persecuted and even eradicated. This has been the fate – to a greater or lesser extent – of such languages as Breton,

Cornish, Irish, Friesian, Saami, Basque, Ainu, Berber and so on. When a language disappears, it might be said that the lifeblood of the community is drained away. For that reason many speech communities and indigenous minorities fight to preserve their language, and more enlightened states assist in their revival or continued vitality. However, many countries with a strong nationalistic, conservative, intolerant streak resist policies that favor the maintenance of minority languages, especially if it costs the speakers of the majority language money.

Apart from indigenous minorities, many countries have a high rate of immigration which brings other languages into the country. This can be seen as an enrichment or as a danger to the identity of the nation. The latter caused Maggie Thatcher to worry publicly on TV: "But are they one of us?" Fear of diversity appears to be far more common than fear of uniformity. A common sentiment is that expressed by former Senator and Presidential candidate Bob Dole of the US: "A common language is the glue that holds us together." Yet, for any society, there has never been any evidence that more diversity has weakened that society. Historically, I think the evidence points to a greater vitality for a linguistically diverse community than for a linguistically homogeneous one.

An area of study related to language diversity is that of the influence of one language over another. For example, Mühlhäusler (1996) analyzes the detrimental effect that the massive power of English has had on many Pacific languages. And periodically people as far apart as Japan, the Netherlands and France worry that English is either killing off their language or seriously eroding its native powers of expression and richness. Skutnabb-Kangas and Phillipson (1995) speak of *linguicide*, when an imported language (usually English of course) so dominates a country's commerce, educational system and social affairs, that the native language(s) are relegated to an ever-decreasing status.

Another hotly debated issue in many countries is bilingualism. Some school systems promote the study of various languages, others do not. The UK has recently been chastised by the European Community that its record on the teaching of LOTE (languages other than English) is appalling. Whereas other countries in the community are making continuous efforts to ensure that their citizens speak two, three or four languages, and have implemented foreign language study in the elementary school system, the British have failed to promote foreign language study with similar energy.

The Americans are of course the worst of the lot: the study of foreign languages has never been good, but has been in steep decline in recent years. The American government found, after the September 11 terrorist attacks, that in the previous year only nine students in the entire US had majored in Arabic. When the government agencies needed fluent speakers in a variety of languages such as Arabic, Dari and Pashtu, very few were to be found. The typical American is staunchly monolingual, and looks upon people who speak several languages with an amazement usually reserved for circus contortionists, or else with a vague suspicion of lack of patriotism (why would you want to speak those languages – might you have an ulterior motive?). Dennis the Menace referred to a bilingual school mate as someone who could "say the same thing twice, but you can only understand it once."

Why would some societies embrace foreign language study, and see it as a valued asset, whereas others regard it as unnecessary, or at best as an unusual specialization? There is a developmental and a utilitarian way of looking at this issue. Developmentally, one might view bilingual/multilingual ability as a way to broaden the mind, as personal and cultural enrichment, and as beneficial for the development of higher cognitive abilities. From a utilitarian perspective, one views bilingualism as a useful tool for travel, tourism, multinational business, and relations with other countries. In the US, the former view has very little currency, but the second one is a more understandable argument. When the Soviets put Sputnik into orbit, the Americans were shocked to discover that they were behind, and this led to an immediate push to beef up the school system, including the study of foreign languages. Russian suddenly became very popular. After a few years, when a variety of American gadgets were also zooming around the earth, interest began to dwindle again. Currently, the tragic events of September 11, 2001, have led to an increase in the interest in studying Arabic. In some cases this may be with the goal of understanding Islamic peoples better, but in most cases the authorities feel that there is an urgent need for Arabic speakers for reasons of national security.

One untapped resource are the multitudes of immigrants who enter many countries, either for economic reasons or because of a variety of disasters including famine, war, and other crises. Given the fact that a very common response of the host country is that these newcomers put all their efforts into learning the host language, it is found that children of such immigrants forget their native language at an alarmingly rapid pace. There are few educational issues about which there are more misconceptions than bilingual education. As argued at the beginning of the chapter, many people feel that it is beneficial or even necessary to 'forget' the native language in order to learn the second language faster. In spite of the fact that all serious research that has been done shows that bilingual education is more effective than monolingual education for immigrants, emotional, political and xenophobic arguments prevail. On top of it all, many taxpayers in the US, Western Europe, and elsewhere feel a huge resentment towards extra expenditures for immigrant children. Why should my tax dollars be wasted on programs that perpetuate these children's 'foreign-ness' and allow them to avoid learning English?

RELATIONSHIPS BETWEEN LEARNER (CHILD OR SECOND LANGUAGE LEARNER) AND THE LEARNING CONTEXT

I will be brief about this aspect of the ecology of learning, since most of the remainder of the book will address these topics in detail. Returning to the common assumptions that we started the chapter off with, I want to point to the common view that learning is basically a matter of 'putting things in the head'. In the case of language, this means internalizing pieces of language that are selected, sequenced and transmitted in language curricula. Against this, the ecological perspective argues that language development – first and subsequent – occurs as a result of meaningful participation in human events. Such participation, perhaps peripheral at first (Lave & Wenger, 1991), involves perception, action and joint construction of meaning. In such socioculturally organized action, affordances become available as resources for further action. Affordances are not pieces of language 'input,' they are relations between the active learner and elements in the environment. We will have much more to say about this in subsequent chapters, but basically we are arguing a shift from an input-based view of learning to an activity-based view. Within an activity, language is part of action, of physical artifacts, of the actions of others. Learners pick up information from all these sources – physical, social, and symbolic – and use them to enrich their activities. In this way, learners are socialized into the social and cultural practices of the language and the people who use it for various purposes.

CONCLUSION

Language is meaning-making activity that takes place in a complex network of complex systems that are interwoven amongst themselves as well as with all aspects of physical, social and symbolic worlds. It is not immune to social, political and economic influences, and it harbors misconceptions with the same ease as wisdoms.

I have questioned a series of common assumptions about language and learning, and related them to theoretical positions and to classroom practices. The assumptions are not totally false, they all contain some measure of truth, but they can lead to questionable practices if considered in isolation or taken to their extreme.

I include two diagrams in the chapter (from van Lier, 1995) that give two different views of language. First, the pyramid shows the traditional componential view of linguistic units from distinctive feature to text, the second one, the concentric circles, shows a more dynamic view, where messages have interpretive potential along a range of dimensions. The latter also shows that the things that are traditionally considered 'core' features of language may not be the most salient or decisive ones for the construction of meaning.

The chapter also discusses briefly two prominent theories of language: those of Saussure and Chomsky. Some of the differences and similarities between these two theoretical positions are explored.

Ecological linguistics is primarily a matter of relationships, rather than objects. The following relationships are discussed in detail in the chapter:

- Relationships between language and the physical environment
- Relationships between language and the social/cultural environment
- Relationships between and among languages, linguistic diversity
- Relationships between learner (child or second language learner) and the learning context

In sum, then, the theory of language proposed here sees language as activity in the world, and as relationships between and among individuals, groups and the world. It is not a system in the static sense, although its use is systematic.

CHAPTER 3

SEMIOTICS

The making of meaning

INTRODUCTION

Semiotics is often defined as the *science of signs*. This is a very general definition, and since both the word *science* and the word *signs* are interpretable in many different ways, a multitude of conceptualizations of semiotics is possible, not unlike the multitude of conceptualizations of language that I illustrated in Chapter 2. At a more concrete level, we can say that semiotics is the study of sign-making and sign-using practices (van Lier, 2002).

It is my thesis in this book that semiotics and ecology go hand in hand. That is, a semiotic approach to language leads to an ecological perspective on language learning (and use), and an ecological perspective on language leads to a placement of learning within a semiotics of space, time, action, perception and mind. In this chapter, in consequence, I will at times refer to the approach as an *ecological-semiotic* one.

Language, as we saw in the previous chapter, does not exist in a vacuum, and it is of dubious value to study it as a separate system. Whatever the value of such work may be in theoretical terms, a language teacher cannot afford the luxury of treating language as an independent, autonomous system, let alone one that is regarded as an instinctual endowment, a mental organ. Strict innatist proposals such as those espoused by Chomsky (2000), Pinker (1994), and Fodor (1998) are therefore of limited value in the practice of language learning, in the same way that the molecular structure of water does not illuminate practices that lead to the protection or destruction of wetland habitats.[1]

For a child learning L1, or any learner of L2, the job is the *language-to-be-learned*, from the learner's perspective. From a semiotic and ecological perspective, we place ourselves in this person's shoes or sandals, and imagine what it is out there that for some reason is to be learned. What we note immediately is that:

a) the language surrounds the learner in all its complexity and variety;

b) the language is embedded in the physical and social world, and is part of other meaning-making systems;

---

[1] This does NOT deny the value of such theorizing from other perspectives, but argues that educators need a different theory of language, one that is not idealized in these ways.

c) language learning and language use cannot be clearly distinguished from one another, and both form part of activity and interaction.

Here we can look ahead and say, "Wait a minute, in L2 classrooms language can be carefully selected and spaced, brought into lessons in a controlled and sequenced way, so that the teacher and the learner can focus efficiently on exactly one problem at a time, and move ahead in an orderly progression." One can further opine that this controlled approach is necessary in order not to overwhelm and totally confuse the learner, otherwise L2 learning would not be possible at all. This sounds persuasive, but an ecological approach argues that it is not the whole story, as I shall indicate in Chapter 6.

Let me give a small example of what is at stake here. At a dinner party somewhere in the US there were three generations of the host family present, plus a few friends of the family. A small boy (probably between 2 and 3 years of age) stole the show by exclaiming, at regular intervals: "THANK you VEry MUCH!" He used the same intonation as someone who uses the phrase sarcastically, meaning "Thanks - for nothing!" - usually another way of saying, "Get lost!" You can imagine that this cute little rascal caused hilarity and attracted attention by uttering this phrase whenever he got a bit of applesauce or another glass of lemonade. Now, it is interesting to look at this little incident, surely multipliable ad infinitum in a learner's career, from the perspective of the learner. First, we should consider that in all likelihood the boy has no idea what exactly the phrase "THANK you VERy MUCH!", uttered in that intonation and stress pattern, means, when it is used and for what purposes.

He probably DOES know what "Thank you" means, but while that phrase certainly meets with approval from adults keen on seeing their diminutive interlocutors behave in polite and proper ways, it does not nearly get the sort of acclaim that the other phrase does. So, this phrase becomes a tool, an instrument to get attention and to cause merriment, a fabulous achievement for a member of the small fry that usually gets ignored when adult conversation dominates. Why it causes this desired effect is not known to the youngster. He just realizes that it does, and he exploits it to the hilt.

It now remains to be explained how he picked up the phrase in that particular way. Obviously he must have overheard it at some point, in all likelihood not addressed to him. But he must overhear a million utterances all the time, most of them not getting picked up and exploited like this one. So why this one? Here we can only speculate, but it is a safe bet, to begin with, that he knew what all the words meant, in other contexts. That certainly makes a phrase pick-up-able, but it may not be enough. There is probably also a realization of something special, something powerful, something weird, wicked or wonderful about it. This second intuition accounts for the obvious fact that small children pick up whatever we DON'T want them to pick up. So, if we are careless enough to utter certain four-letter words within a small child's earshot, it is dead certain that they will immediately pick up the offending expression and parade it around the house with glee. "Where did you learn that word?" "Oh, Uncle Bob said it when he hit his thumb with the hammer." In sum, the child-language-learner here, surrounded by the fulness of familial language use, carves out his linguistic sphere of influence supported by the relations he sets up with his audience.

A learner's language use is a matter of physical perception, social noticing, and pragmatic success. Learning takes place as a result of these moments of perceiving, selecting, and evaluating the effect of language actions. All of it is folded into all kinds of higgledy-piggledy daily activities, and it is these daily activities that fuel the progression of learning new things.

Another fact to note, as already mentioned above, is that the learner encounters the world 'ready-made' (Rossi-Landi, 1992); both the physical and the socio-cultural world existed before the learner came on the scene, and are confronted in their entirety. This is most evident in the case of the newborn baby, but it also applies to the L2 learner so far as the L2 world is concerned. In Chapter 6 we will discuss in detail what this means for the dynamics of language learning.

In this chapter I will provide a short overview of the development of semiotics (or *semiology, semeotic*) in the 20th century. Three key figures in this development are Ferdinand de Saussure (1983), Charles Sanders Peirce (1992, 1998), and Michael Halliday (1978). There are a number of other important figures such as Lev Vygotsky, Mihael Bakhtin, Charles Morris, A. J. Greimas, Ferrucio Rossi-Landi, Julia Kristeva, Thomas Sebeok and Umberto Eco. A full treatment is impossible within these pages, and the reader is referred to several useful introductions or reference books (Cobley, 2001; Nöth, 1995; Sebeok, 1994).

SIGNS EVERYWHERE

In the introduction I mentioned that semiotics is the study of sign-making and sign-using practices. What are signs, and what is their role in the environment? Signs are not uniquely human phenomena, even though the kinds of signs used by humans are different from those used in the rest of nature. However, as Peirce put it, "Even plants make their living by uttering signs" (Sebeok, 1994, p.70). Flowers, by their bright colors, attract bees and butterflies that will pollinate the plants. Animals, of course, use a great variety of signs, for courtship, territorial claims, protection from predators, and so on.

The human world is full of signs, some natural, some culturally manufactured, some expressly formulated for communicative purposes. Everything we see, hear or feel can become a sign. Indeed, as Bourdieu reports from his work with the Kabyles in Northern Africa: "Morning is the time when everything becomes a sign announcing good or ill to come" (1977, p.152). A cloud means rain, a red sky at dawn also means rain, an umbrella means rain, the noise on the roof means rain, a glistening pavement means rain, *lluvia* means rain, and so on and so forth. Note that the word 'means' means something different in these examples. They all 'mean' rain, but in different ways, and in this realization many of the problems and difficulties of semiotics are contained.

In general, a sign has the following form:

X	means	Y	Z
(something)	stands for	(something else)	... to somebody
	relates to		
	refers to		
	is like, etc.		

Examples:

- smoke means fire to a forest ranger
- a cough stands for "be quiet" to an audience
- a rash indicates an allergy to a doctor
- a compass needle points to the North for an explorer
- 'beanz meanz Heinz' - an advertising slogan
  etc.

Historically, perhaps the first recorded use of the notion of sign is the medical use of *symptom* by the Greek physician Hippocrates, as some noticeable condition that stands for a medical problem or illness. Aristotle laid the foundation for semiotics by defining the sign as the actual *physical sign* itself, the thing or state of affairs it refers to (the *referent*), and the *meaning* it evokes. Throughout history, this western notion of sign has been further elaborated upon by philosophers from St. Augustine to John Locke (who proposed the formal study of signs and named it *semiotics*). From these beginnings the ideas were picked up around the turn of the 20th century by Saussure and Peirce, independently from one another. Around that same time other thinkers such as Bakhtin and Vygotsky were elaborating theories of language and thought that have since become influential in modern (or postmodern) conceptions of semiotics.

FERDINAND DE SAUSSURE

Saussure's book, *Course in general linguistics* (1983), was published posthumously (in 1907) on the basis of lecture notes taken by his students. It has become the founding text of modern linguistics, even though there has been – and continues to be – much controversy as to how much of it is accurately Saussure's work and how much is misrepresented, partially recalled, or written into the text as we have received it (see, e.g., Thibault, 1997). Be that as it may, there is enough in the book to justify its status as the "Magna Carta of modern linguistics" (Harris, in Cobley, 2001, p. 255), as well as one of the beginnings of semiotics. We'll have to give the students the benefit of the doubt, and call their recollections 'Saussure.'

Saussure (1857-1913) is responsible for three basic distinctions in linguistics that have become standard concepts since he introduced them:

- langue and parole
- syntagmatic and paradigmatic

- diachronic and synchronic

Saussure called the totality of human language, the language faculty, *langage*. *Langage* is subdivided into *langue*, the linguistic system, and *parole*, actual activities of speaking. As we saw in Chapter 2, Saussure regarded *langue* as the proper subject for linguistic study, since with *parole* there were too many influences and contributing factors that would have to be studied from the perspective of different disciplines. Thus, Saussure focused on studying the systematicity of language (langue), rather than its actual use in human affairs (parole).

One of his strongest points was that it is impossible to define a particular linguistic concept in isolation from other concepts within the system. As he puts it,

> A language is a system in which all the elements fit together, and in which the value of any one element depends on the simultaneous coexistence of all the others (1983, p. 113).

That is, linguistic phenomena only make sense in terms of their relationships with each other within the system of *la langue*. The analogy of chess has often been used to explain this point (Harris, 1990). If we want to define the notion of 'knight' in chess, this can only be done when setting it in the context of the other pieces, and comparing its moves and special uses to the other pieces. In isolation, without placing it in the context of the game, the chess piece called 'knight' is meaningless. On the other hand, once the knight is seen as a piece in the game, it can be represented by anything, including a rusty bottle cap ('we lost one of the black knights, so we'll use this bottle cap as the black knight'). This relational notion brings Saussure close to a semiotic perspective on language, except that his treatment is confined by considering only the relationships *within* the system of language, rather than considering also the wider context of communicative systems (see further below).

In Saussure's scheme, there are two types of relations: relations of *sequence* (syntagmatic), and relations of *association* (paradigmatic). Syntagmatic relations follow from the linearity of language: one unit (sound, word, utterance, etc.) must necessarily follow another, and a particular unit in discourse receives its value from what precedes and what follows it. So, if we hear "Mary lost her ___" we know that the next word will be a noun. Paradigmatic relations are based on the associations between one unit and another. There are several ways in which these associations work. One is by morphological relationships, so that teach, teacher, taught, teaching, and teachable are related paradigmatically. Another type of paradigmatic relationship is word class, e.g. a pronominal relationship between me-you-him-us, etc. In the above example, Mary may have lost her wallet, her keys, her mind, or her little lamb. All these are paradigmatic choices in the category noun phrase.

Saussure was the first modern linguist because he broke with the tradition of studying languages diachronically, that is, as they changed over time (e.g. the vowel shift in English, Grimm's sound laws, and etymological studies of relationships between related languages, or successive historical versions of a single language). Saussure argued that the synchronic study of language was necessary to show the structure and systematicity of one language at the present time. Diachronic studies would never be able to do that, since they merely show changes along a temporal dimension, rather than addressing the dynamics of language as a complex system.

We now turn to Saussure as a pioneer in semiotics. He states his vision of semiotics (or semiology) early on in the *Cours*:

> It is therefore possible to conceive of a science which studies the role of signs as part of social life. It would form part of social psychology, and hence of general psychology. We shall call it semiology ... It would investigate the nature of signs and the laws governing them. Since it does not yet exist, one cannot know for certain that it will exist. But it has a right to exist, a place ready for it in advance. Linguistics is only one branch of this general science. The laws which semiology will discover will be laws applicable to linguistics, and linguistics will thus be assigned to a clearly defined place in the field of human knowledge. (1983, p. 15-16)

As I mentioned above, Saussure did not extend his linguistic research beyond language, but the quote shows that he was aware of the necessity for semiotics to do so. Saussure limited himself to studying *langue*, and never got to the point where he was able to delve into *parole* systematically (even though he emphasized that the two were intimately connected). The latter is clearly a necessary focus if language is to be placed within the proposed science of semiotics.

The sign in Saussure's semiology is fixed and arbitrary. It consists of two opposing elements: *signifier* (or sound-image) and *signified* (or concept, thought). Even though they are opposite, they cannot be separated. Saussure uses the famous image of a sheet of paper: signifier is on one side, thought on the other. You cannot cut one away from the other, whichever way you cut it, you will always end up with parts of both. The relationship between signifier and signified is arbitrary, as we already saw in Chapter 2 (p.48). Saussure acknowledges onomatopoeia, but argues they are minor phenomena and not integral parts of the linguistic system.

A troublesome and much-debated notion in Saussure's system is *value*. The sign has value, as noted above, not in itself, but because it is part of a system. The value of the knight in chess can only be determined by its relations with other pieces on the board (as part of the *game*, as Wittgenstein [1958] would later say). Thus, there are two sources of meaning in this system: *signification*, or the signifier-signified relationship in itself; and *value*, or the relationship of the sign to other signs in the system (the system being language, of course). One of the things not explored in Saussure – and we must remember, of course, that he staked out semiology as a future science, not one that he himself spent much time developing – is the role of the physical and socio-cultural context in the growth of signs, or the elaboration of meanings.

For such a more expanded view of semiotics, one that goes beyond the *linguacentric* or *glottocentric* (Deely, 1990, p. 4) direction Saussurian followers have often taken, we need to turn to the main founder of modern semiotics, C.S. Peirce.

CHARLES SANDERS PEIRCE[2]

Peirce (1839 – 1914; pronounced *purse*) is considered the greatest US philosopher of all time. Apart from being a scientist, logician and mathematician, he created an elaborate theory of signs that has been gaining prominence steadily during all of the 20th century and into the 21st.

Peirce regularly got into various kinds of trouble[3] during his lifetime (see Brent, 1993), and this contributed to his never obtaining any long-term academic employment or affiliation. He often had to rely for economic and moral support on the generosity and long-suffering loyalty of his most famous pupil, William James. Yet he produced thousands upon thousands of pages of highly complex and often-brilliant writings on a variety of scientific and philosophical topics, the most prominent of which relate to his elaborations of pragmatism, pragmaticism, and semiotics. His influence was carried forward into more recent times by his followers William James, John Dewey, Charles Morris and George Herbert Mead, all of whom have had an influence on language education, but Peirce's semiotics has only recently begun to influence educational linguistics in more direct ways.

Peirce picks up the Aristotelian notion of the three-part sign,[4] and turns it into an elaborate theory of signs, a fully-fledged semiotics. He bases his semiotics on three universal categories: *Firstness, Secondness*, and *Thirdness* (1992, 1998). Firstness is just what is, in itself, with no reference to anything else. This is often called Quality (not in the more practical sense that I use it elsewhere in the book) and is related to feeling, or possibility; Secondness is reaction, relation, change, experience; Thirdness is mediation, habit, interpretation, representation, communication, symbolism.

The triadic Peircean sign is fundamentally different from the Saussurian dyadic sign. While the latter is static, and gains value only in relation to other signs in the system of langue, Peirce's triadic sign is open and dynamic, always changing, and always developing into other signs, in a never-ending process of *semiosis* or meaning making. It continually evolves in various directions, growing into other signs, through interpretive processes. It is triadic because it consists of the dynamic interaction between the *Representamen* (sign or sign vehicle; signifier in Saussure, 1983), the *Referent* or object, that which it stands for, and the *Interpretant*, the meaning or outcome of the sign (which is already another sign). Each of these three correlates can be characterized in terms of Firstness, Secondness or Thirdness, and thus the total number of possible signs according to this scheme is huge, in a mathematical sense.

---

[2] Parts of this section are, with revisions, taken from van Lier, 2002.
[3] Recurring bouts of neuralgia caused acute facial pain and contributed to uncontrolled outbursts of emotion and a difficult temper; in addition his marital situation (e.g., he was living with another woman before being divorced from his wife) was unacceptable in the conservative climate of the time.
[4] Note also the influence of the 13th century scientist Peter of Spain, see Cobley, 2001.

However, for us as language educators, it is important to keep focused on the sign-making processes, or semiosis, in learning contexts. A learning context is constituted of physical, social and symbolic opportunities for meaning making, and the central notion that drives this meaning making is *activity*. Instead of instructional material (facts, skills, behaviors) that is inculcated through processes of presentation, practice and production, an ecological-semiotic approach envisages an active learner who is guided and stimulated to higher, more complex levels of activity, as will be illustrated in subsequent chapters. The directions in which the processes are taken by learners working together or alone cannot and should not be exactly predicted or controlled, a notion that must horrify many educational planners. Yet, it is a direct consequence of taking an ecological-semiotic approach, and is also evident in the experiential approach of John Dewey (see Kohonen, 2001). Stenhouse puts this same idea as follows: "Education as induction into knowledge is successful to the extent that it makes the behavioral outcomes of the students unpredictable." (1975, pp. 82-3).

In an earlier paper (van Lier, 2002) I illustrated the complexities of sign making using the Australian or New Zealand word *pozzie*. To recapitulate briefly, I was in a busy store looking around for a place to put down a big shopping bag so that I could examine the merchandise more easily, and the sales assistant pointed to a bench in the corner nearby, saying: *"There's a good pozzie."* I had never heard the word before, but knew immediately what the intended messsage was. Only later on was I able to relate *pozzie* to the word *position* (I assume that's where it comes from), making an analogy to other Australian and New Zealand words such as *pokie, barbie,* and *garbo* that employ similar abbreviation processes (*poker, barbecue,* and *garbage collector,* respectively). The point of the example is that any activity can spawn a number of semiotic processes, leading to the creation and sharing of strings of signs, creating webs of meaning that extend in many directions.

Learning processes are processes of semiosis. The learning context, in ecological terms, is an *activity space*. When we are active in a learning context, affordances become available for further action. The world around us reveals its relevance for us and begins to offer affordances because of who we are and what we are doing. We perceive these affordances and use them as meaning-making material. In nature these affordances are perceived directly, immediately, since they express the 'fit' between organism and ecosystem. I suggest that the same is true for humans, even though the *immediate* becomes intertwined with the *mediate* (mediated) ever more rapidly as as language socialization (Ochs, 2002) proceeds (cf. also the distinction Rommetveit makes between *felt immediacy* and *re-presentational mediacy* (1998, pp. 354-5). The word 'pozzie' starts out as a linguistic affordance, then becomes imbued with signification, because it allows me to connect my needs with the physical resources (as sources for natural affordances) in the environment. It also affords story telling, and exploring the wonders of New Zealand and Australian word making.[5]

---

[5] In terms of *relevance theory*, the original utterance is immediately relevant in the context of situation (affording a place to put my bag), and then gives rise to a number of contextual effects (cognitive,

Activity, perception, and affordance are the ingredients, the raw materials out of which signs grow, and from which language emerges. In early childhood a child's random hand movement becomes a grasp when the hand encounters the mother's finger (Vygotsky, 1978), a vocalization becomes a call when the mother answers it, an eye movement becomes intersubjective engagement (Trevarthen, 1990). Thus the child's actions become "acts of meaning" (Halliday, 1993, p. 94). At first there are iconic Firstnesses, growing into indexical expressions (Secondnesses) when they are shared, and ending up as symbolic Thirdnesses when they turn into games, grow into speech, form rituals, stories and jokes. However, it is important to emphasize that Thirdness does not *replace* Secondness, nor Secondness *replace* Firstness, rather, they are *added*, transforming signs into more complex signs (*engenderment* in Peirce's terminology) as the process of semiosis progresses.

Signs are not objects out there, nor thoughts in here, but relationships of relevance between the person and the world, physical, social and symbolic. Signs are mediated affordances[6], thus they start out as dialogical relationships between the person and 'something out there.' At first the kaleidoscopic confusion of the world may seem (from our perspective) to be uninterpretable, unmanageable to an infant. We imagine that, just as in a thick fog that is slowly lifting, shapes gradually appear, become recognizable, interpretable, usable. However, things are not a complete soup of confusion for the neonate infant; perhaps even the whole idea of a "wild dance of uncoordinated sensations," as Bühler expressed it (Vygotsky, 1987, p. 291) is irrelevant from the infant's perspective. In the beginning there are *voice* and *face* (as well as touch, taste and smell), affordances perceived directly, and gradually meaningful signs emerge from and around those anchors of security, those Firstnesses. Once affordances have grown into signs, and signs have created the indexical infrastructure to grow language, we use language to reassure ourselves that we know where we are. There is thus a conceptual congruence between Gibson's ecological theory of perception (1979), Peirce's theory of signs (1992, 1998), Bakhtin's dialogical theory of language (1981), Wittgenstein's theory of language as use (1958), and Vygotsky's theory of mental development (1978). All these perspectives share a focus on relations rather than objects, on the interconnectedness of perception and action, and on the social and dialogical nature of sign and language.

To bring the discussion back to second language learning, in the diagram below (adapted from Merrell, 1997b), Peirce's basic 'decalogue' of ten types of signs is presented.

---

conversational, linguistic) that connect my interests to the context, thus increasing the relevance-to-me of the term, to this day (Sperber & Wilson, 1986).

[6] As I will suggest in the next chapter, the relationship between affordances and signs is a difficult and controversial one. Gibson's original notion of affordance, one that is perceived directly, may best be seen as a 'pre-sign' or a 'first-level' affordance in the case of humans, and combines with mediated, social affordances, or 'second-level' affordances that are signs in the Peircean sense.

Peirce's Decalogue of Signs
Adapted from Merrell, 1997, p.210

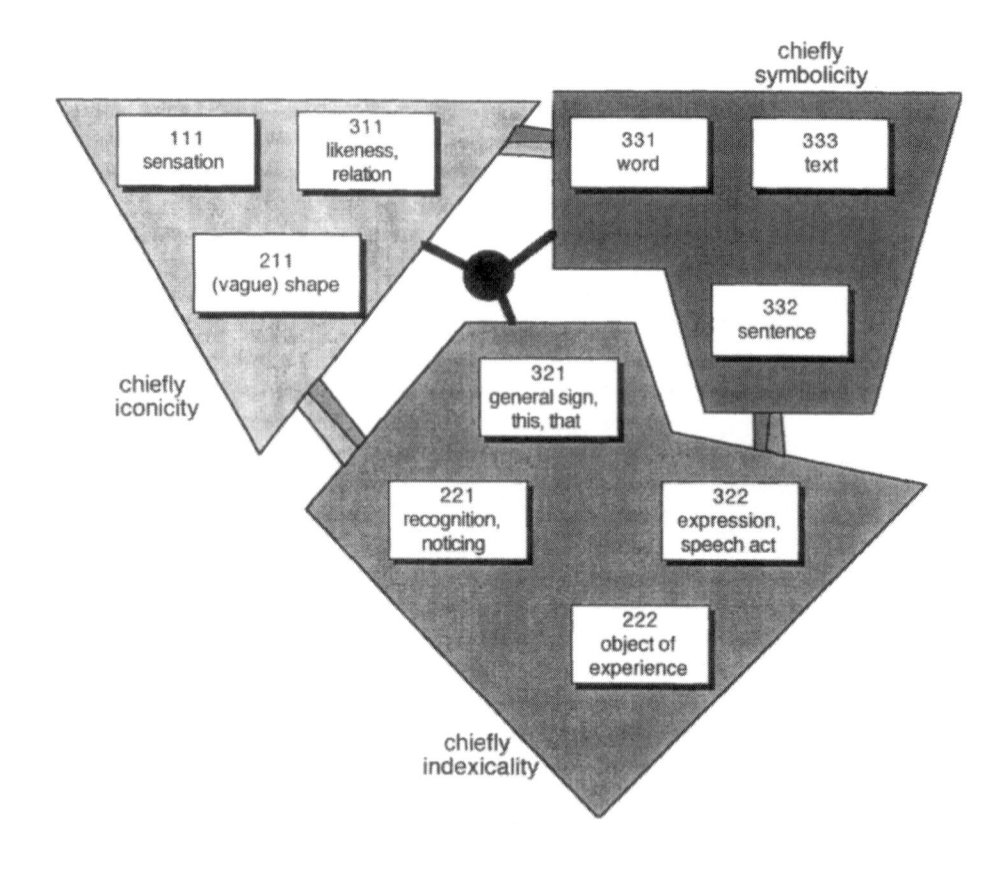

Figure 3:1: The decalogue of signs

In the illustration we see three interrelated realms (planes) of signs (cf. Merrell, 1997a; 1997b; 1998):

***ICONICITY**, which represents:*

- feeling, sensation, smell, taste, direct perceptual experience, self;
- phatic communion (Malinowski, in Jaworski & Coupland, 1999);
- tone of voice, expression, prosody, iconic gestures (McNeill, 2000).

***INDEXICALITY**, which represents:*

- linearity, synchronicity, division, otherness, the social world;
- reaction, interaction, change, dialogue;
- deixis, pointing, deictic gestures (McNeill, 2000);

- joint attention.

SYMBOLICITY, *which represents:*

- reason, logic, representation, integration, argument;
- habit, convention, ritual;
- symbolic gestures (McNeill, 2000).

The picture shows the dynamic flow from one sign type to another. There are conduits between the broad realms of iconicity, indexicality and symbolicity, as well as between all the sign types within these realms. There are specific, well-'traveled' routes of engenderment and de-engenderment[7] among the sign types, allowing signs to grow, expand, contract, link and merge. Engenderment is the process of creating higher signs, e.g. moving from Firstness to Secondness to Thirdness (or, for example, from sensation to expression to narration), and de-engenderment is the process of turning symbols into indices or icons, for example when a metaphor becomes a cliché, or a symbol of freedom (such as a flag, an eagle) comes to function as an icon or a pictorial representation of a country.

Language and language learning are primarily concentrated in Secondness to begin with: linguistic action in the world, especially social interaction with others. Eco calls the beginning of language primary *indexicality* or *attentionality*, "the sign that gets the semiotic process underway." He explains,

> Primary indexicality occurs when we attract someone's attention, not necessarily to speak to him but just to show him something that will have to become a sign or an example, and we tug his jacket, we turn-his-head-toward (2000, p. 14).

This moment first occurs when, around 9 months of age, the child can pay joint attention with someone else to something in the environment, when parent and child can focus on a third object together. Other researchers have also noted the importance of this moment, e.g. Halliday, who calls this the "magic gateway" (1993; see next chapter), and Trevarthen, who refers to it as "secondary subjectivity" (1998). It is no coincidence that at this time in the child's life the process of lexical acquisition begins (at first through syllabic babbling). Before this time, child and parent are mutually engaged in primary intersubjectivity, face to face prosodic interaction, a mutuality that Eco refers to as Firstness or "Voice" (2000, p. 100). This is of course also language in some sense, certainly it is dyadic communication, but it is perhaps better called protolanguage (Halliday, 1993), or first-level affordance.

Several iterations of semiosis (meaning making, i.e. sign making) are required before an affordance in the world can become a *word*, a linguistic action that is (becomes) separable from the activity space in which it occurs. The central process

---

[7] Peirce used the term engenderment to refer to the growth of signs from other signs, into "new and higher translations" (Merrell 1997a, p. 31); conversely, signs can de-engender into embedded, entrenched, automatized or habitual signs (Merrell 1997a, p. 58). Peirce also used the terms generate and degenerate, but given the common negative connotation of the term 'degenerate,' these latter terms are not commonly used now since they might be misleading. Both engendering and de-engendering are processes of meaning making or semiosis.

of language at this beginning moment is *anchoring*, the tying of language to the world, the grasping of the world through language, and the tying of the self to the world, resulting in mind. The general term for this semiotic process is *deixis*, or pointing (Clark, 1996; Hanks, 1995; Levinson, 1983). Gibson (1979) called this the *indicational* process of language, as opposed to higher-level *predicational* processes (see Reed, 1996). Deixis has several functions, the most important of which include indexing, referring and naming. The indexical functions of language are instrumental in sorting out the world, and here the incipient language user explores Firstnesses for affordances that can become signs, and these signs can become engendered into higher signs, including symbolic signs, chiefly through interaction with other users of language.

I suggested in my earlier paper (2002, p. 152) that the indexical plane is the gateway into language, and these early language signs 'pick up' signs from the iconic substrate (in the way that a hurricane picks up power from the warm ocean waters) and engender upwards into symbolic territory, with both immediate and socially mediated affordances that provide signs of increasing as well as decreasing complexity. And every sign invokes and evokes other signs. Language, though it takes shape in Secondness[8], soon begins to engender signs that incorporate iconic, indexical, and symbolic qualities in various combinations and emphases.

Through language we jump straight into the sign world, on the indexical plane. This plane becomes a workbench or desktop from which we make sense of experience and become part of a socio-cultural-historical world (Cole, 1996). Language is thus a way of gaining access, both to the physical world of space, time, and objects (the physical environment), and to the social world of people, events, and societies (the symbolic environment, cf. Bourdieu and Wacquant, 1992), including Lewin's *life space* (1943), Bakhtin's *chronotopes* (1981), and Anderson's *imagined communities* (1991). All these conceptual ways of constructing worlds are 'languaged' and are attempts to come to grips with the social, cultural and historical heritage of the human race. This same heritage also underlies the processes of mediation that characterize Vygotsky's theory of human development (Cole, 1995).

Signs continually develop into other signs, they 'leak' or 'pour forth' into each other, as Merrell puts it (Merrell, 1997b, pp. 210-211). Language development involves both the use of ever more complex constellations of signs (from indicational to predicational, in Gibson's terms [Reed, 1996], from lexical pointers and heuristic speech acts to texts and arguments), and the simplification of complex (symbolic) signs into indices and icons (rituals, routines, metaphors, idioms). So,

---

[8] This is in no way meant to downplay the importance of perception and emotion in language. As mentioned, language has its roots in the Firstness – iconicity - of mother's voice and other voices, and it resonates deeply through the first experiences of being, gradually separating from other perceptual experiences, and taking acoustic shape in the wake of taking emotional shape, but it cannot be expressed or grasped *as language* until it has become Secondness through joint attention. A further point to note is that Firstness does not disappear when Secondness and Thirdness arrive on the scene to craft language- it remains an essential ingredient in all language use. When it is absent, as in some foreign language contexts, the condition might well be regarded as pathological.

signs develop 'upwards' (engenderment) and 'downwards' (de-engenderment) along specific routes of semiosis (Merrell, 1998).

If language learning, both first and subsequent, proceeds in some way as suggested here, there are certain instigative and debilitative circumstances that might occur.

For example, routes to engenderment (and subsequent de-engenderment and re-engenderment) may be blocked, ruptured, denied, in a number of ways. One such way is insufficient proficiency or in more general terms insufficient access to significant signs and sign systems in the surrounding world. Another way might be lack of engagement, in extreme cases anomie. In such circumstances of insufficient access to and/or engagement with indexical language work (and in all cases this also includes non-linguistic action), signs may be predominantly channeled towards iconic and indexical aspects of the world: anxiety, pain, food, survival, danger, work-for-survival. A culture's or society's Thirdnesses (symbolic systems) are cut off, flattened, or funneled into iconic and indexical realms. Or in some cases alternative symbolic systems are set up, in the form of countercultures, imported ethnic cultures, or 'oppositional cultures' (Ogbu, 1991). English language learners in the school system in fact often feel acutely that they are cut off from full participation in the iconic and symbolic affairs of the host country when they complain, as they often do, that only trivialities are discussed in their classes, and that they feel they are treated as if they had nothing of value to say *for themselves* (Walqui, 2000).

Language and other communicative processes thus essentially depend for their success on the open flow between iconic and symbolic systems, activated through the 'desktop' of indexicality. Indices (indexicals, deictic expressions, including pronouns, demonstratives and names) play a key role in this, and often can be used analytically as indicators of the success or failure of a person's linguistic sign work (see e.g., Wortham, 1994). Indexing can also be used to control (either deny or facilitate) access by constructing group membership, drawing boundaries (e.g., through constructing discourses of otherness, or 'othering', Riggins, 1997), or more positively by prolepsis (Rommetveit, 1974).[9] Connecting these suggestions to Bronfenbrenner's ecology of human development, indexing can be instigative or inhibitory or, in Bronfenbrenner's words, the "activity milieu" can "stimulate or stifle psychological growth" (1979, p. 55). As mentioned, close examination of the use of pronouns (e.g., inclusive versus exclusive uses) and practices of naming in discourse can provide significant clues in this respect. Types of interaction that can be particularly revealing are stories, jokes, and conversations, all of them prime vehicles for indexing, and through indexing the integration of iconic and symbolic systems. Access to such speech events, and the ability to participate in their creation and enactment, are crucial for the developing person. See in this respect the insightful work of Bonnie Peirce, which discusses 'the right to speak' (1995;

---

[9] In general, prolepsis means speaking of a future state of affairs as if it already existed. Bakhurst notes, in a remark he attributes to Vygotsky, that "treating children as if they had abilities they do not yes possess is a necessary condition of the development of those abilities" (1991, p. 67).

Bourdieu, 1977), Bourdieu's economic metaphors of linguistic and cultural 'capital' (Bourdieu, 1991; Bourdieu & Wacquant, 1992), and the work of discursive psychologists (Harré & Gillett, 1994; Edwards, 1997; see also Mercer, 1995).

To conclude this section, I am suggesting that sign systems provide the learner with keys to enter into the world, but sometimes the keys are broken, lost or withheld, for a multitude of reasons (including racism and other forms of discrimination, lack of resources, ineffective educational practices, lack of opportunities for participation, excessive psychological distance, and so on). The most important key to becoming a member of a community is the indexing or deictic one, the one that allows for pointing, referring and participating. It allows for the creation and use of relevant affordances and signs, but more importantly it is the workbench or desktop on which the learner may negotiate the free flow among signs and the construction of options for life. Without the deictic key the learning person remains an outsider, but with that key an invitational culture of learning is possible, and the learner may become a *signatory* to that culture.

THE PEIRCEAN SIGN CLOSE-UP

In this section we will look at the various Peircean sign relationships more closely, and we will take another look, now on a more micro level, at how this semiotic system relates to language and language learning.

We can think of semiosis (meaning making, essentially) as consisting of three sources of signification, plus processes of drawing from them resources for compiling signs, plus processes of constantly rearranging and recombining these resources into signs in dialogue with other meaning makers (Wells, 1986) and worldly things. We might say that we are always busy in the kitchen of our under-construction reality cooking up a storm of meaning.

As we have seen, in Peirce's semiotics, signs have a triadic structure, consisting of the sign (or representamen, but I'll use 'sign' for short), the object, and the interpretant. Further, all signs have iconic, indexical and symbolic meanings to varying degrees and in varying combinations. Thus, a sign 'looks like' this:

sign   object

interpretant

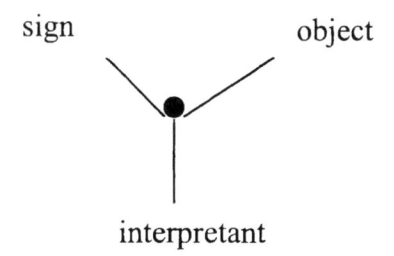

Figure 3.2: Structure of the sign

Each of the three elements of the sign can have iconic, indexical, or symbolic values. At their most abstract level, these elements are also called Firstness, Secondness, and Thirdness by Peirce. Writing the overall sign as s – o – i, it could be a completely iconic sign (1 – 1 – 1) or a completely symbolic sign (3 – 3 – 3), or any combination in between (e.g., 1 – 2 – 2, 2 – 2 – 1, and so on – Peirce gave names such as legisign, sinsign, qualisign to the most common semiotic configurations). Signs continually evolve, gathering semiotic 'material' (meanings) of various kinds, and also shedding semiotic material at various times. In Peirce's words, signs are continually engendered or de-engendered.

Signs are socially constructed, and language of course plays a key role. However, physical objects, cultural artifacts, guidance from others, and bodily movements and postures all conspire to get and keep the process of semiosis going.

A word about the dot or node in the middle. The sign is purposely drawn not as a closed triangle (the way Ogden and Richards, 1923, did; see also Apel, 1981; Merrell, 1997a, p. 133), but as an open, spoked wheel, so as to emphasize its outward-looking and mobile nature. Being metaphorical, the dot is the hub, the center of gravity around which the semiosis gathers force and transforms meaning into meaning, sign into sign. At times Peirce speaks of 'ground' (an uncertain construct), and this may be what the node represents. It may also represent the person's self, as the person centers and coordinates the semiosis. But the node is not some sort of executive 'governor,' a brain-resident homunculus, rather the subject's window to the other, and to the world.

When two learners are focused jointly on the same object (maybe a computer screen, or an 'improvable object' [Wells, 1999] of any kind), they may first of all develop their own signs as an initial step in making sense of it. Then they may use language to share their signs, which then become dialogically coupled in a variety of ways, continually evolving, converging and diverging, and so on, and continually making more language use and action relevant.

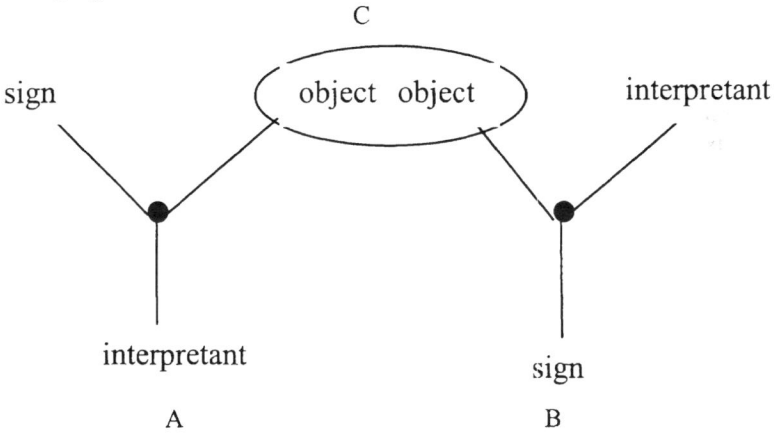

Figure 3.3: Dialogically coupled signs on the indexical plane[10]

---

[10] It may seem as if I have inverted interpretant and sign for A and B, but actually if you rotate one of them one step to the left or right you will see that the structure stays the same for A and B. This is not important, just a visual convention.

70 CHAPTER 3

If we imagine signs as continually rotating clockwise or counter-clockwise (of course, in the imagination only, since they do nothing of the sort in reality), and connecting (coupling) at various points, we can get an idea of how joint meaning making happens. In the example above, A's and B's signs are joined at the indexical level. This simply means that A and B are jointly focusing on a particular object (C), such as perhaps an image on a computer screen. They may both be pointing to it, or looking at it.

Now, let us imagine further that A comes up with a proposed meaning or purpose for the object (or just an evaluative message, "Dude! Cool, huh?"), and mentions that to B. This means that A's interpretant (symbolic) level rotates and joins B's object level. Meanwhile, as a result of A's interpretant, B's sign also rotates and creates a new sign (representamen), so that A's meaning is coupled with B's new sign. Then A or B, or both, may suggest some next action. And so on. Clearly, putting it this way is hopelessly primitive and simplistic, but it may give the reader an inkling of how joint meaning making is accomplished in this triadic sign scheme. Most importantly, this view of the coupling of signs emphasizes the dialogical nature of semiosis, since every successive iteration (rotation in my visual imagery above) of signifying will pick up signifying energy from the other (where 'other' can be co-present interlocutor, institutional habitus, cultural artifact, physical object, and a million other 'others'). The sign is thus always a social sign, it is, paraphrasing Bakhtin, "half someone else's" (1981, p. 345-6). It takes place in the world, not in the mind.

Below I represent Peirce's three triads, or triadic categories, in the form of a table. From left to right, roughly, we move from sensation to relation to interpretation. From top to bottom we move from sign type (representamen, or signifier) to object type (semiotic object) to meaning type (interpretation, uptake). The actual names are not important now, but the point is to show how signs gain in complexity, in engagement, and in depth, through the ongoing inter-activity of the meaning-making subjects.

	Firstness	**Secondness**	**Thirdness**
Type of Representamen	Qualisign	Sinsign	Legisign
Sign-Object Relation	Icon	Index	Symbol
Type of Interpretant	Rheme (Term)	Dicent (Proposition)	Argument (Text)

hypoicons: images ⎯⎯⎯⎯
              diagrams ⎯⎯⎯⎯
                        ⎯⎯⎯ metaphors

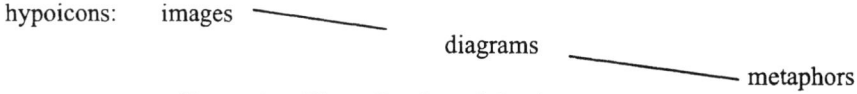

Figure 3.4: Three Triads and the 'hypo-icons'

Underneath the table I have placed the three 'hypoicons' of Peirce, referring to artifacts of various types that relate in different ways to objects or events. Examples would be pictures or portraits of things or people (images); maps and drawings of events, places and relationships (diagrams); and conventional representations of states of affairs, e.g. flags, fashion statements, and peace signs (metaphors).

On the basis of much arcane logical discussion Peirce worked out ten basic classes of sign (refer back to 'decalogue' picture above; Merrell, 1997a, p. 299). These include complex terms such as *rhematic indexical sinsign, dicent indexical legisign*, and so on, and I suggest we need not go into them at this point. As with the table above, it is more important for us to get an idea of the multitude of pathways along which sign making takes place, than to fathom the precise logical provenance of each class.

SEMIOSIS AND LANGUAGE LEARNING

How do we relate these various puzzles of semiosis to language learning? I already gave some hints in the discussion following the earlier decalogue picture (Figure 3.1). That was mostly at the global end of the spectrum, relating to the accessibility of social-cultural-historical symbolicity to learners, particularly if they are not members of the host culture. I also suggested that the way into language is through indexicality and deixis. I further hinted at close connections between iconic and symbolic sign systems mediated by indexical work.

To begin to answer the question posed in the previous paragraph, I would like to refer back to the concentric circles diagram in Chapter 2 (Figure 2.3, page 46). It should be clear that Firstness (mainly iconicity, the first block in the decalogue) in language refers to the mutuality that is expressed in intonation, tone of voice, facial expression, and similar features of speech, those areas traditionally – and misleadingly – referred to as 'paralinguistic,' the outer layers of the diagram. I also mentioned that, whenever there is an interpretational conflict or ambiguity in a particular speech action, affordances in the outer layers tend to override those in the inner layers. We can therefore not learn, use, or interpret language without including the notion of iconicity. 'Language is arbitrary,' many textbooks tell us. At a trivial, formal, morpho-phonemic level that is largely true, but it is totally untrue for any actual utterance in real life.

In an earlier paper (van Lier, 2002) I argued that there are three phases or moments to language and language development: *mutuality, indexicality*, and *predicality*, largely coinciding with the three blocks in the decalogue. The first phase, also called *primary intersubjectivity* by Trevarthen (1990) is characterized by a connectedness between caregiver (most often the mother) and baby, during the first nine months or so of life. Vocal interaction at this point is sensory, direct, immediate, rhythmic, and affective. Language use is primarily voice, rather than speech (even though the mother will use actual utterances, songs, stories and so on).

As I mentioned earlier, the second phase begins when caregiver and infant can jointly focus on an object elsewhere in the environment (rather than just focus on each other). At that point interaction becomes triadic, including infant, caregiver and object of attention. That is generally regarded as the point at which language develops (Reed, 1996, Eco, 2000), hence my earlier remark that language begins with indexicality or deixis. This second phase is the indicational phase, the 'look here,' 'what's that,' and 'gimme that' phase. Trevarthen calls this phase *secondary intersubjectivity* (1990). It is primarily characterized by lexical development and formulaic speech acts.

The third phase, the development of predicational language, moves into the symbolic realm, with the ability to discuss things that are not here and now, and the development of narrative, logical reasoning, and so on. In a word, the emergence of grammar.

The important thing to remember is that one phase does not replace the previous one, rather, it sweeps the previous one along with it, and the new mode of language use incorporates previous modes into multiplex meaning-making processes, gradually transforming the sensory world into a world mediated by language.

When the child goes to school, maybe reaching the fourth grade or so, the symbolic aspects of language become more and more salient, the object in the triadic interaction becoming increasingly abstract and decontextualized. Without the help of the indexical plane, and without the emotional boost provided by iconic support structures, the child would face an uphill battle, and might get lost in confusion.

Now let's apply this to the second language learner, perhaps an immigrant child in the school system. Not only is the pace of development accelerated furiously, all the aspects of the target language, iconic, indexical and symbolic, hit the learner smack in the face, simultaneously. In fact, in school the iconic and indexical aspects may be stripped away in decontextualized curricula (and bear in mind that for the immigrant everything appears decontextualized, since the new context and its metaphors are not yet familiar).

In the case of the foreign language learner, curricula tend to be very linguistic and formal, so that there is almost no opportunity to develop a Firstness, a relation of emotional mutuality with the language. The deep emotional connectedness that we feel when we use our mother tongue may remain elusive, since we are denied systematic opportunities to *speak for ourselves*. Moreover, there may be few opportunities to engage in joint project-based (triadic) work that would allow for the development of indicational skills as a way into more predicational ways of using the new language. We can see, therefore, that a triadic semiotic view such as the one developed by Peirce more than a hundred years ago, can give us important insights about how to organize language education. In summary, the main insights are as follows:

- Language and the physical, social and symbolic world are interconnected in a myriad of ways, and this should be reflected in curricula, materials and classroom practices. That is, language learning should be richly contextualized.
- Language is not just brain-resident or located in an abstract mental realm; it is intimately connected with the body (it is embodied) and with gestures, expressions, interpersonal resonance, and so on. These are not just added-on frills of language, but they are *constitutive* of language and *instrumental* in learning.

- Healthy and robust language use combines Firstness, Secondness and Thirdness (or iconic, indexical and symbolic elements) in equal degrees. Learning contexts must therefore ensure the availablity of rich semiotic resources in all three areas. Learners are people with something to say, and with meaningful goals in life, not just statistics that add to test averages.
- Communicative methodologies may have overstated the notion of face-to-face communication as an interactional model. Perhaps more important is a side-by-side model that employs joint attention to a common focus, an *improvable object* (Wells, 1999) as a basic design feature (leading to project-based learning, see Chapter 6).
- Seeing language from a semiotic perspective and learning from an ecological perspective can thus contribute to a learning environment that is pedagogically rich and stimulating, learner and learning-centered, non-controlling and autonomy-supporting (Deci and Flaste, 1995), and truly thought- and language-provoking for all learners.

MICHAEL A. K. HALLIDAY

Halliday is a student of J.R. Firth (1890-1960), a British linguist who has often been called the first sociolinguist (he used the term 'sociological linguistics'), and who was a pioneer of modern British linguistics. Firth (not to be confused with his namesake, Raymond Firth, a well known social anthropologist from New Zealand, who carried on the tradition of Malinowski[11]) was influenced by – but was not afraid to disagree with – a number of different linguists, anthropologists and philosophers, notably Saussure, Pike, Malinowski, Russell and Wittgenstein.

Firth saw that Saussure, in his signifier-signified and langue-parole distinctions, perpetuated the Cartesian mind-body dualism which he (Firth) strongly opposed (de Beaugrande, 1991, p. 193). Instead, Firth demands that 'we must look to the whole man thinking and acting as a whole, in association with his fellows' (ibid.). Firth further rejects structuralism (attributed to Saussure, among others), suggesting that it leads to a 'dead technical language' (ibid., p.197).

Among his other achievements, Firth elaborated Malinowski's *context of situation*, established the linguistic study of collocation, and argued for a functional linguistics. His work thus contains many elements that suggest an ecological direction, although in his early work (at least) he proudly lauds European cultural supremacy as making 'the most of what the earth has to give' and thus having made 'the world one.' As de Beaugrande points out, this has usually been done "by exploiting, subjugating, or exterminating others" (ibid, p. 217). I would add, and by destroying large parts of the earth's natural resources.

---

[11] Bronislaw Malinowksi was a Polish-born British anthropologist who pioneered participant observation and who emphasized the centrality of speech, including what he called 'phatic communion,' in a culture. He also noted the role of 'the context of situation' in meaning.

Be that as it may, and perhaps giving Firth some clemency as being a creature of his (colonial) times, we can see that Halliday had a brilliant, unorthodox, often iconoclastic teacher, who took a decidedly untraditional view of language and linguistics.

Halliday has developed a functional linguistics that at times has also been called *rank-scale* grammar, *systemic* grammar, *systemic-functional* grammar, or Halliday's term *social semiotic*. Rejecting both Saussure's langue-parole and Chomsky's competence-performance distinctions, Halliday sees language as *meaning potential*, a system of choices that lies before the speaker. The *context of culture* defines the meaning potential (in ecological terms we might say, the semiotic potential, or the affordances), the *context of situation* determines how this potential is realized through choices and in action.

The network of systemic choices yields a 'dynamic grammar' that starts with broad themes like *theme, actor* and *subject*, and is progressively elaborated into more fine-grained levels of delicacy. The central organizational framework of Halliday's system is his three-part set of macrofunctions: *ideational, interpersonal* and *textual*, which are broadly mapped onto the situation types field, tenor, and mode, as visually shown in the diagram below (Figure 3.4). This framework yields a broad but flexible and powerful instrument for the analysis of language use in context (when compared, e.g., to Hymes' much more detailed but essentially taxonomic list of interactional heuristics represented in the well-known acronym S*P*E*A*K*I*N*G[12] (Hymes, 1974).

The ideational function relates to content, experience, what is being done (the nature of the activity), in general the 'aboutness' of the event or speech act. In terms of knowledge structures, it relates to narration, memories and reports, everyday logic, and so on.

The interpersonal function relates to the social circumstances of speech, roles and identities of participants, sociocultural issues, relationships, power and control.

The textual function relates to the ways in which language organizes itself, the ways in which it "delegates a part of itself for interpreting itself," to paraphrase Eco (2000, p. 37). It includes markers and phrases such as *First, second,.. To summarize,... So what you're trying to say is,...* as well markers of cohesion, introductory and summarizing statements, and so on.

One of Halliday's most interesting and influential publications is Learning how to mean (1975), a detailed study of the first 2 years of his son Nigel's language development. He suggests a set of seven functions "in which the child first learns to mean," appearing roughly in the order listed, as follows:

As the child grows up, language crystallizes into the three macrofunctions mentioned above, the ideational, interpersonal and the textual. Interestingly, in the seven children's functions listed above, the interpersonal dominates in the first four, the ideational enters in the fifth ("tell me why"), but the textual remains implicit.

---

[12] The letters stand for: Situation- Participants- Ends- Acts- Key- Instrumentalities- Norms- Genre. Interestingly, whenever I have asked graduate students to analyze speech events using Hymes's acronym or Halliday's simpler scheme of Field-Tenor-Mode, the latter has yielded more food for discussion. However, from an anthropological perspective, Hymes's scheme is more analytically precise.

Instrumental	'I want'
Regulatory	'do as I tell you'
Interactional	'me and you'
Personal	'here I come'
Heuristic	'tell me why'
Imaginative	'let's pretend'
Informative	'I've got something to tell you'
	(Halliday, 1975, p. 37)

Figure 3.5

Still, "Let's pretend" and common informative gambits such as "Guess what?" suggest that even very young children may be developing a sense of textuality. It is important to bear in mind that, in Halliday's view, all language use bears elements of all three macrofunctions, even though markers that carry primarily ideational, interpersonal or textual information may be found in messages.

According to Halliday, and functional linguistics in general, language use determines – at least to some extent – language structure. I am hedging here because I personally do not believe in the deterministic 'language determines thought' – 'thought determines language' philosophy. Even so, the latter is more plausible than the former, but the trick is to think how the two directionalities might be related. I suspect, along with Vygotsky, Wittgenstein and many other thinkers, that language and thought mutually create each other. I also think that neither of them are finished products, static entities that can be held up to the light as objects for comparison. Instead, they are constantly intertwining processes, always growing and changing together, requiring maturation as well as cultural nurturing, perhaps similar to the way grapes and yeast interact to produce a delicious wine.

Halliday explains the semiotic structure of a context of situation as follows:

> The *field* is the social action in which the text is embedded; it includes the subject-matter, as one special manifestation. The *tenor* is the set of role relationships among the relevant participants; it includes levels of formality as one particular instance. The *mode* is the channel or wavelength selected, which is essentially the function that is assigned to language in the total structure of the situation. It includes the medium (spoken or written), which is explained as a functional variable. (Halliday, 1978, p. 110, my emphases)

In an important, more recent paper Halliday further develops the functional language development of children. In it, he emphasizes that when children learn language they are learning the foundation of learning itself. This learning is a semiotic process that "goes on from birth, through infancy and childhood, and on through adolescence into adult life" (1993, p. 93). In modern cultures, it includes not only the 'natural' language of the culture and the community, but also the institutionalized language of writing and academic subject matters. He proposes 21 features of language learning, from birth to the academic language of secondary schooling. As we will see, when we look at these features in more detail in the next chapter, Halliday's summary in many ways parallels that of other child language

76 CHAPTER 3

researchers and semioticians who investigate language development in an ecological perspective.

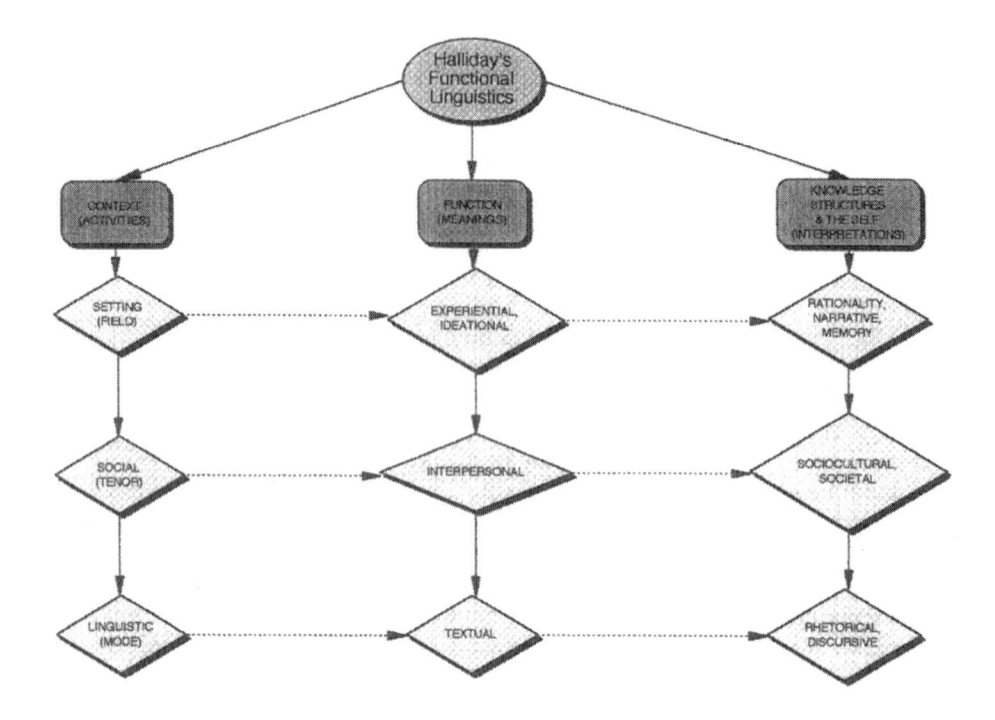

Figure 3.6 Halliday's macrofunctions

CONCLUSION

In this chapter I have given an overview of some of the most important semiotic developments of the 20th century. I singled out Saussure, Peirce and Halliday as the three giants in this field. In general, as the field of semiotics now stands, three types of relationships stand out so far as language is concerned:

1. Relationships within linguistic systems and sub-systems (structural and functional);
2. Relationships between linguistic systems and other systems of communication (gestures, facial expressions, body language in general, a variety of cultural and
   artifactual signs);
3. Relationships between sign making systems and the physical world.

All these meaning making systems and meaning sources are in constant action and interaction, resonating with one another and creating shared information.

Saussure was the first 'modern linguist,' giving us the dichotomies of *langue* and *parole*, *syntagmatic* and *paradigmatic*, and *synchronic* and *diachronic*. Saussure's semiotics has often been criticized as based on a crude sender-receiver model.[13] Furthermore, his semiotic relations only refer to relations within the linguistic systems themselves (his notion of *value*), not with the social or physical world. This is the essence of structuralism, and it unduly brackets off language from its place in the world (the realm of *parole*, an area that Saussure preferred not to deal with).

Peirce is the giant among giants of semioticians. His work influenced that of most 20th century semioticians, including Morris, Mead, Eco, Jakobson and Sebeok (see Nöth, 1995). It also has much affinity with the dialogical work of Bakhtin (Merrell, 1997a). Peirce's semiotics, while being highly theoretical and abstract in its founding constructs, is squarely placed in the rough and tumble of the physical and the social world, and is highly dynamic. We might say it is the quantum physics version of semiotics. There are more dimensions in it than we can bend our brain around.

Halliday's work is closely allied to language learning pedagogy. It is perhaps the easiest semiotic framework for a teacher to get into. It is also, in my view, remarkably compatible with Peircean semiotics, much more than with the Saussurian version, but that remains to be shown in detail.

I have suggested in this chapter that semiotics can be a powerful tool not only to delve into the intricacies of language learning, but also to shed light on societal patterns of facilitation and inhibition. This suggests a connection between semiotics and the sociology of education, and it will be of interest to study the work of scholars in this area, such as Basil Bernstein (2000) and Pierre Bourdieu (1991), from a semiotic perspective. However, this would be a major study in its own right.

In the next chapter we will look more closely at the ways in which meaning emerges, and in particular how language proficiency develops.

---

[13] Saussure scholars do not all agree on this point: it can certainly be argued that Saussure's position was far more nuanced than the sender – receiver model suggests (Thibault, 1997).

CHAPTER 4

EMERGENCE AND AFFORDANCE

INTRODUCTION

> The types of phenomena that should lead the way [in the theory of cognition] must be drawn from perception in the service of action and from action in the service of perception. There are two major reasons for confidence in this choice. First, what is known by humans and other animals is grounded in perceiving and doing. ... Second, the control of perception by action and the enhancement by exploratory action of the opportunities to perceive are so fluent, reliable, and widely manifest in living things that they must be underwritten by principles of the most basic and general kind.... Whatever the cognitive capacities of interest, it can be expected that the laws and principles that make perceiving and acting possible play a central role in shaping the characteristics that define the given capacity (Turvey, 1992, p. 86).

In this chapter I will be looking at two central – and related – concepts in the ecological approach to language learning: *emergence* and *affordance*. Both concepts are part of the foundation of ecology: affordance because it is at the roots of the relationship between the person and the physical, social and symbolic world; emergence because it characterizes the development of complex linguistic abilities.

One of the things I will try to do is to relate the two concepts in meaningful ways, and to relate both to semiotics (both Peirce's and Halliday's), as outlined in the last chapter. I will also extend the notion of perception and action to discuss attention and awareness, or in general, consciousness. Then I will discuss the process of language growth by looking at approaches to grammar development or *emergent grammar* (Hopper, 1998). Related approaches in second language learning will also be discussed, such as *grammaticization* (Rutherford, 1987), *grammaticalization* (Dittmar, 1992), and *grammaring* (Larsen-Freeman, 2003).

EMERGENCE

The whole is bigger than the parts, and it is also often smarter than the parts. This is a major tenet of Gestalt psychology.[1] One of the clearest examples is the ant colony, a smartly organized society of individually fairly simple little animals. Put one ant

---

[1] Gibson criticized Gestalt psychology for not showing what exactly it is that makes the whole more than the sum of its parts. In Gibson's view, Gestalt often turned into some mysterious doctrine (Reed, 1988, p. 55). I think that Vygotsky had similar qualms about Gestalt psychology, although he voiced them in different ways.

on a table, and you will find that it is really quite helpless. If it can find its way home it will be all right, but if not, it will soon perish. The ant colony as a whole builds elaborate structures, organizes raids, runs aphid farms, stores and processes food, etc., a regular industrial and administrative enterprise, but one without centralized leadership. It demonstrates the process of *emergence*, that is, structures such as ant colonies evolve a higher level of sophistication from lower-level rules (Johnson, 2001).

Emergence happens when relatively simple organisms or elements reorganize themselves into more complex, more intelligent systems. In addition, these systems appear to be able to adapt to changing conditions whereas the simpler forms that compose them have no such adaptive abilities (ibid).

Johnson describes the amazing feat of an organism called 'slime mold' that was trained to find the shortest way through a maze by the Japanese scientist Toshiyuki Nakagaki (Johnson, ibid, p. 11). The slime mold is nothing but thousands of single-cell molds that, under certain conditions, coalesce into a single reddish-orange piece of goop, not unlike dog's vomit, that slowly moves across rotting wood or leaves in a forest. There is no central nervous system, let alone a brain, yet this amorphous blob moves about and, it turns out, can even learn to find its way around a maze. When the weather turns cool and damp, the blob splits up again into thousands of single mold cells, all basically just sitting around minding their own business until the collective mood strikes them (rather, they start to emit a certain chemical substance) to get together again.

Let us resist the temptation to describe more curious phenomena or supra-organisms (see Johnson, 2001, for many fascinating examples), and go directly to the issue of emergence in language. I want to begin my discussion of learning in an ecological perspective (see also van Lier, 2000) with an anecdote that involves my son when he was three years old. He grew up speaking Spanish in Peru, and when we moved to the USA he spoke no English. He went through the classic silent period for the first few months, when he would speak no English at all, though he clearly understood a great deal. We did continue speaking Spanish at home, but he went to an all-English Montessori pre-school. In that environment he was clearly quite traumatized at first.

After about two or three months, I was wheeling my cart around the local supermarket, with him sitting in the front. I had just picked up a box of Rice Krispies, the first item in our cart, when another guy came along with a cart that also had just a box of Rice Krispies in it. A humorous coincidence, which Marcus noticed. At that point he produced his first English sentence:

Look! This on this!

We can note several important semiotic phenomena. First, the word "Look!" establishes joint attention to an object in the environment. It's an opening, a summons, and by following his gaze and the direction of his pointing finger, I know what it is we are talking about. But that is just the first part. Now he has to explain why it is that this thing is noteworthy. Having secured my attention he has to justify having done so. He does not have the language to say, "Isn't it a curious coincidence that ... etc...," but by combining his linguistic resources with other semiotic resources, he is able to convey his meaning. In this way the context provides *affordances* (possibilities for action that yield opportunities for engagement and participation) that can stimulate intersubjectivity, joint attention, and various kinds of linguistic commentary. The availability in the context of 'things to talk about' and the availability of resources to engage with them and stimulate further action (including verbal action, which is always social interaction), I would like to call the *semiotic resources* of the environment. A rich semiotic budget of resources, I hypothesize, stimulates the emergence of language. A learning environment is not one in which a teacher throws linguistic signs around like an eccentric billionaire might throw dollar bills, nor one in which bills of various linguistic denominations are doled out piecemeal by a grammar miser. Instead, we hope to teach the learners how the *linguistic market* works. This is quite a different proposition from teaching rules of grammar and vocabulary.

How do learners learn the rules of the linguistic market place? Let us divert for a moment and ask: How do kids learn the rules of playing soccer (see van Lier, 1996)? Certainly not by being lectured on them for several years. They learn them by participating in certain practices. Two pivotal practices in this respect are a) playing the game; and b) participating in stories and comments about the game perhaps combined with watching games. When they start playing, children tend to run after the ball in a single swarm, kicking it around in seemingly random directions. Then at some point a 'feel for the game' emerges. The game reorganizes itself (not for all players at once, but for some) from 'running after the ball wherever it rolls' to 'moving the ball around collaboratively in strategic ways.' At that point the rules of the game become learnable, in an interaction between bottom-up discovery, and top-down instruction, within the social context of playing the game.

Another example I gave in the 1996 book was that of Benji Langdon, who determined to replicate the mathematical genius of idiot-savant twins. In his case he tried and tried, practiced and practiced, with no apparent progress until suddenly, overnight, his poor abused brain cells reorganized themselves, migrated in droves to the right brain, and he was able to perform the same tricks as the twins.

Emergence thus can have different trajectories, can come about in different ways, and may or may not involve a dramatic 'ahah Erlebnis' or epiphany. Given this heterogeneity, what really is emergence (as different from just plain 'learning,' or maybe as a special perspective on learning)? Recall that emergence is a reorganization of simple elements into a more complex system. In language, such emergence has been documented in several ways. One is the establishment of a phonological system. Researchers, among them Janet Werker and Patricia Kuhl, have found that around nine months to one year of age infants complete the establishment of a phonological system. Before that time they can distinguish phonemic contrasts from another language that are indistinguishable to native speakers of their own language (Werker & Tees, 1984). After that time (i.e., when the neurons in the brain are committed to the phonological system of English), they can no longer hear the distinctions. This commitment occurs fairly rapidly, and is the basis upon which syllabic (reduplicative) babbling is built, which then fairly quickly leads to vocabulary development. In this way, innate dispositions in interaction with the social and physical environment bring about the gradual emergence of linguistic resources.

Below we will look more closely at the processes by which language learning happens, or how language emerges within a context that stimulates learning.[2]

EMERGENTISM

The notion of emergentism is associated first with the philosopher John Stuart Mill, who distinguished mechanical causes from chemical causes. In chemical processes, the mixture of several reactants produces results that are in no way the sum of the elements, but often something quite different, such as a new gas or liquid (Wilson & Keil, 1999, p. 267). By just looking at hydrogen atoms and oxygen atoms you will never get the idea of water. The idea of emergentism (and emergence) both in the physical and in the social sciences, is that the result of events or activities may be dramatically different from the initial inputs to those events or activities, and may not be reducible to them. This is actually a key element also in the developmental psychology of Vygotsky.

The traditional paradigm of scientific research cannot handle such apparent disconnections between cause and effect, and usually some other factor such as innatism or instinct is then invoked to explain the surprising development. But, as Bateson has pointed out (1979), to rely on instinct, genetics, or other putative explanations in fact is to provide no explanation at all.

What are the sorts of things that emerge in nature, the sorts of things that cannot be predicted? Things like climatic changes, earthquakes, hurricanes, and avalanches? The establishment or collapse of ecosystems, human societies, or cities (Humphrey, 1992; Johnson, 2001)? In all such cases, the result of some action must be qualitatively different, some reorganization on a different scale, for the word emergence to be warranted. If we put two pebbles on the floor and add two pebbles, it would not make sense to say that a group of four pebbles 'emerges.' Nor, in the strict sense of emergentism, can we speak of emergence if we have a hillside full of pebbles, and we add one pebble, and a landslide happens. The addition of the pebble 'causes' the landslide, and even though we cannot give a precise calculation that predicts that this particular addition of one pebble WILL cause a landslide, there is an additive, mechanical process that says that, given enough pebbles on a slope of this kind, a landslide is bound to happen sooner or later.

Emergence presupposes a non-reductive change, from a lower-level phenomenon to a higher-level phenomenon, from individual ants to an ant colony, from a bunch of houses to an organized city, from perception to thought, from pointing to language, etc. *Non-reductive* means that the lower-level elements (things, behaviors, skills) cannot explain the higher-level ones, thus they are qualitatively different, yet the higher level is clearly in some way based on, derived from, or built up from, the lower level. A butterfly emerges from the chrysalis. Opening up the chrysalis

---

[2] Some of the ideas and examples contained in parts of this chapter are drawn from recent papers, e.g. van Lier, 2000 and van Lier, 2002, as well as various unpublished papers based on presentations and seminars.

beforehand and studying it under a microscope will not reveal a hidden butterfly (or butterfly parts), nor can you show, by studying the butterfly, that it came from a chrysalis.

In language learning (and learning in general), the notion of emergence is gaining considerable attention (Elman et al., 1996; MacWhinney, 1999). Yet, the concept is not new. It is closely connected with the old nature-nurture debate that we will briefly review below. One example of emergence in language, diachronically (over time) is the Great Vowel Shift in the English language that happened in the 16th century in England. Basically, some vowels changed in quality, these changes brought about other changes, and eventually a new vowel system emerged. That is, because of some changes in some vowels, the whole system reorganized, reaching a new equilibrium as it were. So, one change can destabilize the system, bring about other changes, and gradually a new system emerges that settles into a new era of stability.

In phonology, vowel systems can be of various kinds: 3, 5, 7, 8 vowels, etc. At times, because of dialect variations, social changes (such as those studied by William Labov on Martha's Vineyard, see Labov, 1972), or language contact, some vowels might merge into one. At that point one might get homophones in the language that might cause confusion. In Southern American English, *pin* and *pen* sound the same. In Northern American English, at least in some dialects, *cot* and *caught* sound the same. A language can deal with a certain amount of homophony, but at some point vowels start to shift and move away, to establish discrete distances again.

In the period between Old, Middle and Modern English (roughly from 1000 to 1500), front vowels in many words became higher, rounded vowels became unrounded, and long high vowels became diphthongs. It sounds like a mess, but looking at it on a vowel chart one can see an emerging pattern:

The chart shows some kind of system at work, but of course in actual life people don't change their pronunciation just because of some externally imposed system. What happened during the Great Vowel Shift is that vowels became higher, so that, e.g., among the front vowels, /næm/ became /neːm/ (name), and /miːs/ became /mais/ (mice). In each case we can see that the vowel moved up one place, or several places in successive steps. When they reached the 'top' (the high front vowel), the next step was a diphthong. At the right side, the back vowels showed a similar pattern, moving from /staːn/ to /stoʷn/ (stone), and /huːs/ to /haʷs/ (house). We can see then that the movement of individual vowels trigger the movement of other vowels, and after a protracted period in which vowel sounds shift into new positions, a whole new system of vowel assignments emerges.[3]

---

[3] There are 'drag' and 'push' theories of sound change. In a 'drag' theory, a vowel shifts, and the next vowel in line is 'dragged' into the space that is vacated. Conversely, in a 'push' theory, the vowel that moves invades the space of another vowel, and 'pushes' that vowel into the next space, thus possibly creating a chain reaction. This leaves unexplained why a sound would change in the first place, and for this there are a number of theories, including sociolinguistic ones (Labov, 1972). For a detailed discussion of the Great Vowel Shift, see Gimson, 1970.

84   CHAPTER 4

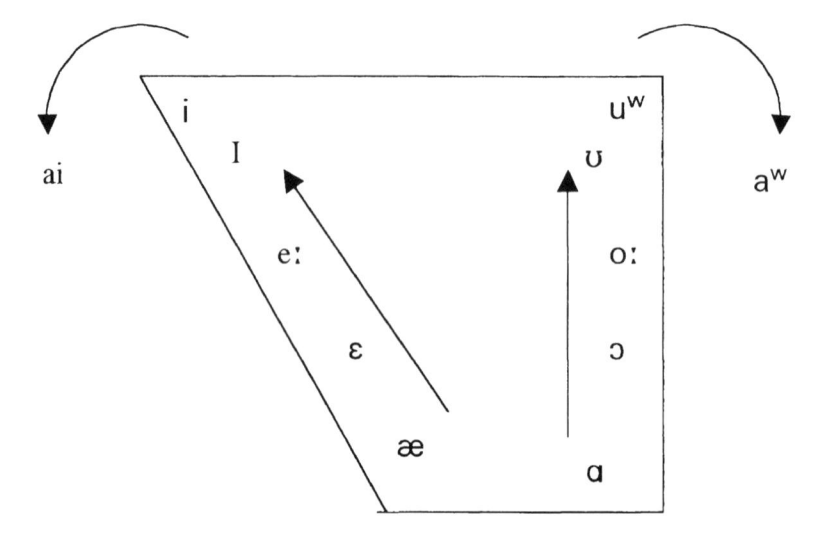

Figure 4.1: The Great Vowel Shift

I have spent some time looking at one famous example of diachronic emergence in language. With this example in mind, we can try to see how this might serve as an analogy for an individual's language learning.

LANGUAGE AS AN EMERGENT SYSTEM

> If "culture" is not an object to be described, neither is it a unified corpus of symbols and meanings that can be definitively interpreted. Culture is contested, temporal, and emergent. Representation and explanation – both by insiders and outsiders – is implicated in this emergence (Clifford, 1986, p. 19).

Language, or a (any) language, including its grammar, is also "contested, temporal and emergent" in the same way that Clifford describes culture. What does it mean for language to be *emergent* in this sense? One example is the Great Vowel Shift shown in the previous section. The vowel system of the language is always in a process of change, with phonemes sprouting allophones, and vowels pushing against other vowels, jostling for space like birds on a wire. At some point, such as when vowel mergers create an unbearable amount of homonymy (caused by homophones, such as *pin* and *pen*, *cot* and *caught*, as illustrated above), the whole system reorganizes itself to establish new neural spaces (given that neurons in the brain are committed to certain vowels) between adjacent vowels. In New Zealand English, so far as I have been able to figure out, *sex* sounds like *six*, and *six* sounds like *sucks*. Maybe *sacks* sounds like *sex*, I haven't been able to establish this.

In grammar or vocabulary things are not particularly stable either. One used to be able to be 'gay' in the sense of being in a good mood, but not any more. 'Terrorism' is achieving new meanings almost daily. In the US, 'did you eat yet' has taken over from 'have you eaten yet,' the distinction between simple present and present perfect having collapsed in a range of contexts. And in the American Midwest, things used to be pretty much the same, but now they are quite different *anymore* (this word now being used also in a positive sense, as 'these days,' see Labov, 1972, p. 309).

Bakhtin (1981) notes an essential tension in language between what he terms *centrifugal* and *centripetal* forces. Centrifugal forces (moving outwards) express creativity, diversification, variety and openness; centripetal forces (moving inwards) express homogeneity, standardization, and centralized control over forms and meanings.

So, on the one hand, speakers want to embroider and invent, sounding new and different, signaling their individual and group identity. On the other hand, speakers (and often official agencies and institutions, such as schools) wish to establish official standards and guidelines for 'correct' language, thus attempting to reduce variations in use.

Schooling usually means conforming to a standard in terms of expression and genre, it implies 'sounding the same,' which is sounding like an educated speaker. Outside of school things may be different: the home dialect may be different from the school dialect (the official language), and may express loyalty, intimacy, understanding. Thus the growing student may become bidialectal.

In these and many other ways, languages shift and change, either through internal processes, or through external pressures and social processes. In this sense we can say that language, not just 'a' language (like French or Farsi), but 'language' in its more general sense, is emergent, not fixed, in flux rather than static. Like culture, it is contested, open to processes of inclusion and exclusion, prescribed and proscribed patterns of use, permeated by value judgments, markers of identity, and signs of success.

THE NATURE-NURTURE DEBATE: A BRIEF REVISIT

To put the notion of emergence into a historical context, it is useful to hark back to the innatist versus environmentalist issue, discussed in more detail in Chapter 2. Over the course of history there have been two major ways of looking at language development (I'm talking about first language now). The first is well illustrated by the following quote from St. Augustine:

> When they (my elders) named some object, and accordingly moved towards something, I saw this and grasped that the thing was called by the sound they uttered when they meant to point it out. Their intention was shewn by their bodily movements, as it were the natural language of all peoples: the expression of the face, the play of the eyes, the movement of other parts of the body, and the tone of voice which expresses our state of mind in

seeking, having, rejecting, or avoiding something. Thus, as I heard words repeatedly used in their proper places in various sentences, I gradually learnt to understand what objects they signified; and after I had trained my mouth to form these signs, I used them to express my own desires (quoted in Wittgenstein, 1958).

In this view, language development consists of learning the names for things, and of imitating what the adults say around you. This can be seen as the environmentalist or 'nurture' approach (see further below). On the other hand, we have the view expressed by the German linguist Wilhelm von Humboldt in the 19th century, who opined that language "cannot really be taught, it can only be awakened in the soul" (quoted in Dakin, 1974). This is the characteristic nativist or 'nature' perspective.

In Chomsky's UG (Universal Grammar, e.g., 2000), the actual language, all the sentences and utterances used in the presence of the developing child cannot predict (or perhaps better: cannot guarantee) the eventual outcome of the adult language system. In other words, language competence is *underdetermined* by the exposure to language that the child experiences. Chomsky's conclusion from this quite reasonable observation is that, whatever the end result is over and above what the child may have heard, this must have been there all along, from the start, as an innate endowment. After all, something cannot come from nothing. Against this, the emergentists (see above) argue that something new (and different) can indeed come, perhaps not from 'nothing,' but from something quite different. That is, the fact that the child ends up with a stable linguistic system that is uniform in its basic essentials across all speakers, regardless of what the precise data were that she was exposed to, this fact does not mean that it must have been there all along. It may emerge from quite different premises. This is the emergentists' argument, and it harks back quite strongly to Piaget's lifelong view of learning as the *construction* of knowledge, as well as Vygotsky's view of learning as a *transformation* from social functions into symbolic functions.[4]

EMERGENT GRAMMAR

The emergentist approach to grammar asks several unusual questions about language, unusual because they question various assumptions language learners and teachers have long held but rarely examined.

Are the rules of language – i.e., its grammar – fixed, or are they constructed in interaction, in practices of socialization, and in the use of language as a tool of thought and social life? Traditionally, language is seen as consisting of a prefabricated structure that exists either as a biologically inherited endowment (a universal grammar, or UG, as in Chomsky's linguistics), or as a cultural-historical monument that has grown into what it is over the millennia of human social intercourse (as Saussure suggested).

Perhaps we do not need to make an either-or choice at this level. Clearly, language is shaped by human needs and human characteristics. We cannot make

---

[4] Although Piaget and Vygotsky approach this issue from quite different directions, and they mean something different by emergence and development.

language by rubbing our legs together like the crickets do, nor by flapping wings that we do not have, nor by emitting intricate scents like the moths do, and so on. We use an articulatory system that uses our mouth, larynx, and other physical tools (for example, in the case of sign language), a conceptual structure that uses our brain, and a prosodic system that uses our emotional processes and bodily gestures. These things in themselves will produce a language that is human and not otherwise. How a biological system or a socio-cultural-historical system would produce a detailed grammar is a more controversial question. Perhaps less controversial is the consideration that a biological system *in interaction with* a socio-cultural-historical system could produce a language system in an incipient member of a speech community.

Let me take this last interactional suggestion as the most reasonable option, and see how the process of 'producing' a language might happen in this meeting of biological and environmental systems. Or let me suggest first how it might *not* happen. It might not happen in the following ways:

1) Language does not just 'grow' with minimal triggering from the environment – the UG perspective;

2) Language does not have to be learned rule by rule, by dint of instruction and practice – the traditional grammar perspective;

3) Language is not just imitation and association based on observed examples – the traditional behavioristic perspective.

Having proposed how language acquisition does *not* happen, how do we propose that it *does* happen, or how language *emerges* in an individual? To begin to answer this question I go back to a crucial distinction made by the philosopher Donald Davidson between *prior theory* and *passing theory* (Davidson, 1986; see also van Lier, 1996) in language use and interpretation:

> For the hearer, the prior theory expresses how he is prepared in advance to interpret the utterance of the speaker, while the passing theory is how he *does* interpret the utterance. For the speaker, the prior theory is what he *believes* the interpreter's prior theory to be, while his passing theory is the theory he *intends* the interpreter to use (Davidson, 1986, p. 442).

We can leave aside Chomsky's objections [5] to Davidson's conclusion [that "there is no such thing as a language" (ibid, p. 446)], but continue to focus on the question of how linguistic abilities arise in contexts of language use.

Language is much less regular in a general sense than grammatical descriptions or prescriptions suggest. Corpus linguistics has shown surprising limitations on large-scale regularity in all areas of grammar and vocabulary use. Moreover, as

---

[5] Chomsky (2000) considers Davidson's argument "largely correct" (p. 69), but argues that an empirical study of "everything that people are capable of doing" is senseless, returning to the Cartesian reductionist practice of isolating well-defined pieces for empirical scrutiny (2000, pp. 69ff; see our earlier discussion on this point in Chapter 2; see also van Lier 2000).

shown above in the example of the Great Vowel Shift, as well as in numerous dialect studies, sound systems are also in a constant state of change.

A crucial characteristic of language is the mapping of structure onto function, or the relationship between form and meaning. This relationship is constantly being interpreted and reinterpreted in every act of speaking, as part of the negotiation of meaning that accompanies every dialogical interchange. As with Davidson's passing theory, new meanings are routinely created for old forms, both accidentally and on purpose.

According to the emergentist perspective, grammar is not a prerequisite of communication, rather it is a byproduct of communication (Hopper, 1998). Regularity and systematicity are "produced by the partial settling or *sedimentation* of frequently used forms into temporary subsystems" (Hopper, ibid, p. 158). Language learning happens in neither of the two extremes mentioned above: not because of the activation of an innate biological module, and not either because of inductive imitation and association. Language learning emerges from participation in linguistic practices, such practices always being steeped in historical, cultural and institutional meaning systems.

I will now briefly look at how emergentism has been interpreted in second and foreign language learning situations.

GRAMMATICALIZATION

Grammaticalization is basically the idea that the acquisition of grammar (or in more general terms, the formal complexities of the language, which are mainly phonological and morpho-syntactic) occurs not as a result of an accumulation of explicitly learned rules, but rather as the result of cognitive and/or social activity using the language in meaningful ways. It is thus largely synonymous with emergent grammar as described above.

In L1 acquisition grammaticalization is well documented as a non-linear example of emergence. Bates and Goodman put it as follows:

> The successive bursts that characterize vocabulary growth and the emergence of morphosyntax can be viewed as different phases of an immense nonlinear wave that starts in the single-word stage and crashes on the shores of grammar a year or so later (1999, p. 41).

The "shores of grammar" that appear on the lexical horizon around the age of two are the beginning of rapid morphosyntactic development that is built on a foundation of vocabulary and formulaic (unanalyzed) phrases. By age five the process of language development in L1 is largely complete. However, as I mentioned in Chapter 2, this is not the end of the story. Many years of language study, both formal and informal, are required before the growing person is a fully articulate member of the speech community. In non-literate societies adult members must be able to participate in rituals, meetings, story telling, market negotiations, and so on. In literate societies educated members must learn to read and write and master a variety of decontextualized discourses, each with their own grammatical and discursive structures (the development of academic language).

In L2 acquisition, something like grammaticalization has long been a part of certain approaches to SLA, such as Krashen's comprehensible input theory (1985). In that view, just by being exposed to lots of comprehensible input the learners will subconsciously acquire the complex structures of the language. In fact, Krashen argues, explicit teaching of grammar is virtually useless, since it only produces learned knowledge about language that is not usable in everyday communication. So, grammatical knowledge (or skill) develops automatically from listening to messages that are comprehensible. Krashen maintains that speech does not cause acquisition, rather, acquisition causes speech (ibid.), thus denying a meaningful role for language use and language practice, something I will disagree with in a later chapter. A problematic aspect of Krashen's theory is that it is impossible to show precisely how these processes (the emergence, the internalization, the 'microgenesis,' in a Vygotskyan sense[6]) come about. Presumably, because the acquisition process is largely subconscious, the workings of the process are not open to inspection, and acquisition just happens.

Another grammaticalization process quite well known in SLA is the *restructuring* that occurs in information-processing theories (McLaughlin, 1987). In this view, incoming information (input) is processed in the brain, and interacts with existing mental representations, and the new information brings about restructuring in the mind. This can be spontaneous, and it can also be the result of practice, hypothesis testing, and other efforts. So, in a sense, restructuring is another word for cognitive emergence. However, there are several problems with the information processing approach, the main ones being a lack of attention to social interaction, and the assumption that language is a fixed code that results in uniform cognitive representations (see Chapter 2 for more detailed discussion). We should note therefore that this cognitive restructuring process in information processing assumes a quite different perspective than Hopper's emergent grammar and routines (Hopper, 1998).

As an approach to grammar teaching, grammaticalization proper starts with the work of Rutherford, who calls it *grammaticization*. Rutherford distinguishes two approaches to teaching grammar: the *mechanical*, and the *organic*. The mechanical approach proceeds by the notion of *accumulated entities* (1987, p. 5), that is, "the steady accumulation of more and more complex language entities" (ibid.). Such a view does not take into account that there are certain innate principles that determine the way language complexities evolve from one another, nor does it take into account how social intentions and demands interact with language resources to produce discourse types of various kinds, with grammatical complexification that is brought about functionally and interactionally. Thus, Rutherford advocates an approach to grammar he calls *consciousness-raising*, which allows for the learners to construct their own developing grammars on the basis of examining their own

---

[6] The term microgenesis was first introduced by Heinz Werner, as follows: "Any human activity such as perceiving, thinking, acting, etc. is an unfolding process, and this unfolding, or 'microgenesis', whether it takes seconds or hours or days, occurs in developmental sequence" (Werner, 1956, p. 347; see also Valsiner & van der Veer, 2000, p. 306).

Interlanguage and discursive practices. Here, the focus is on examining the "actual metamorphosis of interlanguage" (1987, p. 38).

In this way, Rutherford, and others who propose a similar approach (e.g., Larsen-Freeman's *grammaring*, 2003), say that neither Krashen's approach of just providing *comprehensible input* that contains linguistic structures just beyond the learner's level ("i+1"), nor the information-processors' *restructuring* (which may well be closely related, even though McLaughlin and Krashen do not see eye to eye on this, see McLaughlin, 1987) are adequate. What needs to happen is a very systematic approach to teaching grammar explicitly, but not by way of explanations or accumulated entities (a succession of drills), but by raising the learners' awareness of what they are trying to say and how they are saying it, and coming up with more efficacious ways of saying that thing. In a sense, then, the grammaticalization approach is trying to take Pit Corder's old idea of the learner's "built-in syllabus" (1967) seriously as a guide to the curriculum.

AFFORDANCES

In an earlier book (van Lier, 1996) I proposed a change from the term 'input' to 'engagement.' Later on (van Lier, 2000) I proposed to change our SLA terminology from 'input' to 'affordance.' Why these problems with the term 'input'? What's in a name, anyway?

Input comes from a view of language as a fixed code and of learning as a process of receiving and processing pieces of this fixed code. This is variously referred to as 'telementation' (Harris, 1996), the 'conduit metaphor' (Reddy, 1979), or the view of the learner (particularly the learner's brain, of course) as a computer, into which data is 'inputted.' In Chapter 2 I discussed some of the problems with this perspective, including some of the pedagogical problems that can result from such a perspective.

A wide range of views, variously named constructivist, constructionist, interactionist, experiential, dialogical, situated, sociocultural, and so on, reject the view that language (or any other phenomenon, worldly or mental) is ready-made for consumption. Rather, we construe and construct it as we go along. A word or an expression never means the same thing twice, in any conversation or across conversations. Dictionary meanings may be useful anchoring points that are distilled from numerous occasions of use and reflections on those occasions of use. But in actual, situated use any word or expression is negotiated anew every time, albeit on a platform of shared presuppositions. This was well expressed by Bakhtin who noted that a word is always "half someone else's" (1981, p. 345). In fact, Bakhtin went further and maintained that all language is dialogical, it does not exist unless it is shared. This is echoed by Wittgenstein, who concluded that, "Yes, meaning something is like going up to someone" (1974, p. 157).

On this understanding, that language as well as other sources of meaning in the world are not ready-made or ready-given, let's explore the concept of affordance. I will begin with a range of quotes from the literature to give a flavor of the sorts of

WHAT ARE AFFORDANCES?

Affordances are relations of possibility between animals and their environments (Neisser, 1987, p.21).

We could benefit from considering participants' orientations to the production and recognition of structural patterns in talk as social affordances: immediately recognizable projections, predictions and perceived consequences of making this (and not that) utterance at any given time (Forrester, 1999, p. 88).

Affordances consist in the opportunities for interaction that things in the environment possess relative to the sensorimotor capacities of the animal (Varela, Thompson & Rosch, 1991, p. 203).

[The linguistic world]... is full of demands and requirements, opportunities and limitations, rejections and invitations, enablements and constraints - in short, affordances (Shotter & Newson 1982, p. 34)

In the above quotes, notions such as relations, possibility, opportunity, immediacy and interaction are prominent. Affordance refers to what is available to the person to do something with. Some things clearly and directly signal their relevance for a person in a particular situation. For example, if I want to cross a creek, a flat rock rising above the water immediately indicates to me that I can step on it in order to get across. Perhaps it signals nothing of the sort to a small child, whose short legs and limited balancing capacity put the rock out of reach. On another occasion, when the tourists are long gone, the rock, warmed by the sun, affords a great pozzie (see p. 64) for a small snake to bask on in the sunshine.

GIBSON'S PERSPECTIVE ON PERCEPTION AND ACTION

Gibson defines affordances as "what [the environment] *offers* the animal, what it *provides* or *furnishes*, either for good or ill" (1979, p. 127, emphasis in the original). Affordances are detected, picked up, and acted upon as part of a person's resonating with, or being in tune with, her or his environment. According to Gibson, to perceive the world is to co-perceive oneself. This means that when we perceive something, we perceive it as it relates to us. So, the object, the *semiotic object*, Peirce would say, is not 'as it is,' but 'as it is to me.' At its most primordial level, an affordance is perceived and acted upon directly, immediately, because the organism is what it is, the animal is what it is, the child is who she or he is. The mother's breast needs neither explanation nor representation for the baby, it affords nourishment directly. The same can be said for the mother's voice: it affords the deepest level of nascent intersubjectivity. The mother's (actually, I shouldn't leave the father out at this point) finger affords grasping, and that affords physical play, and that affords vocalization, and that affords.... conversation, ultimately.

In a sense, the notion of affordance is related to *meaning potential* (Halliday, 1978), so long as we do not define meaning as sitting inside words and sentences (or in objects). More accurately, it is *action potential*, and it emerges as we interact with the physical and social world. Preconditions for meaning to emerge are action, perception and interpretation, in a continuous cycle of mutual reinforcement:

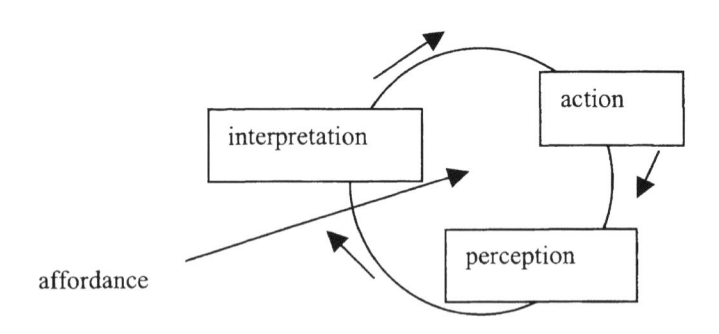

Figure 4.2: Affordance

When we look at meaning in this way, it becomes an active relationship, or engagement, with the environment in which we find ourselves.

One of Gibson's most important – and most contested – findings is that perception of affordances is in the first instance direct and immediate, rather than indirect and mediated. Gibson protests strongly against those who would say that we see only what we want to or are conditioned to see, through the lens of our prior expectations or mental representations. He says that we should not see ourselves as limited by predetermined ways of seeing, as programmed to see things in a certain way, but rather, that we are able to perceive the world creatively, and relate to it directly.

What does it mean for perception to be direct, or for affordances to be immediate, and why would this be of interest to language learning? It appears that it is easier to argue the case for direct perception with animals than it is with humans, though Gibson steadfastly refused to draw a clear distinction between the two. Certainly, his insistence on the primacy of direct perception attacked several of the sacred cows of early cognitivism: *memory, representation* and *schema* foremost among them.

Auyang mentions three powerful advantages of Gibson's theory of affordances that set it apart from earlier behaviorist or gestaltist views, and that I will relate here to language learning:

1. It replaces fixed-eye vision by mobile-eye vision. Expanding from this to human development, the affordance perspective assumes an active learner establishing relationships with and within the environment. In terms of language learning, affordances arise out of participation and use, and learning opportunities arise as a consequence of participation and use.

2. It brings out the rich complexity of environmental factors. Note that the linguistic environment immediately increases in complexity when we envisage a learner physically, socially, and mentally moving around a multidimensional semiotic space. However, since the affordances match the learner to the environment, it is the activity that determines what is picked up, not the complex environment. Therefore, a simple learning activity is possible in a complex environment (given appropriate guidance), and the environment remains there as a potential proximal source of instigative processes.

3. It is not based on an assumption of arbitrary impulses that strike the perceptual organs, and that can only become meaningful after being interpreted (mediated) by mental representations. Rather, it assumes that invariant properties in the environment can directly resonate with the actively perceiving organism (or learner). In terms of language learning, the learner can directly perceive and act on the ambient language, without having to route everything through a pre-existing mental apparatus of schemata and representations (2000, p. 62).

Critics of Gibson's theory of affordances and direct perception – and there have been many (see e.g. Ullmann, 1980) – complain that this ecological approach does not leave room for the individual person, with a mental life, with memories, with well-established cognitive representations, with a large repertoire of expectations, and so on.

Perhaps affordances can best be seen as 'pre-signs,' that is, they may be the fuel that get sign-making going. Recall that, according to the above picture, action, perception and interpretation are one holistic circle. But they may go through many iterations before linguistic meaning and symbolic meaning emerge, and then merge into cultural meaning.

If this is the case, then meaning making builds on affordance and direct perception as a necessary *prerequisite* at first, and as a necessary *ingredient* later. In Peirce's scheme, "Thirdness cannot be divorced from Secondness and Firstness, symbols emerge from the terrain, oftentimes unsteady, of icons and indices" (Merrell, 1997a, p. 73). I suggested in Chapter 3 that indexicality is the 'way into' language. However, the pump must be primed by iconicity, by Firstness, and Firstness is first-level affordance. Let's work through an example.

I am in France, and I don't know any French. French is a learnable language in that situation, but I haven't started on that yet, or maybe I am not even sure if I *want* to start. After all, those guttural 'r's, and those rounded front vowels, are quite unsettling to hear, let alone to produce. I visit someone in her office, and she says, "asseyez-vous." I have no idea what that means, but there is a chair there, and she is pointing to it with an outstretched hand. So, the chair offers its usual affordance (it offers 'sitting in'), and she offers permission for me to carry out that action. So I sit and say "thank you."

In the first instance, the first moment, the words "asseyez-vous" have no meaning in themselves, but in the context they come to be seen as part of a sitting-down routine. The chair directly affords sitting for me (other objects, such as potted cactuses and toaster ovens do not), but the social context does not automatically afford sitting. It must, in this office, be afforded by a specific set of words and gestures. If the gestures are universal enough, then the words, incomprehensible though they may be, will become social affordances, the immediate chair-sitting affordance is supplemented by a socially mediated invitation, and I can sit down. So, immediate and mediated affordances act in consort to link language to actions via perception. In language learning it seems to me that these connections are crucial for learning opportunities to emerge.

CULTURAL ARTIFACTS AND OTHER AFFORDANCES

A chair is a cultural artifact. So are hammers, spoons, books and doorbells. We might want to draw a difference between a physical object that is a natural affordance, and one that is a social/cultural affordance. Why? Human artifacts have their intended uses built into their design, and therefore carry historical-social-cultural information in that design. They may therefore signal affordances in special and obvious ways for humans. Clearly, a chair is designed for seatability. A button is designed for pushing. And so on. Donald Norman (in his book *The Psychology of Everyday Things,* 1988) in fact used the theory of affordances to discuss the design of objects, and this was extended later on for the design of computer interfaces and web site designs. His article on the Internet (http://www.jnd.org/dn.mss/affordances-interactions.html) discusses some of the problems associated with the proliferation of meanings of the term.

EXPANDED MEANINGS OF AFFORDANCE

As the discussion above suggests, in recent times the notion of affordance has been expanded to include various sub-categories that expand the construct beyond the original meanings discussed in the work of James Gibson (see also E. J. Gibson, 1991).

Reed distinguishes between *natural* and *cultural* affordances, the latter having to do with "historically specific meanings and values" (1988, p. 310).

Shotter and Newson (1982, see above) include all sorts of linguistic "enablements and constraints" in the notion of affordance. These are clearly social affordances of a higher order, and must be seen as indirect and mediated, in the sense of Peirce's signs that include the interpretant.

Forrester (1999) adds a further dimension, the detection of conversational affordances as part of making sense of talk in interaction. These might include turn-taking signals, back channels, intonation patterns, and various attitudinal markers. In similar ways, McArthur and Baron discuss the notion of social affordances (1983), in which they include various kinds of 'attunements,' such as those that signal compliance, various kinds of emotion perception, impression management, etc.

The extent to which these extensions fruitfully expand the concept of affordance, or perhaps dilute it from Gibson's original conception is a difficult but important question. While I think it is valuable to extend the reach of the concept of affordance into the realm of language learning, we must continually bear in mind the defining features of the concept, here expressed in linguistic terms:

a) an affordance expresses a relationship between a person and a linguistic expression (a speech act, a speech event); it is *action potential*; it is a *relation of possibility*, as Neisser put it (see above);
b) linguistic affordances are specified in the linguistic expression, and available to the active interlocutor (or addressee) who may pick up one or more of those affordances as they are relevant at the moment;
c) the affordances picked up serve the agent – depending on his or her abilities – to promote further action and lead to higher and more successful levels of interaction.

In sum, then, language affordances, whether natural or cultural, direct or indirect, are relations of possibility between language users. They can be acted upon to make further linguistic action possible. At his point, affordance links up with the Vygotskyan concept of *microgenesis* (on which more later).

Gibson's theory of affordances and direct perception leaves unaddressed the issue of what features of the environment are relevant. At the most basic level, the question is an evolutionary one. Organisms relate to certain invariant features of their environment naturally. They are in tune with these affordances, they 'resonate' with them (cf. Grossberg's notion of *adaptive resonance*, 1980), and they perceive them directly. The flower is relevant to the bee, and an empty shell of a certain shape and size is relevant to a hermit crab. To a certain extent, this same evolutionary, direct relevance applies also to humans. A flat hard surface is 'walkable-on,' a pebble is 'throwable,' and so on. In the case of manufactured objects (cultural artifacts), the intended use is designed into the artifact itself, it signals its purpose (e.g., a hammer, a doorknob, a shoe). These design features entail a special kind of relevance, and this has led to a special field of study that has also extended to the design of computer interface and web design conventions (Norman, 1988; no date).

Language use in communication raises the need for a theory of relevance of some sort. Affordances in communication are intermingled with and hooked into a myriad of other meaning-producing signs and sign chains. While first-level affordances (such as the conversational affordances mentioned in Forrester, 1999) continue to be directly available in terms of what they 'mean,' other signs require both design from the utterer's perspective and interpretation from the hearer's perspective.

If we reject, as I have done in several places above, the fixed-code theory of communication that assumes that ready-made messages are coded at one end, transmitted, and then decoded in identical form at the other end, then we need in its place a constructivist theory of message construction and interpretation. Some of the most influential theories of this nature include Grice's *cooperative principle* (and the maxims of quality, quantity, relation and manner, 1975), Sperber and Wilson's *theory of relevance* (1986), and Keller's *principle of rationality* (1998). Basically, the speaker or performer of an action wants to be understood rather than misunderstood, and the interlocutor attempts to understand the speech or action in the way that it is intended to be understood. There is an array of interpretive processes that are engaged, including those relating to cognition, social perceptions and goals, and physical reactions, and they include direct, first-level affordances (signaling attitude, emotion, stance, and so on) as well as mediated signs and sign sequences of many kinds, following a variety of semiotic trajectories upwards and downwards the Peircean range (see the preceding chapter).

The following diagram expresses what I believe as the essential role of affordance in our life. It preserves the essential notion of relationship, or what biologists call 'coupling' (structural or social – see further Maturana and Varela, 1992). Relevance (not shown) emerges in a third dimension, as a result of the interaction between perception/activity (through affordance) and agent/environment relationships. The result is semiosis (or meaning making).[7]

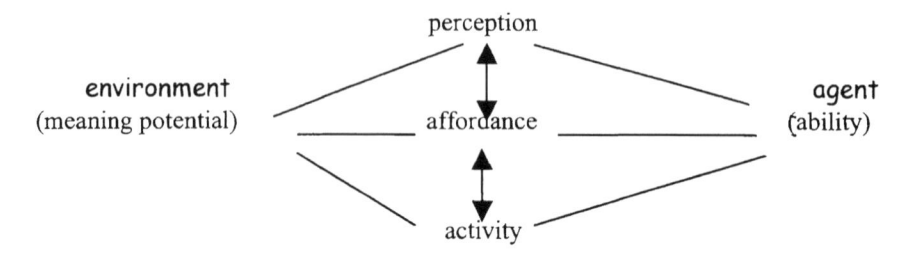

Figure 4.3: Affordance in context

The environment is full of meaning potential, especially if it has a rich semiotic budget, which may not be true of all classrooms, textbooks, or pedagogical interactions. The agent (the learner, in our case) has certain abilities, aptitudes, effectiveness, fitness, or whatever psychologists, biologists or anthropologists might call it (see Greeno, 1994, p. 338). Affordances are those relationships that provide a 'match' between something in the environment (whether it's a chair or an utterance) and the learner. The affordance fuels perception and activity, and brings about meanings – further affordances and signs, and further higher-level activity as well as more differentiated perception.

MEDIATION

Mediation is a central concept in sociocultural theory. In Vygotsky's original conception of this idea, tools mediate activity. That is, if I want to get an apple from a tree, and the apple is too high to reach, a stick or a ladder will mediate. So, mediation in this view is tool using. As argued above, whether the tool is a

---

[7] Another way of looking at the complex notion of relevance from an ecological perspective would be to say that relevance emerges from perception and action by an agent in an environment, but that would of course deny the crucial human element of reflective rationality, and the notions of self and identity that I will examine in the next chapter.

human/cultural artifact or a convenient object encountered in the environment, is not crucially different.

Now, one way to mediate our activities is by using language. In the case of the apple, a child can call to a nearby adult, and ask, "Daddy, can you get that apple for me please?" If she does not yet have enough language for that request, she might look at the adult, establish joint attention (by saying something like "Dah!" or "Papi"), point to the apple, and let the adult do the rest. "Oh, would you like that nice shiny apple? Forget it, it's mine." No, of course we need a happy ending, so the adult says, "Oh, would you like that nice shiny apple? Daddy will get it for you." In this way, language contributes to the mediation effort, but it may be heavily supported by other, gestural (indexical) signs.

So, language is mediated by gestures and other bodily expressions (McCafferty, 2002, McNeill, 2000). And activity (especially cognitive activity) is mediated by language. Good examples of this are the use of private speech in language learning (Ohta, 2001) and the phenomenon of inner speech, which can function, among other things, as mental rehearsal (Guerrero, 1994).

Language learning, in a Vygotskyan (sociocultural) perspective, is mediated by all the semiotic resources that are available in the learning environment, including of course in the classroom. These resources are not passively available, or 'just there,' they are actively brought in and created, shared and used (*appropriated*, in a term used by Barbara Rogoff (1995), and originally from Bakhtin) under guidance from the teacher and other learners.

In my 1996 book I identified the most important criteria (or conditions) for language learning as a combination of *access* and *engagement*. This pair of terms is general enough for most theories of learning to be able to fit around it, but it does concentrate our focus towards the essentials, whereas most theories tend to fly off at tangents in all sorts of directions. What do these essentials tell us?

First, language must be around in the environment, of course. But that is not enough. Just a while ago I listened for about five minutes to a woman speaking in Maori on the radio. I could not understand a single word, and I doubt that I could learn the language even if I listened for several hours every day for a month of Mondays. I could probably get a good feeling for the phonology and the prosody of the language, and I might be able to produce some impressive-sounding imitations, but I doubt I would ever end up speaking Maori in fluent and meaningful ways.

For language learning to occur we need access to the information in the environment. This information cannot just be transmitted to us, we must *pick it up* while being engaged in meaningful activities. That is, according to the ecological – semiotic perspective, we must first be active, then pick up language information that is useful for our activities. We may need assistance to be able to use and internalize the information, but we cannot be just passive vessels ('empty buckets,' as Montessori put it, 1917/1965) into which the information is poured. No, we must be engaged in activity and have information around that is available to be picked up and used. This is what I mean by access and engagement.

Access and engagement require perception and activity (active perception might be a good way to put it, or we might also say, perception-in-action). One of the key elements that unite action and perception is attention, that is, getting information from the environment while doing something, in order to do something else. Attention therefore combines perception with action, with the aim of improving our dealings with the world.

As I noted in my 1996 book, and in another study in 1998 (and of course, as has been noted many times before, I am not claiming originality), there are different kinds and levels of attention. Also, it is important to point out, attention relates to *awareness* and *consciousness*. There are two ways of looking at this, one relates to the intensity or level of attention focusing, the second relates to kinds of awareness and consciousness. To review, here are two diagrams that illustrate these two ways of looking at the same phenomenon:

perceiving an object:

consciousness

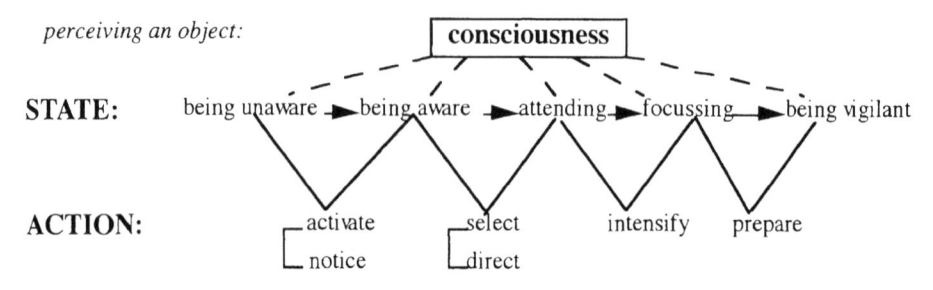

STATE: being unaware → being aware → attending → focussing → being vigilant

ACTION: activate / notice   select / direct   intensify   prepare

Figure 4.4: Degrees of attention

Here is a brief gloss of this diagram, and what it means for learning. If we are not aware at all of something, we will clearly not pick up information about that something. If we are aware, our cognitive processes will be activated while we are incorporating the information into our activities. As we continue to be active, and our activity interacts with the environment, we select what we pay attention to, we direct our focus to certain particulars or details, we may focus more intensely, we may prepare for more action, and so on.

This second diagram is different from the preceding one. In the preceding diagram there was basically an increase in the *intensity* of engagement as a result of perception and action. In this diagram we see different *kinds* of engagement depending on the depth of our human involvement.

Animals can play the entire gamut in the first diagram, and this is well illustrated in the following quote from Price:

> The cat as he crouches ready to spring ... is prepared for any one of many possible mouse-movements. We have seen that this preparedness for alternatives is one of the characteristic features of animal (and human) vigilance. But this is not all. The cat is prepared to jump in the appropriate direction, whichever of these alternatives is realized. ... Practical reason, rather than theoretical, is Pussy's strong point. (1969, pp. 127 and 129).

In Gibson's ecological theory, perception, attention, and action form one whole, they are not separate activities or processes. Rather, they each form and inform the others. The various levels and kinds of attention and consciousness in diagrams 1 and 2 must be seen as occurring during learning-oriented activity, whether individually, in group work, or in whole-class instruction (see Sullivan 2000 for some insightful commentary on cultural differences between these participation modes).

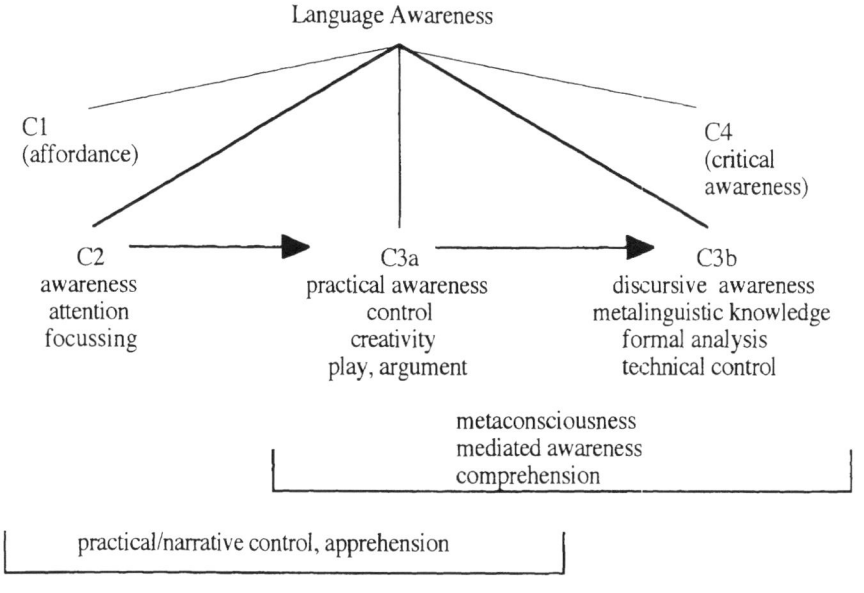

```
                        Language Awareness
                               /|\
                              / | \
                             /  |  \
   C1                       /   |   \                    C4
   (affordance)            /    |    \                   (critical
                          /     |     \                  awareness)

   C2         ────▶      C3a         ────▶       C3b
   awareness             practical awareness     discursive awareness
   attention             control                 metalinguistic knowledge
   focussing             creativity              formal analysis
                         play, argument          technical control

                              metaconsciousness
                              mediated awareness
                              comprehension

   practical/narrative control, apprehension
```

Figure 4.5: Levels of awareness

About Figure 4.4 I will just say that levels of attention vary from relaxed to vigilant, and from peripheral to focal, depending on the particular activity the learners are engaged in. It cannot be said that one level is more conducive to learning than another, all have their place. Thus, I feel that language learning is at times incidental and implicit, and at times it may require concentrated attention. Both conditions – and all other gradations in between – can yield learning in various circumstances.

Figure 4.5 needs more elucidation. It is headed *Language Awareness*, meaning that the learner is at some level and in some measure aware of language, in other words, has *perceptual experience* of language, rather than just using it in transparent ways. When children learn their L1, it is a matter of debate when they become aware of language *as language*. It is often pitched at around 4 or 5 years of age, although research indicates that, in bilingual children at least, awareness begins much earlier (Genesee, 2002).

In a second language, learners must be aware of language right from the start, since they focus on the language as an object-to-be-learned, and cannot help but look at L2 utterances as objects, rather than as actions. However, I must point out that Roy Harris emphasizes that in an integrationalist approach to language all language use, at whatever level or in whatever context, has a metalinguistic aspect, which he calls the *reflexivity* of language (1997, p. 258). I agree with this comment, and in my 1998 paper I therefore said that the academic sorts of metalinguistic knowledge, the technical language used in schooling to describe, analyze and reflect on language, are epiphenomenal, whereas awareness of language (the reflexivity that Harris talks about) occurs in all language use, and is therefore an integral part of it. This is in contrast to most writing about metalinguistics. Now back to the diagram.

Level 1 here is called *affordance*. As we have seen, affordance (to be precise, first-level affordance) is a direct (unmediated) relationship between an organism and some quality or property in its environment. We now have to see what a language affordance is or can be. The first candidate is the mother's voice, which the baby presumably perceives directly, unmediated. I would like to associate this level of affordance with Peirce's Firstness, the realm of direct feeling, quality, emotion. Oliver Sacks, in his account of healing his torn leg (not by medicine, surgery, or exercise, but by inner forces stimulated by music) after being badly mauled by an angry bull in Norway, calls it *grace*: "... full-bodied vital feeling and action, originating from an aboriginal, commanding, willing, 'I'"(1984, pp. 121-2). Eco calls this first beginning of semiosis "voice" (2000, p. 100). This first experience of voice is a part of the establishment of primary intersubjectivity, the reciprocal bond between caregiver and infant. This is where Firstness (quality, feeling) meets Secondness (reaction, response, dialogicity).

A crucial thing to bear in mind is that first-level affordance does not go away as soon as Secondness arrives on the scene. As I argued in the previous chapter, it remains there, in words and utterances, as one of the ingredients that make meaning (produce semiosis). It may be more or less prominent, hidden or overt, but it is there, as one of the elements of every sign that is created. We may not talk much about it, perhaps not be aware of it all the time, and it does not feature in the dictionary. But that does not mean that it is unimportant.

Shotter expresses the notion of linguistic affordance as follows:

> Just as the child comes to appreciate the "suckability" of a perceived teat or the "graspability" of a cup handle, so he apprehends in an equally direct manner, I suggest, the moral force underlying a serious maternal prohibition, and begins to distinguish between a deliberately harmful insult to his person and one which is merely ... play. He perceives these social barrier reefs and high seas, the harbours, havens and horizons directly in people's stony silences and fixed expressions, in their nods, winks, grimaces, gestures, stances, and smiles (1984, p. 95, quoted in Reed, 1988, p. 310).

These affordances relate to prosodic features, voice quality, and body language accompanying messages. The suggestion is that they are communicated directly, without any need for mediation, and then become part of the meanings generated. Indeed, as I suggested in relation to the diagram of the concentric circles (see Chapters 2 and 3, see also van Lier, 1995), these 'outer circles' of interpretation often tend to have a decisive influence in instances of ambiguity of meaning. They are therefore not to be brushed off as irrelevant.

Level 2 is a deliberate act of focusing attention, of noticing a linguistic feature. It may follow a first-level affordance, and then it means entering into new acts of making meaning (semiosis). It may also be the result of someone drawing our attention to something, as in the example of Marcus saying, "Look!" At this level of perception is also what Dick Schmidt (Schmidt & Frota, 1986) has called 'noticing the gap,' i.e., a realization that some language used out there is different from our current language knowledge, and we then may use this as a learning opportunity. This may be the case in the example of Phillip in the extract below (taken from van Lier, 1998):

Lea:	Your mami slept on the bed.
Phillip:	My mami sleeped on the truck.
Lea:	Your mami slept on the roof.
Phillip:	My mami sleeped ... slipt on the car.

As argued in that paper, Phillip here may be noticing the discrepancy between his 'sleeped' and Lea's 'slept.' Two preconditions may have to exist for Phillip to move his Interlanguage in the direction of Lea's language (both are four years old). First, he must assume that Lea is the more proficient speaker, which is actually the case, since Lea is a native speaker, whereas Phillip is bilingual German-English. But this is not necessary if another precondition is met: if Phillip has heard 'slept' in the environment on a large enough number of occasions – peripherally, without noticing the discrepancy between his 'sleeped' and everybody else's 'slept' – this may, in the terminology of the *competition model* (MacWhinney, 1987), provide sufficient *cue strength* now for Phillip to move his language in the direction of 'slept,' even if Lea is not linguistically ahead of him in other respects.

This is an important point. It is often assumed – among students and teachers alike – that interaction among equal peers will not lead to improvements in learning. After all, for learning to occur a more advanced learner's input or judgment will be necessary, or so the argument goes. This is actually not at all the case: so long as there are sufficient examples of target language use (cues) in the environment, learners amongst themselves can orient to those cues and act upon them appropriately in interactions. As Rogoff has pointed out (1993; see also Donato, 1994; Ohta, 2001, p. 87; and see Chapter 6), interaction among learners at equal levels can be a very efficient context of learning. This collaborative learning process among equals is stressed by Piaget throughout his work, though not by Vygotsky, in whose writings a more capable interlocutor is assumed to be necessary for a Zone of Proximal Development to exist. I think, along with Rogoff and others, that both Piaget and Vygotsky have a valuable point to make here. It is likely that different sorts of learning and processes of learning occur in both these conditions, and that they are both valuable when occurring in a flexible community of learning, in a suitably balanced way, and taking into account local cultural practices (Sullivan, 2000).

Level 3 adds active control to the awareness menu. First, in level 3a, an element of playing with language and a manipulation of linguistic expression, perhaps in story telling, acting out and acting up, creating puns, imitating others, and so on. Next, as a result of schooling especially, an academic level of analytical control, a more technical manipulation of the linguistic code and a detached analysis of its structures and functions.

Finally, at level 4, we have a critical perspective, in which the social and political aspects of language are examined, including the use and abuse of power, the manufacture of public opinion, deception and moral use, and so on (some of the things that were mentioned in Chapter 2).

All in all, then, awareness and consciousness (which we will come back to in the next chapter) occur at several levels of intensity as well as in several different contextual forms, depending both on communicative purpose and developmental skill. Learning runs the gamut of all these levels and kinds, and an educational environment should provide multiple opportunities for deploying all of them through diverse activities.

HALLIDAY'S LANGUAGE-BASED THEORY OF LEARNING

I want to close this chapter with a brief look at an important paper that Michael Halliday published in 1993. This paper encapsulates his social-semiotic view of language and education. In it, he argues that all learning is language learning, and therefore theories of learning should take language development much more centrally into account. I want to relate his overview to the notions of emergence and affordance, as outlined in this chapter.

He takes us step by step through the development of language from early childhood into adolescence, including the very important (and lengthy!) period of schooling – an episode of language learning that is usually ignored by language acquisition researchers, who tend to concentrate on pre-scholastic or extra-scholastic language development.

Halliday's interesting overview must be examined in far greater detail, but now I just want to mention the broad sweep of his proposal, focusing specially on the ways in which his account coincides (I think in quite remarkable ways) with Peirce's semiotics and Gibson's ecological psychology.

I will list the 21 features of Halliday's language – based theory, and draw some immediate ecological connections in the column next to them. We can then elaborate on some of the ideas later, as the need arises. I am probably recasting some of Halliday's points into Peircean semiotic terms, and into an ecological mould, but I hope this is a justifiable extension.

Halliday's scheme is clearly very ambitious and all-encompassing. Unfortunately, for our purposes, Halliday has not made a connection to Peirce, Gibson, or Vygotsky. Even though Halliday's commitment to a semiotic and ecological approach to language is quite evident, there is considerable interpretive work to be done to reconcile terminologies and concepts (although Wells, 1999, provides an interesting and useful comparison between Vygotsky's and Halliday's work). The above table merely gives some preliminary suggestions to broaden the relationships among the various contributors to an ecological perspective.

Table 4.1: Halliday's language-based theory of meaning

Halliday's Features	Semiotic-Ecological Interpretation
1. Symbolic acts ('Acts of Meaning'): starting to construct signs.	Here the Peircean would say, they are not yet symbolic, they are iconic and incipiently indexical. They are Trevarthen's *primary intersubjectivity*.
2. Iconic (natural) symbols: Constructing signs that resemble what they mean.	Clearly iconic; direct perception.
3. Systems of symbolic acts: Organizing signs into paradigms (protolanguage).	Indexical speech acts: "I want," "gimme," "hold me," etc.
4. The lexicogrammatical stratum: Constructing a three-level semiotic system (language).	phonology – grammar – semantics. Mediation: "doing things with words" begins.
5. Non-iconic (Conventional) symbols: Taking up signs that do not resemble their meanings.	Naming and reference.
6. "Trailer" strategy: Anticipating a developmental step that is to come.	Seems like an intermezzo here: maybe it's proleptic exploration: "frontier texts".
7. "Magic Gateway" Strategy: Finding a way in to a new activity or to a new understanding.	This is the key moment of secondary subjectivity, or triadic interaction: The move into grammar.
8. Generalization (classifying, taxonomizing): Naming classes ("common" terms) and classes of classes.	Development of lexical processes of naming and classifying. Distinguishing between names and between concepts.
9. The "Metafunctional" principle: Experiential and interpersonal meanings (from single function utterances, either pragmatic [doing] or mathetic [learning], to multifunctional ones, both experiential and interpersonal).	Developing a sense of story and conversation.
10. Semogenic strategies: Expanding the meaning potential (refining distinctions, moving into new domains, deconstructing linked variables).	In Vygotskyan terms, linking the interpersonal to the intrapersonal.
11. Construal of "Information": From rehearsing shared experience to imparting unshared experience.	Here the focus is on construction: putting ideas into coherent text (discourse).
12. The interpersonal "Gateway": Developing new meanings first in interpersonal contexts.	The Vygotskyan hub: interpersonal meanings become intra-personal ones. After 7, this is the second watershed. Language "colonizes" cognition. The construction of *identity*.
13. Dialectic of system and process: Constructing language from text, constructing text from language.	Venturing into new meaning-making events on the basis of formulaic and ritual acts.
14. Filtering and he "Challenge" zone: Rejecting what is out of range and working on what is accessible.	Another "intermezzo" I feel (like 6): learners will judge what is or is not within reach at any time.
15. Probability – The quantitative	Here we begin *academic language*

foundation: Construing relative frequencies.	development.
16. Discourse: The third metafunction: Construing a parallel world of semiosis.	This is misleading. Here the textual world (genre awareness) comes in, but I feel parallel semiosis may be problematic. Maybe metaconsciousness. Note that Harris might have a problem with this.
17. Complementarities: Construing experience from different angles of vision.	I think from feature 15 onwards we are moving upwards in terms of academic skills development.
18. Abstraction and literacy: Understanding abstract meanings and moving into the written mode.	Continuing the academic process, construction of higher mental functions, in Vygotsky's terms.
19. Reconstruction and regression: Backing off into an earlier semiotic "moment" while reconstruing both content and expression.	Here students have to recast their knowledge into more abstract, decontextualized academic language, The shock that the personal and the academic are different.
20. Grammatical metaphor (Nominalizing, Technologizing): From commonsense grammar to the grammar of objects and technical hierarchies.	This is the third "Gateway" I feel: the realization that meanings are encoded in language expressing ideologies and separating identities from actions, thus neutralizing moral/ethical issues.
21. Synoptic/Dynamic complementarity: Reconciling two semiotic models of human experience.	Understanding the relationship between personal experience and the experience of education and workplace experience.

I noted three 'gateways' in the table: 7, 12, and 20. In my interpretation, 7 is the gateway into *grammar* (or *predication*), 12 is the gateway into *identity*, 20 is the gateway into *ideology*. Elaborating further, several broader phases can be proposed:

Feature 1-6: Primary subjectivity, mutuality, indicational language, indexicality;
Feature 7-11: Secondary subjectivity: joint attention, co-construction, triadic interaction, predicational language;
Feature 12-14: Linguistic construction of self, voice;
Feature 15- 19: Academic language development; renegotiating identities;
Feature 20-21: Critical discourse development.

Learning and development are not linear, slowly cumulative and incremental processes that basically just increase in size or volume. Rather, they include series of transformations and emergent configurations of activity and cognition, with phase transitions (the gateways), where the nature of the new processes cannot be reduced to the nature of the preceding ones.

CONCLUSION

This chapter introduces two key concepts of ecological learning: *emergence* and *affordance*. Emergence happens when relatively simple organisms or elements reorganize themselves into more complex, more intelligent systems or collectives. In addition, these systems appear to be able to adapt to changing conditions whereas the simpler forms that compose them have no such adaptive abilities. In language learning, terms like *restructuring* (part of the vocabulary of information processing) and *grammaticalization* relate to the notion of emergence, although not always in an ecological sense. Hopper's *emergent grammar*, (1998), must be seen as quite different from most perspectives on restructuring in the second language literature since he sees language as *activity*, although Rutherford's *organic grammar*, (1987), and Larsen-Freeman's *grammaring*, (1991), share resemblances with Hopper's perspective. In such views language learning is not the accumulation of discrete entities, but rather the creation (construction) of new, more complex systems[8] from simpler elements. To enhance such emergence, researchers recommend programs of awareness raising or consciousness raising (Rutherford, 1987; Larsen-Freeman, 2003; Schmidt, 1994).

Affordances are what [the environment] *offers* the animal, what it *provides* or *furnishes*, either for good or ill (Gibson, 1979). They are relationships of possibility, the result of perceiving an object while co-perceiving oneself. In other words, what I perceive is perceived as it is relevant to me. In this view, perception, action and interpretation are part of one dynamic process.

In recent years, many proposals have been made to extend the notion of affordance in different directions: cultural affordances, social affordances, cognitive affordances, and so on. Such affordances are indirect, or mediated, whereas the original type of affordance in visual perception as researched by Gibson is direct (we might call these first-level affordances).

The chapter ends with a glimpse at Halliday's 21 features of language learning, and a tentative beginning of relating them to the ecological-semiotic framework proposed in this book.

---

[8] The word *system* here may work for some perspectives on grammaticalization, but as we have seen, not for Hopper, who focuses on emergent practices, remembered routines, and processes of use.

CHAPTER 5

THE SELF AND LANGUAGE LEARNING

If you want to know yourself,
Just look how others do it;
If you want to understand others,
Look into your own heart.

- Johann von Schiller (1759-1805)
Tabulae Votivae, 1797

INTRODUCTION

The notions of self and identity have had a long and checkered history in the social sciences, but only a relatively short and tentative one in applied linguistics. Philosophers – notably Descartes – have often regarded the self (soul, spirit) as a substance quite separate from the body, or else they have, as materialists, denied the existence of any such thing, considering it basically no more than a figment of our inflated imagination. Others have seen it as a real thing, but perhaps in the shape of some controlling intelligence sitting somewhere in our brain, supervising our actions and evaluating what is out there for us, a sort of overlord, governor, or central command station (in that case, of course, we ask who is the 'me' that the central command is reporting to, and then we enter a situation of infinite regress).

In this chapter I will show that a semiotic and ecological approach sees the self as a real entity, but one that is dialogically and socially constructed. As Butterworth puts it, "the ecological approach proposes that the self exists objectively from the outset by virtue of its embodiment" (1999, p. 204). This does not mean that the self is a ready-made, innate faculty, but that humans are so constituted that in their activity in the world, both external (about the environment) and internal information (about the body and its activity) is created. This forms the basis of what Neisser calls the *ecological self* (1988), and is similar to what Damasio calls the *proto-self* (1999). According to some researchers, this initial self has an innate social structure, that is, in the newborn baby it is present as a 'virtual other', a neural structure that is designed for social cognition, beginning with *protoconversation*, an early form of social interaction attested in neonate babies (Bråten, 1998; Trevarthen, 1990, 1998). A key characteristic of an ecological approach is the close, inseparable connection between body and mind (hence the term 'embodied mind;' see Varela, Thompson & Rosch, 1991; see also Giddens, 1991; Damasio 1999;[1] Ruthroff, 2000).

---

[1] Damasio makes the interesting suggestion that the body *as represented in the brain* is "the forerunner for what eventually becomes the elusive sense of self." He continues: "The deep roots of the self, including the elaborate self which encompasses identity and personhood, are to be found in the ensemble

To begin with, I want to explore how self and language relate, in particular, what kind of a theory of language we need in order to accommodate the semiotic/ecological self. The most important requirement is that language is not an a priori, finished body of words and structures, but an emergent set of resources for enacting linguistic activities.

Using language is not a simple, neutral business of transmitting information to another person or to the world at large. Whenever we say something we do not only provide a piece of information about something or other, we also at the same time provide information about two other important matters: Who we are ourselves, and who we think our listeners or readers are. Or, phrasing it another way, our language use gives information about what we think of ourselves and what we think of the people who may be listening (or reading).

Language use is a form of action, and action is a form of relating to the world, an instance of 'structural' or 'social coupling,' as Maturana and Varela (1992) call it, using terminology from biology. Discourse, definable as language use in context, therefore is not communicating something from A to B in a sender-receiver sort of way, but it is situated activity. As Bakhtin puts it:

> An utterance does not merely refer to its object, ... but it *expresses* its subject in addition: the units of language, in themselves, are not expressive.... In oral discourse, a specific, expressive intonation marks this dimension of the utterance. The utterance enters in relation to past utterances which had the same object, and with those of the future, which it foresees as answers. Finally the utterance is always addressed to someone (Todorov, 1984, p. 42).

You might then ask, what about grammar books and dictionaries? Surely they tell us about language as it really is, and not about activity in the world? Let's examine this for a moment.

What are dictionaries for? Why would I want to look up the word *table*? I already know that what I am sitting at right now is called a table. So, maybe I want to know what other ways that word can be used in. Such as, 'table of contents,' or 'water table,' or 'to table a motion.' Another person might want to look it up to see where the word *table* comes from – the Latin word *tabula*. The only person who might want to look it up because he or she does not know what it means is one who is learning English as a foreign language. That person may want to establish that *table* in English means roughly the same as *mesa* in Spanish.

What does the grammar book tell us? As the cynic sees it, the grammar book is about the dissection of linguistic cadavers. Dead bones (sentences) are piled up, sequenced, labeled and catalogued, like in a paleontological museum. One can certainly learn from these linguistic remains, especially if a visit to the real living habitat of the particular language is out of reach. Of course, the linguistic museum (a.k.a. the grammar book[2]) should never be mistaken for the real community of speakers that use the language. Unfortunately, however, academic grammarians and grammar teachers, through "innumerable acts of correction" (Bourdieu, see

---

of brain devices which continuously and *nonconsciously* maintain the body state within the narrow range and relative stability required for survival" (1999, p. 22, italics in original).

[2] I should be kinder to grammars (in any case, I love museums of natural history), and I must mention that there is a new generation of grammar books that are based on corpora of actual language.

quotation below), perpetuate the grammar book version of the language across generations of students, often neglecting to connect it systematically to the living language, focusing instead on examining the students' memory of arcane paradigms and rules and creating the impression that it is the grammar book that contains the 'real' language, and what is used in the world outside is merely an imperfect, degenerate version thereof. As a result, when students spend six or eight years studying a foreign language in school, and then find themselves in a country where it is spoken, they are in for a shock! Conversely, when children get to school thinking that they know their own mother tongue, they find to their dismay that there is a whole academic language out there that needs to be conquered by dint of many years of hard labor.

> ... [L]egitimate language is a semi-artificial language which has to be sustained by a permanent effort of correction, a task which falls both to institutions specially designed for this purpose and to individual speakers. Through its grammarians, who fix and codify legitimate usage, and its teachers who impose and inculcate it through innumerable acts of correction, the educational system tends, in this area as elsewhere, to produce the need for its own services and its own products, i.e., the labour and instruments of correction (Bourdieu, 1991, pp. 60-61).

Both the dictionary and the grammar book have their uses; I am certainly a great fan of them, but they do not 'contain' the language in any useful sense of that concept. If you hold up the biggest grammar book and the biggest dictionary of language X (should you have the muscular power to do so, which may be a real problem) and say, "Language X is contained in these two tomes!" I will be skeptical to say the least. I suggest you would be closer to the truth of that statement if you held up a children's classic in that language (something like *Winnie-The-Pooh, Max und Moritz,* or *Le Petit Prince*), or pointed to two people sitting at a cafeteria table with a carafe of wine or a pot of tea (here you change the word 'tomes' to 'conversationalists' of course). This is very simply the same way that 'the humpback whale' is contained in the animal swimming in the ocean and its membership in its social group, rather than in the collection of bones (possibly connected by wires to simulate the skeleton) in the paleontological section of the museum of natural history.

The point of all this is to emphasize once again that language is not a 'fixed code' (Harris, 1996) that exists independently of users, and that is ready-made for users before they start using it, but rather that it is created, or at the very least assembled from conventional elements, each time it is used, along the lines of the *passing theory* that the philosopher Donald Davidson talked about (1986, p. 446) and that we discussed in the last chapter. In this way, language is intimately connected with the self, as an entity that is always under construction, always emergent.

THE DIALOGIC NATURE OF THE SIGN

As we discussed in Chapter 3, a sign is something that stands for something to somebody. This gives the sign a triadic nature, consisting of Sign (Representamen) – Object (Semiotic Object) – Interpretant (Meaning).

The question we now raise is, what about the originator ('utterer', in Peirce's words) of the sign? Someone produced the sign in order to be understood or to perform some action. The interpretant not only understands the sign (more precisely, understands the *intention* of the sign) but also understands/recognizes the originator/origination of the sign (see also the discussion of *relevance* in the last chapter). This is not quite true of all signs: clouds are a sign of (possible) rain, but they were not produced or uttered by 'somebody.' The same goes for the sound of an avalanche, a patch of ice on the road, a shiny red poison oak leaf, a red spot on a black widow spider, a stinger on a scorpion, a sweet smell on a fruit. All these signs we might call 'natural' signs, not produced by any human or animal agency, that just tell us certain things if we have learned how to interpret them.

Then there are other signs that involve various levels of agency in their production. These include the rattling of a rattlesnake, paw prints in the sand, the smell of a skunk, the growling of a dog.

Then we get to the realm of human signs. First, there are those that clearly have been produced by 'someone,' but it is irrelevant who that is or was. These include cultural (and conventionally understood) signs such as weather vanes, mailboxes, and stop signs.

Next we get clothes, cars, hairstyles, pierced eyebrows, white picket fences and eyeshades. These are intentional. But we also have unintentional ones, like blushing, drooping shoulders, tears, pouts, and perspiration.

Then we get flags, pictures of eagles, bears and kiwis on bank notes, and national anthems.

This is followed by nods and winks, 'the finger,' and all kinds of 'body language.'

We are getting closer to language now, indeed, you might say we are already IN language. Next thing, someone says something, and the notion of sign is transformed into a different realm.

Linguistic signs form a special case of signs. They don't just float around unattached; they are made, grown, proposed, offered (etc.). How can that be made to be part of semiotic theory?

Peirce usually did not explicitly single out linguistic signs, or at least, did not often talk ONLY about linguistic signs, rather about signs of all kinds, physical, manufactured, linguistic, and so on, as an organic process of semiosis. Here is a telling quote to illustrate this vision:

> Thought is not necessarily connected with a brain. It appears in the work of bees, of crystals, and throughout the purely physical world; and one can no more deny that it is really there, than that the colors, the shapes, etc., of objects are really there. ... Not only is thought in the organic world, but it develops there. But as there cannot be a General without Instances embodying it, so there cannot be thought without signs. (Peirce, 4.551, quoted in Johansen, 1993, p. 190).

As educational linguists, we are specially language-oriented, so we need to spend a bit more time figuring out the linguistics of semiosis, particularly how people come to understand each other. I will begin with three example texts that illustrate some of the dynamics.

TEXT 1
  A. Well!
  B. ((silence))

What do we think of when we are presented with the above speech activity? It could be just about anything – our imagination might run amok. Is it an expression of triumph, despair, encouragement, impatience? And why does B remain silent? We cannot tell. This example is quite different from some other possible exchanges, such as:

TEXT 2:
  A: Petronella, do you take Filbert as your lawfully married husband?
  B: I do.

In this case, we surmise that a wedding is taking place. Why? Because the words here are recognizably and typically used in such a ceremony. We recognize the words as belonging to the ritual of marriage ceremonies. They are conventional, and context-bound. So we can confidently say, 'Well, I guess Petronella and Filbert are getting married.' But in the case of Text 1 we can say no such thing. 'Well' can – and is – said in all kinds of situations, it might mean just about anything. It doesn't help either that B is not cooperating with us by keeping silent.

Now for some enlightenment. Text 1 comes from Volosinov (1973; see Merrell, 1997a, p. 28). There are two people in the room. One says, 'Well.' the other does not say anything. According to Volosinov, several contextual sources of information are missing for a plausible interpretation:

a) shared physical surroundings;
b) shared background knowledge; and
c) shared situation definition.

This would help in explaining Text 1. But the differences between Text 1 and the Petronella example still remain. Within their respective situations, the interpretations may be equally simple and understandable, but they cannot be the same, since stripping the contextual information away makes Text 1 incomprehensible, but the Petronella exchange remains perfectly comprehensible. In the latter case, the language brings its own context, we might say; in the first case we (as uninformed outsiders) have to bring an imagined context to it. In both cases, the language is tied to the context, but it is tied in very different ways. That aside, let's get enlightenment on Text 1 from Volosinov:

> ... both interlocutors looked up at the window and saw that it had begun to snow; both knew that it was already May and that it was high time for spring to come; finally, both were sick and tired of the protracted winter...(ibid.).

So, on this reading, there are 'jointly seen,' jointly known,' and 'unanimously evaluated' elements in this one word, and the utterance directly depends on these for interpretation. All of these are also relevant in the wedding example, but there the joint seeing, knowing, and evaluating are predicted by virtue of the ritual that brings forth the words. Even if we did not know that every marriage ceremony includes the words uttered, just knowing that we are in such a ceremony will make the worlds carry their performative meaning. The ceremony (ritual), provided it is recognized as such, acts as a carapace for the words.

Now let's look at an entirely different situation, though it also starts with 'Well,' just as Text 1. Do we get more information here, and if so, where does that information come from?

TEXT 3
'Well!' the young man said.
'Well!' she said.
'Well, here we are,' he said.
'Here we are,' she said, 'Aren't we?'
'I should say we were,' he said, 'Eeyop! Here we are.'
'Well!' she said.
'Well!' he said, 'well.' (Birk, 1972)

I think we all know what this is about. We're here in the midst of romance. Yet, as we can see, there are no overt expressions of love or devotion, of passion or surrender. So, how do we know the plot? Words like 'well,' 'here we are,' and 'eeyop' in themselves are poor instigators of meaning, but in a particular context they can be saturated with meaning. What is it in this context that gives them the fullness of meaning that they clearly have?

In Malinowski's terminology, the above would be a perfect example of 'phatic communion,' that is, talk that is just made to foster social relationships, or to keep channels of communication open. There is absolutely no information transfer in the standard sense of symbolic content shared or transmitted; there is no politics, literature, golf, dry cleaning or backyard composting being discussed. Yet, vast rivers, perhaps cataracts, of emotional information are pouring back and forth between these two people. In contradistinction to Text 1, this is quite transparent in Text 3. The question is, why?

A possible answer is that the signs are closely tied to different affordances available in the context in which the signs are used. Affordances are not neutral or objective. Sure, the invariants in the objects are there whether or not someone is around to pick them up, but they only become affordances when they are attended to (i.e., noticed) and used for action, (they are not *subjective*, either: they are subject-object relationships). In all three texts the linguistic contribution is very much embedded in the context. In all three cases an interpretation requires extensive contextual information. To complicate matters further, in all three cases the linguistic action(s) are an integral part of *creating* the context. This brings to mind what we said about context in Chapter 2.

If we think in this way about the sign, as arising out of a context of affordance, action, and perception, then we begin to see that all signs, especially the higher ones – including language – are dialogical, that is, are produced and interpreted with an interlocutor in mind (including, as both Bakhtin and Vygotsky would argue, when they are written on a page or produced as private or inner speech), they are social acts.

Let's take again the case of Text 1, the utterance, "Well!" The utterer, the man standing by the window gazing out at the nasty weather, produces a linguistic sign that is conventional (symbolic). It is interpretable as such by the listener, who knows that "Well!" must be a comment on something in the environment. He looks at A, sees him looking out at the weather, and now he (B) also looks out at the weather. Provided that A sees B doing this, the dialogicity of the exchange is complete, and B need not (he might, of course, but need not) offer a verbal rejoinder such as, well, "That sucks" (or whatever). This is possible because of the shared perception of the snow (triadic interaction), the common knowledge of the lateness of Spring (shared background knowledge of calendar, seasons in Moscow, etc.), and shared knowledge of each other's feelings about this business (mutuality, or intersubjectivity).

Another way of describing the sequence of events is:
1. The snow is a natural affordance, and relates to A as a source of disappointment, impatience, disgust (mostly iconicity, Firstness).
2. A's verbal utterance "Well!" carries the potential for sharing these feelings with B, and at the same time may have the intention of drawing B's attention to the falling snow outside the window (mostly indexicality, Secondness).
3. B's gaze completes the dialogic cycle of semiosis.

Note that in the single word "Well!" there are several affordances and signs, and sequences of affordances and signs, all of which contribute meaning and sharing of meaning. Like the silver ball in the pinball machine, the word lights up, buzzes, flashes, and rings a number of bells in the semiotic environment. Some of the affordances and signs are present in the room and beyond the window, others are evoked in the social setting and the minds of A and B. Highly simplistically and conflated, the event can be shown as follows, preserving the triadic nature of the sign (where S = sign [representamen], O= object, I = interpretant).

This is an attempt at reproducing how the meaning making is produced by the people in the room. All semiosis, while possibly starting out as a natural or perceived affordance, consists of signs becoming signs becoming signs ... and so on, chaining, foregrounding, backgrounding, distilling, expanding aspects of the meaning potential in the environment, physical, social and symbolic. The utterer(s) and interpretant(s) themselves become signs, objects and interpretants as well, as they construct, deconstruct and reconstruct through signs what it is that they wish to establish or achieve in this particular interaction. Signs therefore do not exist outside of human interaction, and they always exist as activity in the world, connected to speakers, hearers, and the objects (physical or symbolic) that they are addressing.

Now we can return to Bakhtin/Volosinov and bring in his statement that "the word in language is half someone else's" (Bakhtin, 1981, p. 239). All signs, as soon as they move beyond natural affordances, are dialogical, since they will include both indexicality and symbolicity. And even natural affordances (things like sit-on-ability of tree stumps and walk-on-ability of hard surfaces) are dialogical, involving an agent and the physical world.

114   CHAPTER 5

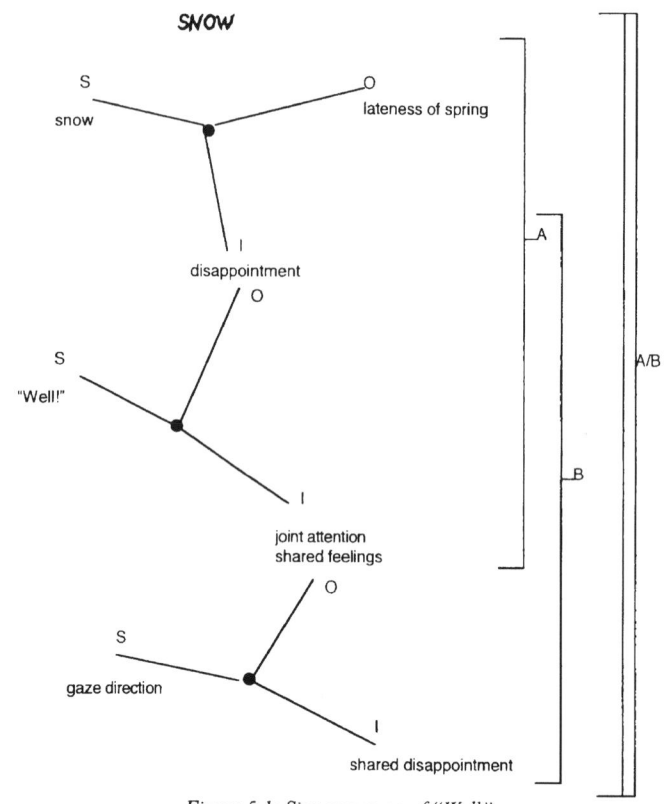

Figure 5.1: Sign sequence of "Well"

As soon as signs begin to involve cultural artifacts or other people, they become dialogical in a social or socio-cultural-historical sense. From this perspective we can move into the discussion of self.

THE DEVELOPMENT OF THE SELF

Like consciousness (see next section), the self is not something we are born with in a ready-made, fully-fledged sort of way. According to a number of researchers (Bråten, 1992; Butterworth, 1999; Damasio, 1999; Neisser, 1988; see also p. 110), the structures for the development of the self may be innately specified in some way, ecologically and perhaps even dialogically. However, the actual development of the self occurs as a consequence of interaction with and in the physical world over the first years of life and is increasingly bound up with language. Psychologists and philosophers have for a long time attempted to define (or define away) the notion of mind/identity/self, at times seeing it as a separate entity (alongside or within the body), at other times as a mere figment of our imagination. An influential view of the self is that of Friedrich Nietzsche, who argues that the self is not given or fixed, but created by each individual (Poster, 1993, p. 66). Poster also notes that Foucault, influenced by Nietzsche, asserts that "we have to create ourselves as works of art" (ibid.), and Sartre relates the self to his notion of *authenticity*, which is ambiguous in terms of universality or self-creation (ibid.). Sartre says that if you try to be authentic just to be authentic, then you are not authentic, but on the other hand, he also says that authenticity is not given, but that it has to be earned (1957). How this is to be accomplished (earning authenticity without wanting to be authentic) never becomes very clear.

However hard it is to come up with an explanation or description that everybody can agree with, there is no doubt that all humans have an awareness of themselves as persons who act, interact, speak, feel and think. We can think back to something that happened to us when we were ten years old (let's say we were in a small rowing boat on a lake), and we know that it was "I", and not somebody else, that it was "my" mother who was watching from the shore, etc. When we see a photograph we have no trouble pointing to a person in it and saying, "that's me."

How do we come to experience our life as a self? A useful beginning is Gibson's revolutionary statement that when we perceive the world we always also perceive ourselves. Perception is thus not just one-way seeing, it's two-way seeing (and two-way hearing, etc.). This is central to the notion of affordance, since to establish a relationship of affordance with something (a physical, social or symbolic entity) we have to see/hear (sense, in general) that something *in relation to* ourselves. Indeed, if it is totally unrelated or unrelatable to ourselves, then we may in fact not see it. van Manen recounts the following dramatic example of this:

> In his introduction to *Person and World*, van den Berg tells an anecdote of a native of the Malaysian jungles (van den Berg and Linschoten, 1953). In order to learn what impression a large and modern city would make on an inhabitant of the jungle, one had placed this man unexpectedly and without much ado in the middle of the large city of Singapore. One walked with him through the busy streets in order to provide the native with ample opportunity to observe whatever the metropolis could offer. When at the end of the trip one asked him what had struck him most, he did not, as one might have expected, talk about the paved streets, the brick houses, concrete buildings, cars, streetcars and trains. Instead, he mentioned how to his amazement one person could carry so many bananas. What he appeared to have seen was a street vendor who transported his bunches of bananas on a push cart (1990, pp. 115-6).

The self is not just a detached observer taking in the world through the windows of the mind, but it is an ongoing project of establishing one's place in the world. If it were the former, it would be like a little person inside, a homunculus, looking out from within the body. Then we would have to specify who would tell the homunculus where to look, and if that were "I" (the self), then we would be back exactly where we were before, it would be an infinite progression of selves inside selves.

According to Neisser (1988), there are five kinds of self-knowledge that develop separately but that are usually perceived as one unitary object. As we saw above, we are primed for self-knowledge from birth, but we are not born with a fully developed sense or notion of self, so it develops as we grow up. Neisser asks, what are the sorts of self-identifying and self-specifying information that make it possible to establish self-knowledge? He proposes that the self consists of five different aspects that are essentially five different kinds of selves:

[T]hey differ in their origins and developmental histories, in what we know about them, in the pathologies to which they are subject, and in the manner in which they contribute to human social experience (1988, p. 35).

The five selves proposed by Neisser are briefly summarized as follows:
- The *ecological self* is the self as perceived with respect to the physical environment: 'I' am the person here in this place, engaged in this particular activity.
- The *interpersonal self*, which appears from earliest infancy just as the ecological self does, is specified by species-specific signals of emotional rapport and communication: I am the person who is engaged, here, in this particular human interchange.
- The *extended self* is based primarily on our personal memories and anticipations: I am the person who had certain specific experiences, who regularly engages in specific and familiar routines.
- The *private self* appears when children first notice that some of their experiences are not directly shared with other people: I am, in principle, the only person who can feel this unique and particular pain.
- The *conceptual self* or 'self-concept' draws its meaning from the network of assumptions and theories in which it is embedded, just as all other concepts do. Some of those theories concern social roles (husband, professor, American), some postulate more or less hypothetical internal entities (the soul, the unconscious mind, mental energy, the brain, the liver), and some establish socially significant dimensions of difference (intelligence, attractiveness, wealth). There is a remarkable variety in what people believe about themselves, and not all of it is true (1988, p. 36).

Below I present a diagram of Neisser's scheme, in the shape of a multilayered representation of the self. It should be noted that, in later work, Neisser (and others, see Neisser, 1993; Neisser & Fivush, 1994; Neisser & Jopling, 1997) considers the ecological and interpersonal selves as two aspects of a larger *perceptual self*: Both provide critical information about the self (1993, p. viii). The conceptual, private and remembered (extended) selves are quite different, in that they do not rely on perception but "on taking oneself as an object of thought" (ibid.). This makes Neisser's theory of self congruent with the sociocultural perspective of Vygotsky, where perceptual and social-interactive (interpersonal) processes precede and grow into conceptual, intrapersonal processes. The role of speech as a tool and as a specific type of activity, alongside or accompanying other activities such as grasping, gesturing, moving, playing and so on, is a specific focus of Vygotsky's work in this respect.

Let's try and put this at once in the context of language learning, first and second. I would expect that all five selves contribute variably to what we call the learner's *voice*. I think this is actually analogous to Bourdieu's 'feel for the game' that I described in the context of learning to play soccer in the last chapter. As I argued in an earlier book (1996), a learner speaks in his or her own voice when three conditions hold: *awareness* of language and learning, *autonomy* and self-determination in language use and learning processes, and *authenticity* in acts of speaking. Of course, whenever we speak, we also embody/enact other people's speech (Bakhtin, 1981; Maybin, 1994), but we *appropriate* it and thus make it our own (Rogoff, 1995). In other words, the voices of other people resonate in our own speech, but we incorporate and integrate them into our own voice. In the words of Volosinov, we bring our own *accentuality* to appropriated speech (Volosinov, 1973).

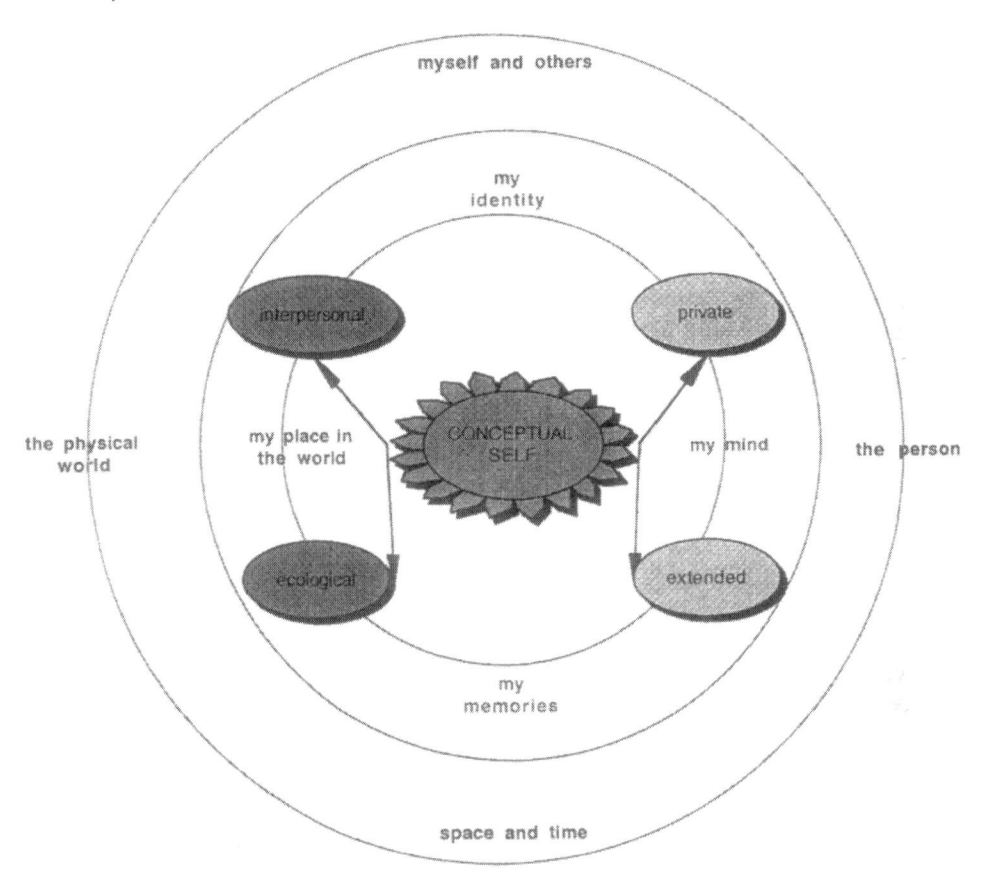

The Self
Based on Ulric Neisser's
"Five Kinds of Self-Knowledge" (1988)

Figure 5.2: Neisser's five selves

In the table below I attempt to place language-learning demands/tasks in the context of Neisser's five kinds of self-knowledge:

Table 5.1: Neisser's selves related to language learning

1. *ecological* the physical environment	Time and space. Deixis. The body. Speech acts. Peirce's Indexical signs. Demonstratives. Pronouns. Prepositions. Names. Categorization.
2. *interpersonal* emotional rapport and communication	Mutuality, reciprocity, intersubjectivity. Rapport. Turn taking. Rhythm, intonation. Conversation. Formality, distance, intimacy. Later: social/societal expectations.
3. *extended* personal memories and expectations, my way of doing things	Memories, remembering. Story telling. Diaries. Looking for learning opportunities. Strategies, initiative.
4. *private* personal uniqueness, separateness, differences from everybody else	Inner and private speech. Self knowledge (Gardner's Intrapersonal intelligence). Learning styles. Self-presentation.
5. *conceptual* identity, roles and status, my 'theory of me', my beliefs about myself	My expectations, investment, motivation. Notions of power, control. Discursive self.

We might see the things on the right as a sort of *proto-curriculum* for the learning of language. In the case of the first language, Neisser presumes that the five selves (aspects of the self, if we prefer to take a holistic stance) develop at different times, along different trajectories, and gradually intermingle, become interpreted as aspects on the theme of 'I' or 'me' (Susan Harter, 1993). In the case of a second language learner, we bring to the task, holus-bolus, whichever cocktail of selves we have concocted in our past. Here two things need to be taken into account:

a) we will approach the second language learning task from the perspective of the conceptual self, which has the other Neisser-selves standing somewhat in the shadows behind it. This conceptual self is all that we believe about ourselves, and as Neisser says, not all of it is true (whatever 'true' means here). It certainly is permanently under construction (although at times it may seem to have become 'stuck' somewhere), and projects itself as our social identity, or range of identities. Indeed, some researchers speak of the notion of 'selving' as a "dynamic and recursive process of organizing, integrating, or meaning-making in individual experience" (Markus, Mullally & Kitayama, 1997, p. 14).

b) our sense of self may be quite strongly determined by socio-cultural factors, so that we cannot assume that 'the self' is an identical construct for all learners from all cultures or ethnicities. For one thing, Rosch claims that in many varieties of Asian philosophy the self as separate from the world does not exist in the way that it does in most Western philosophies. Moreover, she notes that for people who practice meditation a notion such as 'private self' simply does not exist at all (1997). In actual fact, that may be a goal that few practitioners of meditation ever reach completely; however, we need to be mindful of the possibility that self and selving might be conceptualized in very different ways in different religious or philosophical traditions.

Extrapolating, one might perhaps also (in addition to 'selving') coin notions such as 'togethering' for social processes of organizing experience, and 'othering', which at its most negative end would mean casting others in fixed terms as inferior, superior, to be bettered, imitated, despised, oppressed and so on (for one such use, see Riggins, 1997).

Different notions of self in different cultures can be reconciled and made convergent if we see the self, as Peirce, Bakhtin, Vygotsky, Wittgenstein and many others have done, as a social construct rather than an individual one. Neither the mind nor the self are contained in the body (though they are *embodied*), they are intricate webs of meaning making, social activity, relations, connections, contingencies, habits and conjectures, that are anchored both inside and outside our body, and that project outwards as well as inwards. In fact, the notions of 'inside' and 'outside' don't have very clear-cut meanings. This is why writers such as Rom Harré (Harré & Gillett, 1994), John Shotter (1993), Derek Edwards (1997) and others say that our selves, our minds, our attitudes and motivations, are *discursively constructed*, that is, they are created, developed and maintained in interaction with others.

Every act of speaking requires a voice. Even though others' voices resonate in any one person's voice, there still has to be a connection with the speaker's voice, especially in conversation, and in other genres that require an authoritative – i.e., authentic and autonomous – voice. It is often hard for students in school to achieve that voice in their schoolwork. Every school subject (based as it is on a particular branch of science) has its own discursive practices, its own genre. To speak (or write) in 'that way' may clash with the students' perceptions of themselves as members of their own speech community. What does it take for it to become 'all right' or even 'cool' to use the appropriate discourse to present a scientific experiment or to pronounce the foreign language just like the natives of country X do? That is not an easy question, yet it is one that every schoolteacher has to face. It is not just a question of reference group, speech accommodation or oppositional culture (though all these play forceful roles), essentially the dilemma facing the student is, do I want to sound like that or do I not? Can I force my mouth to make those sounds? Don't I sound like a real dork using those words and silly expressions?

I recall one group of Mexican migrant farm workers that I was volunteering to teach English for their citizenship applications. Basically, they just have to memorize the answers to 100 questions, such as, What are the colors of the American Flag? Who is the president of the US? What are the three branches of Government? These answers are short and memorizable in a straightforward predictable fashion. But I had some idealistic notion that perhaps they would want to be able to use English for more social purposes, such as talking about their family, their work, telling stories about their home town in Mexico and their family that is still there, and so on. But they really just wanted to go through the 100 questions in a mechanical manner, practicing and memorizing doggedly whatever it said on the sheet, whatever it might mean.

Then one evening Miguel came back. We hadn't seen him for a while. He looked a bit down. "¿Qué pasó, pues, Miguel?" It turned out that Miguel had flunked his citizenship interview in San Jose. He had practiced his 100 answers as diligently as everyone else, but the immigration agent had asked him to sit down, how is your family, where do you work, etc., and this had so unsettled Miguel that he became tongue-tied and could not speak at all. He was dumb-struck, terrified, staring at the agent, his mouth open but unable to form any of the words that he had been practicing so hard for months in the citizenship classes. When the agent gave him one more chance, and asked Miguel to say the pledge of allegiance, he stretched his arm outward as they do in Mexico, instead of placing it on his heart as is the custom in the US, and the agent felt he had to flunk the hapless Miguel, perhaps suspecting him of fascist tendencies as well as linguistic incapacities.

After this most horrific story, my students were suddenly quite eager to practice conversational English, and put their heart and soul into telling me and each other, in English, about their families in the US and back in Mexico, their kids in school, their work problems, sports, and many other topics that had previously been ruled irrelevant because they did not fit within the 100 questions. I do not mean to say that this learning to chit chat in English is in itself such a worthy goal, a sort of bridge to becoming a good docile citizen of the country, or that conversing in English should replace conversing in Spanish for these immigrants. Indeed, one would hope that more substantial and empowering curricular goals could be established, such as life skills, job skills, parenting skills, and so on. However, for people facing a citizenship interview, clearly not much else besides the list of 100 questions is relevant at that point in time. At the same time, the list becomes a distancing device, an artifact that allows the immigrant to study diligently while at the same time avoiding an investment in voice. The longer-term goal of any language program is therefore to connect the new language to the self, finding a voice, constructing and validating identities or *roles*, in Vygotskyan terminology (Kramsch, 2000, p. 151) and this can only be done through conversation.

The utilitarian motive, the perceived usefulness or urgency of language, is not the only one to give impetus to developing linguistic skills. Bonnie Norton (Norton Peirce, 1995), in her case study of five immigrant women in Canada, identifies several important conditions in the language-learning context:

- participation in communicative events

- access to the target-language community
- relations of power and equitable social structures
- language as constitutive of and constituted by social identity
- opportunities to speak and the right to speak
- investment: motivation as the learner's relationship to the changing social world
- cultural/linguistic capital (Bourdieu, 1991)

Norton Peirce argues that "when language learners speak, they are not only exchanging information with target language speakers but they are constantly organizing and reorganizing a sense of who they are and how they relate to the social world" (1995, p. 18). Learners are not always able to choose freely when and with whom they speak in the target language setting. Doing so requires access, investment, participation and also the right to speak, which may have to be *claimed*. Using Bourdieu's notion of linguistic and cultural capital, which assumes differential access to material and symbolic goods, acts of speaking, and investments in learning, are related to a perceived 'return on investment' (Peirce, 1995, p. 17). Of course, things are not as simple as all that. A long-term expectation of gain may not win out over a short-term fear of failure, defeat or ridicule. In an earlier book (van Lier, 1996) I gave the example of an immigrant woman in New York who has failed to learn English, relying instead on her sister and Latino boyfriend for complex dealings with the English-speaking world. She is undoubtedly aware that knowing English would be advantageous, but she believes she is not smart enough to learn, and is to timid to try. Mainstream monolinguals, in their ignorance and ethnocentricity, often brush such 'failures' off as laziness, comparing them to other cases of successful learning without looking more closely at the circumstances. Failure is seen as an individual's fault, but it is in fact usually at least in part due to societal circumstances and quite often manufactured by the society.

It is fairly easy to see how learning a second language in a host country, as an immigrant or as a visiting student, should be heavily influenced by notions of struggle in terms of self and social identity. The immigrant arrives with a complex notion of conceptual, private and extended self, but then encounters a new and different ecological and interpersonal reality. Whereas in first language development the perceived (ecological and interpersonal) selves develop first and gradually contribute to the growth of the other aspects of the self, here in the new environment the perceived and the established aspects of self are not naturally in sync, and quite often clash quite violently with one another, leading to culture and language shock (Agar, 1994), a traumatic silent period, and a protracted struggle between the perceived outer world and the experienced inner world. The outer-inner clash needs to be resolved for second language acquisition to be successful (for further examples, see Pavlenko & Lantolf, 2000).

When we learn another language (a 'foreign' language) in our own environment, a whole other set of issues comes to the fore, and these also need to be problematized. It is generally assumed that issues of social and psychological distance (to use Schumann's original terms, 1978) do not play a role to any significant extent in a foreign language setting. However, we should not assume that traditional practices of distinguishing between second and foreign language learning can be applied uniformly across all settings. For example, participation in communicative events, and access to the target-language community (the first two conditions in Norton Peirce's account, as summarized above) can be facilitated or hindered in a foreign language as well as in a second language setting. Being in a target language setting does not guarantee access and participation (or engagement and investment), and being in a foreign language setting does not preclude them (for one thing, the Internet, the media, and the increasing diversity of communities all over the world greatly facilitate direct access to numerous languages wherever we go). The ecologies are different, the constraints and resources are different, and thus the means for achieving the necessary access, engagement, investment and participation are different, but the overall job remains the same. As some researchers in foreign language settings have shown, issues of self and identity can also play a role when learning a foreign language. For example, Ohta (2001) has conducted a number of studies analyzing participation in tasks in Japanese as a Foreign Language classrooms in the US. Similarly, Kramsch (2000) has investigated the construction of self in a foreign language through the teaching of literature. In a study of students producing summaries of a story about a Vietnamese immigrant and his son raised in the US, students were able to take a variety of roles or identities, such as narrator, author, commentator, without the pretense of having to reveal a single 'true' self. Further contributions on this topic can be found in Lantolf (2000); see also Norton (2000).

MIND, CONSCIOUSNESS, COGNITION

> ... the mind is not something that is within my brain. Consciousness and mind belong to social coupling. That is the locus of their dynamics.
>
> - Maturana & Varela, 1992, p.234

Vygotsky's work is to a large extent a psychological and philosophical study of the concept of consciousness. This is how Leontiev describes Vygotsky's position:

> Consciousness is not given from the beginning and is not produced by nature: consciousness is a product of society: it is produced. ... Thus the process of internalization is not the *transferral* of an external activity to a pre-existing internal 'plane of consciousness': it is the process in which this plane is formed. (Leontiev, 1981, pp. 56-7, quoted in Bakhurst & Sypnowich, 1995, p. 6)

Another quote containing the same sentiment comes from Stephen Toulmin:

> Etymologically, of course, the term 'consciousness' is a knowledge word. This is evidenced by the Latin form, *-sci-*, in the middle of the word. But what are we to make of the prefix *con-* that precedes it? Look at the usage of the term in Roman Law, and the answer will be easy enough. Two or more agents who act jointly – having formed a common intention, framed a plan, and concerted their actions – are as a result *conscientes*. They act as they do knowing one another's plans: they act *jointly knowing*. (1982, p. 64, quoted in Shotter, 1993, p. 16):

Similar to mind and self, consciousness has traditionally been seen as an individual possession, something contained inside our body. Different cultural traditions put it in different places, perhaps the heart, or the stomach, but in Western tradition it is squarely located in the brain. That is, unless we are of a materialist bent and deny its existence altogether.

Now, as the above quotes suggest, it is also possible to see consciousness as a social construct. Not only Vygotsky and Toulmin see it this way, but also many other thinkers have done so, throughout history. In the Western world these include Spinoza, Vico, Peirce, Bakhtin and Wittgenstein, showing a strong thread of social constructionism throughout Western thought. Other traditions in other parts of the world, from the Americas, Africa, Australasia, to Asia, have always resisted separation of individual minds and consciousness from the world.

In an earlier paper I argued for a close connection between social interaction and consciousness in language learning. I will not repeat the arguments made there (van Lier, 1998), but I should make it clear that if we regard consciousness and mind as social constructs, and as not uniquely contained inside the brain, then a statement such as that language is acquired subconsciously or unconsciously does not make any sense at all. It is surely true that we do not know precisely (or even vaguely) what goes on inside the head while we are 'learning,' but that is a very different statement from saying that learning therefore occurs unconsciously. We might as well say that we do not know what is going on inside our elbow when we are learning to serve at tennis, and that therefore tennis is learned unconsciously.

Mind and consciousness develop as a result of social activity in the world, and learning *consists of* achieving more complex, more effective ('better' would of course be rather loaded terminology) activity in the world.

Interestingly, for Vygotsky consciousness was a combination of affect and intellect, one could not occur without the other, and consciousness would not arise if one were missing. This insight has more recently been given much further impetus by the well-known neuroscientist Antonio Damasio in his book *The feeling of what happens* (1999). In this book he argues that cognition and emotion go hand in hand.

Cognitive activity does of course exist and is very important in language development. The ecological approach would be useless if it ignored the role of cognition in language. It would just go to the other extreme of the early cognitivist approach, the phase that Harré & Gillett call "the first cognitive revolution" (1994, p. 8). That approach ignored the environment, something that also led to language being perceived as a purely mental construct, in Chomsky's theory of universal grammar.

Neisser (1992) says that there are two themes in the study of cognition, which is "like a piece of music with two principal themes that keep weaving in and out" (p. 339). Neisser is an interesting case, since he straddles both the first and the second cognitive revolution, he moved from one to other, and is therefore well equipped to keep both in view, and avoid the extremes of either. He wrote the first major textbook of cognitive psychology in 1967, but since the 1980s he has explored a range of themes in ecological psychology (such as his theory of self that forms the main topic of this chapter). Another example of a philosopher/psychology researcher who has gone through both versions of cognitive science is Jerome Bruner (e.g., 1986).

The first cognitive revolution is characterized by information processing, mental representation, schemata, and computational brain processes. The first pioneers were

Bruner, Miller, Pribram, Norman (the same person who more recently has studied affordances), Schank, Papert, Minsky, and of course Chomsky (for a review, see Gardner, 1985). Many of these people were also heavily involved in computer modeling, indeed, the leading metaphor for the mind/brain in the early days (the 60s) was the computer. Experimental work focused on such things as attention, memory, types and levels of processing, schema formation, and so on. In education this led to the use of advance organizers and various schema-building strategies, designed to promote a better comprehension of a text.

Experiments were typically, as has been common in psychology since the days of Wilhelm Wundt, conducted in highly controlled laboratory settings. Of such experimentation Urie Bronfenbrenner, one of the first ecologically oriented developmental psychologists in the US, complained:

> ...much of developmental psychology, as it now exists, is the science of the strange behavior of children in strange situations with strange adults for the briefest possible periods of time (1979, p. 19).

The second cognitive revolution is heavily influenced by Wittgenstein's later work, particularly the *Philosophical Investigations* (1958), which first appeared in 1953. This revolution, however, is not without its antecedents, among whom we have noted Vygotsky, Peirce and Bakhtin. Harré & Gillett summarize the main tenets of this revolution as follows:

1. Many psychological phenomena are to be interpreted as properties or features of discourse, and that discourse might be public or private. As public, it is behavior; as private, it is thought.
2. Individual and private uses of symbolic systems, which in this view constitute thinking, are derived from interpersonal discursive processes that are the main feature of the human environment.
3. The production of psychological phenomena, such as emotions, decisions, attitudes, personality displays, and so on, in discourse depends upon the skill of the actors, their relative moral standing in the community, and the story lines that unfold (1994, p. 27).

We now see that language is centrally implicated in cognitive as well as social activity, and indeed, language of course connects the cognitive and the social aspects of our activity.

SELF: THE I, ME, AND YOU

As argued above, the *self* is a social construction. So is the closely related notion of *identity*. Indeed, for many psychologists these notions refer to the same construct, to all intents and purposes (Giddens, 1991). Wiley, on the other hand, regards the self as an expression of general, universal nature (and all the things that characterize that nature in uniquely human ways), and identity as an individual self-concept, constructed both from social processes outside the individual, and from within (1994, p. 1). The distinction between self and identity, in this view, is one of degree of generality.

Another way of looking at self and identity may be to regard the former as the personal history of a person, phylogenetically as a member of humanity, and ontogenetically as a particular person. Identity might then be the *project* of this person (with this sense of self) to *place* him or herself in the world, and to *act* in this world in some identifiable manner. Identity is thus both a *project* and a *projection* of the self. Since it contains elements from without and within, it is closely related to the social environment(s) in which the person lives. In fact, as a member of social groupings, including family and institutions, a person's identity can become part of a collective identity, one in which such characteristics as race, religion, class, gender, and so on, can play major role. When they are imposed, identities (and a person can have several socially, politically and institutionally defined identities) can control the individual's self-concept to a greater or lesser degree. By the same token, identities can be negotiated and contested, and to some extent they are always in some process of change. Identities can be more stable or more labile. Identities can also be destroyed, they can be sites of struggle and resistance, and they can pit the self against the society.

For the pragmatists, Peirce, James, Dewey, Mead foremost among them, the self was a dialogical and social construct. It started in dialogue with caregivers, and its "inner life ... was a continuation of interpersonal dialogue" (Wiley, 1994, p. 9). We can see here a remarkable convergence of the American pragmatists' vision and that of their Russian counterparts and (roughly) contemporaries: Vygotsky, Bakhtin, Luria, Leontiev, *inter alia*. The dialogical perspective on self, mind, language and consciousness evolved almost simultaneously – but apparently independently – in the Soviet Union and in the United States.

It is generally assumed that Peirce emphasized semiosis from an individual perspective, but that it was really George Herbert Mead who brought it into the realm of social interaction (through his *Symbolic Interactionism*). However, Wiley shows that this is not the case, quoting several passages from Peirce's writing that show his dialogical outlook (1994). Peirce does not place language central in his scheme of semiotics: it is just one element, one system among many. However, when he speaks about language, it is in strongly ecological and dialogical terms.

The semiotic self as proposed by Peirce and Mead (independently from one another, but both as proponents of pragmatism) consists of semiotic (meaning making) processes that can be highly variable and flexible, thus accounting for human variation and many different projected identities, built on something like Neisser's five kinds of self knowledge: perceived (ecological and interpersonal), conceptual, extended, private.

Peirce described the semiotic self as containing an 'I' and 'you' component: an 'I' of the present, and a 'you' of the projected self in the immediate future. Mead, on the other hand, described it as an 'I' of the present and a 'me' of past selves. Peirce and Mead therefore conceptualize the self in terms of opposite temporal directions, present-future for Peirce, present-past for Mead.

Peirce's triadic process of semiosis, sign-object-interpretant, is dynamic and in perpetual motion (Colapietro 1989; Wiley 1994). As we have seen, the word *sign* carries two meanings: first, naming the overall triad, and second, denoting the first element of the sign. This is somewhat confusing, and in fact the word *representamen* is often used to avoid this ambiguity (one might also reliably use Saussure's *signifier*, though this is defined exclusively in linguistic terms). The representamen can be a written mark or spoken word, but it can also be a thought or a concept in itself, so then the triadic sign becomes thought – object – interpretation of thought (Wiley, 1994, p. 14). Wiley elaborates:

> The sign [representamen] and the interpretant are in a dialogical relationship, discussing the object, so to speak. In addition the interpretant of one moment often becomes the sign [representamen] of the next. (1994, p.14)

Colapietro (1989) suggests a combination of Peirce's and Mead's dialogues, turning the resulting notion of self into three triads:

present	past	future
I	**me**	**you**
sign	object	interpretant

The self is always in a process of self-interpretation, with the 'I' interpreting the past 'me' in order to give direction to the 'you' (Wiley, 1994, p.14).

Wiley proposes further that the self has three levels, and I will argue below that these must be interconnected in order for the language-learning person to develop his or her own *voice*:

1. thoughts;
2. systematic complexes of signs, e.g. the ethnic, class, gender and sexual identities and self-concepts;
3. the generic capacity for semiosis, anchored in the I – you – me structure (1994, p. 15).

The pragmatists' notion of self is a democratic, voluntarist and egalitarian one, and as such it successfully combated the social Darwinism of the late 19th century, which was based on the assumption of inherent racial inequalities, justified slavery, and contained the roots of fascism (Wiley, 1994). The pragmatists' self must not be confused with the notions of individualism and utilitarianism that have periodically surfaced as dominant in the American Zeitgeist, and that have sometimes been lumped together with pragmatism.

It is true that William James considered the utilitarian philosopher Stuart Mill as his major hero, but there were sharp differences between the pragmatism of James and that of Peirce-Mead-Dewey. Indeed, at one time Peirce was so disturbed by his pupil William James's interpretation of pragmatism that he decided to rebaptize his own original version as 'pragmaticism,' a name that he thought was ugly enough to protect it from further 'kidnappers' (Apel, 1981, p. 82).

It is therefore a mistake to identify Peirce's (and to a large extent, Mead's, Morris's, and Dewey's) pragmatism with that of James and others, some of whom later aligned it with a crude utilitarianism (one that is actually also far removed of the original philosophy of John Stuart Mill), individualism (such as that of Ayn Rand), and even now, it seems, at the moment of writing, with a new brand of neo-conservatism. It is clear that 'pragmatic' (i.e., utilitarian) approaches to the corporate market place, to international hegemony, to educational commodification, and so on, have nothing at all to do with the original tenets of pragmatism/pragmaticism as worked out by Peirce.[3]

Peirce's conception of pragmatism is distinguished by the dialogical nature of the sign, by a view of knowledge as produced by a community of interpreters, and by a need for semiosis to be grounded in everyday common sense (what he sometimes called 'critical common-sensism'), the practical world or human reason.[4]

The overall semiotic structure of the self is identical for all humans. Identities, on the other hand, are more contextually determined, and result in various cultural interpretations of race, gender, religion and so on, in general, the politics of identity. This means that social, institutional and political considerations and forces operate at the level of identity, and inequalities are therefore environmentally produced rather than inherited.

This is a very important point for educational policy. If the human self is equal in all cases ('created equal,' as the American constitution asserts), then variation is produced by circumstance. It follows that in our classrooms we should expect students from all backgrounds, rural or urban, colored in various ways, gendered differently, rich or poor, accented one way or another (and so on) to be able to achieve high standards.

Yet, there is an ethos in schools all around the world that endorses differential expectations for different groups. These differential expectations (acting as self-fulfilling prophecies in too many cases) in fact broadcast signs (overtly or covertly) that students of such-and-such description are likely to do better or worse than others of different descriptions, and they therefore implicitly or explicity institutionalize discriminatory practices. The inevitable resulting failure of the inferior-labeled groups is then ascribed to an insurmountable (perhaps racial or genetic, though it is not often spelled out which) incapacity of the group (s) in question to achieve educational success. The ecological-semiotic perspective is absolutely opposed to such forms of stereotyping, and this egalitarian position finds support in all of the ecological and pragmatic-semiotic literature, with caveats as noted above.

As we know, not only at the end of the 19th century (with social Darwinism), but periodically since then, everything from lack of economic success to IQ has been attributed to biological (racial, gender) differences. A notorious case, not too long ago, was *The Bell Curve* by Richard Herrnstein and Charles Murray (1994), which claimed that IQ differences were due to racial differences. In the pragmatists' perspective of the semiotic self, any differences in IQ (or other basic traits) must be due not to biological differences, but to socially produced inequalities at the level of political and politicized identities. Of course, these can and often do coincide with racial, gender and other differences, so that a false connection can be easily made. Stereotyping and categorizing are insidious evils in education, and educators have a

---

[3] For recent Peircean studies from different scientific and philosophical perspectives, see Ketner, 1995. For a historical perspective, see Menand, 2001.

[4] On this point his thinking was remarkably similar to that of Vico, although close connections to and influences from Vico have not been established to my knowledge. Certainly, both Vico and Peirce were sharply critical of Descartes' disembodied and anti-social rationality.

constant duty to actively teach to counteract them, and to remember that the word *kategorein* in ancient Greek meant: "to accuse in public."

In this view, the semiotic self and its identities directly leads to a critical perspective on social activity, including learning. Let's take a look at how this might play out in the classroom at a practical level.

As suggested above, a key variable in second/foreign (I add foreign here, because things may be different in a FL context[5]) language learning is the notion of *voice*. A person has a *voice* when his or her acts of speaking reflect all three of the levels mentioned above: thought, identity, and self. When there is a break between any of these three levels, then the voice is broken. Immigrants and foreign language learners have difficulty in establishing an authentic voice (see above, and van Lier, 1996; see also Kramsch, 1998) in the target language, because thought, identity and self may clash. The self is steeped in all five selves of Neisser's description, but conflicting identities are imposed by the host country or the foreign language. I cannot speak in that foreign language from the depth of my self, and with integrity in my thoughts, the learner might say. Or, more practically, I cannot make my mouth say these sounds and things. The identity that has been allotted to me in this new culture, country or language, creates a barrier between my thoughts and my self, and I feel tongue-tied. I feel "lost in translation," as Eva Hoffman put it (1989). I may limit my use of the foreign language to purely survival or utilitarian concerns (such as the memorization of the 100 immigration questions, as discussed earlier in the chapter), but it will not touch my thinking and my self, nor my private identities which I will only reveal with my own people, in my own language.

If this is the case, then the teacher and the learner face a momentous task, and that is to legitimate the new language vis a vis the thoughts and the self, and make the new identities compatible with the old. One way of doing so is by not denying existing conflicting identities and competing discourses, but rather by exploring them as a means of empowerment (Canagarajah, 1999, following bell hooks, 1989). I think that is also what Bonnie Norton Peirce hinted at in her work with the immigrant women in Canada (1995, 2000). We can only speak the second language when thoughts, identities and self are aligned. In the new culture and language that means the development of compatible identities that do not negate existing ones, nor erode the self. There is a constant struggle for authenticity and voice in the new language (Hoffman, 1989). We will pick this theme up again in Chapter 7.

LANGUAGE USE AND VOICE

In this final section of the chapter I want to first of all add another influence into the mix, illustrating how the ecological approach relates to the views on language of

---

[5] If the foreign language is not commonly used in the environment, then the notion of investment may be quite different: particularly the Firstnesses of speaking maybe absent.

Ludwig Wittgenstein, by quoting a few snippets from his later work (1958, 1974, 1980)[6]:

> *To have a language means to be a member of a community.*
>
> *Yes, meaning something is like going up to someone (1974, p.157).*
>
> *Understanding is knowing 'how to go on.' In the sense in which there are processes (including mental processes) which are characteristic of understanding, understanding is not a mental process (1958, p. 61e).*
>
> *It is misleading then to talk of thinking as a mental activity. We may say that thinking is essentially the activity of operating with signs.*

These remarks emphasize, once again, that language cannot be understood or conceptualized in isolation from the context in which it is used. Language is social activity, not a collection of words and sentences. For Wittgenstein, the meaning of language lies in its use.

Recall also in this context the claim of Donald Davidson that "there is no such thing as a language" (1986, p. 446). Interestingly, as we saw earlier, Chomsky agrees with Davidson on the latter's distinction between a *prior theory* (the knowledge we bring to an encounter) and a *passing theory* (the ongoing procedures we use to make sense of what is said), but turns them into something quite similar to the old competence-performance distinction, something Davidson definitely did not have in mind (Chomsky, 2000, p. 67 ff.). Once again, this allows Chomsky to say that the passing theory is of no interest linguistically speaking, and he is right back where he started. This argument will continue a while longer, I feel.

In my view of things, and I alluded to this in my 1996 book, the passing theory is of great interest linguistically, since it looks at language as process and progress in the world. It relates also to the layers of interpretation I presented in Chapter 2 (see also my *Introducing Language Awareness* book, 1995) and it means addressing the twin questions of what it takes to understand an utterance the way it is intended to be understood, and what it takes to be understood the way one intends to be understood. These are very central questions in language development and classroom language learning.[7]

The dialogical nature of language means that views of self and other are always embedded in acts of speaking, in discourses. In academic language such personal aspects tend to be suppressed so that language becomes pure information and argumentation, but even there views of self and other, and more broadly cultural assumptions and shared views, surface very regularly as examples, asides, hedging, assertion, rhetorical ploys, and so on. And what is more crucial for secondary school students, the appropriation of academic discourse may require shifts of identity that many young people are simply not in a position to make. This is so because, as Heath argues,

---

[6] I have gleaned these and many other remarks from a variety of editions and translations of Wittgenstein's work over the years; unfortunately, I have been unable to link all of them to particular pages in the editions I have currently on my shelves.

[7] See also the dicussion on relevance in the previous chapter.

> An ease with such discourse forms comes only with multiple opportunities to play meaningful roles within groups that talk across these genres of explanation, explication and narrative and that demonstrate understanding in several modes – from dramatic improvisation to paint to photography. Hence, any curriculum must ensure extensive opportunities for students to develop explanations through different means and collaboratively with the guidance of adults and other youths. The latter are important in this socialisation process, because they illustrate peer uses of certain discourse forms and model roles that demonstrate theory building at work. The arts lend themselves most readily to creating such opportunities. Jointly composing the script for a play or interpretation of a given script, planning and painting a mural as a class or providing advertising and programme design for a school-wide musical event demand collaborative theory building and strategy development (2000, p. 125).

Learners approach a second language with a given history and ongoing construction of their social self and identity. In the new language, various aspects of the self must be renegotiated and reconstructed, and this often entails clashes and struggles. This is true in both second and foreign language learning, though the processes and problems can differ in different contexts.

Teachers can encourage students to develop their own 'voice' in the new language (and first-language learners need to do the same thing in the academic registers of their own language) by embedding language in meaningful activity. Focusing on the here and now brings the benefit that indicational uses of language are established first, allowing the learners to develop ecological and interpersonal perceptions in the language, and on the basis of these they can construct translingual and trans-cultural selves (along the lines of Kramsch's 'third place' (1993, drawing on the work of Homi Bhabha, 1992). Thus, in Vygotskyan terms, interpersonal meanings, using language as both tool and sign, can be stepping stones towards symbolic meanings and higher socio-cognitive processes.

CONCLUSION

The first thing to establish when talking about language and self is that language is not a fixed code (Harris, 1996). If it were, then language would have very little to do with self and identity. Instead, language is a process of meaning making (meaning potential in Halliday's terms, semiosis in the parlance of semioticians). As we have seen, not only is language a constantly constructed and reconstructed process, it is also inherently a dialogical process. This dialogicity is usually associated with Bakhtin, but we have seen that the pragmatists, from Peirce to Mead (and including Dewey) have proposed a semiotic process based on the triadic sign, and this triadicity (as different from the Saussurian signifier-signified dyad) turns every sign into a dialogical sign, whether it is made in a speaker-hearer context or not.

I used three texts to illustrate how the self and its identities may be involved in the semiotic process of language use, and the contextual requirements that need to be in place for the assignment of interpretations. According to Volosinov, sources of contextual information include:

a) shared physical surroundings;
b) shared background knowledge; and

c) shared situation definition.

The first of course is mediated indirectly in writing and reading (e.g., in novels, using Bakhtin's notion of chronotope, 1981), and in general the spatial-temporal location of an utterance will determine the extent to which contextual requirements, and what kinds of requirements, are needed for meaning making. The second in many ways is being created in dialogue rather than pre-existing as fixed properties, and the third involves the establishment of intersubjectivity (Rommetveit, 1974) and a shared contextual framework for joint action, or activity space.

I have described the self as an ongoing project of establishing one's place in the world. It does not exist at birth (except in the sense of proto-self, Damasio, 1999), though neuroscientist Stein Bråten (1998) argues that neural structures of a 'virtual other' exist in the newborn child's brain, a suggestion seconded by Colwyn Trevarthen (1990). That is, in these views (and the pragmatists' proposals are aligned with this), the human child is 'designed for' or 'born with' dialogicity.

Ulric Neisser has proposed that humans have five kinds of self knowledge: ecological, interpersonal (together forming the perceived self), extended, private and conceptual selves. These selves gradually develop as a child grows up in a particular social milieu.

I have defined identity as a *project* as well as a *projection* of the self, in interaction with social groups, institutions, and particular political contexts. Identities are formed from within as well as from without, so that they can become a site of struggle for individuals and groups. This is illustrated by Bonnie Norton Peirce's (1995) case studies of Canadian immigrant women, and the circumstances that surround their appropriation of the new language (including opportunities and the right to speak, investment in cultural and linguistic capital, relations of power and control, etc.). It is also illustrated in classroom work in Kramsch (2000), where students explore their voices of author, narrator, commentator and so on.

It is important to note that many current proponents of cognitive science (the 'second cognitive revolution,' as Harré and Gillett, 1994, call it) have gone beyond a view of mind and consciousness as 'brain-resident' and regard all these constructs (including language, self and identity) as at least partially socially constructed in discourse and distributed in the life space.

Recent 'neo-pragmatists' such as Colapietro (1989) and Wiley (1994) have proposed a semiotic self that is based on a combination of the different perspectives of Peirce and Mead, creating in effect a present 'I' that is in constant dialogue with the past 'me' and the future 'you'.

Wiley proposes that the self has three levels, and I have suggested that a person's voice reflects all three levels: *thought*, *identity*, and *self*:

a) thoughts
b) systematic complexes of signs, e.g. the ethnic, class, gender and sexual identities and self-concepts
c) the generic capacity for semiosis, anchored in the I – you – me structure (1994, p.15).

The pragmatists' notion of self is a democratic, voluntarist and egalitarian one, and as such it successfully combated the social Darwinism of the late 19th century, which was based on the assumption of inherent racial inequalities, justified slavery, and contained the roots of fascism. The overall semiotic structure of the self is identical for all humans. Identities, on the other hand, are more variable, and result in various cultural interpretations of race, gender, religion and so on, in general, the politics of identity.

There is currently a great deal of interest in notions of self and identity in the language learning field, and I have mentioned some of the main researchers and publications in this area. Identities are shaped in and through social relationships, by virtue of the fact that the person-in-action perceives his or her own body and actions as well as aspects of the environment (physical, social, symbolic) that are or are becoming relevant. A crucial factor in the establishment of identities (as projects and projections of the self) is the use of language, both by self and by other. In fact, identity and language are mutually constitutive. Speaking is thus never the mere emission of a message, it is always an act of presenting the self, a use of voice in the Bakhtinian and Ecoian sense. Thus, in language learning, the emergence, the management, and the growth of identities must play a central part in the interactions between and among institution, teacher, and learners.

CHAPTER 6

LANGUAGE LEARNING PATHWAYS

INTRODUCTION

In this chapter I address the question of how language learning actually happens. It is widely believed or assumed that language learning occurs in a context of communication and interaction. But how exactly this learning occurs is not so easy to establish. I hope to show that the ecological approach to language learning (both first and second) can shed some light on the actual learning processes that occur.

Some of the difficult concepts to grapple with are Vygotsky's notion of *internalization* (*appropriation*, as some prefer to call it, e.g., Rogoff, 1995, or *interiorization*, as it is called in Vygotsky & Luria, 1994, p. 153), various ways of *scaffolding* learning (Bruner, 1983; Donato, 1994; van Lier, 1996), *prolepsis*, or "evoking the future in the present" (Flynn, 1991, p. 6), and the *Zone of Proximal Development* or *ZPD* (Vygotsky, 1978). It is also important to think about how L1 and L2 learning relate to each other. There surely are many parallels, but just as surely there are also many differences. How can we capture both the similarities and the differences? Two other areas that will be discussed from an ecological perspective are the development of academic language, and project-based learning.

The ecological approach maintains that information is picked up when something in the linguistic surroundings (ambient language) is perceived as significant, i.e., is "behaviorally relevant" (McArthur & Baron, 1983, p. 234). With that in mind, what are the most appropriate instructional contexts for second language learning? We know that the most common arrangement is still rows of desks or tables facing the front of the room where the teacher orchestrates the lesson. This classroom ecology is more conducive to teaching as transmission of information, and to learning as receiving information and individually processing it. When activity, perception, and information pick-up are placed in the center, the ecology of the learning environment may have to be changed. Perhaps work stations, resource centers, open activity spaces, and consultation areas would be more appropriate in such a pedagogical ecosystem.

On the other hand, even rows of tables and cramped classrooms can become a true classroom community if the teacher is successful in establishing good rapport with the students (Sullivan, 2000). In addition, of course, there are cultural differences in acceptable or 'good' spatial designs of classrooms, and changing the

VIEWS ON LANGUAGE LEARNING

In Chapter 5 I quoted St. Augustine's view of language learning. This was basically a view of labeling objects with the right name, and imitating adults when they used those names. Similarly, popular folk views often regard foreign language learning as a matter of replacing one set of labels with another set of labels. But those who actually try foreign language learning in schools or institutes may also develop the view that it consists of the mastery of many intricate rules and structures, perhaps more like mathematics or logic than like free expression or appreciation of language.

I remember a visiting jazz musician speaking to my son's music class in high school. I was outside in the hall (eavesdropping), waiting to pick up my contingent of car pool victims. The musician (a rather well known professional jazz performer) was just finishing his demo with some final words of wisdom. He said that students should think of music as a creative exploration, something that just flows. He felt that the students thought of music more as a rigid set of rules and formulas that had to be learned by heart, *"just like mathematics and foreign languages."* This was a quite interesting comment. Why should foreign language learning be equated with mathematics, rather than with, say, painting, or music, or soccer? After all, as I argued in the last chapter, language use requires an investment of voice, and there is an aesthetic element in language use from this perspective, in the same way that voice and identity are invested in music, painting, and even in more bodily activities such as soccer (and of course dance).

Vygotsky's view on second/foreign language learning is interesting to consider in this context. It certainly differs markedly from his view on first language development, as the following quote from *Thought and language* illustrates:

> It is well known that to learn a foreign language at school and to develop one's native language involve two entirely different processes. While learning a foreign language, we use word meanings that are already well developed in the native language, and only translate them; the advanced knowledge of one's own language also plays an important role in the study of the foreign one, as well as those inner and outer relations that are characteristic only in the study of the foreign language. And yet, in spite of all these differences, the acquisition of the foreign and the native languages belongs to one general class of the processes of speech development (1986, p. 159).

Vygotsky's observation points to differences as well as similarities between L1 and L2 development. Referring back to my discussion of this issue in Chapter 4, I would agree with Elisabeth Bates's suggestion of "less is more", i.e., L1 proceeds as efficiently as it does because the child has limited cognitive capacities, not because he or she has a special kind of language organ (Elman, et al., 1996, p. 349). As I have argued elsewhere (2000), language development in L1 proceeds in three broad phases: *mutuality* (primary subjectivity), *indicality* (secondary subjectivity, triadic interaction), and *predicality*, or grammaticalization. Each phase represents a qualitative transformation of the previous one, a movement towards a higher level of cognitive functioning, in Vygotsky's terms. The movement to a higher level of cognitive functioning is accompanied by a change in physical and social landscape configurations. In the first phase, mutuality, the landscape is one of two subjects, of I and you. The coupling is an interorganismic one, between caregiver and baby, a direct relationship of reciprocity. In the second phase the infant and caregiver can jointly share an attentional focus on a third entity, an object. The crucial development is that they are both aware that the other is attending to the same entity. This phase is characterized by pointing, naming, commenting. The third phase, finally, allows a supersession of the here and now, a grammatical mediation of an expanded reality, a talking about things not here or not here now.

When learning a second language the learner faces these three phases simultaneously at full force. It is not a case of first building up reciprocal rhythms, then joint intentionality, then shared symbolicity; instead, the entire L2 world hits the learner head-on. As Vygotsky appears to suggest, the L1 is called upon to cushion the blow. The incoming avalanche is slowed down by filtering everything through the familiar L1 patternings. At first it seems that it is this L1 buffering that causes the slowdown, and the idea occurs that removing it might speed up the L2 acquisition process. However, nothing could be further from the truth. This is another case where a classic simile from Kant is relevant:

> The light dove cleaving in free flight the thin air, whose resistance it feels, might imagine that her movements would be far more free and rapid in airless space (1934, p. 29).

However, the dove does not realize that but for the air it would plummet down to the ground. Similarly, removing the L1 influence during the L2 development process (if that were at all possible, which it is not) would merely obstruct and delay the latter. The L1 acts as a mediator or a support structure for L2 acquisition, a means of keeping the learning processes aloft.

Another way of looking at it is by way of the concentric circles diagram in Chapter 2 (also, van Lier, 1995). Our interpretation of any linguistic action is like a bar code reader that scans all the layers instantaneously for salient information. The main interpretive law seems to be that outer layers overrule inner ones, in case of any clashes of meaning or ambiguities. In an L2 situation this interpretive sequence is likely to break down, the formal tends to precede the functional, the intellectual tends to precede the emotional (strangely, Thirdness precedes Firstness), and the metaphorical often precedes the literal (due to the Cartesian biases inherent in Western school systems).

Although from an educational, scholastic perspective, these would seem the right directions of meaning making, ecological examination suggests that the obverse is the case in L1. Instead of the formal, intellectual, and metaphorical forming the basis for the functional, emotional and literal, in L1 the latter probably precede the former.

How do we conceptualize second language development in an ecological perspective? How is it different from first language development, and in what ways may it be similar as well?

Here I will be drawing on some of the arguments made in previous chapters, and pulling them together into what I hope will be a coherent perspective on second language development, with parallels drawn from first language development where it seems to be appropriate. In the chart on the next page (Table 6.1)[1] I summarize four common views on second language learning.

1. TRIGGER

In the innatist view (see Chapter 2), language is neither taught nor learned, it basically 'grows' as a 'mental organ.' In the old days this ability was called the LAD or 'language acquisition device', a black-box mechanism to account for the apparent ease with which children acquire their native language. There are several reasons why innate abilities must play a role in L1 acquisition (Lightfoot, 1982). The most important reason is that the linguistic knowledge the child has is *underdetermined* by the data available. What this means is that the child knows more (by the age of four or five) than he/she can possibly have encountered in the environment. The five-year-old child knows the difference between *Paint the barn red* and *Paint the red barn*, and between *When did Peter say he hurt himself?* and *When did Peter say how he hurt himself?* [2]

The assumption is that there must be a rich innate mental structure in the brain that unfolds just by virtue of the child's being in an environment in which the language is used. The exact nature of the exposure is unimportant, it does not matter what kinds of sentences, how accurate every sentence is, and so on. So the precise nature of the input is relatively trivial, since all it does is trigger the growth of the innate system. Indeed, Pinker puts this case so strongly that he speaks of 'the language instinct' (book title, 1994). However, we would do well to heed Hebb's warning that "the term 'instinct' implying a mechanism or neural process into which learning enters, is a misleading term and should be abandoned" (Hebb, 1953, p. 46, quoted in Gibson, 1991, p. 149).

2. INPUT

In second language theory and practice, I do not believe that anyone espouses an extreme innatist view of development, except perhaps for early childhood bilingualism. Even those who espouse an innatist view of first-language acquisition are likely to take a more explicit, learning-centered perspective on second-language acquisition. Krashen, possibly the strongest advocate of an innatist approach in the second-language field, holds that acquisition occurs at a subconscious level when a learner is exposed to comprehensible input in which linguistic forms occur that are just slightly ahead of the learner's current level of Interlanguage, that is, the current level of proficiency or competence in the second language. Conditions that facilitate such subconscious acquisition include (in addition, of course, to rich and efficient internal acquisition mechanisms) a low 'affective filter' that makes the learner receptive to the input (Krashen, 1985).

---

[1] In this chart the term "FonF "refers to a focus on form within a meaning-based task, see Long, 1996. By contrast, "FonFs" refers to a focus on forms, i.e., a traditional grammar-driven perspective.
[2] These examples are taken from the video: The Human Language, Part II.

LANGUAGE	LEARNING	CONDITIONS	TEACHING	ROLE OF L1	META-LINGUISTIC WORK; FonF
TRIGGER	1. GROWTH OF AN INNATELY SPECIFIED SYSTEM	Exposure Characteristics of exposure language unimportant	Speak to learner	L1 irrelevant "submersion"	No focus on form (FonF) or forms (FonFs). Positive input is sufficient
INPUT	2. COMPREHENSIBLE INPUT	Exposure to comprehensible input: i+1 Low affective filter Verbal action (speech) is the result of comprehension	Speak to learner in comprehensible language Promote a positive atmosphere	occasional L1 use to assist comprehension	FonF(s) only produces "learning." Metalinguistic knowledge as "monitor." Role of negative input marginal.
NEGOTIATION	3. INPUT MODIFIED THROUGH NEGOTIATION OF MEANING: "FACE-TO-FACE" COLLABORATION	Input made comprehensible in interaction. Learner receives improved input	Provide opportunities for negotiation through communicative tasks. NS interlocutor often preferred	L1 use to facilitate negotiation, structuring	FonF through interactional modifications. Metalinguistic knowledge is incidental. Negative input through recasts, clarifications.
AFFORDANCE	4. ACTIVITY IN AN ECOLOGY OF LEARNING. "SIDE-BY-SIDE" COLLABORATION	Activity makes linguistic material relevant and available for further action (affordances). Perception integrated with action	Provide access to meaningful activities and encourage learner to be engaged. Scaffolding, awareness raising. Contingent language use is possible	L1 use to provide access and promote engagement. L1 as mediator	Focus on Language (FonL) or Semiotics (FonS) is a natural aspect of language use. Awareness raising to assist attention focusing. Metalinguistic knowledge as positive resource.

Figure 6.1: Four views of learning

Krashen's theoretical position on second language acquisition consists of five loosely interrelated hypotheses, briefly summarized in the following conveniently mnemonic acronym (ANIMA):

Acquisition must be sharply distinguished from learning.
Natural order: there is a natural order of language acquisition in terms of structures and complexity, and this order cannot be circumvented by grammatical syllabuses and drilling.
Input: The learner acquires language when receiving abundant comprehensible input that is at stage i + 1, that is, input that is linguistically just one step ahead of the learner's current level of Interlanguage (as noted above).
Monitor: Linguistic material, e.g. grammatical rules, can be learned, but it is only useful as a monitor, that is, to edit language use consciously under conditions of sufficient time, e.g. when writing an essay or doing an exam. Some people are better than others at monitoring, and there are even 'super-monitors' who can monitor their language in real time while speaking.
Affective filter: It is extremely difficult to acquire language under conditions of low receptivity, high stress, and high anxiety.

There is in my view a lot of truth and common sense in all of these hypotheses, and Krashen has time and again marshaled evidence from empirical studies to support his key position, that of comprehensible input being necessary and possibly sufficient for acquisition to occur. Yet, it also seems to me that, at least in these stripped-down formulations, Krashen misses the key point in each of the topics that the five hypotheses address. Let us therefore take a more expansive view and see how they can contribute positively to our understanding of the field.

ACQUISITION

The opposition between acquisition and learning may be less rigid than Krashen presumes. There are two reasons for suggesting that this may be the case. First, whenever Krashen talks about learning, he appears to refer to the sorts of rote grammar and drill-and-kill methods that have been (probably still are, in many quarters) rampant in many foreign language classes. So it is possible that his claim can be reduced to: bad learning (meaningless drilling, memorization of rules, mechanical translation of sentences and words, etc.) is useless in terms of acquisition. I would agree with that, referring to Whitehead's classic statement that much of school knowledge remains 'inert,' that is, is unusable in real life contexts (1929). However, this is quite different from saying that 'learning,' (deliberate, conscious, purposeful study) is useless per se. I personally think it is always useful and in many cases essential.

The second consideration is that even rote memorization, repetitive drilling, etc., may bear fruit at some point, in the same way that practicing throwing balls may lead to more precision in baseball or football. Krashen's 'no-interface' position may therefore be too strong. On the other hand, some views of language learning that emphasize the need for hard-slog drilling and cramming may also be too strong at the other end of the continuum. Perhaps it would be best to follow Ellis's suggestion that a *'weak-interface'* position between acquisition and learning may be most reasonable (1994). He and others have argued that learning can assist in acquiring skills that are useable in actual settings. That is certainly my experience as a language learner.

A totally different option is to reject the acquisition – learning distinction altogether. In an *emergentist* or *grammaticalization* perspective (see chapter 4), both incidental learning (acquisition, in a comprehensible input situation) and deliberate, focused learning can contribute to the emergence of linguistic abilities. The key (to escape the inertness that Whitehead noted) may be to make sure the incidental, meaningful activities and the deliberate practice activities are related and integrated with one another.

NATURAL ORDER

There is considerable evidence from SLA research that there are natural orders and sequences of linguistic material in second language learning. These orders and sequences (see Ellis, 1994) may not be all that different from L1 development, where they have been well established since the pioneering work of Roger Brown in the early 1970s (Brown, 1973).[3] This means that we cannot easily learn linguistic structures in any random sequence, rather, there is some logical progression in terms of related items and prerequisite knowledge. Traditional grammatical syllabuses have not been very good at taking these issues into account, so that much time may be wasted in trying to teach students things they are not ready to learn. This has been examined and corroborated by Pienemann and his colleagues in the teachability and processability hypotheses (Pienemann, 1998). However, even here, we can store rules learned in rote fashion in our memory and retrieve them later to help us acquire the second language when we are in the thick of things. So, I am sure that my memorized lists of verb inflections, plurals, and case assignments of prepositions (such as, that "aus, bei, mit, nach, seit, von, zu, binnen and gegenüber" take the dative case, something I learned at the age of 14) help me when I need to re-activate my German yet another time.

INPUT

I have argued earlier in this book (see Chapters 2 and 4) and elsewhere (van Lier, 2000) that there are problems with the word 'input.' It is a computational metaphor that places an emphasis on fixed pieces of language that are processed and stored in the brain. It ignores, or at least neglects, the socially active learner,

---

[3] The reader may ask, how rigid might such natural orders be, and how might they be compatible with an ecological outlook? It should be no surprise that there are constraints, caused by complexity of structure and expression, that require a level of readiness or preparedness. But the rigidity of these orders, and the ways in which the complexities of language interact with the exigencies of participation in activity, are not all that well understood at this stage (see Elman, Bates, Johnson, Karmiloff-Smith, Parisi & Plunkett, 1996, for some relevant studies in first-language development).

and the fact that language itself is to some extent recreated every time it is negotiated (i.e., it is emergent).

MONITOR

In reality, monitoring is a constant and necessary component of language use. It involves, minimally, an online awareness of audience design, message design, and interactional design of utterances (van Lier, 1996). In addition, our sense of social identity relates what we feel and who we are to what we say, constantly matching one with the other. We can also recall Harris's suggestion that the metalinguistic element of language is not just some sophisticated or academic add-on, but a constant accompaniment of any act of language use (1996, 1997). Finally, the use of the word 'monitor' as a noun suggests some supervisory center in the brain that inspects the stream of language before, during and after it happens. Instead, the mental, perceptual, and social activity of monitoring is part of the very fabric of the process of using and learning language.

AFFECTIVE FILTER

The affective side of all cognitive and social work is extremely important. The learner must be receptive to learning and invest in it. Research in psychology and neuroscience has shown that the emotional component of cognition is instrumental in stimulating brain functioning (cf. Schumann's discussion of the role of the amygdala, 1990; see also Damasio, 1999; for a recent discussion of the role of affective factors, see Arnold, 1999). One of the problems of Krashen's metaphor of the affective filter is that it encourages a view that this is a single variable that varies just along a single dimension, from 'open' to 'closed.' This view is compatible with a passive, asocial learner who just sits around soaking up comprehensible input. At the level of caricature, we might imagine a roomful of learners just feeling good being exposed to comprehensible input, which may just be simplified, dumbed-down lecturing by a friendly, caring teacher. A cabbage-patch image with a nurturing gardener going around tending the tender plants. This denies the complexity of both affect and the activity of learning. In any complex learning activity a multiplicity of social and cognitive factors play an inseparable role: anxiety, curiosity, interest, excitement, fear, confidence, and so on. An area of research that contributes much to the area of emotional engagement is that of intrinsic motivation and autonomy (Deci & Flaste, 1995; Dornyei, 2001; Kohonen, Jaatinen, Kaikkonen & Lehtovaara, 2001; van Lier 1996). Emotional factors cannot easily or clearly be divided into 'positive' or 'negative' factors. For example, learning can be a stressful activity, to be sure, but neither the presence nor the absence of stress have any uniform relationship with learning. It is likely that the necessity of investment, and the demands of the learning context, will engender periods of stress and anxiety as well as periods of relaxed attention. The old saying: "No pain, no gain" may sometimes be true, and sometimes not.

3. NEGOTIATION OF MEANING

A more active and interactive perspective on input holds that we can make language more comprehensible by engaging in meaningful interaction. While being engaged in challenging tasks, learners need to work actively to comprehend each other's messages, and in this work they focus on those parts of language that need improvement, both receptively and productively. As Long puts it,

> [N]egotiation for meaning, and especially negotiation work that triggers interactional adjustments by the NS or more competent interlocutor, facilitates acquisition because it connects input, internal learner capacities, particularly selective attention, and output in productive ways (1996, pp. 451-2).

A key feature in this interaction-based approach is *selective attention*. The learner, while engaged in a meaningful task, attends to those features of language that require modification for the task to be successful. Here the learner may naturally focus on form (FonF), or his/her attention may be drawn to specific formal features that are deemed to be of importance.

Another important feature is that 'output' is assumed to be a valuable aspect of interaction. Recall that in Krashen's theories speech cannot cause acquisition, only acquisition can cause speech. The idea is that nothing can come out of our mouth (in more precise terms, be formulated for expression) that is not already there, in our brain. This assumes a linear causality from competence to performance:

$$\text{acquired competence} \dashrightarrow \text{performance in speech}$$

In line with Swain's (2000) arguments that output can sharpen learners' awareness of linguistic expression in ways that input simply cannot, practice in speaking in meaningful contexts is seen to have many benefits in terms of language development. For example, when listening to another person speak, syntactic precision is not always essential for reasonable interpretation. But when speaking, we may have to struggle to make our ideas clear in precise grammatical and lexical terms, or else we may be misunderstood. In ecological terms, proficiency emerges gradually, through repeated trials of production and reception, with meaning and precision accruing over time. It seems that in Krashen's view, acquisition is an all-at-once affair: it happens, and then it is useable. In reality it is much more like a social struggle for expression and meaning sharing.

Finally, in this perspective, as in Vygotsky's ZPD, the ideal interlocutor is a native speaker or at least a more competent partner. This creates an expert-novice relationship, in which the 'expert' can guide the 'novice' towards higher levels of language use. Here is a typical example of such negotiated interaction, from the work of Pica (1992):

> NNS: so there's a cross in the center of the paper ...
> NS: what do you mean by cross?
> NNS: traffic cross
> NS: oh, where people can cross or a traffic light

NNS: yes

We can see here that the NS vets and approves, questions and elaborates. The NNS very much follows the NS's interactional lead. This does not mean that the learner does not also work hard to contribute to the meaning making, but s/he does so very much under the tutelage of the NS. And the NS-NNS interaction itself may serve to construct learner incompetence, and thus debilitate NNS performance more than might be the case in more symmetrical encounters (Liddicoat, 1997).

4. AFFORDANCE

In Chapter 4 I proposed some arguments for replacing the 'input metaphor' with an ecological one that emphasizes activity and perception. This does not replace the notion of negotiated interaction and interactional modification described above, but it places it in a wider context. For example, as I will show below, interaction among equal learners can also be beneficial (see also van Lier & Matsuo, 2000). This is in line with recommendations by Barbara Rogoff, who distinguishes three types of proximal learning contexts: guided participation, participatory appropriation, and apprenticeship (1993). This harks back also to recommendations by Piaget, who saw constructive interaction among equals as the ideal learning context (see below). Ironically, therefore, Piaget with his reputation for focusing squarely on individual cognitive processes and development, is here more social-constructivist than Vygotsky, who focuses on guidance under the tutelage of an expert. While Piaget stresses the need for symmetrical cooperation, Vygotsky emphasizes inequality of skills and maturity – although not in a relationship that exploits a power/authority differential. Rogoff points out that these different interactional configurations are likely to stimulate different learning processes (1993, p. 130). In Rogoff (1995) three planes of sociocultural activity are elaborated, and I summarize them in the box on the next page.

In an ecological perspective activity and perception are central, including the sorts of focused attention that Long talks about. In such an activity-centered context learners will use all the tools at their disposal to accomplish what it is they have set out to do or what the curriculum has been set up to focus on. This means interaction with other learners as well as the teacher, and also the use of various resources that may be helpful, including the L1 and various kinds of linguistic and metalinguistic knowledge. In such a scenario, I feel that Focus on *Form* (FonF) can be more appropriately referred to as Focus on *Language* (FonL), since not just forms but all aspects of language (phonology, morphology, meaning, pragmatics, discourse) and other meaning-bearing systems (gestures, artifacts, symbolic content) can become the focus of attention. So, perhaps we should say FonS (focus on *Semiosis*).

> apprenticeship, a form of 'community activity,' which goes beyond the expert-novice dyad: a small group in a community with specialization of roles. A system of interpersonal involvements and arrangements in which people engage in culturally organized activity in which apprentices become more responsible participants (p.143).
>
> guided participation, interpersonal engagements and arrangements, people manage their own and others' roles, and structure situations. Not just face-to-face, but also side by side and more distal.
>
> participatory appropriation, interdependence, not "internalization" (from information-processing); the process is not "one of internalization in which something static is taken across a boundary from the external to the internal" (p. 151). "The dynamic approach of participatory appropriation does not define cognition as a collection of stored possessions (such as thoughts, representations, memories, plans), but rather treats thinking, re-presenting, remembering, and planning as active processes that cannot be reduced to the possession of stored objects" (p. 151).

THE ROLE OF INTERACTION AND CONVERSATION

In this section I will elaborate on the notion of negotiation and interaction as processes that occur during learning tasks. I will focus primarily on conversational interaction, thus setting the stage for an elaborated perspective on pedagogical interaction in the sections that follow. First, here is a useful quote on conversation from Vygotsky:

> In conversation, every sentence is prompted by a motive. Desire or need lead to request, question to answer, bewilderment to explanation. The changing motives of the interlocutors determine at every moment the turn oral speech will take. It does not have to be consciously directed – the dynamic situation takes care of that. (Vygotsky, 1962, p. 99)

Without wishing to upstage St. John, it occurs to me that the story of language development might well start like this: 'In the beginning was the conversation.'

The centrality of conversation in human development and in the construction of reality has been noted by many writers. Here is a small selection of pertinent quotes:

The primary human reality is persons in conversation.
– R. Harré (1983, p. 58)

Conversation flows on, the application and interpretation of words, and only in its course do words have their meaning.
– Wittgenstein, 1967, p. 24e

Conversation, understood widely enough, is the form of human transactions in general.
– A. MacIntyre 1981, p. 197

Exactly how language learning is accomplished remains a mystery. Over the years, memorization of rules and words, imitation of examples, responses to stimuli, and the maturation of innate structures have all had their moment in the limelight, but none of them have been able to provide conclusive or convincing evidence of their rightness. The most recent perspective, that of communication and interaction, has likewise been unable to this date to specify exactly how the task is done.

It would be rather reckless of the ecological approach to claim that it can succeed with clarity where the other approaches have only been able to hint with vagueness. However, ecology does encourage us to probe into the details of human activity to try and find the genesis of language learning there.

One angle is the suggestion that intersubjectivity (both primary and secondary, see Chapter 3) is built into the individual, who is genetically primed to favor interaction as a means of coping in the world. This possibility is discussed by a number of psychologists and social researchers, as well as biologists. As for the latter, Maturana and Varela refer to the structural coupling of cellular organisms (1992; recall also Johnson's discussion of the slime mold, mentioned in Chapter 4). In Chapter 5 I mentioned Stein Bråten's notion of a *virtual other*, the hypothesis that the brain has a specific propensity to perceive and interact with others. As Bråten explains,

> The mind is postulated a self-organizing dyad with an inborn virtual other who invites replacement by actual others. The actual other who replaces the virtual other is directly experienced in felt immediacy. This permits a model of how the developing mind recreates and transforms itself (i) in the intrapersonal domain with the virtual other, and (ii) in the interpersonal domain with actual others. (Bråten, 1992, p. 94).

Trevarthen (1990) picks up on this idea of the virtual other in his discussion of *protoconversation* of newborns. He argues that an 'implicit other' is created in the mind of the infant seeking to communicate with a real other (the mother, in the first instance). Thus, the child is biologically and genetically primed for communication.

Argyle offers the following evolutionary argument for such a view as the human being primed for social interaction:

> One possibility is that the experience of closely synchronised interaction is intrinsically rewarding, the result of evolutionary pressures favouring cooperation (Argyle, 1991, p.10).

Such closely synchronized interaction is possible between adult (particularly a parent or caregiver) and child as well as between two learners. It may be more difficult to achieve between native speaker and non-native speaker, and between teacher and student. According to Piaget, children's interactions with adults usually generate compliance to adults' authority and prevent cognitive restructuring. (Granott, 1993, p. 185).

Charles Crook (1994) discusses Piaget's notion that a symmetrical relationship can be particularly conducive to some kinds of learning. Piaget (1928) argues that there may be varieties of intellectual stimulation arising in work with peers that are less readily furnished within interactions involving more expert adults (Crook, 1994, p. 138). Crook elaborates further:

> [Piaget] argues that the implicit authority characterising children's asymmetrical relations with adults can be counter-productive in some problem-solving situations. It is the symmetry (in authority) of peer-based discussion that most effectively forces useful reflection. It encourages active evaluation of the status of one's own ideas - as legitimate alternatives to those of a partner. The tension arising from two *like* minds coming into conflict prompts resolving argumentation and reflection - rather than deference to authority (ibid., p. 138).

Piaget's position, as summarized here by Crook, can be linked to the notion of *interactional positioning* (the presentation of oneself, in interaction, as a person with such-and-such beliefs, traits, identity, and so on) as an open-ended process, familiar from the work of Bakhtin (1981) and the ethnomethodologists (e.g., Garfinkel & Sacks, 1970). As Wortham points out,

> Reducing interactional positioning to something largely computable through rules outside of context would make analysts more comfortable, because it does not open up the inexhaustible possibilities of recontextualization. But such an approach misses the essentially open character of interactional positioning through speech (2001, p. 43).

This means that the speaker's meaning and identity are not ready-made ahead of time, they are continually renegotiated, reconstructed and 'updated' in every encounter. The importance for learning of these ideas, as contained in conversation, cannot be underestimated. Language use is *contingent* in two senses: it is designed to be understood in a certain way, and it is actually understood in a certain way (van Lier, 1996). The design and the interpretation are two different things, that may converge or diverge. Communication is only successful, and meaning is only created, when the use of language is dialogically congruent in Bakhtin's sense,[4] that is, if the participants each understand what the other is talking about. This does not mean that they have to 'agree' in the traditional sense (there can certainly be intersubjectivity without agreement), but that they have to acknowledge that the other's language use is *receivable*, even if it is not agreed to or accepted.

In conclusion, meaning is created, enacted, and shared in conversation. Language learning, if it is to be at all meaningful, and if it is to be tied to the self and the formation of identities, must therefore be embedded in conversation. Worksheets, grammar books, drills and tests can never be more than distancing devices, unless they are integrally connected to acts of speaking, presentations of self, and projections of identity. This does not mean that they are useless. On the contrary, if pressed into the service of meaningful language-using projects, they can be powerful instigators of deep learning. As van Dam (2002) shows, grammar drill can become ritual dialogue, and similar to the teacher-fronted lesson described in Sullivan (2000), playfulness added to formal practice can become a community-building device (see also Butzkamm, 1980).

VYGOTSKY'S ZONE OF PROXIMAL DEVELOPMENT (ZPD)

Vygotsky developed the notion of a ZPD as a new approach for investigating the interaction between learning and development. A clear and concise discussion of

---

[4] Note that 'meaning' is regarded here as a social construct in Wittgenstein's sense; note also that this is essentially the same as the social definition of semiosis in Peirce.

the construct and its purposes is given in *Mind in society* (1978, p. 84 ff.).[5] The most frequently cited definition of the ZPD is as follows:

> It is the distance between the actual developmental level as determined by independent problem solving and the level of potential development as determined through problem solving under adult guidance or in collaboration with more capable peers (1978, p. 86).

Although most educators are now quite familiar with this notion, its innovative nature must not be underestimated. It is a quite common pedagogical belief that developmental patterns must be nurtured, in a sense similar to the way a plant is cared for, and that the innate growth processes will do the rest. Skills and abilities will blossom if they are just left to unfold in a propitious climate. In fact, that is a common way to interpret Piaget's constructivist legacy, and it also follows from Chomsky's innatist perspective, and Krashen's input hypothesis (see above). Trying to speed up or alter the natural process of development would on this view be interfering with nature – it might in fact be detrimental, or at best futile.

Vygotsky, on the other hand, strongly rejects this "botanical, vegetable character of child development" (Vygotsky & Luria, 1994, p. 99). He argues repeatedly that instruction (and learning) must be ahead of development. In *Thinking and Speech* he puts it as follows:

> Instruction is only useful when it moves ahead of development. When it does, it impells (sic.) or wakens a whole series of functions that are in a stage of maturation lying in the zone of proximal development (1987, p. 212).

As Wells points out in a useful discussion of the ZPD (1999, especially Chapter 10), Vygotsky introduced the notion of a ZPD in two different contexts: *assessment* and *instruction*. With respect to assessment, he examined the differences between testing the mental abilities of children when working on their own, versus those abilities on similar tasks when they received specific kinds of assistance. He showed that the latter condition was a better predictor of their abilities, both present and future. In terms of instruction Vygotsky proposed that conscious awareness and voluntary attention emerge in the ZPD (in collaboration with adults), and these in turn are the key to transforming everyday concepts into higher (scientific or academic) concepts (1987, p. 220).

There have been a number of controversies regarding the ZPD over the years and decades since Vygotsky's work became widely available in the 1960s. One of the reasons may be that, apart from the fairly brief and programmatic discussions referred to above, Vygotsky never discussed the ZPD in the context of practical classroom teaching in any detail. His remarks on the ZPD came rather late in his life, and his untimely death may have prevented a full development of the implications of the ZPD (along with the ideas that ultimately led to activity theory – see Chapter 8).

I will return to some of the developments and proposals below, after a discussion of two concepts that are central to working in the ZPD: *scaffolding* and

---

[5] There is also a discussion of the ZPD in *Thought and language* (Vygotsky, 1962), although the corresponding section in the more recent translation (by Norris Minick) entitled *Thinking and speech* is considerably more detailed and precise (1987, pp. 209 ff.).

prolepsis. I will gradually move towards the more general term *proximal context* (following Bronfenbrenner, 1993), referring to the larger learning ecology rather than merely the expert-novice dyad.

SCAFFOLDING

Scaffolding in learning is a somewhat troublesome notion. According to David Wood, scaffolding is tutorial behaviour that is contingent, collaborative and interactive: "Research on scaffolding *assumes* the existence of a zone of proximal development by implying performance alone would be inferior" (1988, p. 96). In this view, then, scaffolding is the same as contingent teaching, and it takes place of necessity in a proximal context (Bronfenbrenner, 1993) or ZPD (Vygotsky, 1978).

In general terms, scaffolding is assisted performance. A scaffold on a building permits work to be conducted that would not be possible without the scaffold. But the scaffold is temporary: as soon as it is no longer needed it is dismantled. The metaphor has its limitations (as do all metaphors, eventually). The notion of a scaffold is rather rigid and static, but the educational work that goes by its name is dynamic and flexible. Yet, the metaphor is useful if we regard it as a structure that allows the movement of pedagogical activity, that permits efficient and quick access to pedagogical goals, and that is temporary. Apart from that, we should not take it too far.

An early mention of the scaffolding metaphor in learning is Bruner and Sherwood, 1975.[6] Bruner's notion of scaffolding developed during an intensive investigation of six infants (0.7 – 1.5) and their mothers over a period of ten months, as they played games together. One of the most regularly played games was peekaboo, and this became a major focus for the researchers.

The game consists of an initial contact, the establishment of joint attention, disappearance, reappearance, and acknowledgement of renewed contact. These obligatory features or the "syntax" of the game occur together with optional features, such as vocalizations to sustain the infant's interest, responses to the infant's attempts to uncover the mother's face, etc. These "non-rule bound" parts of the game are an instance of the mother providing a "scaffold" for the child (1975, p. 280).

Over time, the game turns into a routine or ritual, but it also allows for variations in the non-rule bound elements of the game. Little by little the roles in the game begin to shift, with the child gradually taking over more of the action, becoming more and more self-directed, and eventually the roles of agent and recipient may become reversed.

What is interesting to note in this early discussion of scaffolding is that scaffolding occurs in the variable rather than the rule-constrained parts of the game, and this is something I will come back to below. Where the rules end, that's where

---

[6] Although a good many years earlier John Dewey used the same metaphor in the context of cognitive development, and Wittgenstein proposed somewhere in his writings that language is a scaffolding for thought

the game becomes variable, and new meanings enter. In other words, improvisation is the fuel of autonomy in learning.

Over the last two decades, the metaphor of scaffolding has increasingly captured the interest and the discourse of the educational community. Although in the early days it was aligned more to the work of Piaget, it soon came to be linked closely to Vygotsky's notion of the ZPD.[7]

While it is fairly clear what scaffolding means in the mother (or caregiver) - infant context, the expansion of the construct in educational settings has led to significant variations in the meanings, practices and definitions of the construct.

One might say that the construct of scaffolding split into two distinct strands in the 80s. One strand can be called interactional scaffolding. As its clearest expression one can signal Scollon's (1976) description of 'vertical construction', a process whereby adult and child jointly construct their utterances across a series of turns. The adult assists the child by filling in, suggesting the next word or phrase, prompting and finishing the child's utterances. When transcribed, the syntax of the utterances is read vertically rather than horizontally, hence the term 'vertically constructed' conversations.

Interactional scaffolding was also explored by several researchers in SLA (see Sato, 1988; see also Larsen-Freeman & Long, 1991, p. 131). This type of scaffolding has also been called 'ratchet-like' by Bruner (Cazden, 1992, p. 103).[8] One might also call it mutual bootstrapping, in that each interlocutor's contribution is boosted by the previous interlocutor's contribution.

In recent years, researchers in the sociocultural theory perspective have also studied scaffolding from an interactional perspective. A well known example is Donato's study of collective scaffolding (1994), which demonstrates how knowledge can be jointly constructed by learners working in groups. A main prerequisite of interactional scaffolding is symmetry between the interactional contributions. For that reason it is most easily observed among interlocutors of equal status, power, and knowledge. However, as Scollon demonstrated (1976), it can also occur between interactants of clearly unequal status, such as mothers and infants, and thus symmetry in interaction can occur in unequal encounters of special kinds.

Interactional scaffolding occurs at the micro level of interaction, the level of *microgenesis*. In itself it can be neither predicted nor premeditated, but as in the case of the peek-a-boo game, micro-interaction is often embedded in larger cultural (and historical, institutional, curricular) structures. There is thus a sense in which microgenesis is facilitated by the larger structures within which it unfolds. Pedagogically speaking, this micro level of pedagogical action has been described as reflection-in-action, pedagogical tact, or mindfulness (van Manen, 1991; Langer,

---

[7] This is not uncontroversial: there are many who feel there is too much predictability and regimented structuring in scaffolding for it to be a true ZPD process. However, I would argue that Vygotsky was not against ritual and routine in education, and secondly, if scaffolding is structured the way that I have indicated above, there is sufficient room for creativity and emergence to do justice to the spirit of the ZPD.

[8] A ratchet is a device that allows movement in one direction in small increments. It can be used in clocks, pulleys, screwdrivers and wrenches, among other tools.

1989). Such moment-to-moment pedagogical action requires 'just-right' and 'just-in-time' responses and interventions, and must be seen as among the most complex and demanding decisions experienced teachers make. They occur within larger planned and institutionalized curricular structures, but can be neither predicted nor controlled by them.

As John Dewey pointed out long ago, the experienced teacher

> ... has acquired the requisite skill of doing two or three distinct things simultaneously – skill to see the room as a whole while hearing one individual in one class recite, of keeping the program of the day and, yes, of the week and of the month in the fringe of consciousness while the work of the hour is in its center (1904, p. 318).

When we therefore apply the concept of scaffolding in pedagogical settings, a range of concerns at various levels of pedagogical activity needs to be borne in mind, and a central task is that of integrating these levels of activity into concerted momentary and long-term action (van Lier, 1996). Just like the peek-a-boo game, the pedagogical game has its rules and constraints as well as its unpredictable and variable aspects. It is particularly in the latter that scaffolding can find a place to grow, and that learning opportunities emerge. It is important for teachers to bear this in mind, since scaffolding is sometimes presented in the form of ready-made instructional activities, without clear indications as to how the handover/takeover is to be effected. However, without this last element, no instruction can be called scaffolding.

We can thus distinguish between scaffolding as vertical construction in interaction, and as "gamelike routines" (Cazden, 1992, p. 106). It seems then that there are two kinds of work involved in successful scaffolding:

a) planning, setting up, and maintaining the scaffolding structure (both building up and dismantling it as required)

b) interactional work on, at or inside the scaffold. In this work it is crucial to be on the lookout for learners' readiness to move outside the scaffold, and to quickly relax the rigging when that happens (to promote handover/takeover).

The two strands of scaffolding, the interactional and the structural, can thus be regarded as aspects of a single pedagogical meta-strategy. In fact, we can propose three related levels or layers of scaffolding (see also van Lier, 1996; Gibbons, 2002):

a) planning task sequences, projects, recurring classroom rituals (macro);

b) planning each activity in terms of sequences of actions, moves (meso);

c) the actual process of interaction from moment to moment (micro).

I will look at these pedagogical processes and practices more closely in the next section.

ASPECTS OF PEDAGOGICAL SCAFFOLDING

There are a number of ways in which scaffolding has been applied in educational settings. Perhaps the first of these was proposed by Bruner and co-workers,

following the research on peek-a-boo mentioned above. Thus, Wood, Bruner and Ross list the following as essential characteristics in scaffolding:
1. Recruiting interest in the task,
2. Reduction in degrees of freedom (simplifying the task),
3. Maintaining pursuit of the goal,
4. Marking critical features of discrepancies between what has been produced and the ideal solution
5. Controlling frustration and risk during problem solving, and
6. Demonstrating an idealized version of the act to be performed. (1976, p. 98; see also Donato, 1994, p. 41)

Within the context of learning to read, Clay and Cazden (1992) adapt the notion of instructional scaffolding as first proposed by Wood, Bruner & Ross (1976) as follows:

1. Setting the topic
2. Increasing accessibility
3. Maintaining interactive ease
4. Prompting the child to [engage in] constructive activity
5. Working with new knowledge
6. Accepting partially correct responses (1992, pp. 120-1).

One can compare, combine and connect these various steps and recommendations as appropriate to different settings, including language lessons. However, at least one potentially conflictive point emerges from a comparison between the two lists above: *simplifying the task* and *increasing accessibility*. There does not need to be a conflict here, for example, one could propose to 'increase accessibility by simplifying the task,' and this might well be appropriate in certain contexts - such as baking a cake for the first time, or telling a story in a second language. Nonetheless, simplifying the task flies in the face of recommendations made in most versions of constructivist pedagogy, as well as studies of socialization in various contexts (Kramsch, 2002). So, constructivist educators (who follow a variety of approaches derived from the work of Dewey, Piaget or Vygotsky) will generally propose that the task should not be *simplified*, rather, it should be *amplified*. Scaffolding is then seen as providing means of access to an activity or text that is unaltered. In educational settings, for example, where English language learners need to take challenging classes in their second language in order to graduate from high school and apply to colleges, it would be counterproductive to simplify the content and the language in which it is couched. Rather, the challenge in such classes is to improve access and to stimulate engagement while keeping the content constant (Walqui, 2000). Similarly, in settings where *legitimate peripheral participation* occurs, complex cultural events and activities are not altered for the benefit of the developing child, but rather, they are allowed access in an incremental, guided and monitored way (Lave & Wenger, 1991).

In earlier work (1996) I proposed the following conditions for scaffolding in language classes:

LANGUAGE LEARNING PATHWAYS 151

1. **continuity**
   (tasks are repeated with variations, and connected to one another (e.g., as part of projects)
2. **contextual support**
   (exploration is encouraged in a safe, supportive environment; access to means and goals is promoted in a variety of ways)
3. **intersubjectivity**
   (mutual engagement, encouragement, non-threatening participation)
4. **contingency**
   (task procedures depend on actions of learners; contributions are oriented towards each other)
5. **handover/takeover**
   an increasing role for the learner as skills and confidence grow; careful watching of learners' readiness to take over increasing parts of the action
6. **flow**
   (skills and challenges are in balance; participants are focused on the task and are in 'tune' with each other)

The picture of scaffolding that I have presented so far emphasizes the improvisational, dialogical side of the process. A different perspective is provided by Koos Winnips, who builds scaffolding into the design of educational software, as shown in the diagram below:

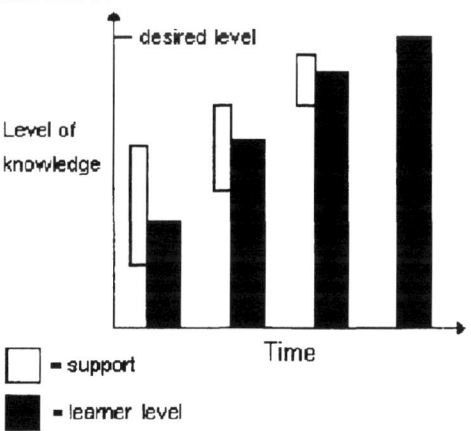

Figure 6.1: Scaffolding and Fading (Winnips, 2001).

The picture (Figure 6.1) illustrates the scaffolding of the development of skills in the design process of educational media through hyperlinked units of learning material (Winnips, 2001).

In Winnips's work, the handover (he calls it *fading*) is built into the design of computer-based learning materials. The design involves the gradual withdrawal of support, and hence fits within the scaffolding metaphor. In my own work I have added the notion of *takeover* to indicate the dynamic, collaborative and dialogical nature of the process, and to emphasize learner agency and autonomy.

PROLEPSIS

As we have seen, scaffolding is a central concept in learning, if this is seen as assisted participation in proximal contexts. A second essential concept is *prolepsis*. As mentioned in the introduction to this chapter, prolepsis is a form of looking ahead, of assuming something to be the case before it has been encountered, a foreshadowing in some sense. Novelists do this all the time when they hint at things to come, or when they omit information, almost as if they thought the reader already knew it. The result of such prolepsis it that the reader (or hearer) creates, rather than passively receives, the information necessary to complete the scene or circumstances that the writer (or speaker) merely hints at. The notion of prolepsis was much discussed by Bakhtin (1981), and further developed in pedagogical directions by Rommetveit (1974), Rogoff and Gardner (1984), Thorne (2000a), among others.

Rommetveit gives as an example a man who says to a colleague that "Yes, we went to see that movie; I liked it very much, but Mary Ann did not," trusting that his interlocutor will be able to figure out (given the situation) that Mary Ann is the speaker's wife, and the interlocutor is thereby drawn into a circle of first-name familiarity with the speaker and his family. As Rommetveit puts it, "the listener is made an insider of a tacitly expanded here-and-now" (1974, p. 88).

In my 1996 book I contrasted prolepsis with ellipsis:

> Ellipsis occurs in sentences or texts when information is left out because it is considered redundant, and the listener (or reader) is supposed to be able to fill in the missing pieces. However, the speaker (or writer) who uses ellipsis does not explicitly check or facilitate the listener's interpretive processes, or invite the listener into a shared intersubjective space. As I explained above, when Rommetveit (1974) proposed the notion of prolepsis, he was thinking of a speaker who gives the hearer clues for the enlargement of common ground without spelling out every detail. Proleptic discourse therefore is aware of gaps in understanding and invites the less-competent into sharing with the more-competent. Whereas ellipsis can be dismissive (or at best indifferent), prolepsis is always invitational and generous (p. 182).

Let's explore a bit further what the literature says about the difficult concept of prolepsis, and try to grasp what its significance for language education might be.

Flynn (1991) describes prolepsis as "the evoking of the future in the present," and its contrast, analepsis, as "the evoking of the past in the present...." Prolepsis is thus a way to refer to what is to come, it is a way to raise expectations, to create suspense and capture the attention of the audience. It would be interesting to see how educators might weave prolepsis and analepsis into their pedagogical discourse, the former to look ahead into new challenges, the latter to link the new to the known, to prior experiences and shared history. Pedagogically, one would expect prolepsis and analepsis to be mutually enhancing.

Taking it a step further, prolepsis can be seen as a game of make-believe in which the educator pretends that the learner knows more than she actually does, and can do more than she has shown to be capable of hitherto. As David Bakhurst says, "the mind projects its mature psychological capacities onto the earlier stages of its development: We see the higher mental functions in the infant's behaviour even when they are not yet present." In a remark that he attributes to Vygotsky, Bakhurst futher says that "treating children *as if* they had abilities they do not yet possess is a necessary condition of the development of those abilities"(Bakhurst, 1991, p. 67).

Vygotsky's biographer, Alex Kozulin (1990) goes even further, suggesting that prolepsis, in the form of 'attributing intent' lies at the root of language development. It is at the very core of the dynamism between learning and development. He quotes from Savage-Rumbaugh to support this idea:

> For those who wonder why the chimpanzee does not develop language in the wild, the answer lies, then, in the absence of a caretaker who is able to attribute communicative intent before its true onset. (1990, p.155)

After this look at some of the things that have been said about prolepsis, it should be clear that it is considered a crucial notion, certainly a cornerstone of equal importance to scaffolding.

Here are some key characteristics of prolepsis (or proleptic discourse):

> What is said (by the speaker) serves to induce presuppositions and trigger anticipatory comprehension (of the hearer) (Rommetveit, 1974, p. 88)

> Novel information is NESTED to what is already known; (the hearer) makes use of pre-established social reality (ibid., p. 91)

> background knowledge is CREATED, instead of ASSUMED (van Lier, 1996, p. 161)

> Prolepsis involves "leaving things out and inviting the hearer to step into an enlarged common space" where minimal clues are given (ibid., p. 161) but completion by the learner is facilitated.

The following extract of mother-child interaction, from the work of Rogoff and Gardner, is a good example of prolepsis:

1. Mother: This should be fun. (*Stands and looks into the grocery bag containing items.*) Okay, now we just got home from the store, okay?

2. Child: Yeah.

3. Mother: And we want to have everything in a certain place, so everyone knows where it goes. Okay, first of all, let's start with this one. (*Points to shelf 1.*) Okay, let's pretend we're going on a picnic (*points again to shelf 1*), and we'll think: what do we need on a picnic? (Rogoff and Gardner, 1984, p. 99).

In turn 1 the mother creates an expectation of something exciting to come. Incidentally, she follows it immediately with an example of analepsis, referring to where they have just come from, thus confirming my earlier suggestion that analepsis and prolepsis are complementary pedagogical acts. In turn 3 the mother sets up an imaginary space (a picnic) inviting the child to 'step in' and consider how to plan such an event.

Proleptic instruction, then, places the learners in a context in which the teacher assumes (or pretends) that the learners know more than they actually do. But contrary to the ellipsis that is common in academic discourse, in prolepsis the conditions are created for the learner to grow into the subject matter. The notion is thus very close to the notion of the ZPD (or proximal context), and also to Lave and Wenger's *legitimate peripheral participation* (1991).

THE ZPD AND SECOND AND FOREIGN LANGUAGE LEARNING

I have previously written about the dangers of interpreting the ZPD in incomplete or misleading ways (van Lier, 1996, p. 192). The ZPD cannot simply be equated with all forms of providing instructional assistance, or breaking tasks into steps of progessive difficulty, and so on. Nor can it be equated with the provision of input that is just one step ahead of a learner's current knowledge base (see below). As Tudge points out, there is a tendency to detach the notion of the ZPD from Vygotsky's overall theory, to detach the tool from its context of use, as it were (1990, p. 156). This tendency can result in a simplification of the construct, since the *idea* behind the construct may be lost from sight.

In the field of second and foreign language learning, the ZPD has from time to time been equated with Krashen's Input Hypothesis, notably the 'i+1' or comprehensible input hypothesis. As explained above, the Input Hypothesis is based on the idea that language acquisition is the result of receiving input that is just slightly ahead of the current level of development. Although this seems indeed quite compatible on the surface, in actual fact there are deep and fundamental differences between the processes and dynamics that each perspective proposes. In a review article, Dunn and Lantolf (1998) examined these differences and concluded that the two perspectives are 'incommensurable.' For two theories or viewpoints to be incommensurate with each other means that the terms and definitions of one cannot be translated into those of the other. In essence, it means that the two approaches speak a different language. Table 6.2 below, summarizing from Dunn & Lantolf's review (1998) argues that this is indeed the case in a number of respects.

At a glance one can see that the left-hand column, that of i+1, relates closely to the input-output, or information-processing perspective that we discussed in Chapter 2 and elsewhere. The right-hand column, the ZPD, corresponds to a sociocultural, ecological, or language socialization perspective. Put another way, using Sfard's distinction between two metaphors of learning, the *acquisition* metaphor and the *participation* metaphor (1998), the left column addresses acquisition, the right column emphasizes participation.

In terms of the unit of analysis, the input theory looks at predetermined elements of language, or structures that are part of a fixed code, predominantly hardwired into the brain and activated through the reception of i+1 input. In the ZPD, on the other hand, the unit of analysis is action (or collaborative activity, i.e., a situated process). In i+1 the learning goal is the acquisition (mastery) of the next linguistic structure or item, but in the ZPD perspective the intended outcomes are the development of more complex activities, of higher mental functions and scientific and academic discourses, and an increasing level of self-regulation.

Table 6.2: The ZPD and i+1 compared

categories of comparison:	i + 1:	ZPD:
unit of analysis	comprehensible input at i + 1, linguistic structures	action, activity
learning outcome or objective	the 'next' linguistic structure or item	more complex activity, higher mental functions, self-regulation
process	subconscious processing	internalization/appropriation and transformation
learner	passive 'loner'	conscious and active social participant
guiding metaphor	hard-wired computer, processor	active organism in ecosystem
model of language	information processing, transmission of information	co-constructing meaning, dialogical
teacher	provide input and keep filter low	guide students' activity, scaffold, support access

The process of acquisition in the i+1 perspective is subconscious; the process also assumes a linear causality between input and acquisition, via unconscious acquisitional processes in the brain. In the ZPD, on the other hand, the development of consciousness is part and parcel of the process of internalization and appropriation, the transformation of interpersonal practices into intrapersonal mental abilities that can be enacted in higher-level individual and social practices.

In the i+1 condition, the learner might be a passive 'loner', or at best an attentive 'receiver' of the input coming her way. Nothing is assumed about co-construction, communities of practice, participation in cultural events, and so on. The ZPD, on the other hand, is created and driven by the activity of the learner, supported and guided by the more knowledgeable peer or teacher. In fact, without full and active participation by the learner, it is impossible to gauge exactly how to set in motion the proximal processes that will stimulate the capabilities that are in the process of developing. Furthermore, they develop on the social plane before they can be internalized on the mental plane. As mentioned earlier, this internalization is not a *reproduction*, that is, an internal replica of an external fact, but it is a *transformation*, that is, a qualitative change occurs in the process.

i+1 assumes a learner as *processor*, a computer that is hard-wired to receive specific kinds of input. The learner in the ZPD is an active *organism in an ecosystem*, in a social-cultural-historical *life space* (Lewin, 1943) or *espace vécu* (Merlau-Ponty, 1962; Kramsch, 2000, p.11). The learner participates (perhaps peripherally at first, see Lave and Wenger, 1991) in this ecosystem, and this gives learning a social nature, "by which [they] grow into the intellectual life of those around them" (Vygotsky, 1978, p. 88).

i+1 assumes a *transmission* view of education, the ZPD a *transformation* view[9], the former adheres to the fixed code of an essentially monological language, the latter assumes an emergent, co-constructed dialogical language. As a result, the teacher in an i+1 context is a *provider*, someone who provides input, albeit while ensuring a positive affective climate, so that the input is not filtered out before it enters the learner's brain. The teacher in a proximal context knows that teaching is *assisted use*, i.e., learner-initiated activity that is guided, supported and stimulated in a variety of ways (primarily through processes of scaffolding, prolepsis and analepsis, as discussed above). The co-cnstructed dialogical language is no longer limited to approved bits of the standard language as promoted by textbooks and tests, but it includes a variety of ways in which learners find their own voice, their right to speak, including the right to draw on their first language (Gomes de Matos, 2002; Cook, 2002).

The comparison above shows that the ZPD cannot be sequestered from the theoretical framework that produced it. Take away the strong theoretical assumptions, and the ZPD becomes little more than a catch-all phrase for any instructional activity by a teacher, however passive the learner and however mechanical the activity.

Yet, this is not the end of the story. As we have seen, Vygotsky's own remarks on the ZPD were brief and sketchy. It is therefore appropriate and necessary for subsequent generations of educators to develop the idea, while taking care to preserve the spirit of the original. I proposed such a development in an earlier book (1996), and I feel it is appropriate to allude to it again here, in the context of our discussion in this chapter.

I believe that it is entirely within the spirit of Vygotsky's developmental and sociocultural theory to look beyond the original definition of the ZPD as occurring between an expert and a novice, or an adult and a child (or a teacher and a learner, of course). Taking the classroom as our ecosystem (a *microsystem* in Bronfenbrenner's contextual theory, 1979), the expert-novice context is not the only, or not even the primary participation structure available. Breaking away from seeing the classroom space configured as rows of desks with receiving heads, oriented towards an elevated talking head at the front, we can envision a differently configured learning space (see Rogoff, 1995). We can think of work stations, group tables, discussion corners, individual quiet places, and common presentation areas. If the weather is good and the mosquitoes are not too numerous, we can include the shady tree or the benches outside.

Within that wider vision of the classroom, the ZPD can become a learning space in which a variety of *proximal processes* (Bronfenbrenner, 1993) can develop, processes that instigate learning. In the expanded notion of the ZPD represented in

---

[9] There are two senses of transformation intended here. First the transformation of social and mental functions that occurs in the process of internalization, as mentioned earlier. Second, a transformation of the educational process itself, since the impetus for learning does not come from the material (input) but from the activities of learners as individuals and groups.

the diagram below (adapted from van Lier, 1996),[10] I note four scenarios for proximal contexts, going beyond the expert-novice (or adult-child, in more general terms) context that Vygotsky used to describe his original ZPD conception.

Clearly, the more-less capable relationship will always be a central participation structure for learning: the more capable partner (whether teacher, parent, or peer) can guide the less capable participants by modeling, scaffolding, and other pedagogical activities. However, there are also many studies now that show that equal peers (i.e., where neither of the participants, or none of the members in the case of a larger group, have the answer to a particular problem or the solution to a particular task, yet, collectively, they can achieve progress (Donato, 1994; Glachan & Light, 1982; Wegerif & Scrimshaw, 1997; Swain & Lapkin, 2000). As we have seen above (p. 149), it was also Piaget's view that in many situations children could learn more by working in a symmetrical relationship with equal peers than with a teacher or other expert. Bronfenbrenner considers that new knowledge resonates among group members, and is shared as a function of collaborative activity in a proximal context.

In the next quadrant of the diagram, I suggest that learners learn also when they themselves act as 'experts' or 'teachers' to each other. By explaining or illustrating difficulties or skills to a less accomplished peer, students clarify and hone their own abilities in the process. Such peer teaching is a special case of what Swain has called *pushed output* (Swain, 2000). In creating a joint ZPD, both the instructing learner and the instructed learner make their ideas clearer, sometimes by trial and error, always by orienting towards mutual comprehension, and by pushing towards clarity of expression. As Wilhelm von Humboldt said, a century and a half ago, we clarify our own ideas by first testing them upon others.

Finally, in all proximal contexts there are opportunities for expanding the ZPD if the learner, when realizing gaps and limitations, seeks to address them by marshaling her own resources and those in her environment (Swain, 2000). It is also the case that, as learners move up the academic ladder, they increasingly have to work on their own, to study independently for periods of time. One might say that in a sense they internalize previously encountered teaching practices as well as social reasoning processes, and become their own 'virtual teacher' as it were. They manage and focus their attention, they select and act upon the affordances they themselves locate in the study environment, and engage in inner instructional dialogue. As Vygotsky himself has pointed out:

> When the school child solves a problem at home on the basis of a model that he has been shown in class, he continues to act in collaboration, though at the moment the teacher is not standing near him (1987, p. 216).

---

[10] In this diagram, the center appears as a fixed space of self-regulation. Some caveats are in order. It is not meant to suggest a sphere of individualism, but includes collaborative social activity. It intends to convey agency, competence, and locus of control. Secondly, the boundaries between self-regulation and the various types of joint regulation should be seen as blurred, movable. The process of self-regulation is not a fixed core, but rather a center that constantly stretches, expands, dissipates, diffuses, and so on, interacting with environmental conditions and social processes of various kinds.

In all then, it seems eminently justifiable to see the ZPD in an expanded sense, not just as an unequal encounter between expert and novice, but also as a multidimensional activity space within which a variety of proximal processes can emerge.

"If one member of a dyad undergoes developmental change, the other is also likely to do so"
(Bronfenbrenner 1979:65)

scaffolding, modeling

assistance from more capable peers or adults

interaction with equal peers

SELF REGULATION

inner resources: knowledge, experience memory, strength

interaction with less capable peers

resourcefulness. self-access

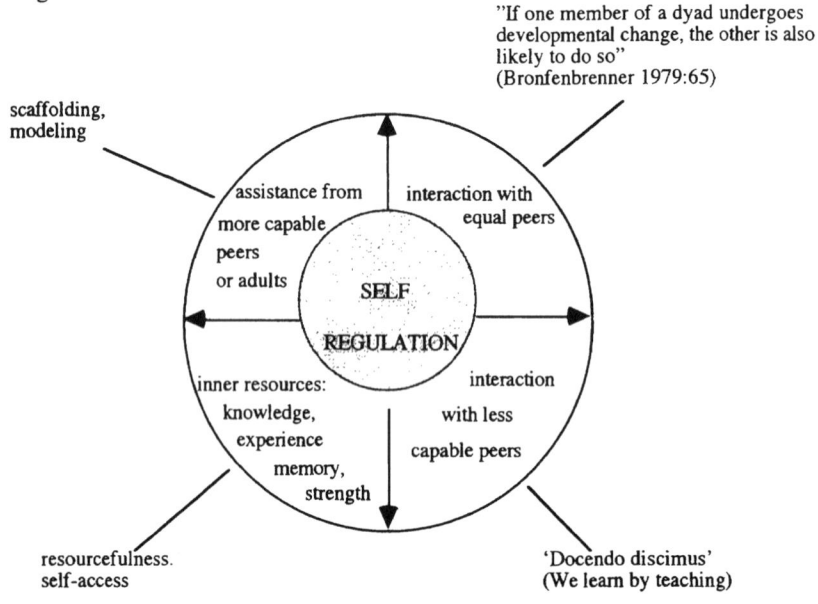

'Docendo discimus'
(We learn by teaching)

Figure 6.2 : An expanded ZPD

PROJECT-BASED LEARNING

We have looked at learning as the result of a variety of activities that occur under appropriate guidance or within a context of collaboration, a *proximal context* (Bronfenbrenner, 1993). Learners benefit from working in different kinds of groupings or participation structures. For some learning, working with a more mature or competent person may be useful. For other learning, perhaps it is useful to work with peers at the same level. Then again, we can also learn much from attempts to assist and teach others. Finally our inner resources, our own 'resourcefulness,' can be instrumental at various points in learning complex abilities.

If we take a 'FonS' (focus on semiosis) perspective, there must be rich resources for meaning making in the classroom and the wider social environment. Then there must also be access to these resources, and the learners must be engaged in activities to want to pick up these resources. When learners are engaged in such a proximal context, affordances of various kinds (direct, social, cultural, conversational, cognitive) become available to be incorporated into the meaning-making process.

An approach to learning of this kind is a project-based or activity-based approach. Prerequisites for such an approach to work are careful structuring with precise guidance, and an expanding menu of options and choices. Such approaches are not new, in fact they were advocated in the early decades of the 20th century by a number of educators and thinkers, including Whitehead, Dewey, Montessori and Vygotsky. Yet, across all that time, the fortunes of activity-based approaches have waxed and waned (Cuban, 1993), as progressive and conservative forces have battled for control of the educational agenda.

Currently (in 2003, in the USA) the push for accountability through test scores is paramount on the official agenda, teaching to the test is the dominant mode of instruction, and the tests are not improving in quality to my knowledge (though they are always increasing in quantity).

However, there are alternative voices as well, as always. There are such approaches as anchored instruction (Bransford et al., 1990); cooperative learning (Slavin, 1983); experiential learning (Kohonen et al., 2001); responsive teaching (Bowers & Flinders, 1990); and reciprocal teaching (Palincsar, David & Brown, 1992). All these approaches, among many others, share a focus on activity, contextualization, authenticity and learner autonomy.

In our own work in Monterey, California with learners of English as a Second Language, we have implemented project-based learning in a variety of ways. In some classes learners have designed websites on topics of their choice. In other classes they have learned how to make documentary movies, and in others they have conducted community-based research. As I mentioned above, such project work requires a tightly designed and richly varied curriculum, with a controlled progression that gradually leads to learner autonomy. At the beginning of such a class, learners may have to learn computer skills and computer terminology, and it is essential that activities are designed that allow them to develop both computer skills and language skills at the same time, through the same activities. This is not easy to do, and it requires very carefully structured materials and activities. It is thus in no way the case that project-based learning (or activity-based learning in general) results in a free-for-all environment. On the contrary, such classes require a high degree of classroom management as well as motivated and well-organized and responsible students (van Lier, 2003).

Teachers working in a foreign language context may object that this is not so easy to achieve in such contexts, since often students speak the same L1, and resources inside and outside of class are not as readily available. While this is no doubt the case to some extent, I strongly believe that project-based learning with rich resources is also possible in most if not all foreign language settings. Those that have Internet access have an unlimited supply of resources of all kinds available at a moment's notice. Those that do not may have community members or tourists around that speak the target language and do not mind visiting class or being recorded, helping with materials and advice, and so on. Then there are video, movie and radio resources, as well as magazines, wrappers and packages from grocery stores and markets, and so on. The resourceful teacher with a class of resourceful students can in most circumstances put together a viable semiotic infrastructure for project work.

ACADEMIC LANGUAGE: THE NORMATIVE SIDE OF LANGUAGE

On various occasions (e.g., Chapter 2) I have mentioned that there are in effect two distinct languages to be learned, both in L1 and in L2. These are the *natural language* (for want of a more felicitous term) children grow into by about five years of age, more or less, and the *normative language*, which contains all the conventions and cultural – academic discourses children struggle with for many years as they grow up to become mature adults, go to school, and strive to achieve a place in their society. I purposely avoid talking exclusively about the academic kind of normative language, since I believe that there are also normative languages in non-literate societies and in non-academic groups in literate societies that require protracted learning efforts. Growing into the academic world is simply one context of discourse socialization, which can in principle be compared to becoming a warrior, a merchant, a farmer - or a gang member for that matter.

In many ways the distinction I have just described is comparable to the distinction Vygotsky draws between *spontaneous* and *scientific* concepts, involving a development from mediation by *tools* (manipulated artifacts, as well as deictic language use) to a mediation by *symbols* (predicational language use and abstract concepts).

While discussing this distinction, Vygotsky proposes the following 'general psychological law':

> ... speech initially develops as a means of communication and mutual understanding, as a communicative, social function. Inner speech (i.e., speech by means of which a human being thinks) emerges later and is the basis for assuming that its formation process occurs only at school age. The path which transforms speech into a means of communication, into a function of collective social behavior, the path which transforms speech into a form of thinking, into an individual psychological function, gives us some idea of the law governing the development of higher psychological functions. The law may be expressed in the following manner: Any psychological function occurs twice in the process of a child's development, first as a function of collective behavior, as an organization of the child's collaboration with his social environment, and then as an individual behavioral operation, as an internalization of psychological activity in the narrow and precise sense of the word. In precisely the same way, speech is transformed from a means of communication into a means of thinking, which characteristically searches for methods to substantiate a judgment; it occurs in a child of preschool age no earlier than the first arguments within the child's collective, no sooner than the necessity arises, stimulating the child's own assertion .... The necessity of logical reflection about an assertion depends on collective operations, such as arguing (1993, p. 129).

This is an argument about the difference between general communicative language development and academic language development.

Foreign language as well as first-language classes tend to be situated inside the 'academic' context of schooling. However, communicative and language experience approaches sometimes deliberately avoid the academic (in reaction to rote-based sentence-driven grammar instruction), and then are charged by many parents and adult students with being too childish or too lax, since they focuses on game-like activities and inconsequential texts.

There will thus be a tension between the natural and the academic in many educational contexts. One way to resolve it is contained in the quote from

Vygotsky, when he says that every function occurs twice, first on the social plane, and then on the mental plane. This emphasizes the process of internalization or appropriation. In terms of academic development, learners need to be able to talk about the concepts required with their teachers and peers, to participate in conversations about the issues, *before* they can be expected to apply the concepts and the modes of reasoning in literate products. This requires a multimodal approach to literacy. Talking, demonstrating, gesturing (and by extrapolation, drawing, painting and making movies) cannot be seen as irrelevant to or separate from developing academic discourses in the required disciplines. They are in fact prerequisites for such development.[11] This means that narrow test-based accountability cultures cut off (for lack of time, since test preparation is of the essence) the very means by which academic success is established. Of course, in the short run students may achieve good test scores, but in the long run they will end up unprepared for the challenges that they will face in their professional life.

CONCLUSION

In this chapter I have tried to come to grips with the nitty gritty or the nuts and bolts of learning in interaction.

I began by comparing four views on language learning:

> trigger
> input
> negotiation
> affordance

Comparing these views suggests some of the ways in which our field proposes how learning occurs, and the ways in which teaching ought to be conducted.

I spent some time looking at Krashen's five hypotheses, because they have had an enormous influence on the second language field as well as on proponents of whole language teaching in the schools. It can be said that there is a lot of truth in them, but also a lot of potential for misleading conclusions. The five hypotheses are:

1. Acquisition versus learning as completely separate processes
2. Natural order of acquisition unaffected by instruction
3. i plus 1 as the ideal input level, just a bit above current ability
4. Monitoring as the result of the learning of explicit grammar
5. Affective filter as facilitating or debilitating acquisition

---

[11] Heath argues that the organization, mapping, planning and description that is part of projects in the visual or dramatic arts are particularly instrumental in the development of academic forms of discourse. She further notes that "practice in such talk must precede development of competence in writing the many kinds of school assignments that require explanation, explication and argumentation (2000, p. 126).

I next looked at negotiation of meaning in tasks, noting that selective attention is facilitated by learners addressing communicative problems. However, the task-based approach has a tendency to devalue general conversation, and I tried to make a case for the value of conversation as a learning process. In a recent study, my co-researchers and I (Nakahama, Tyler, & van Lier, 2001) systematically compared learners' performance in two-way communication gap tasks and in general conversation. We found that on every measure the conversational context yielded more complex interaction and more complex language than the task. It is therefore advisable to look at conversation more carefully as a potentially powerful learning context.

I mentioned that the learner may need various kinds of guidance. Such guidance, in a sociocultural or ecological context is often referred to as scaffolding. A number of different attributes of scaffolding have been suggested. However, going back to the original formulation of the process by Bruner and his colleagues, I noted that scaffolding occurs not in the deliberately planned or ritual parts of a game or task, but rather in the interstices between the planned and the unpredictable, that is, when something new and unexpected happens. This turns the traditional way of looking at scaffolding on its head: we are now saying that scaffolding occurs when planned pedagogical action stops. New and higher skills emerge when new and previously untried actions are undertaken.

This gives the teacher and the learner two separate but tightly interrelated tasks:
- First, structures must be set up to facilitate guided action, since new departures must occur in a safe and familiar context;
- Second, teacher and learners must carefully watch for opportunities to depart, expand, elaborate, and improvise, and during those opportunities a handover/takeover must be effected, so that the new emerges from the known, but on the initiative of the learner.

Scaffolding only occurs in proximal contexts, in other words, in Vygotsky's ZPD.[12] I have argued that this construct must be expanded to include not only an expert-novice relationship, but also an equal peer one, a peer to lower-level peer one, and a self-access, self-regulated on. Thus, I suggest, proximal contexts are peopled with interlocutors of different kinds.

Another important notion in proximal contexts is prolepsis. This means that we assume (pretend) that learners already have the abilities we and they wish to develop. Together with this assumption we create invitational structures and spaces for learners to step into and grow into.

The chapter ends with a look at project-based learning and the development of academic language. It is proposed that there are deep differences between *natural language* (that which any child grows into by about age 5) and *normative language* (those aspects of language that have to be learned by conscious effort, in school or in the community of cultural practices).

---

[12] Steve Thorne (personal communication, 2003) suggests, interestingly, that a learning opportunity may occur later, upon reflection on an earlier activity in the ZPD. This is in line with the fourth quadrant above, and means that a proximal context may have distal effects.

Successful teaching is that which can harness natural language abilities in the service of academic development. The connection between the two is essential if learners are to develop an academic identity that does not clash with their primary (and prior) social identity, that is, if they develop identities that do not clash with one another and thus do not bring unbearable contradictions to their conceptual and semiotic self (see the previous chapter).

There will always be contradictions between identities, and identities change and develop in different ways. Following Canagarajah (1999), conflicting and competing identities can themselves become part of the curriculum, and the struggle of voices is an inherent part of the curriculum.

CHAPTER 7

CRITICAL ECOLOGICAL LINGUISTICS

Education, Policy, Public Opinion and Linguistic Human Rights

... it seems to me that the term 'ecology of language' covers a broad range of interests within which linguists can cooperate significantly with all kinds of social scientists towards an understanding of the interaction of languages and their users. One may even venture to suggest that ecology is not just a name of a descriptive science, but in its application has become the banner of a movement for environmental sanitation. The term could include also in its application to language some interest in the general concern among laymen over the cultivation and preservation of language. Ecology suggests a dynamic rather than a static science, something beyond the descriptive that one might call predictive and even therapeutic. What will be, or should be, for example, the role of 'small' languages; and how can they or any other language be made 'better,' 'richer,' and more 'fruitful' for mankind? (Haugen, 1972, reprinted in Fill & Mühlhäusler, 2001, p. 60).

INTRODUCTION

Over the past several centuries, science has evolved from a separation between church and science in the days of Descartes, to a positivistic phase in the 19th century, an increasing control by commercial interests, and ever-increasing specialization into narrower and narrower research interests. Linguistics arguably became a science with de Saussure's establishment of modern synchronic linguistics (see Chapter 2), and psychology gained scientific status roughly around the same time though the experimental approach of Wundt.

Reed (1996) traces four crises in psychology since the 19th Century, beginning with the failure of introspective psychology that led to Wundt's experimental program, claiming a scientific status for psychology modeled on the more established 'exact' sciences of physics, chemistry and medicine. The second crisis came with the failure of Wundt's program, and resulted in clashes between the early behaviorists such as Watson and Pavlov, and various challenges to this approach by Gestalt psychology, Vygotsky's socio-cultural-historical approach, Piaget's genetic epistemology, and others. Operationalists and logical positivists, radical hard-line forms of behaviorism, took control of the mainstream of psychology, well into the 1950s and beyond. Psychometric measurement and carefully controlled experimentation established a stimulus-response-reinforcement model of human behavior. Then, in the late 1950s there occurred a massive implosion (the third crisis), and a loss of faith in a causal deterministic laboratory-based model. The first wave of cognitivists rejected the positivistic behaviorist model, and looked towards information theory and, increasingly, computer-driven models of Artificial Intelligence, with a focus on schema and script theory, studies of memory and attention, information processing, mental representations, and modularity of brain functions.

The fourth and current crisis results from dissatisfaction with the brain-resident models that ignore activity in the world (including social activity) as well as the dissociation of mind, body and world, and it has since the 1980s resulted in a proliferation of approaches characterized by various conceptions of postmodernism, relativism, connectionist computer models, and numerous approaches to mental functioning in context (resuscitating earlier work by Vygotsky, Dewey, Mead, Lewin, and others who operated outside the mainstream of their own period).

Reed (1996) argues for psychology to become a natural science of human life, a science of *values* instead of a science of *causes*, a science of *meaning* instead of a science of *mechanisms*. This is in reaction to the notion that science is supposed to be neutral and value-free. Such science either leads to knowledge for the sake of knowledge, or to the development of commercially profitable inventions and products. Even in cases where scientific and technological advances are clearly in the public (human) good, they need to be commercially viable before they are seriously acted upon. This can be clearly seen in the lackluster success rate of such innovations as recycling, solar and wind energy, no-emission vehicles, clean and efficient public transportation, and the safeguarding of oceans and forest habitats.

Reed's review of the four psychological crises and revolutions is represented in the table below.

Table 7.1: Crises in psychology

	problem	reaction	revolution
1	Clashes between physiological and interpretive psychology	Scientific psychology arises (Wundt)	Scientific revolution
2	Clashes between the scientific approach of behaviorism and Gestalt psychology, and Vygotsky's challenge	Operationalists and logical positivists; (Skinner, Tolman)	Behaviorism dominates
3	Implosion of the 50s (Hull, Tolman, Skinner): behaviorism unable to answer basic questions	Information theorists, cybernetics, Artificial Intelligence	Cognitive revolution: behaviorism discredited
4	Cognitivism ignores social and other environmental factors. Clashes lead to fragmentation, hyper-reductionism, hyperpost-modernism, hyper-modeling (connectionism)	Psychology as the natural science of human life	Ecological revolution; 'science of value and meaning' (Reed)

This framework of cyclical revolutions does not tell the whole story. While it reminds us of the scientific revolutions described in Kuhn's brilliant book (1970), it does not show the constantly contested nature of all paradigms and orientations. We can identify periods of what Kuhn calls 'normal science', in the lulls between revolutions, where a generally accepted set of basic assumptions leads to a great amount of work in support of hypotheses relevant to the basic (uncontested) position. However, every paradigm is contested, whether from within or from without. I already mentioned Vygotsky, Dewey, Mead, and Lewin as working outside of the dominant positivistic dogma of the first half of the 20th century. It is not very much of a stretch to apply the label ecological to much of their work. Notions such as relations, emergence, patterning, and value, among others, permeate their work. Theory and practice, the individual and the social, and object and subject are juxtaposed and their dynamic interaction is examined. The context of research is always central.

The above is a perspective on a century or so of psychological history; let us now add a perspective on language over the same period, roughly speaking. The first reference I have been able to find referring explicitly to ecological linguistics is Trim (1959) in a paper on language history and change. Next, Haugen (1972) published several papers on ecological linguistics, looking at language change, language contact, and related issues, but referring also to an earlier paper by Carl and Frances Voegelin and Noel Schutz in 1967. These were anthropological linguists, and I suppose it is natural that an ecological perspective would appear in field work (as it did later in the work of Gregory Bateson).

Currently, a number of linguists identify their work as ecological, including Makkai, 1993; Halliday, 2001; Harris, 1996; Hornberger, 2002. Most of these use ecology as a metaphor in a macro sense, that is, to refer to language contact, language shift and related issues, in the way that the opening quote from Haugen above suggests.

During the era of structural linguistics (roughly, up to the 1960s), there was a close connection between linguistics and anthropology, as evidenced in the work of the Voegelins, much of Haugen's work, Sapir and Whorf, among many others (for current work see Leanne Hinton and Kenneth Hale on the maintenance and revitalization of Native American Languages, e.g., Hinton & Hale, 2001). In such a context it was natural that the relations between language and the environment, and between languages, played an important role in linguistic theorizing. The same was true in the UK, where the influence of the anthropologist Malinowski was strong both in the work of Firth and later that of Halliday (see Chapter 3). While linguistics in that period was structuralist and strongly influenced by behaviorism, it was also open to the examinations of connections with other world systems, and particularly anthropology which itself was strongly structuralist (see the work of Levi-Strauss). The close connection came to an end with Chomsky's (1959) devastating attack on behaviorism and its linguistic associations, which galvanized behaviorism's opponents into launching the first cognitive revolution. Chomsky built an impermeable wall between the individual and the social, first by separating competence from performance (and ruling the latter irrelevant to a theory of language), and later on the equivalent but even more strongly asocial distinction between I-language and E-language (Chomsky, 1986, 2000). As a counter-current to Chomsky's anti-environmentalist stance, soon after the sea change of the early

1960s the sociolinguistic movement arose, with early pioneers such as Dell Hymes, William Labov, Susuan Ervin-Tripp, and John Gumperz (e.g., Gumperz & Hymes, 1972) arguing in favor of a broad notion of communicative competence and contextual influences on language acquisition and use.

Chomsky's new linguistics had very little of relevance to offer to anthropology and the other social sciences, and a rift occurred between the brain-resident linguists and other cognitive scientists on the one hand (see Gardner, 1985), and sociolinguists, sociologists, anthropologists, and scholars in related fields that emphasized the role of context, on the other. Several theoretical linguists, notably Halliday and Harris (among others, to be sure) did not join the either-or game, the former elaborating a 'social-semiotic' perspective, the latter his 'integrationist' linguistics.[1]

THE EMERGENCE OF THE ECOLOGICAL PERSPECTIVE

> We are beginning to play with ideas of ecology, and although we immediately trivialize these ideas into commerce or politics, there is at least an impulse still in the human breast to unify and thereby sanctify the total natural world, of which we are (Bateson ,1979, p. 27).

The introduction shows that two closely related sciences, psychology and linguistics, have come to include an ecological perspective among the current array of approaches to their fields. In psychology, early pioneers who explicitly referred to their perspective as ecological were Egon Brunswik (1943) and Roger Barker (1978). Kurt Lewin's work (1943) in organizational psychology can also be called ecological.

A key characteristic of any ecological approach is its contextualized (or *situative*, as Greeno calls it, 1997) character. It can be argued that this inevitably leads to a critical perspective,[2] since whatever happens in the examined context becomes part of the investigation. This critical engagement can be seen in all ecological work, from Brunswik to Gibson, as well as in the more recent work in Neisser's Emory Symposia on Cognition.

One area in which the critical perspective is evident is that of *ecological validity* (EV) in research and testing. Ecological validity first came into psychological prominence through the work of two German psychologists (already mentioned above) who emigrated to the US in the 1930s, Egon Brunswik and Kurt Lewin (Cole, in Wilson & Keil, 1999). As quoted by Bronfenbrenner (1979, p. 28), Brunswik defined EV as follows:

---

[1] Both Halliday and Harris identify themselves as linguists rather than as sociolinguists. Indeed, Halliday has claimed that the term *sociolinguistics* is redundant, since all linguistics is per definition social. It is likely that Harris would agree. I need to add that this is not the whole story: other linguists maintain that there is more to language than Chomsky's Universal Grammar, and have formed a separate group called cognitive linguistics, with its own journal (e.g., Lakoff, 1987; Langacker, 1987).

[2] The adjective 'critical' is easily used, but not so easily defined. I define it as any approach (scientific or otherwise) to a state of affairs that applies an explicit and overt rational, moral and ethical stance to the treatment, interpretation and documentation of that state of affairs (a *science of values*, in Reed's [1996] words). As a corollary, a critical approach must be intervention and change oriented.

> An investigation is regarded as ecologically valid if it is carried out in a natural setting and involves objects and activities from everyday life.

Brunswik saw it as his task to take psychology out of the lab and into the regular contexts in which human activities occur. However, Lewin developed a different notion of EV, one that was based on an individual's *life space*, by which he meant "the person and the psychological environment as it exists for him" (1943, p. 306). Lewin claimed that Brunswik merely carried the laboratory experiments around with him, making them happen in non-laboratory environments. Brunswik, on his part, considered Lewin to be a captive of the life space, prevented from making replicable and generalizable observations (Cole, Hood & McDermott, 1997).

This dilemma between Brunswik's and Lewin's perspective on EV is relevant to the issues of research and assessment in language education. Let's look at an example of the sort of work Brunswik's notion of EV inspired. Researchers asked a number of passers-by on the campus of an Israeli university what day of the week it was, and measured the timing of their responses with a stopwatch. They found that reaction time was anchored to the Sabbath, reactions being slower the further away the actual day was from the Sabbath. This procedure would be perfectly valid from a Brunswikian perspective. From Lewin's perspective, however, 'recalling the day of the week' should be studied by observing people being asked about or asking about the day of the week whenever the occasion arose in their daily activities. A weakness of Brunswik's procedure is the disconnection between the questions (and the stopwatch-bearing questioner) and the person's natural behavior in context. In an actual instance of being asked what day of the week it is, someone in an office might call to a nearby friend, glance at a clock or look at the agenda on the desk. He or she might also crack a joke that "it feels like Friday, but it's only Monday", and so on. Brunswik's subject, on the other hand, might be puzzled for some time by the clearly visible stopwatch. Thus, "remembering what time of day it is" might be a quite different process in a Brunswikian than in a Lewinian research context (Cole, Hood & McDermott, 1997, p. 55).

Bronfenbrenner, like Lewin before him, regards Brunswik's view as 'simplistic and scientifically unsound' (p. 28). In Bronfenbrenner's version, part of EV is 'phenomenological validity,' or the 'correspondence between the subject's and the investigator's view of the research situation' (p. 33):

> Ecological validity refers to the extent to which the environment experienced by the subjects in a scientific investigation has the properties it is supposed or assumed to have by the investigator (1979, p. 29).

As we saw in Chapter 5, Bronfenbrenner strongly criticized the use of laboratory experiments in educational research, arguing for a situated or contextual approach.

Another influence on ecological theory comes from Gregory Bateson's work. Although he is often classified as an anthropologist (cf. his early study *Naven*, about the Iatmul people in New Guinea, 1936), his work on theories of play, schizophrenia, alcoholism etc., as well as his studies of animal communication, shows he was equally important in psychology and biology. Bateson wrote two key works in ecological theory: *Steps to an Ecology of Mind* (1973), and *Mind and Nature: A Necessary Unity* (1979). One of the things Bateson critiques is the notion of explanatory principles such as 'instinct.' He points out that explanatory principles of this sort explain nothing, they merely beg the question they presume to address (see also Chapter 2).

DEEP ECOLOGY IN NATURE AND IN EDUCATION

I argued that it was a teacher's duty to speak frankly to students of college age about all sorts of concerns of humankind, not just the subject of a course as stated in the catalogue. "That's how we gain their trust, and encourage them to speak up as well," I said, "and to realize that all subjects do not reside in neat little compartments, but are continuous and inseparable from the one big subject we have been put on Earth to study, which is life itself."

- Kurt Vonnegut, Jr., Hocus Pocus, 1990, Chapter 18

In Chapter 1 I briefly introduced the distinction between deep and shallow ecology. I defined these two perspectives as a *geocentric*, critical perspective on the one hand, and an *anthropocentric*, or mechanistic/engineering perspective of 'fixing' things that have gone wrong in the environment, on the other. I mentioned also that deep ecology breaks with the Cartesian scientific model of mind-body dualism, and the view of the world as a resource to be exploited or 'developed.' Descartes explicitly set out to study the earth and living organisms as mechanisms: "I have described the earth, and all the visible world, as if it were a machine" (1644; quoted in Abrams, 1996, p. 234). The mechanical metaphor still rules in much of linguistic and cognitive research. Thus, in his recent book Chomsky reiterates his long held view that "generative grammar seeks to discover the mechanisms that are used, thus contributing to the study of *how* they are used in the creative fashion of normal life" (2000, p. 17). Yet, this use of the word 'mechanism', the mechanical metaphor, as Abrams explains, was originally set up merely to make an alliance (or at least a coexistence) between 17th century science and the church possible (1996, p. 238). But the ecological perspective, including not only Gibson (1979) but also the perceptual theory of Merleau-Ponty (1962), states that we perceive the world always as interactive, reciprocal participants. "Perception is always an active engagement with what one perceives, a reciprocal participation with things" (Abrams, 1996, p. 240). It is hard to reconcile this reciprocal participation with a mechanistic metaphor.

The distinction between deep and shallow ecology was first made by the Norwegian philosopher Arne Naess. He defines ecology as "…the interdisciplinary study of the living conditions of organisms in interaction with each other and with the surroundings, organic as well as inorganic" (1989, p. 36). He further coins the term *ecosophy* (ecology + philosophy) to mean " a philosophical world-view or system inspired by the conditions of life in the ecosphere" (ibid, p. 38).

Naess formulates a 'platform' of the deep ecology movement in eight points (see the box below) that I will subsequently compare to a critical ecology of language learning.

It will be instructive to compare the deep ecology manifesto of Naess to the efforts of linguists to establish a critical ecological perspective on linguistics. One such perspective, Terralingua ('Partnerships for Linguistic and Biological

Diversity'), is a recently established (1995) non-governmental organization that one might call a linguistic counterpart to the deep ecology movement. Its founding principles are given in the box on the next page.

According to some linguists and anthropologists, there is a direct link between biodiversity (linked to rainfall) and linguistic diversity (Glausiusz, 2001). The theory is that in areas of greater rainfall there is greater biodiversity, and people living in those regions have a greater diversity of language. By contrast, more arid areas are characterized by fewer languages. This certainly seems to hold for, say, the peoples of the Amazon basin versus the Andean highlands in South America. The Amazon area houses a vast number of different groups (many of them threatened with extinction due to 'development') with different languages, and multilingualism (people speaking three or more languages) is commonplace. In contrast, the languages of the high Andes are basically Quechua (and the related Quichua of Ecuador) and Aymara (both colonized, of course, by Spanish). Quechua, in its various dialects, is spoken along a vast stretch of the Andes, from Colombia down to Chile and Northern Argentina.

A platform of the deep ecology movement
1. The flourishing of human and non-human life on Earth has intrinsic value. The value of non-human life forms is independent of the usefulness these may have for narrow human purposes.
2. Richness and diversity of life forms are values in themselves and contribute to the flourishing of human and non-human life on Earth.
3. Humans have no right to reduce this richness and diversity except to satisfy vital needs.
4. Present human interference with the non-human world is excessive, and the situation is rapidly worsening.
5. The flourishing of human life and cultures is compatible with a substantial decrease of the human population. The flourishing of non-human life requires such a decrease.
6. Significant change of life conditions for the better requires change in policies. These affect basic economic, technological, and ideological structures.
7. The ideological change is mainly that of appreciating *life quality* (dwelling in situations of intrinsic value) rather than adhering to a high standard of living. There will be a profound awareness of the difference between big and great.
8. Those who subscribe to the foregoing points have an obligation directly or indirectly to participate in the attempt to implement the necessary changes (1989, p. 29).

While this is demonstrably true, it is not an automatic endorsement of the benefits of linguistic diversity. The Amazon Indians are in general terms not better off than the Andean speakers of Quechua and Aymara (for a variety of reasons, none of them to do with language). The benefits of diversity – if any – have to demonstrated, not presupposed. What needs to be demonstrated is the superiority of *diversity* over *homogeneity*, and this has not really been done in any scientifically plausible way.

> **Terralingua: a statement of basic principles**
> 1. That the diversity of languages and their variant forms is a vital part of the world's cultural diversity;
> 2. That biological diversity and cultural diversity (of which linguistic diversity is a major component) are not only related, but often inseparable, perhaps causally connected through coevolution;
> 3. That, like biological diversity, linguistic diversity (represented mostly by indigenous languages) is facing rapidly increasing threats that are causing a drastic loss of both languages and the knowledge of which they are carriers, including knowledge about the environment and sustainable resource use;
> 4. That the continued loss of linguistic, cultural and biological diversity will have dangerous consequences for humans and the Earth; and
> 5. That, therefore, the fate of the lands, languages and cultures of indigenous peoples is decisive for the maintenance of biodiversity and linguistic and cultural diversity (Maffi, 2000, p. 19).

The study of ecosystems in nature does not support the view that the more diversity there is in an ecosystem, the healthier that ecosystem is (Allen & Hoekstra, 1992). Rather, the crucial ingredient is that of *balance*. Whether what is true for ecosystems in nature is also true for linguistic ecosystems needs to be demonstrated, and again, to my knowledge this has not been done. What has been shown time and again is the destructive effect of the *reduction* of linguistic diversity (Mühlhäusler, 1996) by various means, such as the prohibition of native language use in schools, colonization by dominant languages, and so on.

With the preservation of linguistic diversity there must be corresponding educational policies. One set of linguistic human rights has been elaborated by Tove Skutnabb-Kangas (2000). It is reproduced in the box below.

This declaration is clearly an ideal that is rarely, if ever, implemented in the vast majority of countries and educational systems in the world. The rights expressed here seem in practice only to be enjoyed by the elite majority speakers of national languages, born and educated in the language of prestige of their society. The current norm in many countries seems to be monolingualism, with bilingualism an academically acquired commodity to enhance career, business opportunities or travel. The exception may be the smaller countries of Europe, and some countries in Africa and Asia (Netherlands, Denmark, possibly South Africa, Singapore, India[3]), where multilingualism has traditionally been spread throughout society. In most other places, official, national, or majority languages encourage a *de facto* or

---

[3] I say "possibly," because in many multilingual countries there is strong social, economic or regional stratification of languages, so that it might be more correct to speak of monolingual groups inside multilingual countries.

default monolingualism except for the 'earned bilingualism' of higher education and careers. On such a scenario, one would have to advise an immigrant child to completely forget her home language while growing up, and then learn it again as a foreign language in high school and beyond. Keeping it active and developing it alongside the majority language somehow seems like cheating, or like subversively promoting the destruction of the very fiber of society. How apparently rational people could ever seriously hold such a view is incomprehensible, unless there is a deeper current of racism and xenophobia underneath it (however vehemently denied).

A UNIVERSAL DECLARATION OF LINGUISTIC HUMAN RIGHTS SHOULD GUARANTEE AT AN INDIVIDUAL LEVEL, IN RELATION TO

THE MOTHER TONGUE(S) (MTS),
that everybody can

identify with their MTs (first languages) and have this identification accepted and respected by others;
learn the MTs fully, orally (when physiologically possible) and in writing. This presupposes that minorities are educated through the medium of their MTs;
use the MTs in most official situations (including schools).

OTHER LANGUAGES,
that everybody whose mother tongue is not an official language in the country where s/he is resident, can become bilingual (or trilingual, if s/he has 2 MTs) in the MTs and (one of) the official language(s) (according to her own choice).

THE RELATIONSHIP BETWEEN LANGUAGES,
that any change of MT is voluntary, not imposed. This presupposes that alternatives exist, and enough reliable knowledge about long-term consequences of the choices.

PROFIT FROM EDUCATION

that everybody can profit from education, regardless of what her MT is.

Indigenous minorities have traditionally fared very poorly in terms of their linguistic human rights (along with their human rights in general, in most cases). One such case, Kurdish, is a much-discussed example, where a former nation has been carved up among four other countries: Turkey, Iran, Iraq and Syria. In many cases the Kurdish language has not been allowed to be used (Hassanpour, 2000, p. 34). A recent report in the Christian Science Monitor (http://www.csmonitor.com/2003/0114/p01s03-wome.html, retrieved January 14, 2003) reports that now Kurdish is permitted to be used on the radio in Turkey, but with strict limitations. There are many other examples of indigenous minorities with languages under pressure. The Berber languages in Morocco and other North-African countries (http://lexicorient.com/cgi-bin/eo-direct-frame.pl?http://i-cias.com/e.o/berber.htm), the Ainu language in Japan (http://www.jlgc.org/ jlgcnews/025/ainu.htm), and so on. According to one account, in 1996 there were 15 native speakers of Ainu left in Japan (http://www.ethnologue.com/). In the US, numerous Native American languages are extinct or on the verge of extinction. Only a handful continue to have any viability at all. Other languages under constant pressure include all the languages of Latin America (except for Spanish and Portuguese), and the Celtic languages of Great Britain – though Welsh appears to have a stronger measure of vitality than either Irish or Scottish Gallic. In many cases attempts are now being made to revive or protect indigenous minorities and their languages, such as Guarani, Quechua and Aymara in Bolivia; Euskera or Basque (http://www.euskadi.net/ euskara/ indice_c.htm), Catalan and others in Spain; Native American Languages in the US (Hinton & Hale, 2001), and so on. The success of such revitalization efforts is uncertain. It is likely to be more successful when it is a bottom-up community effort rather than a program brought in by outside groups, however well-meaning. Interestingly, the Internet appears to be an excellent way for such minority groups to create a sense of community and to share linguistic information, create dictionaries, collect stories and myths, in general, to have their voice heard (witness some of the websites listed above, among many others; a good entry into information about world languages is the website of Ethnologue (http://www.ethnologue.com/).

On the other hand, some minority languages do quite well, such as the Swedish minority in Finland, and the Frisian minority in the Netherlands. Of course, in these cases racial differences are imperceptible, and these minorities have enjoyed economic success and high status for a long time.

In recent decades the issue of immigrant children's education has become a much-debated and fought-over issue. One case is Northern Europe, which imported an enormous amount of cheap labor from Southern European and Northern African countries in the booming 1960s. When these workers (euphemistically called 'guest workers') brought their families over, large numbers of children entered into the school systems. The schools were not prepared to deal with such large numbers of non-native speaking students, and a variety of attempts have been made over the intervening decades to deal with the issue. In a recent survey of six European countries, Broeder and Extra describe the different ways in which these countries treat the issue of educating immigrant children. A summary of their findings appears in the box below.

The immigrant education issue in the US is quite a saga in its own right. In the 1970s the trend was towards maintenance bilingual education, that is, an approach that would safeguard a student's development of the L1. However, from 1980 onwards (the Reagan era), the term *maintenance* became a dirty word and it was struck from all official publications and congressional documents. Then the official nomenclature became *transitional* bilingual education, that is, the L1 was used and tolerated for a limited period of time until the student could be mainstreamed into the regular English-medium classroom. This "limited period of time" was (and remains) a hazy notion that always seemed to long to some and too short to others.

Immigrant Minority Language Education in six European Countries

Belgium.
IMLI (immigrant minority language instruction) is available, but suffers from "a striking lack of direction" (p. 2). About 20 per cent of minority students in Flanders receive IMLI, for up to 20 per cent of the time (supportive model) or up to 50 per cent of the time (bicultural model, this applies only in Brussels).
IMLI often also occurs outside regular school hours, without government intervention. No information available on any one year programs of Dutch as L2 immersion, rather it seems special work in Dutch L2 is carried on as required, supplemented with intercultural education and work aimed at overcoming developmental and learning problems. No time limit is mentioned.

Germany.
So-called preparatory classes in German L2 are recommended, for a maximum of one or two years prior to mainstreaming. In various states IMLI is offered in a number of languages, often with assistance from the embassies of the countries in question, usually limited to five hours per week. There is a lot of variation. Sometimes the IMLI language can be taken for credit instead of another foreign language. Report cards give marks for IMLI. There appear to be trends towards further decentralization, some signs of more focus on mother tongue teaching, but it is still largely perceived as compensatory.

France.
The Ministry predominantly conceives of IMLI as conducive to integration and school success: Immigrant minority pupils will be more successful if they are better acquainted with their community language and culture. In secondary schools there is no IMLI (but often they can take their own language as a 'foreign language'), but in primary schools there is, in various degrees, usually between 1 1/2 to 3 hours. Either for the entire elementary school, or the last four years. The French distance education system (CNED) allows students to take exams in non-Western European languages if their school does not offer them. They get regular credit for passing exams in their native language.

Great Britain.
There is the straitjacket of the National Curriculum. Immigrant groups themselves are responsible for any IMLI there is (not much). ESL and intercultural education are emphasized. Sometimes bilingual assistants are appointed. There is no one-year limit to ESL funding (called Section 11). Local authorities bid or apply for the funds they need, and they must demonstrate those needs.

The Netherlands.
In a 1992 report (*Ceders in de tuin*), the Committee for Immigrant Minority Pupils in Education, proposed a perspective that immigrant minority languages are not primarily sources of problems or deficiencies, but sources of potential knowledge and strength. Overall, 65 per cent (1993 figures) of immigrant minority pupils receive IMLI in elementary school. In secondary school, 8204 students in 1994/5 (no percentage given here). Schools are legally permitted to include IMLI in primary school, up to 2.5 hours within schools hours, plus up to 2.5 hours outside school hours. If there are at least 8 students for a language, the government supports IMLI there. Schools may pool together and share funds and teachers. In secondary schools, IMLI may be optional subjects, electives. There is no one-year limit on Dutch L2. Local needs determine what is done.

Sweden.
By law, immigrants have the obligation to study Swedish L2, and the right to study their own language. Cultural and bilingual arguments and objectives are stressed. Schools have to provide IMLI whenever there are 5 or more students in a language. There is no one-year limit on Swedish L2, which is offered throughout the entire K-12 school system.

(Broeder & Extra, 1997)

Any example of inefficient bilingual education became a weapon in a political fight against bilingual education. Any money spent on any language other than English (or a legitimate foreign language) was perceived as a waste of taxpayers' money, and therefore badly run programs provided ammunition to political groups opposed to bilingual education. Even though serious research studies showed that *good* bilingual programs can provide superior results, there were enough *bad* programs around for politicians and other opponents to ignore the results of those studies (for an overview and history of bilingual education in the US, see Crawford, 1991; for an interesting study conducted in the Netherlands, see Verhoeven, 1990).

Unfortunately, the smart marketing and significant financial resources of the English-Only lobby, coupled with a swing towards traditionalism and conservatism in education among politicians, have now turned the word 'bilingual' itself unacceptable, and it has been substituted now by the word 'immersion' or 'dual immersion.' 'Multiculturalism' is also an unacceptable word, of course. Things have even gone further, and it appears that some politicians now have problems with the word 'literacy,' presumably since this field is crawling with subversive elements espousing dangerous 'critical pedagogy' ideals such as critical thinking, diversity, and critical scrutiny of language use in politics and the media. Clearly, students are not supposed to think (let alone in more than one language!), just to pass tests.

One of the serious problems (and there have been many) that have beset bilingual education programs is the lack of a professional approach to teaching English as a Second Language (ESL). Traditional teacher education programs do not have an adequate ESL component. In addition, ESL teachers have long been very low in the pecking order and rather isolated in the school system. Very often they have had to cobble together a living wage on the basis of a few part-time hours here and there, traveling from school to school, teaching in borrowed classrooms. In recent years this has been somewhat improved, e.g., in California a specialization program called CLAD (Cross-Cultural Language and Academic Development) which gives teachers special training in the basics of second language teaching has been operating in the last ten years or so. However, even the modest success of this program is now undermined since the State of California is discontinuing (as we speak, in early 2003) any special training for ESL, and instead has decided to 'integrate' it into regular subject matter preparation. In effect, of course, this is in line with the conservatives' agenda of stripping all special provisions for immigrant students in the school systems. The original arguments that led to special programs, and that successfully fought against the 'separate but equal' practices of the first half of the 20th century (Lau v. Nichols, 1974; Brown v. Board of Education, 1954) appear to have been forgotten. Added to this is the latest wave of test-driven accountability which inevitably strips all 'inessential' educational activity (such as meaningful ESL, field trips, music, and theatre) from the school calendar, leaving room only for drill and kill activities.

Traditionally, the shift from one language to another language, in the case of immigrants, from their language of origin to the language of the host nation, has taken three generations. According to Stephen May, it involves:

1) initial language contact leading to minority status of the historically associated language;
2) bilingualism where the original language is retained but the new language is also required;
3) recessive use of the old language, limited largely to intraethnic communication;
4) increasingly unstable bilingualism, eventually leading to monolingualism in the new language (May, 2001, p. 145).

However, in more recent times it appears that for many immigrants in many countries, due to pressures from mainstream society and educational practices, the shift occurs in one generation, with the parents often remaining basically monolingual in the native language, and the children in effect becoming monolingual in the target language by the time they are in high school. This leads to a situation in which communication within the family breaks down and no stable cultural patterns can be established or maintained (for an example of this, see Richard Rodriguez's autobiography *Hunger of Memory*, 1981).

Yet, there are strong currents in the US and elsewhere that assume that imported languages are diluting the national spirit and the cohesion of the state. Politicians in the US are fond of referring to English as "the common glue" that holds the nation together (e.g., U.S. Senator Bob Dole in his presidential campaign in the mid-90s). Rather than being worried about the alarming rate at which immigrant families lose their heritage language, and examining the detrimental social and educational effects of such a rapid shift, vociferous segments of the population and their politicians claim that, unless efforts are stepped up to protect the English language, the immigrants will tear the nation apart. Ironically, now in the climate of a 'war against terrorism,' US authorities are scrambling around trying to find trustworthy speakers (i.e. U.S. citizens) of uncommon strategic languages such as Arabic, Farsi, Dari, Korean and so on. Currently there is considerable interest in the preservation of so-called Heritage Languages (that is, the native languages of immigrant minorities) for security purposes.

James Crawford, one of the most active advocates of a more reasoned approach to language issues, puts the conflictive approach to foreign languages in the U.S. in forceful terms, as reported the box below.

Education in most of its institutional incarnations is built on an ethos of homogeneity and conformity rather than one of diversity and transformation.[4] Examining current practices and attempting to change them always has a subversive aura, and is seen as an attempt to challenge the very essence of the social order. Bourdieu's studies of *reproduction* in educational and other institutions, that is, the tendency of such institutions to create the need for their own perpetuation, are very clear about this (1977). In addition, Bourdieu uses the

---

[4] The same might be said about the nation state, which is often also assumed to be 'healthier' if it is monolingual, monocultural and mono-ethnic. Such assumptions can of course not withstand historical scrutiny, yet they live on as a taken-for-granted doxa, championed by the dominant groups. More on this below.

notions of cultural and linguistic capital (1991) to show how access to these forms of capital is not equally available to all.

> After reporting on bilingual education and the English-only movement for the past ten years, I am still amazed by the enormous gap between popular attitudes about language and scientific realities about language, as documented by researchers and educators. Especially ironic is the claim that the dominance of English is threatened in the United States today by the encroachment of other tongues. Many Anglo-Americans worry that minority language speakers are refusing to assimilate, owing to the influence of ethnic separatists and to government programs such as bilingual education, bilingual voting, and bilingual social services, which appear to enable people to live here without learning English. Since the early 1980s, such fears have nourished a movement to declare English the official language at both state and federal levels. Without such legislation, its advocates warn, U.S. national unity will be eroded as language diversity continues to increase and the hegemony of English continues to decline. This perception is widespread, as reflected by public opinion polls and by statements from the new Republican leadership in Congress, which now insists that English needs "legal protection" – that is, legislation to make it the sole medium of government functions.
>
> Objective evidence, however, indicates quite the reverse. It is not English, but minority languages that are threatened in this country. Back in the early 1980s, the demographer Calvin Veltman (1983) completed the most extensive analysis of linguistic assimilation ever conducted in the United States. He concluded that, without the replenishing effects of immigration, all languages other than English would gradually die out in this country, with the possible exception of Navajo. And, I regret to report, Veltman would probably drop that qualifier today, following two decades of rapid erosion for Navajo and other Native American languages.
>
> James Crawford,
> http://www.ncbe.gwu.edu/miscpubs/stabilize/ii-policy/hypotheses.htm

A dramatic case of this notion of reproduction and capital was the case of *Ebonics* in Oakland, a few years ago. A brief description of this episode should be illustrative of the homogenizing forces of education. *Ebonics* is basically another word for African American English, generally regarded as a dialectal variant of English. However, some people at times have claimed the status of *language* for this variety, which has made some white citizens furious. In Oakland, a resolution was made to proclaim Ebonics a language, and thus it should qualify for bilingual education funding. As a mere second dialect it would not receive any such funding and could safely be ignored. This attempt backfired into a major national furor and the Oakland City Council quickly backtracked, but of course the can of worms was opened. It was considered unthinkable that schools would teach Ebonics instead of English (of course, nothing of the sort was claimed by anyone, but tolerating and respecting a child's home language/dialect is apparently synonymous to teaching it, and this is an attack on the dominant language: English).

The following is a small piece of talk from an elementary classroom which was shown on the TV news during the beginning of 1997, when the Oakland Ebonics resolution caused this sudden outburst of controversy all over the USA. Since it was shown on TV, and since the place, time, teacher, and children all remain anonymous, I assume that it is ethically acceptable to discuss it. Suffice it to say that teacher and children are African-American, insofar as the viewer can tell. In any case, the purpose is not to criticize teacher, children or lesson, rather to use the example to draw connections between classroom talk and the wider society, including Bourdieu's notion of reproduction and linguistic capital.

> T: Morning boys and girls. We are going to correct the daily edit.
> ((written on blackboard:))
> *The sun have gave the earth heat*
> *for millions of years.*
> What kind of language ... is the word <u>earth</u> ... <u>earth</u> ... ah Alejandre
> A: Standard English
> T: It's standard English. But if I said earf, what kind of English is that, ah Nancy?
> N: Non-standard English
> T: Non-standard English

This example was one among several shown on the news to reassure the anxious (or irate, in some cases) public that schools were not actually teaching Ebonics, rather, they were using it to assist in teaching children standard English. The rationale is that it is pedagogically ill-advised to denigrate or outlaw the child's variety of language. It is better to build on it, as one builds on other prior experiences in the education of children.

However, 'using Ebonics in the classroom' is interpreted by many as identical to 'teaching Ebonics', given that most critics have little patience to listen to HOW it is used, for what reasons, and with what pedagogical justification (the same is true for the use of other languages in education, say Spanish). In the present example, the use of Ebonics is rather special: it consists of holding it up as non-standard English, within the context of an exercise of correction. So, we do not have here Ebonics and American English (which, in theory at least, you could present as equal languages, or dialects), we have non-standard and standard English. The message is that, in school at least, language use involves the use of standard rather than non-standard English, and non-standard English is to be corrected. While the teacher does not explicitly say that non-standard is inferior to standard English, the context of the exercise: "We are going to correct the daily edit" signifies that standard English is an improved version of non-standard English.

Note that, when you have one language and another language, say French and Korean, you cannot 'correct' the one and thereby achieve the other. All you can do is translate *from* one *into* the other. In the case of a non-standard version, however, or in the case of anything designated as a 'dialect', correction can improve the lower version and raise it to the standard. It also becomes possible now to compare the two versions in terms of what the non-standard does not have or do vis a vis the standard. Thus, an 'Ebonics glossary' that appeared in a number of newspapers explained that in Ebonics "the verb BE is not conjugated and may be dropped", and "a final S may be added or dropped". Ebonics is defined from the vantage point of 'correct English.' Its speakers do something to standard English, or fail to do something, thus producing something that deviates from the standard. To see this effect more clearly, imagine that a British newspaper defines American English in terms of statements like "NT in the middle of words is pronounced as N: 'interested' becomes 'innerested'. "The words LATTER and LADDER sound the same". "NEWS and TUESDAY are pronounced as NOOS and TOOSDY". In this way, the image can easily be created that American English is an inferior version of British English. British English becomes the standard, thus defining the American cousin in non-standard terms. Efforts to elevate one dialect or another to the status of standard (thus bestowing it the status of 'language,' or 'official' or 'national language', with attendant claims that it has superior structure, purity or systematicity, have no doubt gone on for centuries. The particular case of African-American English or BEV (Black English Vernacular, the same variety as the Ebonics we discussed above), was shown in many studies by Labov and others (Labov, 1972) to have the same degree of systematicity as any other version of English.

Now back to the classroom. It is clear that what the teacher and the children are doing is not unrelated to what the world outside says about standard and non-standard language. It is also clear that, were they to do something quite different, let's say write poems in African-American English or Ebonics, certain things might happen. Looking at Bronfenbrenner's model of nested ecosystems (1979; see next chapter), things might happen between the home and the school (some parents might complain, for example). Within the school certain things might happen: the principal or other teachers might object. Next, the school district, perhaps pressured by local officials, parent groups, the local TV station, a local radio talk show, might raise hell. And so on. Thus, language in the classroom is defined in accordance with the way language is defined in society. One of the consequences is the continued received opinion of the inferiority of the dialect, and by association, its speakers. Another is that the person who wishes to succeed academically and professionally must put aside the dialect and embrace the standard (bidialectalism not being a well-understood or well-accepted phenomenon in most countries). For the children, there is now an early and persistent message, heard loudly outside the classroom and reinforced inside it, even though perhaps in kinder, gentler ways, that there is something wrong with the dialect. Immediately the child is faced with a clash of loyalties: loyalty to the goal of education, and loyalty to those she loves at home and in the neighborhood. The consequences of this clash are not at all well understood.

It is interesting to speculate what would happen if we instituted a course in language awareness, for both teachers and children (and inviting the local media and politicians as well, were they to consider themselves educable). In it we would say, as is surely accepted among all linguists, that all dialects are linguistically equal, that the standard is not automatically 'better', just because it is a standard, etc. That the child should be encouraged to keep her dialect or language, study it, enjoy it, speak it at home and with friends, compare it systematically (but non-judgmentally) with other dialects or languages such as standard American English, and strive to become a proficient bidialectal or bilingual speaker. That we all speak differently in different circumstances, that speakers in a particular area always think that it is the others who have a 'funny accent', and so on.

LANGUAGE POLICY AND LANGUAGE PLANNING

In the section above we looked at both macro and micro perspectives on language education, and we should be getting some idea of how the macro and the micro are interrelated. Understanding these relations (see, e.g., the nested ecosystems view of Bronfenbrenner, 1979, in the next chapter), is crucial to formulating a coherent language policy for educational purposes.

Traditionally a nation and its language have formed one unity. Thus, Korea and Korean are a whole, but the same cannot be said of many other countries. Japan, traditionally considered a homogeneous society, includes the Ainu minority, as well as sizeable immigrant minorities speaking Korean, Filipino, and other languages.

Switzerland, Belgium, Spain and Canada are nations that have from their inception included speakers of various languages. In some cases different languages in one country have ended up on opposite sides in civil wars and other conflicts. The French-Flemish language struggle in Belgium is a well-known case in point. However, in all such cases it is hard – I would say foolish - to maintain that the struggles and conflicts have occurred *because* of the language differences. I think this is about the same as saying that wars are caused by nations having different colored flags. Indeed, in all cases that I am aware of, economic inequality, political oppression, religious intolerance, racism and other reasons are to blame for wars and conflict. Language is often a mere tool in such struggles.

Language policy, and some sorts of planning related to the formulation and administration of policy, is a common aspect of the government of most countries. This applies to what is done with language in education, but also in wider realms of public affairs. The most dramatic examples of language planning occur when a nation becomes independent and needs to develop an infrastructure for all its official institutions. So, for example, what used to be called Serbo-Croatian is now two languages: Serbian and Croatian (or four languages, if we add Bosnian and Montenegrin). Similarly, in post-Franco Spain Catalan was promoted as the official language of Catalonia, with laws governing both its teaching in schools, and rules for its development as an autonomous language (rather than a dialect of Spanish). In the newly independent state of East Timor, the Tetum language will be institutionalized by a linguistics commission. In post-Apartheid South Africa, nine African languages have been added to English and Afrikaans as official languages. In Belgium, no content may be taught in French in the Dutch-speaking schools, and no content may be taught in Dutch in the French-speaking schools, though the other side's language can be taught as a foreign (not second?) language. This raises the interesting question whether content-based foreign language teaching in French or Dutch would therefore be an illegal methodology in Belgium.

Multilingual language policies are increasingly common, in fact, they are more common than monolingual ones. The one-nation – one-language model of the state is no longer the norm. Cases in point are South Africa (with eleven national languages) and Bolivia (with Spanish, Quechua, Aymara, Guarani, and a number of smaller languages all receiving attention in the new national educational reform movement). Such policies require complex multilingual educational structures, including literacy in two or more languages. As mentioned above, in South Africa, the post-apartheid Constitution includes, in addition to the colonial languages English and Afrikaans, nine African languages. The Constitution also includes specific reference to the rights of citizens to use and receive schooling in one of the official languages (plus the Khoi, Nama and San languages, and in sign language – these languages not being accorded 'official' status). However, there is also a caveat of 'practicability' included, and whether or not this turns into a loophole (to avoid promoting some of the languages in practice) remains to be seen. Certainly, as elsewhere, the establishment of the Constitution, and its implementation, are not without controversy (Alexander, 2002; Makoni, 2003).

Nancy Hornberger (2002) looks at three themes of language ecology in relation to multilingual language policies:

1. *Language Evolution*: Languages live and evolve in an ecosystem along with other languages
2. *Language Environment*: Languages interact with their sociopolitical, economic, and cultural environments
3. *Language Endangerment*: Languages become endangered if there is inadequate environmental support for them vis-à-vis other languages in the ecosystem.

These are very much the themes that were prominent in Haugen's work, and also in the more recent work of Mühlhäusler in the Pacific region (1996). The concern is for endangered languages, and the endangerment is linked to both evolutionary and environmental factors. One group of culprits are the so-called 'killer languages,' including English, Spanish, Mandarin, among others. These languages, by virtue of their dominant economic and political power, constantly threaten other languages in their areas of influence. The ecology of language metaphor has the advantage of focusing directly on the issue of linguistic human rights and a concern for the inclusion of minority languages in educational and state institutions.

As an example, Hornberger examines the notion of 'biliteracy,' through a series of nested relationships of development, content, media, and contexts. The development of literacy in more than one language relates to the complex linguistic environment in which the languages are used in society, and it is also influenced by relations of power between the languages and the educational processes. Some of the traditional inequalities that Hornberger signals are shown below. It seems that anguage use, particularly language use that involves literacy, is always wrapped up with power.

Figure 7.1: Biliteracy and power

Contexts of biliteracy:

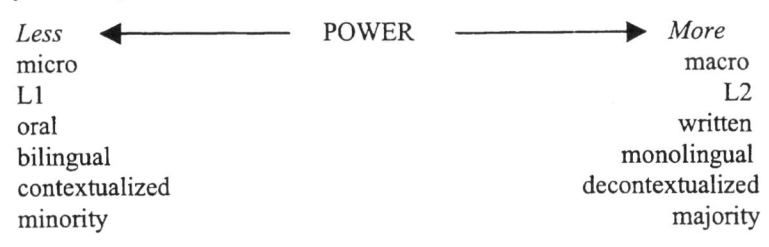

Less ←	POWER	→ *More*
micro		macro
L1		L2
oral		written
bilingual		monolingual
contextualized		decontextualized
minority		majority

From the child's perspective, as research has shown (Genesee, 2002), bilingualism and biliteracy are not a problem, neither cognitively nor socially (though it may be a problem for the adults that are involved in the child's education). Communication is in reality always multimodal, that is, it involves more than just seen or heard language. It also involves artifacts, pictures, gestures, movement and much else. Within such a multimodal view, the child's language serves as a support for the emergence of other modalities, including other languages, both written and spoken. Further, the use of other modalities in practical activity assists in the development of the child's languages.

CULTURE, MIND, VALUE

The word culture has a tremendously wide range of interpretations and definitions. In 1952 Kroeber and Kluckhohn, two prominent American anthropologists, put together a sizeable book reviewing 'concepts and definitions' of culture (1952). This did not solve the problem, because since that time meanings and definitions have proliferated even further. In addition, a common practice is that of distinguishing between 'high' and 'low' culture, or culture with a capital 'C' or with a small 'c,' though many writers frown upon such an elitist or bourgeois distinction. A common joke is that at a congress attended by both linguists and anthropologists, someone was asked, "How can you tell which ones are the linguists and which ones are the anthropologists?" The answer was, "The anthropologists are the ones that don't use the word culture."

Yet, the word *culture* will not go away, which indicates that it fulfills a range of useful functions in education and daily life. It may be a raggle taggle collection of ideas, but we all carry it around with us nevertheless.

How then do we define the term culture? Perhaps the simplest definition is one I once heard at a workshop (unfortunately I don't have the date, place, or name):

Culture is the way we do things around here.

This definition alludes to everyday activity in a certain place ("around here"), to a bounded group of people ("we"), and to a certain commonly accepted norm for the actions by the group in that place ("the way"). The definition thus addresses some of the most central problematic areas for a non-member, and at the same time, its very vagueness dramatically highlights how difficult it is to gain the necessary knowledge and skills to become a member, or at least, to 'understand' the members enough not to cause major misunderstandings and trouble. Nobody can tell you exactly how things are done, because many of the cultural patterns and processes are tacit, that is, they are not consciously enacted and metaconsciously discussed. So as an outsider you just have to 'crack the code' as it were, you have to grow into these cultural ways, and it is unclear how much of it can be taught explicitly as a body of knowledge or as recipes for behavior.

It is also possible to look at culture in a more critical sense, as e.g. Kramsch (1998) and Byram (1997) have done. Questions that arise in a critical perspective address the following issues, among others:

> **Fact**: Culture as an existent body of facts, an accumulated knowledge base;
> **Boundary**: Culture as bounded by national, ethnic, or group boundaries: 'French' culture, 'Latino' culture, 'Pop' culture, etc.
> **Competence**: Culture as a range of skills for behaving and speaking appropriately in certain contexts;
> **Communication**: Culture as the ability to communicate culturally or cross-culturally;
> **Encounter**: Culture as "an encounter in an open landscape" (Tornberg, 2000, p. 248), characterized by contingent dialogue (Bakhtin, 1981).

The categories listed here are not mutually exclusive. They all play a role in the rather vague and amorphous picture off culture painted above. Yet, picking any one of them as salient has important consequences for teaching and learning. Picking the last one, *encounter* (as we must in an ecological perspective), means that all the prior ones in the list are relevant as foci of information, study and critique. Notions such as *fact* and *boundary*, for example, when considered on their own, may suggest homogeneity, constancy and agreement, whereas in a more critical ecological perspective notions such as diversity, change and contest must also be considered.

Clifford says that "culture is contested, temporary and emergent" (1986, p. 19) and as we noted in Chapter 4, the same can be argued for language. In this view, the things that are written and said about culture and language are also part of this emergent, temporal and contested phenomenon. In effect then, both culture and language are *discursively constructed*, that is, they are shaped as they are enacted and discussed, in social contexts. They are *processes*, not just depositories of facts and rules.

Bateson (1979) makes a distinction, in research and theorizing, between *classification* and *process*. Classification thinking is an early stage of thinking that categorizes and sorts things, and builds temporary models. Process thinking is more difficult and more advanced. In practice, elements of both classification and process enter into all sociocognitive activity, including learning. However, it is worth noting Bateson's point that classification is a *tool* for process thinking, not an alternative to it.

When students learn a new language, new cultural processes are of course an integral part of the learning. However, as Kramsch (1993) argues, this does not just involve adding a second culture to the first, and then switching cultural stance every time one switches language. Rather, the bilingual and bicultural (or multilingual, multicultural, transcultural) person develops a vantage point that draws on varieties of cultural information to form differentiated sets of positions (processes of *framing, footing* in Goffman's terminology, 1981) from which to craft new identities. These new positions are what Kramsch refers to as the *third place* (1993).

Learning culture is thus not the collection of a number of facts, a list of knowledge items (such as important dates, festivals, food, typical customs, etc.), rather, it is more like learning the ability to draw on witnessed and shared practices, in the same way that Hopper envisages the process of emergent grammar (1998; see also Chapter 4).

The 'third place' involves the ability to construct meanings that draw on different contexts, on a juxtaposition of contexts, on relevant rememberings from different places and times, while being sensitive to how these meanings play in the current context. In all this juggling of polyphonic and multimodal elements (Bakhtin, 1981) we may be reconstructing our *conceptual self* as well, that is, our system of beliefs about ourselves (Neisser, 1988; see also Chapter 5).

We cannot understand our own language unless and until we come across another one. The same is true of culture, however we define that kaleidoscopic construct. Until then we are immersed in an invisible ether-like element, like a fish in water. But once we're outside of that element we can begin to see what it is, and who *we* are in it and out of it. An unsettling experience, quite literally, but one that ultimately affords deeper understandings and more critical examination of our values and practices.

Our mind, as we have seen, is an essentially social construct. It is the life space between our bodily boundaries and the interlocuting world. It does not reside in the brain, even though our brain is sometimes (not in all cultural traditions, though!) perceived as the main control room. This means that the mind is also a cultural construct. The mind is both embodied and projected into the world. This is what Bateson meant by 'ecology of the mind' (1973). What we think, what we think *about*, and *the way* we think, are thus closely connected to the world in which we move and live and act. In this sense the Sapir-Whorf theory is quite correct, not in a deterministic, but in a *resonating* sort of way. Our body, mind, language use, and activity all resonate with the familiar world around us.

A final world about value. It has been said very often that no theory or research can ever be value-free. We always put our prior theoretical assumptions into whatever it is we are observing or manipulating. The same is true of all language use: there is no value-free or value-less language use, unless it is stripped of all meaning. When we use language, we want to do something, get something done, or express something. These speech actions are performed in a context in which they are interpreted by interlocutors (whether real or imaginary), and we clearly wish them to be interpreted in the way they are intended to be interpreted. Following the concentric circles diagram in Chapter 2, our emotional investment into any act of speaking is encoded in the outer circles, and it is that precisely that conveys our valuation of what it is that is being said. Of course, we can suppress that by being stone-faced or poker-faced, but that is in and of itself an acquired skill, not available to those of us who blush or cry easily. Such signs of valuation occur at the interface between the words and the body.

I do not wish to reduce emotions, beliefs, and values to their physical manifestations (in gestures, expressions or biological phenomena), nor to contrast these to *thoughts* which would then be manifested by logic, syntax and rhetoric. I want to suggest that all these phenomena are much more closely intertwined amongst themselves, and far more intimately connected to the surrounding life space than we realize, or even wish to admit. Singling out the linguistic aspects of communication means the neglect of its embodied and spatio-temporal nature, and that means a disconnect between utterance, world and voice.

Value, virtue (as discussed in Plato's dialogue *The Meno*), belief, and thought do not appear out of the blue, nor out of the depths of the reptilian brain, but they are connections between our selves and our identities and the surrounding world. In a critical ecological view of cultural learning as contingent encounters, moral and political aspects are an integral part of the process. We then consider learners as speakers in their own right (Kramsch, 1998) not just as subjects who display improvable utterances and sentences. This means that learners' identities, values and questions become central components in classroom dialogue.

CRITICAL USES OF TECHNOLOGY

There is no doubt that technology (computers, video, cell phones) has changed the educational landscape. How deep and of what nature this change is as yet unclear. Some say that computers are the ruination of education, others say they are the salvation. Both perspectives marshal evidence for their view, and both make points that need to be listened to. If these camps are both right, then technology use can go either way: it can be beneficial in some circumstances, and it can be detrimental in others.

This is the perspective of many teachers that I have talked to. When I ask them how they feel technology has changed their professional lives, the quite often say, technology has made it more interesting, and also more frustrating. It saves time, and it wastes time. It makes the students interested, and it also distracts the students in negative ways. And so on, not unlike the opening section of Dickens's Tale of Two Cities.

The field of educational technology is too young and recent to make hard and fast predictions about the ultimate effect. Studies of the effect of using computers on learning show very mixed and ambivalent results (Kirkpatrick & Cuban, 1998). One thing however can be predicted with certainty: technology will not go away. Everyone will have to deal with it at some level, and luddism is not an option. Therefore, at this point it seems to me that a reasonable stance is not to either embrace or reject technology uncritically, but to think hard about ways to integrate it in such a way that it enhances our teaching and learning. Can some of those ways we established at this point?

A perennial issue is the so-called 'Digital Divide,' the unequal access to technology at all levels, country by country, area by area, socio-economic class by socio-economic class, school by school, home by home, and student by student. The most obvious way to resolve this is by providing more technology (e.g., computers and connections) to those who have less. This clearly is important, but I would suggest it is not the most important issue. The real issue is to take a hard and critical look at what actually happens in classrooms and in students' lives with technology. As I (and others) have pointed out (van Lier, 2003), differential access, and differential *quality* of access are rampant at all levels of education. A simple example is the type of software or activity used. By and large, richer schools (in richer neighborhoods of course) use more sophisticated software and activities than poorer schools in poorer neighborhoods. In the former, students may be working on web design or digital movie making, whereas in the latter they may be working with prepackaged drill programs.

Computer (and other technology) use can be intellectually stimulating and socially rewarding, if integrated into a well-constructed activity-based curriculum. I have found that in such a context there can be more talk, debate, and laughter at and around computers in a technology-enhanced classroom than in a traditional teacher and information-driven classroom (see also Crook, 1994).

Similarly, interacting with non-present others *through* the computer can also be a rewarding intellectual and social experience, if the curriculum is well-designed (Lam & Kramsch, 2003). Our younger students today routinely chat with friends on instant messaging systems, and many of them have even left email far behind, using it only for factual communications with parents and teachers (the 'boring stuff'). Their communicative practices and preferences must be taken into account when designing educational programs at a distance.

Many educators take a skeptical view of the role of technology in education so far. Cuban, in a case study of high schools in and around the famed Silicon Valley, finds that computers are 'oversold and underused' (2001). I would add that they are also heavily misused. Postman, in a series of publications (e.g., 1993), questions the corporate and business aspect of the technological revolution, finding that as more and more money gets spent on computers and wiring, less and less time is available for all-round valuable educational experiences, from field trips to art to physical education. Bowers takes a scathing look at the pedagogical consequences of the computer boom in education, arguing that in effect it exacerbates cultures of commodification, sees education as the delivery of information, a mindset that equates information with knowledge, the notion that technology is a tool for controlling the environment, and a view of human development as an individual rather than social process (Bowers, 2000).

Technology can be seen either as a tool to overcome marginalization and inequality, or as an instrument in the destruction of native cultures (Warschauer, 1998). When I worked in the Peruvian Andes in the 1980s, some radio stations were used to send messages to and from remote rural communities, call for assemblies, and play local music (notably, the radio station of the ̣s group in Puno). At the same time, other radio stations brought pop ̣vs and opinions from the big cities. A double-edged sword, in other words. The computer no doubt has those dual possibilities as well. Marginalized communities can have their own websites and listservs where they can try to revitalize their language and that serve as a meeting place for community members living far away. Recently, I found to my amazement that my small native village in the southern Netherlands has a flourishing and sophisticated website where all manner of things regarding local history, dialect, events and so on are being discussed. Admittedly, we are not talking about a developing country, but as Warschauer points out, many threatened language groups around the world have also taken advantage of the power of the Internet to collect and share traditional stories and preserve their language and customs, as well as promote local causes.

These are positive developments that occur alongside many other less positive ones. It is up to the local users – teachers, community leaders, students – to steer the technology in positive directions. It is surely unlikely that leadership in this respect will come from corporations or politicians. Unfortunately, unselfish foresight and wisdom are in short supply in those circles.

CRITICAL LANGUAGE STUDIES

Under this umbrella I will primarily discuss Critical Applied Linguistics as developed by Pennycook (2001; forthcoming), and to some extent critical pedagogy, critical discourse analysis, and critical language awareness. All these, and others besides (critical feminism, critical philosophy, critical literacy, and so on) share many family resemblances.

The use of the word 'critical' implies that we think outside the narrow confines of our particular box. Early on in the book I rejected the notion that applied linguistics takes ideas from linguistics and applies them in education or other areas of work (such as factories, court rooms, doctor's offices, and so on). This would make the applied linguist into a consumer or grocer of theoretical knowledge, a sort of go-between between linguistics and the real world of language use. Instead, I proposed the term educational linguistics to indicate that the language profession should be a theory-producing one, namely the production of a theory of educational practice. Such a theory does not automatically come about by applying linguistic and educational theories, which themselves are usually quite far removed from actual practices.

Critical language studies, a term that I think is more consistent for reasons just mentioned than critical applied linguistics, has an agenda that includes a necessary range of principles or premises. I will not provide a litany of these, but it seems to me that the most crucial one must be some form of idealism, moral commitment, or ethical purpose. I am not talking here about religious zeal, or a holier-than-thou righteousness, but definitely a clear articulation of what we see as the goals of the language-educational enterprise. It can probably not be mandated what political or philosophical flavor these goals should articulate. For example, there is no inherent reason why they should be, to just mention some ideological oppositions, Marxist or capitalist, humanitarian or utilitarian, agnostic or religious, and so on. All I can do, as a critical educator, is to lay my principles on the table and say, this is what they are, take it or leave it. Critical language education should be neither proselytizing nor indoctrinating, because then it basically ceases to be critical, it just becomes dogma, and dogma controls thought and action, and that is not being critical. This also means that our students should be entitled to reject, contest and ignore our particular viewpoints, and be able to do so without dire consequences for their grades or graduation chances.

So, if we take out the notion of indoctrination, what is left of critical language studies? How do we steer a course between docility and zealotry? I think the answer is contained in two simple, related phrases:

- think for yourself
- speak for yourself

This means exactly what it says. The students should develop their own ways of thinking, based on their own developing positions, going in their own chosen direction. At the same time they should do so with full participation in the socio-cultural groups of which they are members. They should furthermore learn to speak in ways that connect their words to their thoughts, and that connect both to their self, their identities, and their social affiliates. This means, they should develop their own – socially situated – authoritative *voice* in the target language.

This does mean that they will have to learn to examine language use critically, with all the exposure of power, manipulation and institutionalized deception that it contains. But it does not mean that we as teachers can mandate one single approved interpretation. So, on the one hand we should avoid "adherence to a particular form of politics " as an unduly limited project (Pennycook, forthcoming, p. 25), on the other hand, accepting "any and every political view point is equally or even more limited" (ibid). I suppose the best one can do is to clearly articulate one's own critical perspective on language learning and practice what one is preaching. That is one side. The other side is how we implement this critical approach in the classrooms in which we, and the teachers we assist, are working.

How do we steer that critical course in the classroom? Of course, as teachers we probably would like the students to think as we do. However, we must also realize that they may already have well-argued and deep-seated opinions and beliefs, and we should perhaps hesitate before imposing our own views on them. Also, as a result of their own critical thought processes and activities, our students may end up thinking differently than we do, which means they have learned to think for themselves. Perhaps our goal should be that they articulate their thinking clearly and effectively in the target language, even if we do not personally like the ideas that are articulated. So now, what does this mean for our critical classroom perspective?

Pennycook (forthcoming, p.7) makes a useful distinction between three main features that define critical work in language teaching:

- domains or areas of interest
- a self-reflexive stance (questioning one's own assumptions)
- a transformative pedagogy (educational change)

Let's look at each one of these in turn for a minute from the perspective of one single context of educational work: teacher in-service work in an immigrant setting (primarily Mexican farm workers in Salinas, California).

DOMAINS OR AREAS OF INTEREST

This will vary from practitioner to practitioner, and from class to class. For example, when I work with teachers of adults in after school programs, all the issues that immigrant adults – workers, parents, professionals – face on a daily basis can be part of the curriculum. This will certainly include discrimination, exploitation, and cultural clashes. On a more positive note it will also include biliteracy for life skills, social and occupational rights, medical services, management of household resources, education of children, parenting skills, and so on and so forth. But of course it may also include more ludic elements from singing songs to doing skits to BBQs and soccer games.

A SELF-REFLEXIVE STANCE

At all times during any educational program, such as the in-service course mentioned here, all participants must reflect on their work: teacher educators, teachers and students alike. Are the needs of the teachers taken into account? Are the activities and lessons proposed realistic in the context in which the teachers work? Do the teachers adequately examine what their vision is, and what their expectations are? Do the students invest in the learning that is going on, is the English they are learning meaningful to them, if so in what ways?

A TRANSFORMATIVE PEDAGOGY

ESL classes for adults can be difficult settings for learning. They are usually after work, drop-in, and therefore the population is always changing, and the levels of proficiency in the class can vary widely. Very often people come into class (possibly for the first time, possibly after an absence of several weeks) and are given some worksheets that appear to be roughly at the level of the student. If the worksheet is too easy, the students get a more difficult one, if it is too difficult, they will get an easier one. Transforming the pedagogy in such a class might involve creating peer-tutoring groups and mini-projects, during which a new member can come in at any time in a legitimate peripheral role at first (Lave & Wenger, 1991) and as a more active participant when ready. Thus, an individual worksheet-based system has been transformed into a collaborative project-based environment that can handle heterogeneous and unpredictable populations.

Key components of critical classroom work at any level are *awareness*, *autonomy*, and *authenticity* (van Lier, 1996). Awareness raising about language, about language use (in the community and elsewhere), about learning, about motivation and goals, about success and failure, is essential. Taking this awareness outside the classroom (in community projects, field work, and so on) yields two clear benefits: First, it encourages learning processes to continue outside of (and in between) classes, and second, it reduces the gap between school and community. Eventually, learners have to do their own learning in collaboration with their community. They need guidance and assistance, but they also need to develop autonomy so that they can take charge of their own actions and language use. Only in this way do they develop the confidence to extend their language use outside class hours and after the course finishes (i.e., to engage in lifelong learning).

Thirdly, students need to develop their own voice and identity in the target language. When they speak or write, they must be able to connect their self to the language, express their own identities, and voice their thoughts effectively. Only in this way does their language use become authentic.

Fourthly and finally, there is still a residue of colonial attitude to the exportation of language teaching methodologies, teachers, and textbooks from the Anglo-centric world (Holliday's 'BANA,' or Britain, Australia, North America; 1994). The assumption is that modern methods that 'work' in a Western context should also work elsewhere, and they may be transported lock stock and barrel to other countries. However, as Holliday points out, this may result in 'tissue rejection,' that is, in institutionally and culturally incompatible practices. Instead, local methodologies should be developed with local expertise, taking local educational history, institutional practices, and deep-seated issues of national and ethnic identity into account. In recent years, through the work of Holliday (1994), Pennycook (1995), Coleman (1996), Canagarajah (2001) and others, more attention is being paid to locally appropriate methodologies and classroom practices.

CONCLUSION

In this chapter I have tried to show how an ecological approach is also a critical one. I have defined a critical approach as one (scientific or otherwise) that applies an explicit and overt rational, moral and ethical stance to the treatment, interpretation and documentation of a particular state of affairs, and one that is therefore intervention and change oriented.

I have provided a brief overview of historical development in psychology and linguistics to show how an ecological and critical perspective emerged in both these disciplines. I elaborate on the notion of *ecological validity* in the work of Brunswik, Lewin and Bronfenbrenner.

Going back to the notion of *deep ecology*, I summarize the basic principles of deep ecology as proposed by the Norwegian philosopher Arne Naess, and compare these to the set of principles formulated by the group Terralingua ('Partnerships for Linguistic and Biological Diversity'). I note that ecological theory does not support the notion that more diversity is always better, but that what is most important in any ecosystem is *balance*. Reduction of social and linguistic diversity by colonization, linguistic dominance, and prohibition of indigenous or immigrant languages are in that respect destructive practices in linguistic ecosystems.

From there I move on to discussing the notion of linguistic human rights, and quote from a declaration proposed by Tove Skutnabb-Kangas. I quote a number of languages that are currently endangered, along with their cultures and customs. A related issue is the education of indigenous or immigrant children and the role of the native language in education. In practice, the native language is treated very poorly in educational settings all over the world. Recently, California turned the clock back by virtually eliminating all native-language use in its schools. Gone are the days when children were whipped for using their native language, but in California today a teacher can be sued for using the child's native language, and lose his or her job. The face of primitivism may have changed, but its substance is still very much among us.

I summarize from a report by Broeder and Extra (1997) on immigrant minority language education in a number of European countries. Bilingual education is and has been a much contested practice, and has always been a highly politicized issue. Currently in many places there is a backlash against bilingual education, and there seems to be little room for the child's mother tongue in a climate of testing and narrow accountability.

Nowadays, immigrant families shift from their native language to the host language far more quickly than they used to. Instead of three generations, it now often takes only one. What this does to social well-being and stability, and the formation of stable identities in young people is not well understood, but the consequences might be dire. I quote from Jim Crawford's website to highlight some of the negative consequences of enforced English monolingualism in the US. I also use the example of *Ebonics*, the proposed use of African American English in the Oakland schools, to highlight the political dimension of language use in schools.

I briefly mention language planning and language policy, e.g. the notion of official and national languages, and multilingual policies, leading to pedagogies of biliteracy or multiliteracy, as described by Hornberger (2002).

Next I examine culture, noting that there are a multitude of conceptions and definitions of that concept. I focus on the notion of culture in everyday life, on practices in which people participate. Culture is "an encounter in an open landscape," as Tornberg (2000, p. 284) puts it. Further, following Clifford, "culture is contested, temporary, and emergent" (1986, p. 19), it is discursively constructed.

I attempt to tie the notions of culture, mind and value together in a practical perspective; using language is grounded in all three if we treat learners as speakers in their own right (Kramsch, 1998).

Technology is of course an inescapable part of today's education, and I argue that it can be a blessing as well as disaster. I propose that teachers need to integrate technology into a curriculum that is socially rewarding and intellectually stimulating. Here I think our focus should be not on course packages, but rather on what is called *open software*, that is, word processing, presentation and multimedia design programs that stimulate creativity and encourage project work. It is important to avoid the commodification of education through technology, and to focus on rich educational experiences, whether or not expensive and sophisticated gadgets have played a role in their creation.

In the final section I look at critical language studies, noting that this involves two very basic rules: think for yourself, and speak for yourself. I reject any critical approach that aims at indoctrination or that proselytizes, since that can only lead to dogma. As Pennycook (forthcoming) points out, of course there is a difficult line to walk between pushing an agenda and accepting any and every political viewpoint. Here we need to be guided by our own "science of values," in the words of Edward Reed (1996).

CHAPTER 8

ECOLOGICAL RESEARCH

INTRODUCTION

In the preceding seven chapters many different issues have been discussed from an ecological perspective. We have looked at language, semiotics, emergence, self, among other phenomena, and I have proposed that the ecological approach is a coherent alternative, theoretically and practically well-motivated, to other ways of teaching and researching language education . But if we are committed to or even just interested in the ecological outlook, how do we approach our work environment in ecological ways, in research and in practice?

In the last chapter we looked at ecological validity as a precursor to a critical ecological approach. In this chapter I will address the nature of ecological research in a broader perspective. I suggest that the main criteria are:

- It is contextualized or situative, focusing on relationships in the setting
- It has spatial and temporal dimensions
- It is (at least potentially) interventionist, i.e. change-oriented and critical
- It is ecologically and phenomenologically valid, particularly in terms of a correspondence between researchers' and participants' situation definition.

Each of these criteria brings with it a range of other requirements and options. For example, a contextualized piece of research must decide what it is that is meant by context. This is no easy task, since innumerable definitions of context exist (see also Chapter 2). In this chapter I show several ways of dealing with this, in particular Bronfenbrenner's nested ecosystems, Engeström's activity theory, and Checkland's systems practice.

Ecological research considers factors of space (the physical, social and symbolic parameters of the site in question) and time (both in terms of past and of future, and the present as it evolves with its past/future dimensions). This sort of work is often associated with longitudinal descriptive/interpretive work, such as ethnography. Many ethnographies take long to develop, sometimes a lifetime (Malinowski, 1967; Geertz, 1973; van Maanen, 1988). Sometimes it is advisable to follow a complete natural or life cycle of the focal unit, which may be a hard thing to define. For example, is the basic cycle of school learning a school year? A semester? A lesson? To an extent such a notion of cycles is arbitrary, since its boundaries are determined by forces that are not part of the cyclical process itself (for an interesting socio-ecological study see Lemke, 2002). Ecological research should aim to determine the natural time spans of the phenomena under investigation, including the temporal perceptions and constructions of the participants (which may or may not coincide with the temporal boundaries set by institutions and official calendars). A good example of a natural time span or cycle is the agricultural one of dry and rainy seasons, of tilling, sowing, planting, harvesting, and so on. Such a cycle of seasons is sedimented deeply into the cultural, ritual and social practices of rural people. However, in my work in the Peruvian Andes I found that the agricultural cycle was incompatible with the imposed school calendar, causing serious disruptions in school as well as on the land. School started just when children were most needed as helpers in the fields, and holidays did not take families' needs into account. The school calendars were set by the central government for urban convenience, not considering rural agricultural families' needs.

In addition to ethnographies, a common method of educational research is the *case study*. Here a bounded case (often an individual, or a small group – such as a classroom) is investigated over a longer period of time to characterize its workings and development. Similar to the discussion of temporal cycles above, the boundaries (temporal and spatial) of a case study are not easy to determine. Indeed, one authoritative account of case study research methodology, Miles and Huberman (1994), considers the boundaries inherently "somewhat indeterminate " (p. 25).

In biological ecological research, some of the more favored ecosystems to study are those that have fairly clear boundaries, such as ponds and small islands. In such environments it is somewhat easier to track and account for "the totality of relationships of an organism with all other organisms with which it comes into contact," to quote from Haeckel's definition of ecology (1866). This is more difficult to do in open or mixed ecosystems such as oceans and tropical forests. In all ecosystems, energy enters and leaves the system in a number of ways. Even in a pond, animals visit and leave seeds or fish eggs (stuck to the feet of ducks, for example), rain falls, water evaporates, mosquitoes hatch and fly off to bother humans, and so on.

Moving from the pond to the language classroom, there are also boundary issues in the latter. The learners spend an hour or so in the classroom, but before that they have been elsewhere, and after that they will go to other places. There is no doubt that their activities elsewhere have an effect on what happens in the classroom, and the same naturally goes for the teacher. Classroom research, including my own (1988; see Chapter 2 for some further discussion) has often treated the classroom as a bounded system, and studied the interactions and language in it without explicit connections to other contexts. I continue to think that such work (often micro-ethnographic or conversation-analytical) can be very valuable, but an additional focus of interest is the range of connections between the classroom and other contexts. Some of the models suggested below, particularly Bronfenbrenner's nested ecosystems (1979), do just that.

Research that is interventionist is usually called *action research*. Action research was pioneered by Kurt Lewin, the psychologist we have mentioned in earlier chapters as well. Lewin thought that theory was too important to be left to the theorists. He is thus an early proponent of the theory of practice, a term associated with the work of Bourdieu (1977). Action research is often problem-oriented, and it introduces a change, the implementation of which is then monitored, studied and reported. Action research can vary from more shallow to deeper, analogous to the shallow and deep ecology discussed in Chapters 1 and 7. The shallow type just focuses on fixing a problem, the deeper kind aims to bring about critical and deep change, such as a transformation of a particular slice of reality.

The final criterion mentioned, ecological or phenomenological validity, is similar to the emic (as opposed to etic) perspective in ethnography. The emic perspective requires that the analytical notions and constructs used in the research are compatible with those that the participants in the setting use. It is thus similar to the phenomenological requirement mentioned by Bronfenbrenner (see the last chapter). An etic perspective, on the other hand, would impose pre-established categories and systems on the setting studied, with the danger of course that the subject matter of the research will be misrepresented. Ideally, etic tools and emic sensitivity should go hand in hand in contextualized research.

There are other forms of research that are compatible with an ecological perspective: narrative research, autobiographies, discourse analysis, conversation analysis, and more. So long as the four basic criteria I started out with are observed, the research can reasonably be called ecological. On the other hand, both qualitative and quantitative methods of analysis can be used, depending on what it is that is relevant to the research question.

COMPLEXITY, CHAOS AND ECOLOGY

Over the last decade or so there have been several papers and presentations exploring the relevance of chaos or complexity theory for educational linguistics (and also for theoretical linguistics). Examples include Bowers, 1990; Edge, 1993; Larsen-Freeman, 1997, 2002; and van Lier, 1998.

The points listed below provide some of the reasons for taking a complexity/ chaos perspective in ecological and educational linguistics. I assume that most readers will readily agree with most of them, although perhaps some question marks will be raised by the relationship between causality and understanding. I will touch upon this issue in various places below.

The notions of chaos and order have had a long history in philosophy and science, though in the perennial quest for predictability, causality and proof they have had to take a back seat until mathematical models and computer programs were powerful enough to put some substance on old ideas. Chaos theory hit the popular consciousness in the 1980s, with the publication of James Gleick's book *Chaos* (1988), and the book (and subsequent movie) *Jurassic Park* (Crichton,

1991) followed soon thereafter. Since then a large number of general as well as scientific publications around these topics have appeared, including some in educational and theoretical linguistics, as mentioned above.

Complexity:
- A 'learning act' never automatically or necessarily follows a 'teaching act.'
- Teaching does not cause learning.
- In learning, there are multiple causes and reasons. Some of these are predictable, but there are also coincidences and accidents.
- Learning may occur at any time in any place: just as likely between lessons as in lessons, just as likely in the bath as in the classroom.
- God dwells among the details, as Stephen Jay Gould tells us (1993); the devil is also in the details. We had better get the details right!
- Causes do not explain complex systems; knowing causes does not equal understanding.
- Any 'small' change may have enormous consequences, or none at all. The same is true of any 'big' change.

Complexity theory (I will use 'complexity' rather than 'chaos' since the former is more encompassing) has its canonical metaphors and analogies. One is the famous butterfly effect, that says something like: A butterfly that flaps its wings in the Amazon rain forest may cause a storm in New York one month later. Another is the tap that trickles irregularly, but if the flow of water is increased little by little, at one point the drip pattern will suddenly turn into a steady stream. In other words, something that is disorganized, chaotic, may become organized and patterned due to a minor change, which may arise from outside or inside the system. In complexity terminology, there are various kinds of *attractors* that bring about sudden transformations in complex systems. Such systems, variously called complex adaptive systems, non-linear systems, self-organizing systems, among other terms, do not function in neat, linear cause-effect ways.

> The flapping of a single butterfly's wing today produces a tiny change in the state of the atmosphere. Over a period of time, what the atmosphere actually does diverges from what it would have done. So, in a month's time, a tornado that would have devastated the Indonesian coast doesn't happen. Or maybe one that wasn't going to happen, does (Stewart, 1989, 141).

How could complexity theory be relevant to SLA? What does language learning have to do with dripping taps, butterfly wings, and complex systems of various kinds?

Traditional research in SLA, being of a reductive nature (as argued in Chapter 2) assumes a simple causal relationship between input and output. For example, if we want to find out if a particular method of vocabulary acquisition works, we first provide instances of a word in the input, and then we look for instances of that word in the student's output at a later date. If we find it there, then we consider the item learned (or acquired, depending on our theoretical persuasion). If we don't find it, we cannot conclude anything. This sort of research follows a cause-effect model, similar to Newtonian physics. It may provide some information, but it is like putting a puzzle together using the shape of each individual piece only, and not using the evolving picture (it's like putting all the pieces blank side up).

Learning language, whether first or subsequent, in the classroom or in the wider community, is a complex process (or project, if we look at it from the learner's perspective), influenced by a multitude of factors. These factors cannot be reduced to single linear relationships, i.e., a *cause* (such as a method, a task, an example, a drill) and a subsequent *effect* (a memorized word or structure, spontaneous use of a targeted item in discourse, a correct answer on a test, etc.).

Understanding a complex process is never just a matter of delving into causes and effects in the linear manner just described. It must be done holistically, yet at the same time with great attention to detail (as Gould emphasized above). Crichton, in his novel *Jurassic Park* (1991) calls the linear thinking of traditional science 'thintelligent' as compared to the new science of chaos and complexity. Other writers, including Bateson (1979) and Capra (1996), emphasize the need for studying *processes* rather than causal mechanisms or fixed structures. As mentioned in the last chapter, Bateson (1979) made a distinction between two kinds of thinking: *classification*, a more or less simplistic and preliminary way of thinking, and *process* thinking, which he considered a more sophisticated, complex and advanced form of thought. Capra (1996, pp.158-161) similarly distinguishes between *pattern* or *structure* (as components of context), and *process* (as the *activities* that take place to produce the patterns and structures). I would add that, once the patterns are 'sedimented' into structures, these structures then provide constraints (positive and negative) that channel, guide, and delimit the processes and stabilize the patterns of relationships. This can be visualized as follows:

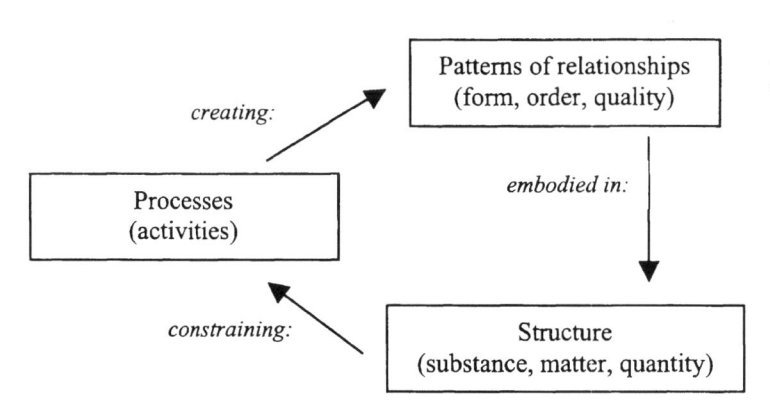

Figure 8.1 Process, Pattern, Structure

A chaos/complexity way of thinking can have a number of consequences for language learning theory and practice. In the box on page 202 I hinted at some of them, such as the limitations of a search for causes, and the importance of focusing on detail (the 'pedagogical moment,' as van Manen puts it, 1991). Elaborating from those starting points, I would like to draw on the pioneering paper of Larsen-Freeman (1997), who suggests a number of potential contributions of chaos/complexity to the language learning field (I will paraphrase Larsen-Freeman's headings and descriptions here, interpreting and adding from my ecological perspective):

1. The blurring of boundaries and dichotomies.

The reader has seen numerous dichotomies in this book (as well as elsewhere, to be sure). Nature versus nurture, competence versus performance, langue versus parole, macro versus micro, the list goes on and on. Chaos/complexity encourages us to see complementarities (interactions) instead of dichotomies; the interactions between complementary perspectives are the key focus of research, avoiding the entrenchment of theories into one extreme position or the other.

2. A warning against drawing premature conclusions, as well as against rejecting contrasting viewpoints.

Reductionist research procedures tend to get locked into one end of a dichotomy, at times fiercely rejecting the other end. When that happens "simple solutions to complex problems" (Larsen-Freeman, 1997, p. 158) become attractive, and are often defended *ad absurdum*. This is arguably the case with Krashen's insistence that only comprehensible input can cause acquisition (1985), and with Pinker's questionable characterization of language as an 'instinct' (1994). Sometimes a point of view is incompatible with another point of view. At such moments it may be worth considering that incompatibilities are often windows through which we are better able to see reality (Natsoulas, 1993).

3. A fresh light on language learning phenomena.

Although very few practitioners will say this explicitly, research, curriculum and testing assume a linear progression, a piecemeal and incremental rate of progress, and a regular process of gradual mastery. Although plateaus of stagnation and spurts of growth are duly noted, and such phenomena as backsliding are acknowledged, they are marginal blips on the radar screen. For example, when backsliding is discussed, the one example that is brought up is the fact that children produce correct irregular past tenses first, and then will incorrectly regularize these past tenses (went – goed, and so on) once they learn the regular past rule. Interesting though this is, it is a meager empirical description of a supposedly common phenomenon. By throwing out the underlying (tacit) assumptions of regularity and incremental growth, chaos/complexity might have quite salutary effects on curriculum and syllabus design, which by and large still derive from those assumptions.

4. Refocuses our attention in the light of emergent phenomena.

The classic view of language teaching and learning is one where an item is presented, then practiced, and finally produced freely. An item is received (put in/taken in), processed, stored, and then made available for use. This seems a bit like a mechanical production unit. You put in malt and hops at one end, stir it about and let it ferment, filter and store the resulting liquid, and out comes a delicious batch of beer.

Chaos/complexity regards all complex systems as inherently unstable ("far from equilibrium," as Prigogine has put it; see Prigogine and Stengers, 1984). Basically, the learner's interlanguage is an unstable language situated in an unstable linguistic environment, including the unstable target language.

5. Discourages cause - effect-based theories.
Causality certainly plays a part in language learning and theorizing. But linear causality can never be more than a minor, relatively uninteresting part of the complex of processes, patterns and structures.

6. Emphasizes the importance of detail.
Chaos/complexity tells us that the smallest changes can have the greatest consequences. In language teaching and learning, some minor event – a learner noticing a particular vowel change (as in the example *sleeped – slept* in Chapter 4) may set in motion a far-reaching restructuring of the learner's interlanguage, the emergence of a whole array of new patterns.

7. Warns against reductionism by finding a focal unit that keeps sight of the whole.
Recall Vygotsky's example of a molecular view of water: hydrogen+oxygen (H_2O), and the impossibility of explaining the fire-extinguishing power of water by examining the chemical composition of water. The whole cannot be explained on the basis of the parts. Therefore, any analysis of details must be intimately and continually connected to the whole. The detail must project to the whole, as it were.

In terms of language, all sorts of units have been used in research: morphemes, words, eye movements, milliseconds of delays in recalling lexical items, all kinds of errors and corrections, grammaticality judgments, and so on. No doubt all of these can supply interesting information about learning processes, yet unless they are connectable to the complex of processes of learning, and particularizable to each individual person that is in a particular learning situation, these piecemeal findings are uninformative.

SOME ILLUSTRATIONS OF CHAOS, COMPLEXITY, AND ECOLOGY

"Have you lost your way, sir?" said he.
"All paths," the Philosopher replied, "are on the earth, and so one can never be lost."
- James Stephens (1912), *The crock of gold*

In this section I want to give a small selection of observations, sayings, quotes and citations that illustrate various properties of chaos/complexity and ecology. The purpose is to provide food for (open-ended) thought, and to push the boundaries of the field outwards.

ON TRUTH AND PROOF

> Truth is a mobile army of metaphors. Nietzsche (1954).

> My chief consolation lies in the fact that truth bears its own impress, and that my story will carry conviction by reason of the internal evidences for its accuracy. Samuel Butler (1872), *Erewhon*.

What these quotes suggest is that truth is not a fixed, scientific fact that can be proven by scientific experiment. Experiment proceeds by a search for proof, not truth. Truth belongs to speech, to stories, to wisdom. Proof belongs to cause-effect mechanics. Truth is heard, proof is seen (see further below).

A simple non-linear system:
scissors
paper
stone

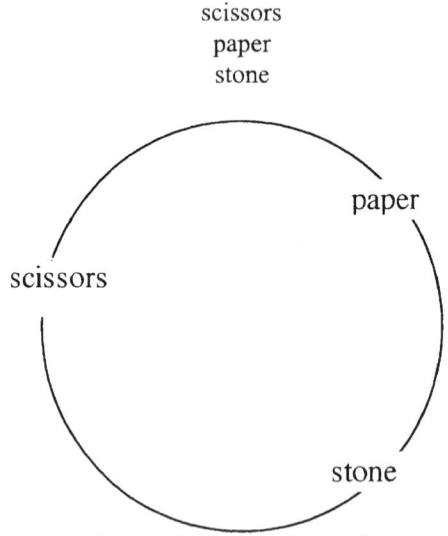

Figure 8.2: Scissors, Paper, Stone

In this game (*jankempon* in Japanese), which I assume all readers are familiar with in one form of another, two fingers represent scissors, a flat hand represents paper, and a fist represents stone. Scissors cut paper, papers enfolds stone, stone knocks scissors. This is not a hierarchy:

scissors > paper > stone > scissors > paper > stone...

Nothing is 'caused' by anything in this game. It represents a conventionalized set of relationships. How many of the human systems, concerns, activity types, and developmental processes are of the linear cause-effect type, how many might be of a different, non-linear type? According to Capra (1996), in the real world there are no hierarchies, only networks. Hierarchies only exist in our attempts at organizing the physical world, and in our own power-and-control oriented social structures and institutions (according to biblical accounts, the first hierarchies were those of the angels in heaven).[1]

CAUSALITY

Let's take a simple example. A rock hits a window and the window breaks. Several statements can be made about this event, as suggested below. In each case, just for fun, I try to find a parallel statement about language learning.

    a) The glass broke because a rock hit it
            ... The student learned because she received comprehensible input
    b) The glass broke because it was brittle
            ... The student learned because the affective filter was low
    c) The glass broke because Cody was fooling around throwing rocks
            ... The student learned because there were lots of interesting activities
            she could participate in.
    d) Cody is always fooling around because his mom just lets him run wild.
            ... etc.

Here you can see that knowing a cause (the rock hit the window; the learner received comprehensible input) does not equal providing a full account of any particular event.

PROBABILITY AND CHAOS

Just take a coin and prepare to flip it. Before doing that, what can you predict will happen, and what can you not predict?

- I can predict with 50 % probability that the coin will land heads up
- I cannot predict how many times it will flip and bounce, how it will roll, where precisely it will land
- I just flipped a coin. I *know* that it has landed either tails or heads up, but I can't find it anywhere. Where did the darn thing end up?

It is interesting to reflect on such combinations of the predictable and the unpredictable. In language learning we may find parallels. For example, we may have developmental stages that are quite regular and predictable, yet they may occur in trajectories that are themselves wholly or partially unpredictable. Learners come to class every day with their regular developmental stages, yet this cannot predict what happens during today's lesson.

PREDICTABILITY AND ORDER

> The level of structure that people seek is always in direct ratio to the amount of chaos they have inside. (Tom Robbins, *Skinny legs and all*, p. 403)

---

[1] Social animals also develop hierarchies, e.g. the 'pecking order' of chickens, and the hierarchical group orders in ants, baboons, gorillas and rats. But it is important to realize that hierarchies are social constructs, not physical or biological ones.

> The insane have a terrific obsession for logic and order, as do the French.(Henry Miller, *Black Spring*, 1963)

We seem to worship order and revile chaos. Yet, as the above quotes, - both tongue-in-cheek to be sure - show, there seems to be an interdependence, some kind of dynamic, between the two. Our classes tend towards the ordered, organized and predictable, and I am sure both teachers and students want it that way – up to a point. I have argued before (1996) that the planned must be balanced by the improvised in any good lesson. I have also argued in this book, in Chapter 6, that the essence of progress in a scaffolded proximal context is the unpredictable. The unpredictable yearns for order, and the predictable yearns for change. We all harbor order and disorder in ourselves, and maybe we vary in our degree of tolerance for one or the other. Be that as it may, language lessons may need a playful tussle between the two, as I assume do the French and everybody else.

GENERALIZING

> The power of generalizing ... gives men much superiority in mistake over the dumb animals. (George Elliot, *Middlemarch*)

> The most common of all scientific mistakes is that of generalization. (Konrad Lorenz, 1990)

Many educational researchers, myself among them, grew up with the belief that the ultimate yardstick of the relevance and success of any piece of research was its *generalizability*. I have since come to the conclusion, in line with the two quotes above, that generalizing is indeed a vastly overrated criterion. In fact, I agree with Elliott and Lorenz that a preoccupation with generalizing has led to a lot of crooked thinking. I now think that what is far more important, particularly in the human and action-based sciences, is *particularization*, i.e., the ability to judge the relevance of one scientific activity in the context of another.

MICRO AND MACRO

One of the most basic issues in social science research is whether to take a micro or a macro approach, or to make an attempt at integrating micro and macro aspects of the phenomena investigated. The British sociologist Giddens calls the frequent confrontation between micro and macro sociological studies "a phony war if there ever was one" (1984, p. 139). He specifically warns against a "division of labour" between the two perspectives, where the micro perspective focuses on the activities of "free agents", and the macro perspective on the constraints operating on free agency (ibid., p. 139). A basic question we need to resolve is how to shape educational research and reform without falling into the chasm between a deterministic and highly subjective macro view ('top-down or nothing') and an objective but uncritical technical nitpicking. Even though at times micro researchers are accused of ignoring larger structures, while macro researchers are accused of neglecting social interaction, a preference to work in either a micro or a macro context cannot be attacked as wrong, such accusations and attacks presumably being what Giddens refers to as 'phony.' The following quote from

Jonathan Turner is a succinct, balanced statement of the relationship between micro and macro approaches:

> I believe that micro and macro sociology are separate kinds of analyses, each valid in its own right. Micro sociology examines the properties of social interaction, whereas macro sociology studies the properties of populations of individuals. For most purposes, micro sociology brackets out of consideration macro dynamics, while the latter takes the fact that individuals interact as given. This is a reasonable division of intellectual activity; and in fact, until more mature theories of micro and macro processes are developed, it is wise to sustain this division (1988, p. 14).

Ecological research models (and contextualized models in general) all attempt to somehow bridge the micro-macro gap. In Chapter 1 I mentioned that ecology operates on the notion of *scale*, and in any research examination of the focal scale may also require examination of scales above and below the focal one (see also Lemke, 2002).

In Chapter 6 we briefly noted Rogoff's three planes of participation: *participatory appropriation* on the personal plane, *guided participation* on the interpersonal plane, and *apprenticeship* on the community plane (Rogoff, 1995). If these planes are conceptualized as spatio-temporal ecological scales, then causality cannot cross from one scale to another (Lemke, 2002, p. 92, commentaries), but rather there are cyclical interrelationships of many kinds at the boundaries (Lemke speaks of social-semiotic and social-ecological processes). Rogoff's three planes can be seen as equivalent to the three aspects of Leontiev's activity model: *operations*, *actions* and *activity* (Leontiev, 1981). Further, one might bring in other notions, such as (1) *module* (at the purely cognitive level, as in Fodor, 1998; we would have to translate that into *socio-cognitive* processes, or *microgenesis*), (2) *domain* (of collaborative activity, co-construction, or as language game, Wittgenstein, 1958) and (3) *field* (Bourdieu, 1991; compare also the notions of *life space* (Lewin, 1943, *espace vecú* (Merleau-Ponty, 1962), *chronotope* (Bakhtin, 1981) and *forms of life* (Wittgenstein, 1958). This is quite an avalanche of contextual terminology, so let me try to organize it in table form. The concepts will not fit neatly, but at least the reader may be able to rearrange them more easily, and compare, add or subtract concepts.

Table 8.1: Comparative contextual layers

operations	microgenesis module (Fodor)	appropriation (Bakhtin, Rogoff)	semiosis (Peirce)
actions	domain co-construction	guided participation (Rogoff)	language game (Wittgenstein)
activity (all three above: Leontiev)	field (Bourdieu)	apprenticeship (Rogoff) community of practice (Wenger)	life space (Lewin); espace vecú (Merleau-Ponty); chronotope (Bakhtin)

Not everything comes neatly in threes, of course, and in the following we see that the spatio-temporal pie can be carved up in many different ways, or that it can be at times best left uncarved. Be that as it may, it should be clear that the world in which our activity unfolds is a multidimentional, multilevel, and multiscalar affair, with multiple influences of all kinds criss-crossing, cycling and looping in untold ways. We can at best only glimpse a partial snapshot of this whole.

ECOLOGICAL RESEARCH MODELS

In the remainder of this chapter I will review three different research models that attempt to deal with the research context in a systematic way. As we discussed in previous chapters, ecological research is contextualized research, and the complexities of context as a research notion need to be brought into some sort of coherent framework.

Such a framework must not only categorize or classify the context into components, but more crucially show how different aspects of context relate to each other and to the subject under investigation.

In previous chapters the notion of context has come under discussion several times. This is not surprising given its centrality in an ecological approach. We have quoted Drew and Heritage's criticism of a "bucket theory" of context (see Chapter 2; Drew & Heritage, 1992), and complained about highly subjective pick-and-choose approaches. We have argued that a context is that which is relevant to the participants themselves. However, we have also seen that at times there may contextual forces at work that the participants themselves are not even aware of, let alone can address overtly in their joint activity. A strict ethnomethodological procedure would require that contextual information or particulars that are not visibly/audibly oriented to in the interaction must be ignored, however tempting their inclusion might be. A laudable, and methodologically defensible stance. However, in educational work (or any practical work for that matter), such a luxury may not always be affordable. In sum, this business of context is no easy matter.

The three models of contextualized research illustrated here have been chosen because they have practical applications in educational settings. There are other proposals that could be included, such as Layder's sociological perspective that aims to bridge the macro-micro divide, which he calls a "realist approach" (1990). For that matter, one might include the types of studies done by Bourdieu under the umbrella of *theory of practice* (1984; 1988); Giddens's theory of *structuration* (1984) and Bhaskar's *critical realism* (1989) could also be used to generate instances of research adhering to the ecological principles outlined in the earlier chapters. Finally, a recent arrival on the scene of contextualized educational research is *design-based research*, first proposed by Brown (1992) and Collins (1992), and aimed at integrating empirical work with theory building, and instructional design with engineering perspectives.

All these perspectives share a number of principles and procedures. There are contextualized, they regard the educational context as a complex, messy system, they view learning as emergent, and they conceptualize research as a series of cyclical activities. Interestingly, but perhaps not so surprisingly, none of the contextualized research models and frameworks mentioned here appear to be aware of each other's existence. This seems a pity, since they could all probably learn from each other's perspectives on similar sets of problems.

The ecological approach is not yet another addition to this list of contextual methods. As mentioned before, ecology is not a single method or even theory, it is more of a world view and a way of working, and it can motivate a wide variety of research and practice. The following three examples are merely offered as possible enactments of an ecological worldview in educational settings. But before I move on to the discussion of these three examples of ecological research, I need to clarify an important philosophical point regarding the notions of *proof* and *truth*, already alluded to above.

A NOTE ON PROOF AND TRUTH

> We know that any understanding must be based finally upon natural language because it is only there we can be certain to touch reality (Heisenberg, 1965, p. 112).

Ecological research aims to understand a complex environment, and the search for proof, causal connections and correlations is not necessarily the best or surest way towards understanding. Proof and scientific explanation tend to reflect the dominance of the visually oriented modes of inquiry associated with the natural sciences, from Galileo to Descartes to today. Descartes said, "Truly we shall learn how to employ our mental intuition from comparing it with the way we employ our eyes" (Descartes, *Rules for the direction of the mind*, Rule ix; cited in Hacking, 1975, p. 31).

Show me! certainly packs more of a punch than *Tell me!* The former suggests skepticism and level-headedness. It is also the motto of the state of Missouri, but there is no state that has the motto: Tell me! The latter sounds like an eager, somewhat naïve listener. However, in human affairs, truth and understanding are from ancient times associated with telling, the telling of stories, and in dialogue. Truth is auditory, proof is visual.[2] As Spinoza said:

> The first meaning of true and false seems to have had its origin in narratives; a narrative was called true when it related a fact which had really occurred, and false when it related a fact which had nowhere occurred (Spinoza, *Thoughts on metaphysics*, I, vi.3; cited in Hacking, 1975, p. 7).

Language is in origin an auditory affair. The (written) sentences of theoretical linguistics are never heard outside of linguistics classes. If they were, they would make little sense. The Firstnesses, feelings and sensations, constituting the auditory iconicity of language, resonate deeply in the youngest children, constantly mingling with the visual and other modalities. Direct perception in language, mediated though it always is by language itself, by the other, and by historical-cultural meanings, goes directly to the origins of communication and mutuality. So far as research is concerned, it is relevant to give due recognition to the primacy of the oral and the aural, and to legitimate the telling of stories as appropriate scientific reporting. From the detailed ethnographic descriptions of Clifford Geertz (1973) to the meticulous documentaries of Erving Goffman (1981), the well-told semiotic

---

[2] Even the Bellman knew this, when he assured his crew that "What I tell you three times is true." Lewis Carroll: *The Hunting of the Snark* (available in many editions of *Alice*, as well as in several online versions).

story is as effective, informative and convincing as the most sophisticated statistical data treatment.[3]

It is no secret that in the social sciences the notion of proof, i.e., an incontrovertible link between a cause and an effect, is an illusion. There may be various degrees of possibility, probability and plausibility, but scientific proof is a pipe dream. In his treatise on educational phenomenology, Max van Manen argues that in the search for plausibility the anecdote can play an important role. Not for the purposes of generalizing, but for a number of other reasons, such as the following:

1) Anecdotes form a concrete counterweight to abstract theoretical thought.
2) Anecdotes express a certain disdain for the alienated and alienating discourse of scholars who have difficulty showing how life and theoretical propositions are connected.
3) Anecdotes may provide an account of certain teachings or doctrines which were never written down. (e.g., Plato's dialogues about Socrates)
4) Anecdotes may be encountered as concrete demonstrations of wisdom, sensitive insight, and proverbial truth.
5) Anecdotes of a certain event or incident may acquire the significance of exemplary character (van Manen, 1990, pp. 118-9).

Similarly, Harold Rosen argues for the importance of story in educational research, since stories have the power to compel, to lead us to reflect, to involve us personally, to transform our practice, and to judge our own interpretive powers (Rosen, 1986, p. 224). Arguably, these are extremely important and worthwhile goals of research in education.

In the US, we are currently (at the time of writing, in early 2003) once again living in a climate in which 'basic' (i.e., large scale, randomized, statistical) research is emphasized. Official preferences carry a lot of power since researchers have to compete for funds, and if the official line favors randomized statistical studies with experimental treatments, then narrative, contextualized and many kinds of qualitative research will not get funded. As a result, ecological research and related contextualized forms of research employing *narrative* (for an overview, see Clandinin & Connolly, 1995; for a collection of second language learning studies, see Bailey & Nunan, 1996) *discursive methods* (Potter & Wetherell, 1987), and other *interpretive approaches*, will once again become endangered species in the educational environment.

Research thus implies a struggle for legitimacy. As I have mentioned several times on earlier pages, research in the social sciences has traditionally attempted to emulate research in the physical sciences. It is demonstrably the case, as almost all physicists will readily admit, that such methods are inappropriate for the study of human development and activity, yet the chimera of numerical exactitude still holds an almost irresistible attraction for researchers, and even more so for policy

---

[3] For some guidelines on how to judge the quality of ethnographic and semiotic writing, see Clifford & Marcus, 1986).

makers, in the fields surrounding the education of our learners. Perseverance and eventual success are the only ingredients that may eventually assure equal attention for ecological (contextual and interpretive) research.

BRONFENBRENNER'S BIOECOLOGICAL MODEL OF DEVELOPMENTAL RESEARCH

The fact that ecological research is research in context or situated research, entails a number of consequences, though it does not necessarily rule out any particular type of research or research methods, even including laboratory experimentation (but see Bronfenbrenner's criticism below and in earlier chapters). A major consequence of the contextual requirement is that any research must be seen as a piece of the ecological puzzle, i.e., an effort must be made to see where and how it fits.

As we saw in the last chapter, Bronfenbrenner takes a dim view of psychological laboratory experimentation, arguing that it lacks ecological validity (1979). Instead, Bronfenbrenner proposes a type of research he calls PPCT: Process, Person, Context, Time (1993; sometimes with the addition of O, or Outcome). Briefly,

- *Process*
  It is always more difficult to research a process than a product. Even when a process is researched, it is often measured by a product as the dependent variable, for example a process of listening comprehension aided by interactive adjustments is measured by a subsequent test of comprehension. Process research in its purest form would judge a process in terms of the process, or progress in the process. So, the learning process would be judged in terms of improvements in the processes of learning.
- *Person*
  This entails looking at persons as persons, not as subjects, undifferentiated and uninteresting except in terms of the investigated trait or function. It can take a long time to understand learners, especially when we take seriously what we all know: that they are all different. In addition, people should not just be passive recipients of research, but active co-researchers, wherever possible.
- *Context*
  As we have seen, context is a very complex concept (see Duranti & Goodwin, 1992). It potentially encompasses the whole world. But, of course, for participants in a particular setting, not the whole world is relevant. Certain affordances become available partly because we are who we are. Research, therefore, might study the environment that is relevant to the people in question, as they signal that relevance in their actions and words.
- *Time*
  Ecological research is research over time, not brief, one-shot probes.

Processes of action, perception and learning unfold gradually over time, and research must document relevant processes and changes longitudinally.

The PPCT model means that the most suitable forms of ecological research are action research (or other intervention studies), case studies, ethnographies, and various forms of collaborative research. We can look here also at biological research, where ethology is a common way to study ecosystems. This type of research was popularized by biologists such as Konrad Lorenz and Nico Tinbergen, who received Nobel prizes for their work on imprinting. Perhaps ethology in biology is equivalent to ethnography in the human sciences. However, we have one advantage (though it has drawbacks, too, of course): we can talk to the people in the setting to be researched, and we can research ourselves too.

In ecological research, several notions are looked at in different ways than in more traditional research. Generalizing, for example, is extremely difficult in a setting with innumerable variables which all interact in constantly changing ways. Causality, especially of the linear variety ('X causes Y') is impossible to attribute. On the other hand, quantification can be just as useful as in more controlled forms of research, so long as the items that are quantified are clearly understood, and the reasons for quantifying are clear.

THE EDUCATIONAL SETTING AS A HIERARCHY OF NESTED ECOSYSTEMS

The context of education can be characterized as a set of ecosystems, each one nested inside the next (Bronfenbrenner, 1979; 1993). Each system has its own set of actors and artifacts, and its own patterns of operations and relations. Also, each ecosystem operates on its own time scale and cycles of events. According to Bronfenbrenner, we can divide the hierarchy into microsystem, mesosystem, exosystem, and macrosystem. A brief description of each follows, from Bronfenbrenner (1993):

- *Microsystem*
  A microsystem is a pattern of activities, roles, and interpersonal relations experienced by the developing person in a given setting with particular physical, social, and symbolic features that invite, permit, or inhibit engagement in sustained, progressively more complex interaction with, and activity in, the immediate environment (p. 15).
- *Mesosystem*
  A mesosystem comprises the linkages and processes taking place between two or more settings containing the developing person. Special attention is focused on the synergistic effects created by the interaction of developmentally instigative or inhibitory features and processes present in each setting (p. 22).
- *Exosystem:*
  The exosystem comprises the linkages and processes taking place between

two or more settings, at least one of which does not contain the developing person, but in which events occur that directly influence processes within the immediate setting in which the developing person lives (p. 24).

- *Macrosystem*
  The macrosystem consists of the overarching pattern of micro-, meso-, and exosystems characteristic of a given culture, subculture, or other extended social structure, with particular reference to the developmental instigative belief systems, resources, hazards, lifestyles, opportunity structures, life course options and patterns of social interchange that are embedded in such overarching systems (p. 25).

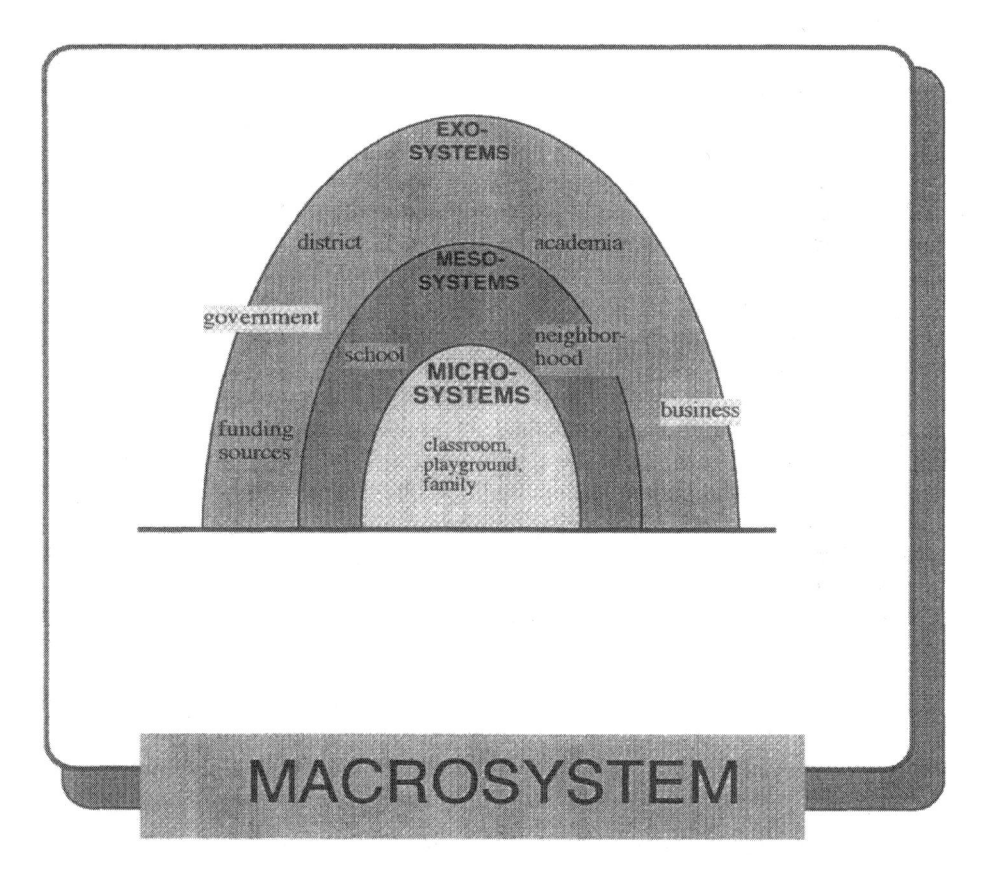

After Bronfenbrenner, U. (1979). *The ecology of human development*. Cambridge, MA: Harvard University Press.

Figure 8.3: Bronfenbrenner's nested ecosystems

210   CHAPTER 8

The value of Bronfenbrenner's model lies not in the nested set of systems, but in the focus on the relationships among them. These 'linkages' allow the researcher to track instigative and debilitative forces between one ecosystem and another. For example, a crucial issue in any educational setting is the potential gap between the school and the home. This needs to be studied from a microsystemic perspective (a study of home and school) as well as from a mesosytemic perspective (the level of school policy, neighborhood patterns of life and customs, etc,). A teacher, administrator or researcher visiting the students' homes or would also be taking a macrosystemic perspective, since he or she would not be member of that microsystem. In this way, educational research can take a micro-macro perspective (see Heath, 1983, for a good example of research that goes in this direction, although not based on Bronfenbrenner's model). A further interesting potential of the model is that it allows for an investigation of how trends or activities on one scale can influence those on another scale. For example, in the *Ebonics* example discussed in the last chapter, public opinion as expressed in (and to some extent created by) the media and various interest groups can influence quite dramatically what happens in the classroom. Chains of decision-making processes go in all directions, and it can take a sustained effort and a multi-scalar analysis to track their influence.

Even though the Bronfenbrenner model emphasizes linkages across systems, the main analytical work in most cases will be anchored at the macrosystemic classroom level. However, to investigate the instigative and debilitative processes that occur there, in other words, to assess the extent to which the classroom is a proximal context, a causal or decontextualized experimental study will be inadequate. Test results and isolated variables do not add up to a systemic understanding of an environment. Therefore, indicators of success in a proximal environment must be identified, and evidence of their occurrence must be observable and documentable. Bronfenbrenner proposes several such indicators, e.g. differentiation in perception and response types, autonomy in terms of activity and the structuring of the learning environment, coping under stress, increased knowledge and skills in particular areas, and the establishment of rewarding and effective social relationships (Bronfenbrenner & Ceci, 1994; van Lier, 2000).

ACTIVITY THEORY

A currently very influential framework for investigating activity in context is Engeström's model of activity theory (1999). As represented below, this consists of several triangles that are connected in various ways. First there is the triangle of subject > object > mediating artifacts/tools; next there is the triangle of subject > object > community. Then other triangles can be traced that bring in other aspects of the context, such as division of labor, values and rules, and so on. The idea is to represent an interconnected system of physical and symbolic aspects of the environment within which the activity occurs.

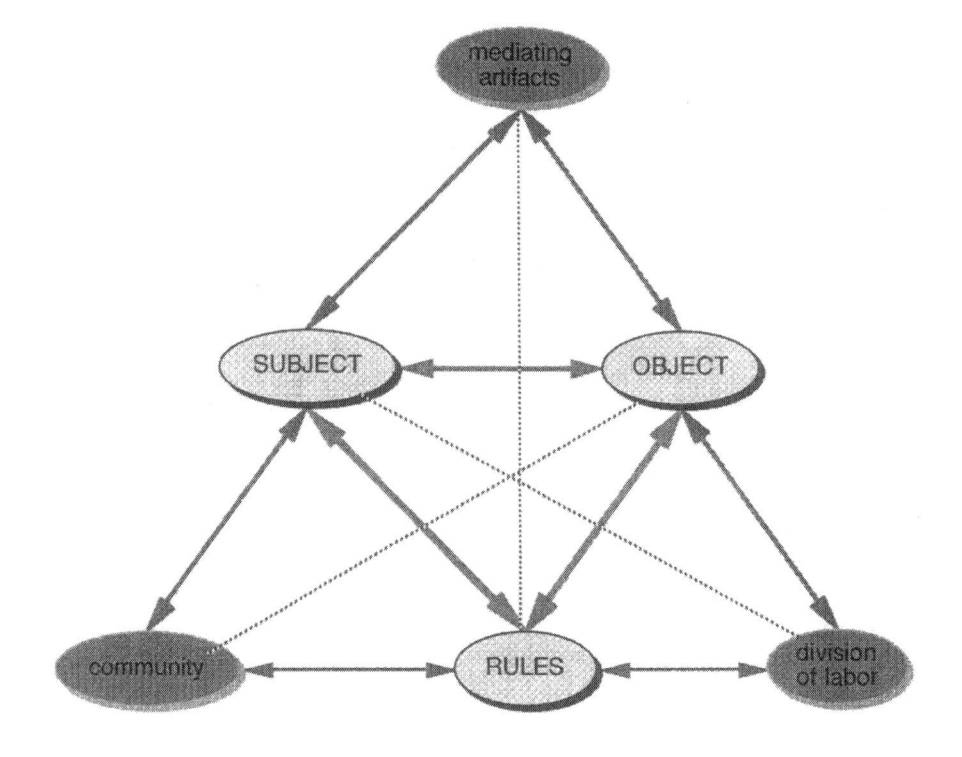

ENGESTROM'S ACTIVITY THEORY MODEL

Figure 8.4: Activity theory

There is no doubt that this model is a very effective way of connecting learning activities with their context of enactment. It is particularly useful for showing inherent contradictions and tensions between different influences in the setting. However, in the early versions of activity theory this and other models (e.g., Leontiev, 1981) paid little attention to the actual dynamics of the interaction and the processes of learning.

There are many ways in which the values of the components have to be written into the framework subsequent to an interpretation of those values by other means. For example, the crucial category "subject" can be "an individual or sub-group whose agency is chosen as the point of view in the analysis" (Wells, 2000, quoting from Engeström's web page). The original framework is therefore more a heuristic for description than an explanatory model. For example, when two learners are working together, side by side, do we focus on the activity of the individual learner or on the dyad as our unit of analysis? We make that decision on the basis of some reasoning (outside of the framework), and then we write in the appropriate specification on the subject node. Goals, purposes, attention, value, motive -- these are some of the crucial notions that have to be brought to bear on the framework, but that are not part of the framework itself. Similarly, perception, cognition and emotion are central ingredients of learning that need to be foregrounded in any account of pedagogical activity. The framework is thus an etic mold into which the interaction is cast (or one might say, it forms a backdrop in front of which activity is enacted), rather than en emic reconstruction of the interaction in situ.

However, in more recent process-based descriptions, this criticism may be less valid. In a recent study Engeström employs detailed analyses of speech, functional analyses of artifacts, and "expansive cycles" of learning actions and social cognition (1999; see also Thorne, 2000b). In these analyses participants' perspectives (particularly in terms of *motives* and *goals*) drive the interpretation, thus using the activity framework as a guideline rather than an interpretive straitjacket. The following diagram presents an 'ideal' example of an expansive learning cycle for collaborative teams in work or educational situations (Engeström, 1999, p. 384). Clearly, such a process model has much in common with current proposals for action research (e.g., McNiff, 1993), as well as the soft-systems methodology of Checkland (1981) illustrated below.

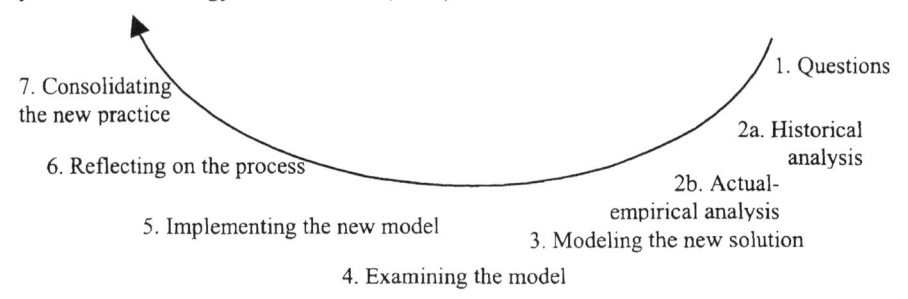

7. Consolidating the new practice
6. Reflecting on the process
5. Implementing the new model
4. Examining the model
1. Questions
2a. Historical analysis
2b. Actual-empirical analysis
3. Modeling the new solution

Figure 8.5: Cycles of activity research

A major task remains here, as it does in most other models attempting to bridge the macro/micro gap: how to integrate the moment-to-moment microgenetic processes with the social, cultural, historical and institutional patters and structures within which they are enacted. This is an area in which, since the pioneering work of Vygotsky, insufficient progress has been made. As we saw in Chapter 1, Vygotsky integrates description and explanation using Lewin's phenotype (outward reality) and genotype analysis (essence and origin) in combination and juxtaposition. For example, phenotypically (externally) a whale looks much like a fish. Genotypically, in terms of its biology and evolution, it looks much more like a cow. Vygotsky applied this dual analysis to the study of the development of speech (1978, p. 62). Speech thus has an external manifestation (phenotype) and a developmental (genotype) nature. Only by considering both perspectives is it possible to see, e.g., private speech on the one hand as similar to social speech, and on the other hand as an external manifestation of inner speech. Once this dual perspective is taken, it becomes possible to understand the role of private speech in the development of self-regulation.

Thorne (2000b) attempts a similar analysis for computer-mediated communication (CMC), that is, talk in chat rooms or via email. At the phenotypic level, he analyses online language use in terms of social dynamics, community building, and the distribution of rights and duties of talk. At the genotypic level, he examines how CMC relates to face-to-face conversation, and how it is influenced (and structured, transformed) by the technological artifacts (computers, chat rooms, software programs, computer labs, and so on) that mediate the communication – the verb *mediate* here including concepts such as *facilitate, constrain, control*, and so on (Thorne, 2000b).

SYSTEMS THEORY

Systems theory was developed independently by Alexander Bogdanov in the early years and decades of the Russian revolution, and by Ludwig von Bertalanffy in the 1940s in Germany and the US (Capra, 1996). Bogdanov's version remained unknown outside the Soviet Union, largely because it was strongly attacked and even vilified by Lenin in his struggle for power (Bakhurst, 1991).

Systems theory focuses on contextual thinking and process thinking, much along the lines we have described above. von Bertalanffy focused on self-regulating (homeostatic) systems and formulated a new theory of *open systems* (1968).

During the same period, under the influence of the new communication technologies and theories, Norbert Wiener attempted to unify general systems theory with communication theory, and coined the term *cybernetics* (1948).

During the 1970s, information processing (a cognitive science offshoot of communication theory) eclipsed cybernetics (and to a certain extent systems theory as a whole) in terms of the focal attention of psychologists and educational researchers. Information processing is incompatible with an ecological worldview (and hence with systems theory and cybernetics) in a number of respects (Capra, 1996; Damasio, 1999):

1. Ecology does not treat information as discrete, fixed items;
2. Information is not passively received, but constructed by the living organism through interaction in the environment;
3. Information, being created interactively, is always colored by emotion;
4. Mind and body form one inseparable unity, so that locating information in the brain is inadequate;
5. Human activity and the information constructed by it is morally purposeful.[4]
6. Information theory (though information *processing* to a lesser extent) assumes a linear causality.

Thus, information theory for a time obscured the relevance of systems theory and cybernetics for psychology, education, and linguistics (among other fields).

---

[4] The fact that this does not seem to apply to human-made institutions such as some corporations and some governments is of course deeply troubling to those who hold an ecological world view.

Meanwhile, however, new insights in physics, mathematics and biology had begun to push the boundaries of Newtonian science, and studies of fractals, dissipative structures, nonlinear equations, and so on, gradually led to the emergence of the sciences of chaos and complexity. Names such as Poincaré, Thom, Mandelbrot, Edward Lorenz and Prigogine are associated with the development of chaos/complexity, some of the characteristics of which we described above.

With the advent of chaos/complexity science in the human or social sciences (Cilliers, 1998) systems theory and systems thinking have once again emerged as an approach to social-scientific research that escapes the straitjacket of linear causality as a fundamental doxa.

Systems theory, being process-oriented and context-based, offers specific suggestions on how to research complex processes such as language learning in ecological ways. A procedure worth looking at in this respect was developed by systems theorist Peter Checkland (1981), and has been recommended for ecological research by Allen and Hoekstra (1992). This procedure is considerably more detailed and practical than other ecological models, contains specific steps for action, and is therefore a good candidate for adapting to educational research. Educational settings are, in the terminology of ecology, 'soft systems', that is, they are not determined by linear causal laws. Rather, they are 'messy,' in that processes are controlled by a number of different, often competing or conflicting agents and events. However, one must assume that there are enough constants and discernible tendencies in the setting to allow for formal research to be possible.

The original procedure contains eight steps that are interdependent, even though they are not necessarily implemented in a strict sequence. These steps alternate between broadening and narrowing perspectives, or between global, macroscopic perspectives and detailed, microscopic perspectives. They also alternate between concrete analysis and abstract conceptualization, and between non-interventive research and intervention in the form of action research. It is clear that such an approach to research requires a great deal of time and a clear focus, not to mention patience in gradually putting the many pieces of the puzzle together.

As Checkland himself recommends, it is not essential in a soft-systems research model to see progress through the eight steps as a rigidly sequential procedure. We are not dealing in our case simply with a management system (such as a multinational corporation), or an ecological task such as an oil spill cleanup or forest management, but with education, specifically language education, and the nature of the inquiry is such that basic questions need to be addressed, including what we mean by language (and how it relates to context), what our basic learning theory is, and what kinds of goals and expectations we have for the learners in our schools. In other words, a clear epistemological basis, as well as a scrupulous examination of moral values and goals, are part of the investigation, which therefore cannot be construed as merely technical or engineering work.

A SOFT SYSTEMS APPROACH TO ECOLOGICAL RESEARCH

I EXPLORATORYSTRAND
  Narrowing the focus

Rich description

Definitions (CATWOE*)

II MODELING STRAND
Building a model

Reality check

III INTERVENTION STRAND
Advisable changes

Action research
(intervention)

IV EVALUATION STRAND

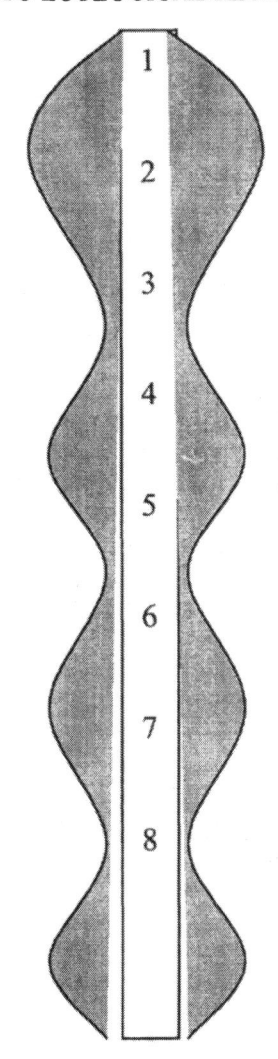

* DEFINITIONS (examples might include technology use in education, the accountability movement in US schools, the effects of privatization, and many other focal areas. The six areas in the acronym form part of the *root definition* that characterizes the problem situation):

C   *Client/Beneficiary/Victim*: teachers, students, parents, for whom the change 'works' or does not work.

A   *Actors*: teachers and students; resource persons, administrators who move and innovate; technicians; coordinators; trainers; corporations; sales people; financial/budget officers; local, state, federal authorities and legislators.

NOTE: One might attempt to scale these people according to their scope of influence.

T   *Transformations*: how does the change (e.g. the influx of technology, the increased use of high-stakes tests) affect the clients' work and lives?

Money, time, amount of work, knowledge required, motivation, results, etc.

W   *Worldview*: educational vision, views of technology, notions of standards and accountability, lifelong learning, etc.

O   *Ownership*: who controls the changes? Who/what determines quality of services, resources, curriculum? What are the real/perceived power structures?

E   *Environment*: time/space considerations. What moves things or slows them down? E.g., in technology: level of expertise, availability of up-to-date machinery, software; budgets, replacement cycle; in standards-based reform: mechanisms of accountability, tests and consequences, curriculum change. Here we also look at constraints and resources in the environment

(Based on Checkland, 1981, and Allen & Hoekstra, 1992)

Figure 8.6: Checkland's Soft Systems model

I will illustrate Checkland's Soft-Systems Methodology (SSM) by looking at one of the few applications of this approach to educational problematics, Magnuson's (2003) investigation of the effects of accountability policies on the education of English Language Learners (ELL), especially those with limited formal schooling in their home countries (LFS-ELL) in the State of Minnesota. In recent years the US federal government has increasingly sought to establish high standards and mechanisms to hold schools accountable for the achievement of those high standards (including mandatory improvement targets and the threat of withholding funding and other penalties for inadequate performance). Not surprisingly, the way that achievement of standards and performance targets is established is by means of an ever-increasing number of high-stakes tests across the school system.

The current version of the Elementary and Secondary Education Act under the George W. Bush administration is called "No Child Left Behind," and it expressly purports to provide equal educational opportunities for all socio-economic and ethnic groups, including ELL. Magnuson sets out to examine how the three-part system of standards – accountability – testing affects the educational opportunities of the LFS-ELL population in Minnesota.

Magnuson conducts surveys and interviews with policy makers (Directors, State Legislators) nationwide and in Minnesota, canvassing their views on the likelihood that the new policies will benefit the LFS-ELL population less, equally, or more than the mainstream student population. In addition, he conducts in-depth sessions with two focus groups of teachers from two schools in the Twin Cities area, and it is with these focus groups that he applies a systems methodology. The key to a systems approach is extensive engagement with the people in the system (or organization, in this case the school system), and in successive focus group sessions Magnuson draws visual representations of the issues that are being discussed, on the basis of transcriptions of the discussions. These representations are shared and discussed (also across the focus groups) and form the basis for the next round of discussions. In this way it is possible to arrive at a *root definition* of the problem area, which for the teachers turns out to be (in abbreviated form): *Teachers want LFS-ELL, through meeting state requirements of the accountability system, to receive a diploma.* A simple enough statement if taken at face value, yet it encapsulates the many tensions and contradictions in the system and the current changes that are being implemented. For example, there are two types of tests in the new system: those that aim for *individual accountability* (i.e., individual scores for students that may determine their graduation chances) and those that address *system accountability* (i.e., those that determine the success rate of the school as a whole, and that have consequences for funding, but not for individual students). The individual-accountability tests are important in view of the root definition given by the teachers, yet the system-accountability tests are most important for the school. The students, however, may not take the latter tests seriously since there are no personal consequences attached to the scores. The teachers are caught between the conflicting demands of the two kinds of accountability.

Numerous other conflicting forces, demands and obstacles emerge from this research, but the overall conclusion is that none of the stakeholders involved actually believe that the new rigorous standards and tests will benefit the LFS-ELL (or ELL in general) equally, let alone more (which would be necessary if they were to catch up) than the mainstream students.

Research such as this could be expanded to include participatory work with other constituencies such as administrators, politicians, parents and students, though this would clearly be a huge undertaking. It would, however, allow for other *root definitions* of stakeholder groups to emerge, and the comparisons between the various root definitions might be very revealing and interesting. A final point worth noting here is that systems theory is change-oriented, that is, if it locates areas where improvements are needed, then the researcher is supposed to work together with the participants to implement change. In this particular case, however, it turned out that none of the participants felt they had any power whatsoever to effect meaningful change (this applied even to the lawmakers, many of whom had voted against the legislation in the first place).

The above visual representation of Checkland's framework (adapted from Allen & Hoekstra, 1992, p. 310), and its subsequent illustration in an educational context (Magnuson, 2003), can be compared to Engeström's application of activity theory, in fact, all three models discussed in this chapter, Bronfenbrenner's nested ecosystems and the PPCT framework, Engeström's activity theory, and Checkland's soft systems approach are frameworks for contextualized, case-based, and interventionist action research, very much in the spirit of much of Vygotsky's and all of Lewin's work.

What all such models do is carefully to prepare for action (intervention) by analyzing the situation in depth before jumping in and making changes. It should be noted that all models of ecological research invest a great deal of effort in understanding the context, describing and modeling that context, and only then propose specific interventions, usually in tentative ways first, and only gradually in more fundamental and committed ways. It is clear that any 'scaling up' or application of the findings of such research has little to do with generalization, but everything with *particularization*, that is, the recontextualization and adaptation of findings in other settings.

CONCLUSION

In this chapter I have looked at some of the implications for research and research methods of an ecological approach. Of course, since ecological research is by definition contextual or situated, experimental laboratory research is not an option. This means that notions such as *proof* and *generalizability* may not carry the same weight as they do in traditional research modeled on the physical sciences. I contrast such exact terms (usually backed up by numerical indicators) with terms like truth, plausibility, understanding and interpretation, which are 'softer' terms that are less easily boxed in by operational formulas. However, definability does not equal importance.

After briefly discussing controversial, but sometimes taken for granted notions such as proof, truth, generalizability, and micro versus macro research, I introduce chaos/complexity theory, signaling it as a highly promising inspiration for language learning research in the future, even though to date we have not been able to apply it fully to language learning or education in general (though see Larsen-Freeman, 1997; 2002).

Ecological research is contextualized, and contextualized research does not have a very strong track record in education (particularly because of a predilection for controlled experimental methods). In this chapter I describe and review three contextual approaches to educational research that can be called ecological in nature.

First, I describe Bronfenbrenner's bio-ecological model. This consists of a principled focus on Process, Person, Context and Time. Bronfenbrenner has conceptualized the notion of context as consisting of several interrelated nested ecosystems: microsysem, mesosystem, macrosystem and exosystem. By tracing the connections between all these systems a rich perspective of influences and practices can be obtained.

The second model is that of activity theory. Early views can be interpreted as rather static and etic representations of context, e.g., in Leontiev's original description of operations, actions and activity, but in later developments and applications, particularly in recent work of Engeström and associates (1999), and also in Thorne's investigation of computer-mediated communication (2000b), it can also generate dynamic and emic descriptions of activity in specific contexts.

The third model, Checkland's soft systems methodology, derives from practical research in organizations and institutions. Based on systems theory, this methodology aims to characterize what is happening in a particular organization or context of work, and then proposes changes leading to more effective functioning.

This model distinguishes itself by promoting the active participation of the members of the system being studied.

I argue that all three models (and there are others) share a number of ecological features, such as a focus on process, a rich view of context, and a goal of bringing about improvements in the functioning of the entities (organizations, schools, classrooms, etc.) under investigation.

EPILOGUE FOR LANGUAGE TEACHERS

Having reached the end of the book – together with those long-suffering readers who have made it this far – I feel it may be beneficial to take an overall look at the various claims and proposals I have made in the preceding chapters, and pull together some ways in which the ideas of ecological, semiotic, and educational linguistics can be of practical value to the language teacher and the language learner.

I started out the book by talking about educational linguistics, and it is appropriate to close with another look at it, from the vantage point of the intervening chapters. I began by arguing for a close connection between language and education, at the theoretical level between linguistics and educational theory, and at the practical level between language teaching and pedagogy. I argued that these close connections do not currently exist but that they should, because all education – indeed all learning, as Halliday (1993) asserts – is permeated by language. What I have been trying to promote here is an ecological educational linguistics.

The study of language use and language learning and their role in educational success are important whether one takes an ecological or sociocultural perspective or not (for a range of perspectives, see Trappes-Lomax & Ferguson, 2002). However, I suggest that the ecological and sociocultural perspectives on various aspects of language in education taken in this book can be of particular benefit for current and future teachers, especially language teachers of course, but not only language teachers. Below, I will point to some of these benefits using some of the main concepts that recur throughout the book.

A first set of key concepts is *action/perception, interaction, relation, environment*. Just observe any natural object in the environment, whether it is a rock, a stream, a tree, a bug, a bird or anything else. How does this object relate to the environment? Does it perceive and act (ecologically speaking, if it perceives, it acts, and if it acts, it perceives)? Translating this set of concepts in classroom terms, we can draw a number of inferences that affect the ways in which we think about teaching and learning. The first is that perception is tied to action.

The importance of perception in language learning (after a long period of neglect) is increasingly recognized. It is prominent in the ideas of noticing, attention, and focusing (e.g., focusing on form, see Long, 1996). The ecological perspective adds the role of direct perception, that is, the immediate noticing of certain characteristics of speech (including gestures, tone of voice, and so on), as first-level affordance. Assessment of relevance in interactional contexts is often direct and immediate, not requiring prior cognitive inferencing or processing. Social and cognitive processes in fact usually kick in *after* initial relevance is established, and if there are no initial affordances it may actually be difficult to establish meaning from scratch. Affordances are relationships, they signal connections between learner and environment, and they are the basis for further action, interaction and cognition.

For the classroom this means that language must be richly contextualized and semiotically interconnected with all available meaning making systems, and synchronized with learners' activity patterns. The unit of learning is therefore the learner in action in a learnable environment, appropriating meaning (and linguistic forms) in action, and jointly with others building structures of effective functioning. Learners must be engaged, so that the learning emanates from them, rather than being delivered to them.

The most natural curriculum from an ecological perspective is a project-based one. Carefully structured projects are clear about goals and procedures, but at the same time allow for learners' interests and creativity to develop. They also allow for learners to work together and learn from one another. However, there are situations in which project-based work might appear difficult if not impossible to realize. For example, flexible seating arrangements (tables in circles, work stations, etc.) maybe be impossible in large classes where desks may be attached to the floor. High stakes tests may put pressure on classroom time to be spent on drills and test practice. In foreign language settings resources on which student can draw for their projects may be less than abundant. In addition, when all students speak the same native language, how can authentic foreign language work be promoted? All these questions and constraints have been noted by many teachers, and they need serious consideration, or else the ecological perspective runs the risk of being restricted to elite second language and academic language contexts (Holliday, 1994; Coleman, 1996; Canagaraja, 1999).

In spite of the difficulties noted, it should be possible to apply ecological ideas in any work context. It must be reiterated that ecology is not some method or theory, but a world view and a particular way of working. The connections between perception, action and context can be kept in mind in any context, and the importance of engagement and attunement can similarly always be recognized.

Even cramped classes with large numbers of students can become environments for linguistic exploration through language play, as Sullivan (2000) shows. Similarly, even disconnected sentences constructed for grammar practice can become jumping off points for interesting exchanges that explore learner initiative (Butzkamm, 1980; van Lier, 1988; Holliday, 1994). Mechanical tasks from commercial computer programs can lead to exploratory learning when learners work together side by side, sharing a computer screen (Wegerif & Scrimshaw, 1997). The use of the first language does not have to be a negative influence; in fact it can mediate second-language use in important ways (Brooks, Donato & McGlone, 1997).

Without ignoring or wishing away the very real and often debilitating constraints that adhere in many institutional settings, a teacher who keeps a clear view of the basic ecological principles can ignite sparks of interest that in turn can set in motion perceptual, social and cognitive processes that instigate learning. Having observed countless classes and videos of classes, the difference between an engaged classroom community, and one that is just going through passive motions of receiving instruction, is startling. Of course, it is difficult to quantify in terms of percentage scores or instructional objects, but it is abundantly visible (and thus *documentable*, in ethnographic terms, and in the indicators suggested in

Bronfenbrenner, 1993, as discussed above) in terms of perceptual and postural orientation and intensity, interpersonal engagement, and in the initiative employed by the learners (van Lier, 1988).

This first set of concerns can be put together under the umbrella of *action*, the idea of the learner as an agent of his or her own learning, and all the consequences that flow from taking such a view. The other side of the coin are the kinds of *assistance* that can be provided for the active learner. In earlier philosophies of language learning it has been assumed that language *use* must be sharply distinguished from language *learning*. This has been particularly true of audiolingual (i.e., behavioristic) and cognitive approaches to language learning (skill-getting before skill-using, Rivers & Temperly, 1978)[5], but it is even true of many current practices, including content-based or task-based learning, and many approaches to academic language development. From an ecological perspective, however, the distinction must be rejected forcefully.

Let me briefly use some ecological ideas to tease apart the false use-learning dichotomy. First, the skill-getting and skill-using distinction should be seen as dynamic interplay, not an either-or choice. Second, the ecological perspective regards teaching as *assisted use*. Third, learning is *situated*, that is, it occurs in the context of meaningful activity. Language practice of the skill-getting kind is part of a bigger picture of language learning: in order to achieve more effective functioning in some aspect of language, learners may need to engage in practice. For example, if learners need to record an introduction to a computer-based presentation they are making, they may want to practice their delivery a number of times to get it right. The crucial idea here is that practice occurs in the context of meaningful purposes and goals; it has a specific reason. Practice that occurs outside such a specific motivation, such as grammatical practice just in order to follow a book or test program, may end up as the sort of inert knowledge that Whitehead (1929) decried almost a century ago.

Language is not a system of communication that occurs in a vacuum. On the contrary, it is an integral part of many connected meaning-making systems, in other words, it's part of semiotics. In Chapter 2 I presented a diagram of concentric circles that shows how important gestures, intonation, social and cultural knowledge of various kinds, and so on, are. Meaning-making processes draw on all those systems and clues, in interpretive processes of complex kinds. As I suggested above, the first level of interpretation is often through affordances, and these also carry the emotional aspects of communicative action that are just as important as the cognitive aspects.

An ecological approach sees the learner as a whole person, not a grammar production unit. This involves having meaningful things to do and say, being taken seriously, being given responsibility, and being encouraged to tackle challenging projects, to think critically, and to take control of one's own learning. The teacher provides assistance, but only just enough and just in time (in the form of

---

[5] To give due justice to Rivers and Temperly, they argue that a key issue is how to relate skill-getting and skill-using in meaningful ways. The points they raise are still very relevant to a consideration of the role of practice in any meaning-based approach.

pedagogical scaffolding), taking the learner's developing skills and interests as the true driving force of the curriculum.

In sum, then, ecology is presented here as a way of thinking about teaching and learning that should be applicable in all situations, and as a way of working that takes the engaged and active learner as a starting point. It is not a finished system or theory, nor is it a method of teaching. It is just a way of thinking about teaching and learning in all its complexity, a way of looking at language as a tool of many uses, and as a key component of all human meaning-making activity. It envisions classrooms as busy workshops with lots of activity and learners who have things they want to accomplish, and who, with the help of teachers, fellow learners, and other sources of assistance, find the tools they need to achieve their goals.

REFERENCES

Abrams, D. (1996). The mechanical and the organic: Epistemological consequences of the Gaia hypothesis. In P. Bunyard (Ed.), *Gaia in action: Science of the living earth* (pp. 234-247). Edinburgh: Floris Books.
Agar, M. (1994). *Language shock: Understanding the culture of conversation.* New York: William Morrow.
Alexander, N. (2002). Linguistic rights, language planning and democracy in post-apartheid South Africa. In S. Baker (Ed.), *Language policy: Lessons from global models* (pp. 116-129). Monterey, CA: Monterey Institute of International Studies.
Allen, T.F.H. & Hoekstra, T.W. (1992). *Toward a unified ecology.* New York: Columbia University Press.
Anderson, B. (1991). *Imagined communities* (Second Edition). London: Verso.
Apel, K-O. (1981). *Charles S. Peirce: From pragmatism to pragmaticism.* Amherst, MA: University of Massachusetts Press.
Argyle, M. (1991). *Cooperation.* London: Routledge.
Arndt, H. & Janney, R. W. (1983). The duck-rabbit phenomenon: Notes on the disambiguation of ambiguous utterances. In W. Enninger & L. M. Haynes (Eds.), *Studies in language ecology* (pp. 94-115). Wiesbaden: Franz Steiner Verlag.
Arnold, J. (Ed.). (1999). *Affect in language learning.* Cambridge: Cambridge University Press
Auer, P. (Ed.). (1998). *Code-switching in conversation: Language, interaction and identity.* New York: Routledge.
Auyang, S. A. (2000). *Mind in everyday life and cognitive science.* Cambridge, MA: MIT.
Bailey, K. M. & Nunan, D. (Eds.).(1996). *Voices from the language classroom.* Cambridge: Cambridge University Press.
Bakhtin, M. (1981). *The dialogical imagination.* Austin: University of Texas Press.
Bakhurst, D. (1991). *Consciousness and revolution in Soviet philosophy.* Cambridge: Cambridge University Press.
Bakhurst, D. & Sypnowich, C. (Eds.). (1995). *The social self.* London: Sage Publications.
Barker, R. (1978). *Ecological psychology.* Stanford, CA: Stanford University Press.
Bates, E. Elman, J., Johnson, M., Karmiloff-Smith, A., Parisi, D., & Plunkett, K. (1998). Innateness and emergentism. In W. Bechtel and G. Graham (Eds.), *A Companion to Cognitive Science.* Oxford: Basil Blackwell. Available online at http://crl.ucsd.edu/~elman/.
Bates, E. & Goodman, J. C. (1999). On the emergence of grammar from the lexicon. In B. MacWhinney (Ed.), *The emergence of language* (pp. 29-80). Mahwah, NJ: Erlbaum.
Bateson, G. (1936). *Naven.* London: Wildwood House.
Bateson, G. (1973). *Steps to an ecology of mind.* London: Granada.
Bateson, G. (1979). *Mind and nature: A necessary unity.* London: Fontana.
Beaugrande, R. de (1991). *Linguistic theory: The discourse of fundamental works.* London: Longman.
Bernstein, B. (2000). *Pedagogy, symbolic control and identity: Theory, research, critique* (revised edition). Lanham, MD: Rowman & Littlefield.
Bhabha, H. K. (1992). Post-colonial authority and post-modern guilt. In L. Grossberg, P. Nelson & P. Treichler (Eds.), *Cultural studies.* London: Routledge.
Bhaskar, R. (1989). *Reclaiming reality: A critical introduction to contemporary philosophy.* London: Verso.

Birk, D. (1972). You never speak a dead language. An informal account of the origins and some applications of functional theory. In G. Thornton, D. Birk, & R. A. Hudson (Eds.), *Language at work* (pp. 25-56). London: Longman for The Schools Council.

Bloomfield, L. (1933). *Language*. Chicago: University of Chicago Press.

Bourdieu, P. (1977). *Outline of a theory of practice*. Cambridge: Cambridge University Press.

Bourdieu, P. (1984). *Distinction: A social critique of the judgment of taste*. Cambridge: Cambridge University Press.

Bourdieu, P. (1988). *Homo Academicus*. Stanford, CA: Stanford University Press.

Bourdieu, P. (1991). *Language and symbolic power*. Cambridge, MA: Harvard University Press.

Bourdieu, P. & Wacquant, L. (1992). *An invitation to reflexive sociology*. Chicago: University of Chicago Press.

Bowerman, M. & Levinson, S. C. (Eds.). (2001). *Language acquisition and conceptual development*. Cambridge: Cambridge University Press.

Bowers, C. A. (1993). *Critical essays on education, modernity, and the recovery of the ecological imperative*. New York: Teachers College Press.

Bowers, C. A. (2000). *Let them eat data: How computers affect education, cultural diversity, and the prospects of ecological sustainability*. Athens, GA: University of Georgia Press.

Bowers, C.A. & Flinders, D.J. (1990). *Responsive teaching: An ecological approach to classroom patterns of language, culture, and thought*. New York: Teachers College Press.

Bowers, R. (1990). Mountains are not cones: What can we learn from chaos? In *Georgetown University Round Table on Languages and Linguistics 1990* (pp. 123-135). Washington, DC: Georgetown University Press.

Bransford, J. D., Sherwood, R. D., Hasselbring, T. S., Kinzer, C. K., & Williams, S. M. (1990). Anchored instruction: Why we need it and how technology can help. In D. Nix & R. Spiro (Eds.), *Cognition, education, and multimedia: Exploring ideas in high technology* (pp. 115-141). Hillsdale, NJ: Erlbaum.

Bråten, S. (1992). The virtual other in infants' minds and social feelings. In A. H. Wold (Ed.), *The dialogical alternative: Towards a theory of language and mind* (pp. 77-97). Oslo: Scandinavian University Press (Distr. OUP).

Bråten, S. (Ed.). (1998). *Intersubjective communication and emotion in early ontogeny*. Cambridge: Cambridge University Press.

Brent, J. (1993). *Charles Sanders Peirce: A life*. Bloomington, IN: Indiana University Press.

Broeder, P. & Extra, G. (1997). *Immigrant minority languages in primary and secondary education. A comparative study of six European Union countries*. Tilburg, NL: Research Group on Language and Minorities, University.

Bronfenbrenner, U. (1979). *The ecology of human development*. Cambridge, MA: Harvard University Press.

Bronfenbrenner, U. (1993). The ecology of cognitive development: Research models and fugitive findings. In Wozniak, R. H. & Fischer, K. W. (Eds.), *Development in context: Acting and thinking in specific environments* (pp. 3-44). Hillsdale, NJ: Erlbaum.

Bronfenbrenner, U. & Ceci, S. J. (1994). Nature-nurture reconceptualized in developmental perspective: A bioecological model. *Psychological Review*, 101, 568-586.

Brooks, F.B., Donato, R. & McGlone, J. V. (1997). When are they going to say "it" right? Understanding learner talk during pair-work activity. *Foreign Language Annals, 30*, 524-541.

Brown, A.L. (1992). Design experiments: Theoretical and methodological challenges in creating complex interventions in classroom settings. *Journal of the Learning Sciences, 2*, 141-178.

Brown, R. (1973). *A first language: The early stages*. Cambridge, MA: Harvard University Press.

Brumfit, C. (1997). The teacher as educational linguist. In L. van Lier & D. Corson (Eds.), *Encyclopedia of Language and Education, Volume 6: Knowledge about language* (pp. 163-172). Dordrecht: Kluwer Academic.

Bruner, J. (1983). *Child's talk*. New York: Norton.

Bruner, J. (1986). *Actual minds, possible worlds*. Cambridge, MA: Harvard University Press.

Bruner, J.S. & Sherwood, V. (1975). Peekaboo and the learning of rule structures. In J.S. Bruner, A. Jolly & K. Sylva (Eds.), *Play: Its role in development and evolution* (pp. 277-85). Harmondsworth: Penguin Books.

Brunswik, E. (1943). Organismic achievement and environmental probability. *The Psychological Review, 50*, 255-272.

Butler, S. (1872/1967). *Erewhon*. New York: Airmont Publishing.
Butterworth, G. (1999). A developmental-ecological perspective on Strawson's "The Self". In Gallagher, S. & Shear, J. (Eds.), *Models of the self* (pp. 203-11). Thorverton, UK: Imprint Academic.
Butzkamm, W. (1980). Verbal play and pattern practice. In Felix, S. (Ed.) *Second language development: Trends and issues* (pp. 233-248). Tübingen: Günther Narr.
Büchler, J. (1955). *Philosophical writings of Peirce*. New York: Dover Books.
Byram, M. (1997). *Teaching and assessing intercultural communicative competence*. Clevedon, UK: Multilingual Matters.
Canagarajah, A. S. (1999). *Resisting linguistic imperialism in English teaching*. Oxford: Oxford University Press.
Canagarajah, A. S. (2001). Critical ethnography of a Sri Lankan classroom: Ambiguities in student opposition to reproduction through ESOL. In C. N. Candlin & N. Mercer (Eds.), *English language teaching in its social context* (pp. 208-226). London: Routledge.
Capra, F. (1996). *The web of life: A new scientific understanding of living systems*. New York: Anchor Books.
Cazden, C. B. (1992). *Whole language plus: Essays on literacy in the United States and New Zealand*. New York: Teachers College.
Checkland, P. (1981). *Systems thinking, systems practice*. New York: Wiley.
Chomsky, N. (1959). Review of B. F. Skinner: Verbal behavior. *Language, 35*, 26-58.
Chomsky, N. (1986). *Knowledge of Language*. Cambridge, MA: MIT.
Chomsky, N. (2000). *New horizons in the study of language and mind*. Cambridge: Cambridge University Press.
Cilliers, P. (1998). *Complexity and postmodernism: Understanding complex systems*. London: Routledge.
Clandinin, D. J. & Connolly, F. M. (1995). *Teachers' professional knowledge landscapes*. New York: Teachers College Press.
Clark, H. (1996). *Using language*. Cambridge: Cambridge University Press.
Clay, M.M. & Cazden, C.B. (1992). A Vygotskyan interpretation of reading recovery. In C. B. Cazden, *Whole language plus: Essays on literacy in the United States and New Zealand* (pp. 114-35). New York: Teachers College.
Clifford, J. (1986). Introduction: Partial truths. In J. Clifford & G. E. Marcus, *Writing culture: The poetics and politics of ethnography* (pp. 1-26). Berkeley, CA: University of California Press.
Clifford, J. & Marcus, G.E. (1986). *Writing culture: The poetics and politics of ethnography*. Berkeley, CA: University of California Press.
Cobley, P. (2001). *The Routledge companion to semiotics and linguistics*. London: Routledge.
Colapietro, V. M. (1989). *Peirce's approach to the self: A semiotic perspective on human subjectivity*. Albany, NY: State University of New York Press.
Cole, M. (1995). Socio-cultural-historical psychology: Some general remarks and a proposal for a new kind of cultural-genetic methodology. In J. V. Wertsch, P. Del Rio, & A. Alvarez (Eds.), *Sociocultural studies of mind* (pp. 187-214). Cambridge: Cambridge University Press.
Cole, M. (1996). *Cultural psychology: A once and future discipline*. Cambridge, MA: Harvard University Press.
Cole, M. (1999). Ecological validity. In R. A. Wilson & F. C. Keil (Eds.), *The MIT encyclopedia of the cognitive sciences* (pp. 257-259). Cambridge, MA: MIT.
Cole, M., Hood, L. & McDermott, R. (1997). Concepts of ecological validity: Their differing implications for comparative cognitive research. In M. Cole, Y. Engeström, & O. Vasquez (Eds.), *Mind, culture and activity* (pp. 49-56). Cambridge: Cambridge University Press.
Coleman, H. (1996). *Society and the language classroom*. Cambridge: Cambridge University Press.
Collins, A. (1992). Towards a design science of education. In E. Scanlon & T. O'Shea (Eds.), *New directions in educational technology*. New York: Springer Verlag.
Cook, V. J. (2002). Language teaching methodology and the L2 user perspective. In V. J. Cook (Ed.), *Portraits of the L2 user* (pp. 327-343). Clevedon, UK: Multilingual Matters.
Corder, S. P. (1967). The significance of learners' errors. *International Review of Applied Linguistics, 5*, 161-9.
Coupland, N. & Jaworski, A. (1997). *Sociolinguistics: A reader*. New York: St. Martin's Press.
Crawford, J. (1991). *Bilingual education: History, politics, theory and practice* (second edition). Los Angeles, CA: Bilingual Educational Services.
Crichton, M. (1991). *Jurassic park*. New York, NY: Knopf.

REFERENCES

Crook, C. (1994). *Computers and the collaborative experience of learning.* London: Routledge.
Cuban, L. (1993). *How teachers taught: Constancy and change in American classrooms, 1890-1990.* New York: Teachers College Press.
Cuban, L. (2001). *Oversold and underused: Computers in the classroom.* Cambridge, MA: Harvard University Press.
Dakin, J. (1974). *The language laboratory and language teaching.* London: Longman.
Damasio, A. (1999). *The feeling of what happens: Body and emotion in the making of consciousness.* New York: Harcourt Brace.
Damasio, A. (2003). *Looking for Spinoza: Joy, sorrow and the feeling brain.* Orlando, FL: Harcourt.
Davidson, D. (1986). A nice derangement of epitaphs. In E. Lepore (Ed.), *Truth and interpretation: Perspectives on the philosophy of Donald Davidson* (pp. 433-446). Oxford: Basil Blackwell.
Deci, E. & Flaste, R. (1995). *Why we do what we do: The dynamics of personal autonomy.* New York: Putnam's Sons.
Deely, J. (1990). *Basics of semiotics.* Bloomington: Indiana University Press.
Dennett, D. (1991). *Consciousness explained.* Boston: Little, Brown and Company.
Dewey, J. (1904). The relation of theory to practice in education. *Third Yearbook*, Part 1 (pp. 9-30). Bloomington, IL: National Society for the Study of Education.
Dewey, J. (1938). *Experience and education.* London: Collier Books.
Dittmar, N. (Ed.). (1992). Grammaticalization in second language acquisition. *Studies in Second Language Acquisition, 14*, 3 (Thematic Issue).
Donato, R. (1994). Collective scaffolding. In J. P. Lantolf and G. Appel. (Eds.), *Vygotskyan approaches to second language research* (pp. 33-56). Norwood, NJ: Ablex.
Dornyei, Z. (2001). Motivation and second language acquisition. In Z. Dornyei and R. Schmidt (Eds.), *Motivation and second language acquisition.* Honolulu: University of Hawaii Press, Second Language Teaching and Curriculum Center.
Drew, P. & Heritage, J. (Eds.). (1992). *Talk at work: Interaction in institutional settings.* Cambridge: Cambridge University Press.
Dunn, W.E. & Lantolf, J. P. (1998). Vygotsky's Zone of Proximal Development and Krashen's $i + 1$: Incommensurable constructs, incommensurable theories. *Language Learning*, 48, 3, 411- 422.
Duranti, A. & Goodwin, C. (Eds.). (1992). *Rethinking context: Language as an interactive phenomenon.* Cambridge: Cambridge University Press.
Durkheim, E. (1964[1895]). *The rules of sociological method.* London: Collier-Macmillan.
Eco, U. (2000). *Kant and the platypus: Essays on language and cognition.* New York: Harcourt Brace.
Edge, J. (1993). The dance of Shiva and the linguistics of relativity. *Applied Linguistics*, 14, 43-55.
Edwards, D. (1997). *Discourse and cognition.* London: Sage.
Elliott, G. (many editions) *Middlemarch.* London: Penguin Classics. (Orig. publ. 1871-2).
Ellis, R. (1994). *The study of second language acquisition.* Oxford: Oxford University Press.
Ellis, R. (2003). *Task-Based Language Learning and Teaching.* Oxford: Oxford University Press.
Elman, J., Bates, E.A., Johnson, M. H., Karmiloff-Smith, A., Parisi, D. & Plunkett, K. (1996). *Rethinking Innatism: A connectionist perspective on development.* Cambridge, MA: MIT.
Engeström, Y. (1999). Innovative learning in work teams: Analyzing cycles of knowledge creation in practice. In Engeström, Y., Miettinen, R. & Punamäki, R-L (Eds.), *Perspectives on activity theory* (377-404). Cambridge: Cambridge University Press.
Engeström, Y., Miettinen, R. & Punamäki, R-L (Eds.). (1999). *Perspectives on activity theory.* Cambridge: Cambridge University Press.
Feyerabend, P. (1975). *Against method: Outline of an anarchistic theory of knowledge.* London: Verso.
Fill, A. & Mühlhäusler, P. (Eds.). (2001). *The ecolinguistics reader: Language, ecology and environment.* London: Continuum.
Firth, A. & Wagner, J. (1997). On discourse, communication and (some) fundamental concepts in SLA research. *Modern Language Journal, 81,* 285-300.
Flynn, P. J. (1991). *The ethnomethodological movement: Sociosemiotic interpretations.* Berlin: Mouton de Gruyter.
Fodor, J. (1998). *Concepts: Where cognitive science went wrong.* Oxford: Clarendon Press.
Forrester, M. (1999). Conversation and instruction within apprenticeship: Affordances for learning. In Ainley, P. & Rainbird, H. (Eds.), *Apprenticeship: Towards a new paradigm of learning* (pp. 86-97). London: Kogan Page.
Foucault, M. (1977). *Discipline and punish: The birth of the prison.* New York: Pantheon.

REFERENCES 229

Freire, P. (1972). *Pedagogy of the oppressed*. New York: Herder and Herder.
Gallagher, S. & Shear, J. (Eds.) (1999). *Models of the self*. Thorverton, UK: Imprint Academic.
Gardner, H. (1985). *The mind's new science*. New York: Basic Books.
Gardner, H. (1993). *Multiple intelligences: The theory into practice*. New York: Basic Books.
Garfinkel, H. & Sacks, H. (1970). On formal structures of practical actions. In J. C. McKinney & E. A. Tiryakian (Eds.), *Theoretical sociology* (pp. 338-366). New York: Appleton Century Crofts.
Geertz, C. (1973). *The interpretation of cultures*. New York: Basic Books.
Genesee, F. (2002). Portrait of the bilingual child. In Cook, V. (Ed.) *Portraits of the second language user* (pp. 170-196). Clevedon, UK: Multilingual Matters.
Gibbons, P. (2002). *Scaffolding language, scaffolding learning: Teaching second language learners in the mainstream classroom*. Portsmouth, NH: Heinemann.
Gibson, E. J. (Ed.). (1991). *An odyssey in learning and perception*. Cambridge, MA: MIT Press.
Gibson, J. J. (1979). *The ecological approach to visual perception*. Hillsdale, NJ: Erlbaum.
Giddens, A. (1991). *Modernity and self-identity: Self and society in the late modern age*. Stanford, CA: Stanford University Press.
Gimson, A. C. (1970). *An introduction to the pronunciation of English*. London: Edward Arnold.
Glachan, M. & Light, P. (1982). Peer interaction and learning: Can two wrongs make a right? In G. Light (Eds.), *Social cognition*. Brighton: Harvester Press.
Butterworth & P. Light (Eds.), *Social cognition*. Brighton: Harvester Press.
Glausiusz, J. (2001). The ecology of language: Link between rainfall and language diversity. In A. Fill & P. Mühlhäusler (Eds.), *The ecolinguistics reader: Language, ecology and environment* (pp. 165-166). London: Continuum.
Gleick, J. (1987). *Chaos: Making a new science*. New York: Penguin Books.
Goatly, A. (2001). Green grammar and grammatical metaphor, or language and myth of power, or metaphors we die by. In A. Fill & P. Mühlhäusler (Eds.), *The ecolinguistics reader: Language, ecology and environment* (pp. 203-225). London: Continuum.
Goffman, E. (1981). *Forms of talk*. Oxford: Basil Blackell.
Goldsmith, E. (1998). *The way: An ecological world view* (second edition). Athens: University of Georgia Press.
Gomes de Matos, F. (2002). Seond language learners' rights. In V. J. Cook (Ed.), *Portraits of the L2 user* (pp. 305-323). Clevedon, UK: Multilingual Matters.
Gould S. J. (1993) *Eight Little Piggies*. New York: Norton.
Granott, N. (1993). Patterns of interaction in the co-construction of knowledge: Separate minds, joint effort, and weird creatures. In R. H. Wozniak & K. W. Fischer (Eds.), *Development in context: Acting and thinking in specific environments* (pp. 183-207). Hillsdale, NJ: Erlbaum.
Greeno, J. G. (1994). Gibson's affordances. *Psychological Review, 101*, 336-342.
Greeno, J. G. (1997). On claims that answer the wrong questions. *Educational Researcher, 26*, 5-17.
Grice, H. P. (1975) Logic and conversation. In P. Cole & J. L. Morgan (Eds.), *Speech acts. Syntax and Semantics*, 3 (41-58). New York: Academic Press.
Grossberg, S. (1980). Direct perception or adaptive resonance? In S. Ullman, Against direct perception (385-6). *The Behavioral and Brain Sciences* (1980), 3.
Guerrero, M. C. M. de. (1994). Form and functions of inner speech in adult second language learning. In J. P. Lantolf & G. Appel (Eds.), *Vygotskian approaches to second language research* (pp. 83-115). Norwood, NJ: Ablex.
Gumperz, J. & Hymes, D. (Eds.).(1972). *Directions in sociolinguistics: The ethnography of communication*. New York: Holt, Rinehart & Winston.
Hacking, I. (1975). *Why does language matter to philosophy?* Cambridge: Cambridge University Press.
Haeckel, E. (1866). *Allgemeine Anatomie der Organismen*. Berlin.
Halliday, M.A.K. (1975). *Learning how to mean*. London: Arnold.
Halliday, M.A.K. (1978). *Language as social semiotic*. London: Arnold.
Halliday, M.A.K. (1993). Towards a language-based theory of learning. *Linguistics and Education, 5*, 93-116.
Halliday, M.A.K. (2001). New ways of meaning: The challenge to applied linguistics. In E. Fill & P. Mühlhäusler (Eds.), *The ecolinguistics reader* (pp. 175-202). London: Continuum.
Halliday, M.A.K. & Martin, J. (1993). *Writing science: Literacy and discursive power*. Pittsburgh: University of Pittsburgh Press.
Hanks, W. F. (1995). *Language and communicative practices*. Boulder, CO: Westview Press.
Hargreaves, A. (1994). *Changing teachers, changing times*. New York: Teachers College Press.

References

Harré, R. (1983). *Personal being: A theory for individual psychology.* Oxford: Blackwell.
Harre, R. & Gillett, G. (1994). *The discursive mind.* Thousand Oaks, CA: Sage Publications.
Harris, R. (1990). *Language, Saussure and Wittgenstein: How to play games with words.* London: Routledge.
Harris, R. (1996). *Signs, language and communication.* London: Routledge.
Harris, R. (1997). From an integrational point of view. In G. Wolf & N. Love (Eds.), *Linguistics inside out: Roy Harrris and his critics* (pp. 229-310). Amsterdam: John Benjamins.
Harter, S. (1993) Visions of the self: Beyond the me in the mirror. In J. E. Jacobs (Ed.), *Developmental perspectives on motivation.* Nebraska Symposium on Motivation, Vol. 40, 1992 (pp. 99-144). Lincoln, NE: University of Nebraska Press.
Hassanpour, A. (2000). The politics of a-political linguistics: Linguists and linguicide. In A. Fill & P. Mühlhäusler (Eds.), *The ecolinguistics reader: Language, ecology and environment* (pp. 33-34). London: Continuum.
Haugen, E. (1972). *The ecology of language: Essays by Einar Haugen* (Edited by Anwar S. Dil). Stanford, CA: Stanford University Press.
Heath, S. B. (1983). *Ways with words.* Cambridge: Cambridge University Press.
Heath, S. B. (2000). Seeing our way into learning. *Cambridge Journal of Education, 30,* 121-132.
Hebb, D. O. (1953). Heredity and environment in mammalian behavior. *British Journal of Animal Behavior, 1,* 43-47.
Heisenberg, W. (1965). The role of modern physics in the development of human thinking. In F.T. Severin (Ed.), *Humanistic viewpoints in psychology.* New York: McGraw-Hill.
Heritage, J. (1987). Ethnomethodology. In A. Giddens & A. Turner (Eds.), *Social theory today* (pp. 224-272). Stanford, CA: Stanford University Press.
Herrnstein, R. & Murray, C. (1994). *The bell curve: Intelligence and class structure in American life.* New York: Free Press.
Hinton, L. & Hale, K. (2001). *The green book of language revitalization in practice.* New York: Academic Press.
Hockett, C. (1968). *The state of the art.* The Hague: Mouton.
Hoffman, E. (1989). *Lost in translation: A life in a new language.* New York, NY: Dutton.
Holliday, A. (1994). *Appropriate methodology and social context.* Cambridge: Cambridge University Press.
hooks, b. (1989). *Talking back: Thinking feminist, thinking black.* Boston: South End Press.
Hopper, P. J. (1998). Emergent grammar. In M. Tomasello (Ed.), *The new psychology of language: Cognitive and functional approaches to language structure.* Mahwah, NJ: Erlbaum.
Hornberger, N. (2001). Educational linguistics as a field: A view from Penn's program as it approaches its 25th anniversary. In R. Cooper, E. Shohamy, & J. Walters (Eds.), *New perspectives and issues in educational language policy: A volume in honor of Bernard Dov Spolsky* (pp. 271-296). Philadelphia: John Benjamins.
Hornberger, N. H. (2002). Multilingual language policies and the continua of biliteracy: An ecological approach. *Language Policy, 1,* 27-51.
Humphrey, N. (1992). *A history of the mind.* London: Chatto & Windus.
Hymes, D. (1974). *Foundations of sociolinguistics: An ethnographic approach.* Philadelphia, PA: University of Pennsylvania Press.
James, C. (1998). *Errors in language learning and use: Exploring error analysis.* New York: Longman.
Jaworski, A. & Coupland, N. (Eds.). (1999). *The discourse reader.* London: Routledge.
Johansen, J.D. (1993). *Dialogic semiosis: An essay on signs and meaning.* Bloomington, IN: Indiana University Press.
Johnson, S. (2001). *Emergence: The connected lives of ants, brains, cities, and software.* New York: Scribner.
Kant, I. (1934 [1787]). *Critique of pure reason.* London: Dent.
Keller, R. (1998). *A theory of linguistic signs.* Oxford: Oxford University Press.
Ketner, K. L. (Ed.). (1995). *Peirce and contemporary thought: Philosophical inquiries.* New York: Fordham University Press.
Kirkpatrick, H. & Cuban, L (1998). Computers make kids smarter – right? *TECHNOS Quarterly for Education and Technology, 7.* (http://www.technos.nct/tq_07/2cuban.htm , Downloaded July 20, 2000).

REFERENCES 231

Kohonen, V. (2001). Towards experiential foreign language education. In V. Kohonen, R. Jaatinen, P. Kaikkonen, & J. Lehtovaara (Eds.), *Experiential learning in foreign language education* (pp. 8-60). London: Longman.

Kohonen, V., Jaatinen, R., Kaikkonen, P., & Lehtovaara, J. (Eds.). (2001). *Experiential learning in foreign language education*. London: Longman.

Kozulin, A. (1986). Introduction. In L.S. Vygotsky, *Thought and language*. (Transl. A Kozulin). Cambridge, MA: MIT.

Kozulin, A. (1990). *Vygotsky's psychology: A biography of ideas*. New York: Harvester Wheatsheaf.

Kramsch, C. (1993). *Context and culture in language teaching*. Oxford: Oxford University Press.

Kramsch, C. (1998). *Language and culture*. Oxford: Oxford University Press.

Kramsch, C. (2000). Social discursive constructions of self in L2 learning. In J. Lantolf (Ed.), *Sociocultural theory in language learning* (pp. 133-154). Oxford: Oxford University Press.

Kramsch, C. (Ed.). (2002). *Language acquisition and language socialization: Ecological perspectives*. London: Continuum.

Krashen, S. (1985). *The input hypothesis*. London: Longman.

Kroeber, A. L. & Kluckhohn, C. (1952). *Culture: A critical review of concepts and definitions*. New York: Vintage Books.

Kuhn, T. (1970). *The structure of scientific revolutions*. Chicago: The University aof Chicago Press.

Labov, W. (1972). *Sociolinguistic Patterns*. Oxford: Basil Blackwell.

Lakoff, G. (1987). *Women, fire, and dangerous things: What categories reveal about the mind*. Chicago: University of Chicago Press.

Lam, W. S. E. & Kramsch, C. (2003). The ecology of an SLA community in a computer-mediated environment. In J. Leather & J. van Dam (Eds.), *Ecology of language acquisition* (pp. 141-158). Dordrecht: Kluwer Academic.

Langacker, R.W. *Foundations of Cognitive Grammar, volume 1: Theoretical Prerequisites*. Stanford, CA: Stanford University Press.

Langer, E. (1989). *Mindfulness*. Reading, MA: Addison-Wesley.

Lantolf, J. (Ed.). (2000). *Sociocultural theory and second language learning*. Oxford: Oxford University Press.

Lantolf, J., & Thorne, S. (forthcoming). *The sociogenesis of second language development*. Oxford: Oxford University Press.

Larsen-Freeman, D. (1997). Chaos/complexity science and second language acquisition. *Applied Linguistics, 18,* 141-165.

Larsen-Freeman, (2002). Language acquisition and language use from a chaos/complexity perspective. In C. Kramsch (Ed.), *Language acquisition and language socialization: Ecological perspectives* (pp. 33-46). London: Continuum.

Larsen-Freeman, D. (2003). *Teaching language: From grammar to grammaring*. Boston, MA: Heinle and Heinle.

Larsen-Freeman, D. & Long, M. H. (1991). *An introduction to second language acquisition research*. London: Longman.

Lave, J. & Wenger, E. (1991). *Situated learning: Legitimate peripheral participation*. Cambridge: Cambridge University Press.

Layder, D. (1990). *The realist image in social science*. London: Macmillan.

Leather, J. & van Dam, J. (2003). Towards an ecology of language acquisition. In J. Leather & J. van Dam (Eds.), *The ecology of language acquisition* (pp. 1-29). Dordrecht: Kluwer Academic Publishers.

Lee, P. (1996). *The Whorf theory complex: A critical reconstruction*. Amsterdam: John Benjamins.

Lemke, J. (2002). Language development and identity: Multiple timescales in the social ecology of learning. In C. Kramsch (Ed.), *Language acquisition and language socialization: Ecological perspectives* (pp. 68-87). London: Continuum.

Leontiev, A.N. (1981). The problem of activity in psychology. In J. V. Wertsch (Ed.). *The problem of activity in contemporary psychology* (pp. 37-71). Armonk, NY: M.E. Sharpe.

Leontiev, A. N. (1997). On Vygotsky's creative development. In Vygotsky, L.S. *The collected works of L. S. Vygotsky, Volume 3. Problems of the theory and history of psychology* (pp. 9-32). New York: Plenum Press.

Levinson, S. (1983). *Pragmatics*. Cambridge: Cambridge University Press.

Lewin, K. (1943). Defining the 'field at a given time.' *Psychological Review, 50,* 292-310.

Lewin, R. (1993). *Complexity: Life at the edge of chaos*. London: Phoenix.
Liddicoat, A. (1997). Interaction, social structure, and second language use: A response to Firth and Wagner. *The Modern Language Journal, 81,* 313-317.
Lightfoot, D. (1982). *The language lottery: Toward a biology of grammars*. Cambridge, MA: MIT Press.
Long, M. (1996). The role of the linguistic environment in second language acquisition. In W. C. Ritchie & T. K. Bhatia (Eds.), *Handbook of second language acquisition* (pp. 413 – 468). San Diego: Academic Press.
Lorenz, K. (1990). *On life and living*. London: St. Martin's Press.
Lovelock, J. (1979). *Gaia*. Oxford: Oxford University Press.
MacIntyre, A. (1981). *After virtue*. London: Duckworth.
MacWhinney, B. (Ed.). (1987). *Mechanisms of language acquisition*. Hillsdale, NJ: Erlbaum.
MacWhinney, B. (Ed.). (1999). *Emergence of language*. Mahwah, NJ: Erlbaum.
Maffi, L. (2000). Linguistic and biological diversity: The inextricable link. In R. Phillipson (Ed.), *Rights to language: Equity, power, and education* (pp. 17-22). Mahwah, NJ: Erlbaum.
Magnuson, P. (2003). The interplay between Minnesota's accountability system and adolescent English Language Learners with limited formal schooling. Unpublished Ph.D. Thesis, University of Minnesota.
Makkai, A. (1993). *Ecolinguistics. ¿Toward a new **paradigm** for the science of language?* London: Pinter Publishers.
Makoni, S. (2003). From misinvention to disinvention of language: Multilingualism and the South African constitution. In S. Makoni, G. Smitherman, A. Ball, & A. Spears (Eds.), *Black linguistics: Language, society, and politics in Africa and the Americas* (pp. 132-152). New York: Routledge.
Malinowski, B. (1967). *A diary in the strict sense of the term*. London: Routledge & Kegan Paul.
Markus, H. R., Mullally, P. R. & Kitayama, S. (1997). Selfways: Diversity in modes of cultural participation. In U. Neisser & D. A. Jopling (Eds.), *The conceptual self in context: Culture, experience, self-understanding* (pp. 13-61). Cambridge: Cambridge University Press.
Maturana, H. R. & Varela, F. J. (1992). *The tree of knowledge: The biological roots of human understanding*. Boston: Shambala.
May, S. (2001). *Language and minority rights: Ethnicity, nationalism and the politics of language*. London: Longman.
Maybin, J. (1994). Children's voices: Talk, knowledge and identity. In D. Graddol, J. Maybin & B. Stierer (Eds.), *Researching language and literacy in social context* (pp. 131-150). Clevedon: Multilingual Matters.
McArthur, L. Z. & Baron, R. M. (1983). Toward an ecological theory of social perception. *Psychological Review, 90,* 215-238.
McCafferty, S. (2002). Gesture and creating zones of proximal development for second language learning. *The Modern Language Journal, 86,*192-203.
McKay, S. L. & Hornberger, N. H. (1996). *Sociolinguistics and language teaching*. New York: St. Martin's Press.
McLaren, P. (1998). *Life in schools: An introduction to critical pedagogy in the foundations of education*. New York: Addison Wesley Longman.
McLaughlin, B. (1987). *Theories of second language learning*. London: Edward Arnold.
McNeill, D. (Ed.). (2000). *Language and gesture*. Cambridge: Cambridge University Press.
McNiff, J. (1993). *Teaching as learning: An action research approach*. London: Routledge.
Mead, G. H. (1934). *Mind, self, and society*. Chicago: University of Chicago Press.
Medawar, P. B. (1967). *The art of the soluble*. London: Methuen.
Meltzoff, A. N. & Prinz, W. (Eds.). (2002). *The imitative mind: Development, evolution and brain bases*. Cambridge: Cambridge University Press.
Menand, L. (2001). *The metaphysical club: A story of ideas in America*. New York: Farrar, Straus and Giroux.
Mercer, N. (1995). *The guided construction of knowledge: Talk between teachers and learners in the classroom*. Clevedon: Multilingual Matters.
Merleau-Ponty, M. (1962). *Phenomenology of perception*. London: Routledge & Kegan Paul.
Merrell, F. (1997a). *Peirce, signs, and meaning*. Toronto: University of Toronto Press.
Merrell, F. (1997b). Do we really need Peirce's whole decalogue of signs? *Semiotica, 114,* 193-286.
Merrell, F. (1998). *Sensing semiosis: Toward the possibility of complementary cultural "logics."* Basingstoke, UK: Macmillan Press.

Miles, M. B. & Huberman, A. M. (1994). *Qualitative data analysis.* Thousand Oaks, CA: Sage Publications.
Miller, H. (1963). *Black spring.* New York: Grove Press.
Miramontes, O. B., Nadeau, A., & Commins, N. L. (1997). *Restructuring schools for linguistic diversity: Linking decision making to effective programs.* New York: Teachers College Press.
Montessori, M. (1917/1965). *Spontaneous activity in education.* New York: Schocken.
Mühlhäusler, P. (1996). *Linguistic ecology: Language change and linguistic imperialism in the Pacific Region.* New York: Routledge.
Naess, A. (1989). *Ecology, community and lifestyle.* Translated and edited by D. Rothenberg. Cambridge: Cambridge University Press.
Nakahama, Y., Tyler, A. & van Lier, L. (2001). Negotiation of meaning in conversations and tasks: A comparative discourse analysis. *TESOL Quarterly, 35,* 377-405.
Natsoulas, T. (1993). Perceiving, its component stream of perceptual experience, and Gibson's ecological approach. *Psychological Research, 55,* 248-257.
Neisser, U. (1987). From direct perception to conceptual structure. In U. Neisser (Ed.), *Concepts and conceptual development: Ecological and intellectual factors in categorization.* Cambridge: Cambridge University Press.
Neisser, U. (1988). Five kinds of self-knowledge. *Philosophical Psychology, 1,* 35-59.
Neisser, U. (1992) Two themes in the study of cognition. In H. L. Pick, P. van den Broek, & D. C. Knill (Eds.), *Cognition: Conceptual and methodological issues.* Washington, D.C.: American Psychological Association.
Neisser, U. (Ed.). (1993). *The perceived self: Ecological and interpersonal sources of self-knowledge.* Cambridge: Cambridge University Press.
Neisser, U. & Fivush, R. (Eds.). (1994). *The remembering self: Construction and accuracy in the self-narrative.* Cambridge: Cambridge University Press.
Neisser, U. & Jopling, D. A. (Eds.). (1997). *The conceptual self in context: Culture, experience, self-understanding.* Cambridge: Cambridge University Press.
Nietzsche, F. (1954). On truth and lie in an extra-moral sense. In W. Kaufmann (Ed.), *The Viking Portable Nietzsche* (pp. 46-7).
Norman, D. A. (1988). *The psychology of everyday things.* New York: Basic Books.
Norman, D. A. (no date) *Affordance, conventions and design.* Retrieved on 5-10-2002 from: http://www.jnd.org/dn.mss/affordances-interactions.html
Norton Peirce, B. (1995). Social identity, investment, and language learning. *TESOL Quarterly, 29,* 9-31.
Norton, B. (2000). *Identity and language learning: Gender, ethnicity and educational change.* New York: Longman.
Nöth, W. (1995). *Handbook of semiotics.* Bloomington, IN: Indiana University Press.
Nystrand, M. (1992). Social interactionism versus social constructionism. In A. H. Wold (Ed.), *The dialogical alternative: Towards a theory of language and mind* (pp. 157-174). Oslo: Scandinavian University Press.
Ochs, E. (2002). Becoming a speaker of culture. In C. Kramsch (Ed.), *Language acquisition and language socialization: Ecological perspectives* (pp. 99-120). London: Continuum.
Ogbu, J. U. (1991). Immigrant and involuntary minorities in comparative perspective. In M. A. Gibson and J. U. Ogbu (Eds.), *Minority status and schooling: A comparative study of immigrant and voluntary minorities* (pp. 3-33). New York: Garland Publishing.
Ogden, C. K. & Richards, I. A. ([1923] 1985). *The meaning of meaning.* London: Routledge.
Ohta, A. S. (2001). *Second language acquisition processes in the classroom: Learning Japanese.* Mahwah, NJ: Erlbaum.
Oyama, S. (2000). *Evolution's eye: A systems view of the biology-culture divide.* Durham, NC: Duke University Press.
Paikeday, T. (1985). *The native speaker is dead!* Toronto: Paikeday Publishing.
Palincsar, A., David, I. & Brown, A. (1992). Using reciprocal teaching in the classroom: A guide for teachers. Unpublished manuscript: The Brown/Campione Research Group.
Passmore, J. (1978). *Science and its critics.* London: Duckworth.
Pavlenko, A & Lantolf, J. (2000). Second language learning as participation and the (re)construction of selves. In Lantolf, J. (Ed.) *Sociocultural theory in language learning* (pp. 155-178). Oxford: Oxford University Press.

Peirce, C. S. (1992 and 1998): *Selected Philosophical Writings*, Vols. 1 and 2. Bloomington, IN: Indiana University Press. Vol. 1: Edited by Nathan Houser and Christian Kloesel, 1992; Vol. 2, Edited by The Peirce Edition Project, 1998.

Pennycook, A. (1995). English in the world/ The world in English. In J. W. Tollefson (Ed.), *Power and inequality in language education* (pp. 34-58). Cambridge: Cambridge University Press.

Pennycook, A. (2001). *Critical applied linguistics*. Mahwah, NJ: Erlbaum.

Pennycook, A. (forthcoming). Critical applied linguistics. To appear in A. Davies & C. Elder (Eds.), *Handbook of Applied Linguistics*. Oxford: Blackwell.

Phelan, P. & Davidson, A. L. (Eds.). (1993). *Renegotiating cultural diversity in American schools*. New York: Teachers College Press.

Phillipson, R. (Ed.). (2000). *Rights to language: Equity, power, and education*. Mahwah, NJ: Erlbaum.

Piaget, J. (1928). *Judgement and reasoning in the child*. London: Routledge and Kegan Paul.

Piaget, J. (1978). *Success and understanding*. Cambridge, MA: Harvard University Press.

Pica, T. (1992). The textual outcomes of native speaker-non-native speaker negotiation: What do they reveal about second language learning? In C. Kramsch and S. McConnell-Ginet (Eds.), *Text and Context Cross-Disciplinary Perspectives on Language Study*. Lexington, MA: D.C. Heath.

Pienemann, M. (1998). *Language processing and second language development: Processability theory*. Philadelphia: John Benjamins.

Pinker, S. (1994). *The language instinct*. New York: William Morrow.

Poster, M. (1993). Foucault and the problem of self-constitution. In J. Caputo & M. Youny (Eds.), *Foucault and the critique of institutions* (pp. 63-80). University Park, PA: The Pennsylvania State University Press.

Postman, N. (1988). *Conscientious objections: Stirring up trouble about language, technology, and education*. New York: Vintage Books.

Postman, N. (1993). *Technopoly: The surrender of culture to technology*. New York: Vintage Books.

Potter, J. & Wetherell, M. (1987). *Discourse and social psychology: Beyond attitudes and behaviour*. London: Sage Publications.

Price, H. H. (1969). *Thinking and experience*. London: Hutchinson.

Prigogine, I. & Stengers, I. (1984). *Order out of chaos: Man's new dialogue with nature*. New York: Bantam Books.

Pullum, G. (1991). *The great Eskimo vocabulary hoax and other irreverent essays on the study of language*. Chicago: The University of Chicago Press.

Rampton, B. (2002). Ritual and foreign language practices at school. *LPI Working Paper No. 9*. Albany, Antwerp, Gent, London and Toronto: Working Papers on Language, Power & Identity.

Reddy, M. (1979). The conduit metaphor. In R. Ortony (Ed.), *Metaphor and thought*. Cambridge: Cambridge University Press.

Reed, E. S. (1988). *James J. Gibson and the psychology of perception*. New Haven, CT: Yale University Press.

Reed, E. S. (1996). *Encountering the world: Toward an ecological psychology*. New York: Oxford University Press.

Riggins, S.H. (1997). The rhetoric of othering. In S. H. Riggins (Ed.), *The language and politics of exclusion: Others in discourse* (pp. 1-30). Thousand Oaks, CA: Sage Publications.

Rivers, W. M. & Temperley, M. S. (1978). *A practical guide to the teaching of English as a second language*. New York: Oxford University Press.

Rodriguez, R. (1981). *Hunger of memory*. Boston, MA: D.R. Godine.

Rogoff, B. (1993). Children's guided participation and participatory appropriation in sociocultural activity. In R. H. Wozniak & K. W. Fischer (Eds.), *Development in context: Acting and thinking in specific environments* (pp. 121-153). Hillsdale, NJ: Erlbaum.

Rogoff, B. (1995). Observing sociocultural activity on three planes: Participatory appropriation, guided participation, and apprenticeship. In J. V. Wertsch, P. Del Rio, & A. Alvarez (Eds.), *Sociocultural studies of mind* (pp. 139-164). Cambridge: Cambridge University Press.

Rogoff, B. & Gardner, W. (1984). Adult guidance in cognitive development. In B. Rogoff & J. Lave (Eds.), *Everyday cognition: Its development in social contexts*. Cambridge, MA: Harvard University Press.

Rommetveit, R. (1974). *On message structure*. New York: Wiley.

Rommetveit, R. (1998). Intersubjective attunement and linguistically mediated meaning in discourse. In S. Bråten (Ed.), *Intersubjective communication and emotion in early ontogeny* (pp. 354-371). Cambridge: Cambridge University Press.
Rosch, E. (1997). Mindfulness meditation and the private (?) self. In U. Neisser & D. A. Jopling (Eds.), *The conceptual self in context: Culture, experience, self-understanding* (pp. 185-202). Cambridge: Cambridge University Press.
Rosen, H. (1986). The importance of story. *Language Arts*, 63 (3), 226-237.
Rossi-Landi, F. (1992). *Between signs and non-signs*. Amsterdam: John Benjamins.
Rutherford, W. E. (1987). *Second language grammar: Teaching and learning*. London: Longman.
Ruthrof, H. (2000). *The body in language*. London: Cassell.
Sacks, H. (1963). Sociological description. *Berkeley Journal of Sociology, 8,* 1-16.
Sacks, O. (1984). *A leg to stand on*. New York: Harper.
Sartre, J. P. (1957). Being and nothingness. London: Methuen.
Sato, C. (1988). Origins of complex syntax in interlanguage development. *Studies in Second Language Acquisition*, 10, 3, 371-395.
Saussure, F. (de) (1907/1983). *Course in general linguistics*. La Salle, IL: Open Court.
Schmidt, R. (1994). Deconstructing conscsciousness in search of useful definitions for applied linguistics. *Revue de l'AILA/AILA Review*, 11, 11-26.
Schmidt, R. & Frota, S. (1986). Developing basic conversational ability in a second language: A case study of an adult learner of Portuguese. In R. Day (Ed.), '*Talking to learn': Conversation in second language acquisition* (pp. 237-326). Rowley, MA: Newbury House.
Schumann, J. (1978). Social and psychological factors in second language acquisition. In J. Richards (Ed.), *Understanding second and foreign language learning* (pp. 163-78). Rowley, MA: Newbury House.
Schumann, J. (1990). The role of the amygdala as a mediator of acculturation and cognition in second language acquisition. In *Georgetown University Round Table on Languages and Linguistics 1990* (pp. 169-176). Washington, D.C.: Georgetown University Press.
Scollon, R. (1976). *Conversations with a one-year old*. Hawaii: University of Hawaii Press.
Sebeok, T. A. (1994). *Signs: An introduction to semiotics*. Toronto: University of Toronto Press.
Sfard, A. (1998). On two metaphors for learning and the dangers of choosing just one. *Educational Researcher, 27,* 4-13.
Shotter, J. (1984). *Social accountability and selfhood*. London: Blackwell.
Shotter, J. (1993). *Conversational realities: Constructing life through language*. London: Sage.
Shotter, J. and Newson, J. (1982). An ecological approach to cognitive development: Implicate orders, joint action and intentionality. In G. Butterworth and P. Light (Eds.), *Social Cognition: Studies of the Development of Understanding*. Sussex: Harvester Press.
Skutnabb-Kangas, T. (2000). *Linguistic genocide in education, or worldwide diversity and human rights?* Mahwah, NJ: Erlbaum.
Skutnabb-Kangas, T. & Phillipson, R. (Eds.). (1995). *Linguistic human rights: Overcoming linguistic discrimination*. Berlin: Mouton.
Slavin, R. E. (1983). *Student team learning: An overview and practical guide*. Washington, D.C.: National Education Association.
Sperber, D. & Wilson, D. (1986). *Relevance: Communication and cognition*. Oxford: Basil Blackwell.
Stenhouse, L. (1975). *An introduction to curriculum research and development*. London: Heinemann.
Stephens, J. (1912). *The crock of gold*. London: Macmillan.
Stewart, I. (1989). *Does God play dice? The mathematics of chaos*. Oxford: Basil Blackwell.
Sullivan, P. N. (2000). Playfulness as mediation in communicative language teaching in a Vietnamese classroom. In J. P. Lantolf (Ed.), *Sociocultural theory and second language learning* (pp. 115-131). Oxford: Oxford University Press.
Swain, M. (2000). The output hypothesis and beyond: Mediating acquisition through collaborative dialogue. In J. P. Lantolf (Ed.), *Sociocultural theory and second language learning* (pp. 97 – 114). Oxford: Oxford University Press.
Swain, M. & Lapkin, S. (2000). Task-based second language learning: The uses of the first language. *Language Teaching Research, 4,* 251-274.
Thibault, P. J. (1997). *Re-reading Saussure: The dynamics of signs in social life*. London: Routledge.

References

Thorne, S. L. (2000a). Second language acquisition theory and the truth(s) about relativity. In J. P. Lantolf (Ed.), *Sociocultural theory and second language learning* (pp. 219-244). Oxford: Oxford University Press.

Thorne, S. L. (2000b). Beyond bounded activity systems: Heterogeneous cultures in instructional uses of persistent conversation. Proceedings of the Thirty-Third Annual Hawaii International Conference on System Sciences (CD-ROM), IEEE Computer Society, Los Alamitos, CA.

Todorov, T. (1984). *Mikhail Bakhtin: The dialogical principle*, (translated by Wlad Godzich). Minneapolis: University of Minnesota Press.

Tomasello, M. (2001). *Cultural origins of human cognition*. Cambridge, MA: Harvard University Press.

Tornberg, U. (2000). On foreign language teaching and learning in a discursive space. English summary of Ph.D. Dissertation, University of Örebro, Sweden.

Toulmin, S. (1982) The genealogy of 'consciousness.' In P.F. Secord (Ed.), *Explaining human behavior: Consciousness, human action, and social structure* (pp. 53-70). Beverly Hills: Sage.

Trappes-Lomax, H. & Ferguson, G. (Eds.). (2002). *Language in language teacher education*. Amsterdam: John Benjamins.

Trevarthen, C. (1990). Signs before speech. In T. Sebeok & Sebeok-Umiker, J. (Eds.), *The semiotic web* (pp. 689-755). The Hage: Mouton.

Trevarthen, C. (1998). The concept and foundations of infant intersubjectivity. In S. Bråten (Ed.), *Intersubjective communication and emotion in early ontogeny* (pp. 15-46). Cambridge: Cambridge University Press.

Trim, J. L. M. (1959). Historical, descriptive and dynamic linguistics. *Language and Speech, 2,* 9-25.

Tudge, J. (1990). Vygotsky, the zone of proximal development, and peer collaboration: Implications for classroom practice. In L. C. Moll (Ed.), *Vygotsky and education: Instructional implications and applications of sociohistorical psychology* (pp. 155-172). Cambridge: Cambridge University Press.

Turner, J. (1988). *A theory of social interaction*. Stanford: Stanford University Press.

Turvey, M. (1992). Ecological foundations of cognition: Invariants of perception and action. In H. L. Pick, Jr., P. van den Broek & D. C. Knill (Eds.), *Cognition: Conceptual and methodological issues* (pp. 85-117). Washington, D. C.: American Psychological Association.

Ullman, S. (1980). Against direct perception. *The Behavioral and Brain Sciences, 3,* 373-415.

Valsiner, J. & van der Veer, R. (2000). *The social mind: Construction of the idea*. Cambridge: Cambridge University Press.

van Dam, J. (2002). Ritual, face, and play in a first English lesson: Bootstrapping a classroom culture. In C. Kramsch (Ed.), *Language acquisition and language socialization: Ecological perspectives* (pp. 237-265). London: Continuum.

van Lier, L. (1988). *The classroom and the language learner*. London: Longman.

van Lier, L. (1994a). Educational linguistics: Field and project. In J. Alatis (Ed.), *Georgetown University Round Table on Languages and Linguistics 1994* (pp. 199-209). Washington, D.C.: Georgetown University Press.

van Lier, L. (1994b). Forks and hope: Pursuing understanding in different ways. *Applied Linguistics, 15,* 328-46.

van Lier, L. (1994c). Some features of a theory of practice. *TESOL Journal, 4,* 6-10.

van Lier, L. (1995). *Introducing language awareness*. London: Penguin UK. See also http://maxkade.miis.edu/Faculty_Pages/lvanlier/

van Lier, L. (1996). *Interaction in the language curriculum: Awareness, autonomy and authenticity*. London: Longman.

van Lier, L. (1998). The relationship between consciousness, interaction and language learning. *Language Awareness, 7,* 128 – 145.

van Lier, L. (2000). From input to affordance: Social-interactive learning from an ecological perspective. In J.P. Lantolf (Ed.), *Sociocultural theory and second language learning: Recent advances* (pp. 245-259). Oxford: Oxford University Press.

van Lier, L. (2002). An ecological-semiotic perspective on language and linguistics. In C. Kramsch (Ed.), *Language Acquisition and Language Socialization. Ecological perspectives* (pp. 140-164). London: Continuum.

van Lier, L. (2003). A tale of two computer classrooms: The ecology of project-based language learning. In J. Leather & J. van Dam (Eds.), *Ecology of language acquisition* (pp. 49-63). Dordrecht: Kluwer Academic.

van Lier, L. & Matsuo, N. (2000). Varieties of conversational experience: Looking for learning opportunities. *Applied Language Learning, 10*, 2.
van Maanen, J. (1988). *Tales of the field*. Chicago, IL: University of Chicago Press.
van Manen, M. (1990). *Researching lived experience: Human science for an action sensitive pedagogy*. New York: SUNY Press.
van Manen, M. (1991). *The tact of teaching*. Albany, NY: SUNY Press.
van der Veer, R. & Valsiner, J. (1991). *Understanding Vygotsky: A quest for synthesis*. Oxford: Basil Blackwell.
Varela, F. J., Thompson, E. and Rosch, E. (1991). *The embodied mind: Cognitive science and human experience*. Cambridge, MA: The MIT Press.
Verhoeven, L. (1990). Language variation and learning to read. In P. Reitsma and L. Verhoeven (Eds.), *Acquisition of reading in Dutch* (pp. 105-120). Dordrecht: Foris.
Volosinov, V. N. (1973). *Marxism and the philosophy of language*. Cambridge, MA: Harvard University Press
von Bertalanffy, L. (1968). *General system theory*. New York: Braziller.
Vonnegut, K. (1990). *Hocus pocus*. New York: Putnam Press.
Vygodskaia, G. L. (1995). Remembering father. *Educational Psychologist, 30*, 57-59.
Vygotsky, L.S. (1962). *Thought and language*. (Transl. E. Hanfmann & G. Vakar). Cambridge, MA: MIT.
Vygotsky, L. S. (1978). *Mind in society*. Cambridge: Cambridge University Press.
Vygotsky, L. S. (1986). *Thought and language*. (Transl. A Kozulin). Cambridge, MA: MIT.
Vygotsky, L. S. (1987). *Thinking and speech*. (Transl. N. Minick). In The Collected Works of L. S. Vygotsky, Volume 1: Problems of general psychology. New York: Plenum Press.
Vygotsky, L. S. (1993). The collected works of L. S. Vygotsky, Volume 2: *The fundamentals of defectology*. New York: Plenum Press.
Vygotsky, L. S. & Luria, A. (1994). Tool and symbol in child development. In R. van der Veer & J. Valsiner (Eds.), *The Vygotsky reader* (pp. 99 – 174). Oxford: Basil Blackwell.
Waldrop, M. M. (1992). *Complexity: The emerging science at the edge of order and chaos*. New York: Simon & Schuster.
Walqui, A. (2000). *Access and engagement*. Washington, D.C.: Center for Applied Linguistics and Delta Systems.
Warschauer, M. (1998). *Electronic literacies: literacies, language, culture, and power in online education*. Mahwah, NJ: Erlbaum.
Wegerif, R. & Scrimshaw, P. (Eds.). (1997). *Computers and talk in the primary classroom*. Clevedon, England: Multilingual Matters.
Wells, G. (1986). *The meaning makers: Children learning language and using language to learn*. Portsmouth, NH: Heinemann.
Wells, G. (1999). *Dialogic inquiry: Towards a sociocultural practice and theory of education*. Cambridge: Cambridge University Press.
Wells, G. (2000). Dialogue in activity theory. Unpublished paper, based on a presentation at AAAL, Vancouver, March 2000.
Wenger, E. (1998). *Communities of practice: Learning, meaning, and identity*. Cambridge: Cambridge University Press.
Werner, H. (1956). Microgenesis and aphasia. *Journal of Abnormal and Social Psychology*, 52, 347-353.
Werker, J. F. & Tees, R. C. (1984). Cross-language speech perception: Evidence for perceptual reorganization during the first year of life. *Infant Behavior and Development, 7*, 49-63.
Wertsch, J. V. (1985). *Vygotsky and the social formation of mind*. Cambridge, MA: Harvard University Press.
Wertsch, J. V., Del Rio, P., & Alvarez, A. (Eds.). (1995). *Sociocultural studies of mind*. Cambridge: Cambridge University Press.
Whitehead, A. N. (1929). *The aims of education*. New York: The Free Press.
Wiener, N. (1948). *Cybernetics*. Cambridge, MA: MIT.
Wiley, N. (1994). *The semiotic self*. Chicago, IL: University of Chicago Press.
Wilson, R. A. & Keil, F. C. (Eds.). (1999). *The MIT encyclopedia of the cognitive sciences*. Cambridge, MA: MIT.
Winnips, J. C. (2001). Scaffolding-by-Design: A model for WWW based learner support. Dissertation. Enschede: University of Twente. Online: http://scaffolding.edte.utwente.nl/

Wittgenstein, L. (1974). *Philosophical grammar*. Berkeley: University of California Press.
Wittgenstein, L. (1980). *Culture and value*. Chicago, IL: University of Chicago Press.
Wolf, G. & Love, N. (Eds.). (1997). *Linguistics inside out: Roy Harris and his critics*. Amsterdam: John Benjamins.
Wood, D. (1988). *How children think and learn*. Oxford: Basil Blackwell.
Wood, D., Bruner, J. & Ross, G. (1976). The role of tutoring in problem-solving. *Journal of Child Psychology and Child Psychiatry, 17,* 89-100.
Wortham, S. (1994). *Acting out participant examples in the classroom*. Amsterdam: John Benjamins.
Wortham, S. (2001). *Narratives in action: A strategy for research and analysis*. New York: Teachers College Press.

INDEX

Academic language, 103t, 222, 223
  grammaticalization/acquisition of, 88
  as normative language, 160–61, 162
  suppression of personal aspects in, 129–30
  Vygotsky on, 160–61
Activity space
  learning context as, 62
  word creation by semiosis in, 65–66
Activity theory
  critical/activist versions of, 17
  in ecological research, 210–13, 211f, 212f, 217–18, 218
  microgenetic processes in, 212
  in SCT/ecology, 19–20, 21
Affordances, 4–5, 90–91, 90–105, 91, 94–95, 96, 96f, 104–5, 223
  cultural artifacts as, 94
  ecological theory and perspective of, 14
  in EL relationships, 45t, 53, 221, 223
  expanded meanings of, 94–96
  Gibson's theory of, 91–94, 92f, 95
  in learning, 62–63, 99f, 100
  mediated/immediate, 16, 62–63, 65–68, 94, 96–102
  in SCT/ecology, 21
Allen, T. F. H., 214
Anderson, B., 66
Anthropocentric worldview, 3
  shallow ecology distinguished by, 170
Argyle, M., 144
Aristotle, 9, 33, 39, 58, 61
Augustine, Saint, 58, 85–86, 134
Auyang, S. A., 92
Avicenna, 9

Bacon, F., 9
Bakhtin, M. M., 8, 14, 16, 16n8, 18, 33, 57, 58, 63, 66, 70, 77, 85, 90, 108, 112, 113, 131
  on consciousness, 123–24
  dialogic perspective on self of, 125
  dialogicity of language associated with, 130, 145
  on prolepsis, 152
Bakhurst, D., 67n9
  on prolepsis, 153
Barker, R., 21, 168
Baron, R. M., 94
Barry, D., 33
Bates, E. A., 88, 134
Bateson, G., 5, 33, 185. *See also* Ecology of mind
  classification distinguished from process by, 184–85, 197, 197f
  on theory of ecology, 169–70
Beaugrande, R. de, 73
The Bell Curve (Herrnstein and Murray), 127–28
Bernstein, B., 15, 77
Bhaskar, R., 204
Bilingual education, 51–52, 174–76, 192
  Crawford on, 177–78, 192
  Ebonics use as, 178–80
Bogdanov, A., 213
Bourdieu, P., 57, 66, 68, 77, 109
  Neisser's selves v., 116
  on reproduction/linguistic capital, 121, 179
  theory of practice associated with, 195, 204
Bowers, C. A., 187
Bråten, S., 131, 144
Broeder, P., 174–75, 192
Bronfenbrenner, U., 15, 21, 67
  bioecological model of developmental research of, 207–8, 218
  contextual theory of, 156–57, 158
  EV in work of, 169–70, 191
  nested ecosystems of, 180, 181, 193, 195, 208–10, 209f, 217–18, 218
  v. cognitive science, 124
Brown, A. L., 204
Brown, R., 139

Bruner, J. S., 15, 33, 147
  cognitive science experience of, 123–24
  on scaffolding in SLA, 148
  scaffolding requirements of, 149–50, 162
Bruno, 9
Brunswik, E., 21
  ecological psychology of, 168
  EV in work of, 168–69, 191
Bühler, 16, 18, 63
Bush, G. W., 47
  "no child left behind" and, 11, 216
Butler, S., 200
Butterfly effect, 196
Butterworth, G., 107
Byram, M., 184

CA. *See* Conversation analysis
California English Language Development Test (CELDT), 29
Canagarajah, A. S., 163
Carroll, L., 39, 205n2
Cazden, C. B., 150
CELDT. *See* California English Language Development Test
Chaos: Making a New Science (Gleick), 195
Chaos/complexity theory, 39–40
  Anasazi collapse viewed using, 8
  Cartesian definition of science v., 42
  deep ecology linked to, 4
  in ecological research, 195–202, 217
  illustrations of, 199–202
  language learning and, 8–9
  systems theory revived by, 214
Checkland, P.
  SSM of, 214–18, 215f–216f, 218
  systems practice of, 193
Chomsky, N., 29, 31, 32, 33, 36, 38, 42, 42n11, 53, 55, 86, 123, 124, 146. *See also* E-language; I-language
  Descartes and, 34
  mechanical metaphor used by, 170
  v. behaviorism/linguistic associations, 167–68, 168n1
  v. Davidson's prior/passing theory, 87, 87n5, 129
Clay, M. M., 150
Clifford, J., 84
  on culture, 184, 192
Colapietro, V. M., 126, 131
Cole, M., 12
Collins, A., 204
Competence, 34
  performance v., 34–35, 35f

replaced by I-language, 42
Comprehensible input theory, 89–90, 146, 154–56, 155t
  and grammaticalization in SLA, 89, 139
  McLaughlin v., 90
  ZPD v., 15, 154–56, 155t
Comte, A., 34
Consciousness
  in language learning, 98–99, 98f
  in self and language learning, 122–24
Context
  in Bronfenbrenner's bioecological model of developmental research, 207
  'bucket' theory of, 41, 204
  in CA, 40
  characterized as nested ecosystems, 208–10, 209f, 218
  in ecological research, 217–18
  ecology and study of, 11
  EL and, 37–40
  Firth's elaboration of Malinowski's, 73–74
  of language learning, 40–43
  relationships between learner/learning, 52–53
  in SCT/ecology, 18, 21
Conversation analysis (CA)
  context in, 40
Corder, S. P., 90
Course in General Linguistics (Saussure), 58
Crawford, J., 177–78
Crichton, M., 195–96, 197
Critical language studies
  domains of, 190
  in EL, 188–91, 192
  self-reflexive stance in, 190
  transformative pedagogy in, 190–91
Crook, C., 144–45
Cuban, L., 187
Culture, 183–84, 192
Cybernetics
  deep ecology linked to, 4
  in systems theory, 213

Damasio, A.
  on cognition/emotion, 123
  proto-self of, 107
Darwin, C., 9, 33
Davidson, D., 87–88, 87n5, 109, 129
de Saussure, F. *See* Saussure, F. de
De-engenderment. *See* Engenderment
Deep ecology
  in nature/education, 170–81, 191
  platform of, 171

shallow v., 3–8, 21, 170–72
Terralingua as linguistic counterpart to, 170–72
Deixis
  and anchoring, 65–66
  EL and relationships in, 45t, 46
  in language learning, 71, 118t
Descartes, 3, 34, 39, 107, 127n4, 165, 170, 205
Dewey, J., 14, 61, 62, 125, 147n6, 149, 150, 159, 167
Diversity in SCT/ecology, 19, 21, 50
Donato, R., 14, 148
Drew, P., 40, 204
Dunn, W. E., 15, 154
Durkheim, E., 34

Ebonics, 178–80, 192
  in nested ecosystem perspective, 210
Eco, U., 57, 65, 74, 77, 100
Ecocentric worldview, 3, 20
Ecological linguistics (EL), 4–8, 43, 44, 167
  anti-environmental linguistic practices v., 49
  chaos/complexity theory in, 195–96
  context in, 37–40
  critical, 6, 165–92, 188–91, 192
  culture/mind/value in, 183–86, 192
  dialogical view of learner autonomy in, 8
  diversity in, 7, 50, 171–81
  ecological perspective in, 168–81, 221–23
  Eskimo vocabulary in, 45t, 46
  inseparability of science/values in, 6
  interpretation in, 43, 44f
  language learning as activity in, 7–8
  language learning as emergence in, 5
  language/context in, 5
  learner/context relationships in, 52–53
  linguistics in context as, 42–43
  patterns/systems opposed to rules/structures by, 5
  policy/planning in, 181–83, 192
  quality in, 5
  relations in, 4–5, 44–53, 45t
  variability in, 6–7
Ecological psychology, 21, 168
Ecological research, 193–95, 193–219
  activity theory in, 210–13, 211f, 212f, 217–18, 218
  Bronfenbrenner's bioecological model in, 207–8, 218
  Bronfenbrenner's nested ecosystems in, 217–18

  causality in, 201
  chaos/complexity theory and ecology in, 195–99, 218
  chaos/probability in, 201
  Educational setting as nested ecosystems in, 208–10, 209f
  generalization in, 202
  micro v. macro approach in, 202, 204, 218
  models in, 204–5
  predictability/order in, 201–2
  SSM approach to, 214–18, 215f–216f
  systems theory in, 213–18
  truth/proof in, 200–201, 200f, 205–7, 218
Ecological validity (EV), 168–69
  as criterion of ecological research, 195
  in EL, 191
Ecological worldview, 3, 222
  benefits to SCT from, 21
  incompatibility of information processing with, 213
  v. rational worldview, 3, 20
Ecological-semiotic approach, 55, 62
Ecology. *See also* Deep ecology; Ecology of mind
  Bateson's influence on theory of, 169–70
  context in, 11
  critical SCT and, 19
  deep v. shallow, 3–8, 21, 170–72
  in ecological research, 195–202
  educational quality addressed by, 12
  Haeckel's definition of, 3, 194
  of human development, 67–68
  language of, 45t, 46–47
  as prescriptive metaphor, 20, 22
  qualitative v. quantitative approaches in, 21
  SCT and, 12–22
  semiotics and, 55
  in social sciences, 8–12
Ecology of mind, 14, 21, 185
Education, 2
  deep ecology in, 170–81
  Halliday's semiotic framework for, 77
  measuring success of, 11–12
  technology in, 186–88, 192
Educational linguistics, 2
  chaos/complexity theory in, 195–96
  Chomskyan/Saussurian perspective on, 34–35
  linguistics in context as, 42
Edwards, D., 119
Einstein, A., 33, 39
EL. *See* Ecological linguistics

E-language, 42. *See also* Performance
Eliot, G., 202
Ellis, R., 139
Emergence, 79–90, 104–5. *See also*
    Emergent grammar
    of culture, 184, 192
    ecological theory and perspective of, 14
    grammaticalization and processes of,
        88–90
    Great Vowel Shift as example of, 83–84,
        84*f*
    of language in learners, 5, 45*t*, 198–99
    nature/nurture in, 85–86
    relationships between language and, 84–85
    in SCT/ecology, 18
Emergence/affordance, 79–84, 79–105
Emergent grammar, 5, 79, 86–88
    restructuring v. Hopper's, 89, 105, 105n8,
        185
    similarity of grammaticalization and,
        88–90
Engenderment, 63
    in decalogue of signs, 65–67, 65n7
Engeström, Y., 17, 20
    activity theory of, 193, 210–13, 211*f*,
        212*f*, 217–18, 218
English as a Second Language (ESL)
    lack of professional approach to, 176
    transformative pedagogy in, 190
ESL. *See* English as a Second Language
Ethnomethodology
Extra, G., 174–75, 192

The Feeling of What Happens (Damasio),
    123
Feyerabend, P., 39
Fill, E., 22, 46, 47
Firth, J. R., 73–74
    Malinowski's influence on, 167
    v. Chomsky's competence/performance,
        74
    v. Saussure's dualism, 73–74
Flynn, P. J., 152
Fodor, J., 55, 203
Forrester, M., 94
Foucault, M., 17, 114–15
Frankl, V., 33
Freire, P., 15
Freud, S., 16, 33

Galileo, 9, 10, 33, 38, 39, 205
Gardner, W., 152–53
Geertz, C., 205–6

Genotypes, 13n7
Genotypic analysis
    phenotypic analysis v., 13, 212–13
    in Vygotsky's developmental method, 14*f*
Geocentric worldview, 3
    deep ecology distinguished by, 170
Gibson, E.
Gibson, J. J., 14, 16, 21, 63, 63n6, 66, 79n1,
        91, 105
    ecological psychology of, 102
    on self-perception, 115
    theory of affordances of, 91–94, 92*f*, 95,
        98
Giddens, A., 107, 202, 204
Gillett, G., 123
Gimson, A. C., 83n3
Gleick, J., 195
Goatly, Andrew, 49
Goffman, E., 205–6
Goodman, J. C., 88
Gould, S. J., 196, 197
Grammaticalization, 79
    in emergence/affordance, 88–90, 105, 139
    Rutherford's grammaticization v., 89–90
Greimas, A. J., 57
Grice, H. P., 95

Haeckel, E., 3, 194
Halliday, M. A. K., 15, 18, 20, 31, 33, 34,
        38, 49, 57, 65, 76, 79, 130
    contributions to semiotics by, 73–76, 77
    as ecological linguist, 167–68, 168n1
    language-based theory of learning of,
        102–4, 103*t*–104*t*, 105, 221
    macrofunctions of, 74–75, 76*f*
    Malinowski's influence on, 167
Hargreaves, A., 2
Harré, R., 119, 123, 143
Harris, R., 15, 20, 28, 33, 38, 99, 104*t*, 140
    as ecological linguist, 167–68, 168n1
Haugen, E., 43, 167, 182
Heath, S. B., 129
Hebb, D. O., 136
Heritage, J., 40, 204
Herrnstein, R., 127–28
Hippocrates, 58
Hocus Pocus (Vonnegut), 170
Hoekstra, T. W., 214
Hoffman, E., 128
homo docilis, 17
Hopper, P.
    restructuring v. emergent grammar of, 89,
        105, 105n8, 185

Hornberger, N. H.
  as ecological linguist, 167
  on policy and language ecology, 182–83, 192
Human rights, linguistic, 172–73, 191–92
Hymes, D., 74, 74n12

i+1. *See* Comprehensible input theory
Iconicity
  in language learning, 71–73
  related to layers of meaning, 71
  in semiosis, 63–68, 64*f*
Identity
  and self in learning process, 107–32
  self v., 124–28, 131–32
  and voice in curriculum, 163, 191
I-language, 38, 42. *See also* Competence
Improvable objects, 69, 73
Indexicality
  in language learning, 71–73
  in semiosis, 63–68, 64f

Jakobson, R., 33, 77
James, W., 61, 125
  Peirce v. pragmatism of, 126–27
Johnson, S., 80
Joyce, J., 44
Jurassic Park (Crichton), 195–96, 197

Kant, I., 135
Keller, R., 95
Kluckhohn, C., 183
Kohler, 16
Kozol, 33
Kozulin, A., 153
Kramsch, C., 14, 131
  on culture, 184–85
  on self in language learning, 122
Krashen, S., 15, 32
  comprehensible input theory of, 89–90, 146, 154–56, 155*t*, 198
  SLA hypotheses of, 136–40, 161
Kristeva, J., 57
Kroeber, A. L., 183
Kuhl, P., 81
Kuhn, T., 166–67

Labov, W., 83
Langdon, B., 81
Language. *See also* Academic language; Theories of language
  awareness of, 99*f*
  Bakhtin's dialogical perspective on, 8, 14, 16, 18
  dialect v., 38n7, 50, 178–80
  dialogical nature of, 16n8, 129–30
  in education, 1–3
  as emergent system, 84–85, 108
  iconicity of, 45, 45*t*
  meaning-as-use view of, 14, 63
  relationships between different, 50–52, 176–78, 181–83, 192
  relationships between environment and, 45–47, 47–50
  telementation view of, 28
  units of, 30*f*
  use/value, 185–86, 192
  Wittgenstein's philosophy of, 16, 128–29
Language education. *See also* Bilingual education; Critical language studies; English as a Second Language
  ecological approach to, 4–8, 133, 193
  and educational linguistics, 2
  of European immigrant children, 174–75, 192
  and language pyramid, 36
  Piaget's developmental stages in, 35
  as science of values, 6, 168n2, 192
Language learning. *See also* Second language acquisition
  acquisition hypothesis v., 138–39
  attention in, 98*f*
  conditions for, 120–22
  conditions for scaffolding in, 150–51
  consciousness in, 98–99, 98*f*, 122–24
  context of, 40–43
  deep ecology in, 170–81
  ecology of, 2, 14–17
  as emergence, 5, 198–99
  Halliday's language-based theory of, 102–4, 103*t*–104*t*
  Halliday's seven functions of, 75*f*
  interaction/conversation in, 143–45
  Neisser's selves v., 116–19, 118*t*
  pathways of, 133–63
  project-based, 158–59, 222
  prolepsis in, 133, 152–54
  scaffolding in, 147–52, 223–24
  semiosis in, 62–68, 71–73, 130
  semiotic resources mediate, 97
  symmetrical relationships in, 157–58
  use-learning dichotomy in, 223
  views on, 134–43
  voice in, 119–22, 128
  Vygotsky on, 134–35

ZPD in, 101, 133, 154–58, 158*f*
Language pyramid, 30*f*, 36
Langue, 34
   abstraction of language from context with, 42
   parole v., 34–35, 35*f*, 59
Lantolf, J., 14, 17, 25, 122
Lantolf, J. P., 15, 154
Larsen-Freeman, D., 105
   on chaos/complexity and language learning, 198–99
   grammaticalization v. grammaring of, 90
Lave, J., 154
Layder, D., 204
Learning How to Mean (Halliday), 74
Leontiev, A. N., 14, 122, 125
   activity model of, 203, 218
Lewin, K., 13, 16, 21, 66, 167, 212, 217
   ecological psychology of, 168
   EV in work of, 168–69, 191
   as pioneer of action research, 195
Lewin, R., 8
Life at the Edge of Chaos (Lewin, R.), 8
Linguicide, 51
Linguistics. *See also* Educational linguistics
   anthropology closely connected with, 166–67
   diversity, 45*t*, 50–52
   integrationist, 20, 28, 33
   Saussure's work in, 58–60
   as science, 33–37
   situated or contextualized, 20
   social semiotic, 20
   in theories of language, 33–37
Locke, J., 58
Long, M., 142
   on negotiation of meaning, 141
Lorenz, K., 33, 208
   on generalization, 202
Luria, 14, 125

MacIntyre, A., 143
Magnuson, P., 216–17
Makkai, A., 167
Malinowski, B., 73, 112
   Firth/Halliday influenced by, 167
Martin, J., 49
Maslow, A., 33
Maturana, H. R., 108, 122, 144
May, S., 176–77
McArthur, L. Z., 94
McCafferty, S.
McLaughlin, B., 90
McNeill
Mead, G. H., 14, 33, 61, 77, 131, 167
   Symbolic Interactionism of, 125–26, 130
Meaning
   dialogical nature of, 21
Medawar, Peter, 37
Mediation
   affordance and, 18, 96–102
   of communication by computers, 213, 218
   in perception, 16
   in SCT, 12–13, 96
   in Vygotsky's developmental method, 14*f*
Mendel, G., 33
Merleau-Ponty, M.
Merrell, F., 66
Microgenesis, 203, 203*t*
   in activity theory, 212
   interactional scaffolding in, 148–49
   Vygotskyan concept of, 95
Microgenetic realm. *See* Ontogenetic domain
Mill, J. S., 82, 126
Miller, H., 202
Mind and Nature: A Necessary Unity (Bateson), 169
Mind in Society (Vygotsky), 146
Minsky, M., 124
Montessori, M., 19, 33, 97, 159
Morris, C., 57, 61, 77
Mühlhäusler, P., 22, 47, 51, 182
Murray, C., 127–28

Naess, A.
   on deep ecology, 3, 170–72, 191
   on quality of life, 5–6
Nakagaki Toshiyuki, 80
The Native Speaker is Dead! (Paikeday), 31
Naven (Bateson), 169
Neisser, U., 21
   ecological self of, 107
   on self-knowledge, 115–19, 117*f*, 118*t*
   on study of cognition, 123
Newson, J., 94
Newton, I., 9, 33, 39
Nietzsche, F., 3, 200
   creation of the self and, 114–15
Norman, D. A., 94, 124
Norton Peirce, B., 67, 131
   on conditions of language learning, 120–22
   on voice in language learning, 128
Nystrand, M.

Occam's razor, 10

Ohta, A. S., 122
Ontogenetic domain, 12
  in Vygotsky's developmental method, 14*f*

Paikeday, Tom, 31
Papert, S., 124
Parole, 34
  langue v., 34–35, 35*f*, 59
Passmore, J., 10
Pasteur, L., 9, 33
Patterns
  rules/structures v. systems and, 5
  in SCT/ecology, 18
Pavlov, I., 165
Peirce, B. N. *See* Norton Peirce, B.
Peirce, C. S., 14, 16, 18, 22, 33, 39, 57, 58, 76, 79, 91, 93, 100, 110, 119, 123–24, 131, 145n4
  congruent theories of signs and, 63
  contributions to semiotics by, 61–71, 64*f*, 77
  dialogical perspective on self of, 125–27, 127n4
  James v. pragmatism of, 126–27
  sign structure of, 68–71, 68*f*, 73, 118*t*, 125–26, 130
Pennycook, A.
  on critical language studies, 189–91, 192
Perception
  ecological theory and perspective of, 14, 63, 221
  ecology of, 14
  felt immediacy of, 62
  mediation of, 16, 205
Performance, 34
  competence v., 34–35, 35*f*
  replaced by E-language, 42
Peter of Spain, 61n4
Phatic communion, 112
Phenotypes, 13n7
Phenotypic analysis
  genotypic analysis v., 13, 212–13
  in Vygotsky's developmental method, 14*f*, 212–13
Phillipson, R., 51
Philosophical Investigations (Wittgenstein), 124
Phonemic awareness
  in CELDT, 29
Phylogenetic domain, 12
  in Vygotsky's developmental method, 14*f*
Piaget, J., 15, 16, 35, 86, 86n4, 101, 146, 150
  genetic epistemology of, 165

ideal learning context of, 142, 144–45
scaffolding alignment with, 148
on symmetrical relationships and learning, 157
Pica, T., 141
Pienemann, M., 139
Pinker, S., 32, 55
  on language instinct, 136, 198
Positivism
  Durkheim influenced by, 34
  in evolution of science, 165
Poster, M., 114
Postman, N., 187
Pribram, K., 124
Price, H. H., 98
Prior/passing theory, 87–88, 87n5, 109, 129
Prolepsis
  in language learning, 133, 152–54, 162
  similarity of ZPD to, 154
  in ZPD, 147, 152–54
Proto-self, 107
The Psychology of Everyday Things (Norman), 94
Pullum, G., 46
Pythagoras, 9

Quality
  of educational experience, 12, 21
  EL and importance of, 5–6
  in SCT/ecology, 18

Rampton, B.
Rand, A., 126
Reduction
  complexity, 10–12, 38
  context, 9–10, 38
  data, 10, 38
Reductionism
  in theories of language, 23–24, 38–40, 199
Reed, E. S.
  on crises in psychology, 165–66, 166*t*
  on language education as science of values, 6, 192
Relations
  EL's view of language as, 4–5
  in SCT/ecology, 18
Robbins, T., 201
Rogoff, B., 20, 101
  learning contexts distinguished by, 142, 203
  prolepsis developed by, 152–53
Rommetveit, R., 62
  prolepsis developed by, 152

Rosch, E., 107, 119
Rosen, H., 206
Ross, G., 149–50
Rossi-Landi, F., 57
Rules
　patterns/systems v. structures and, 5
Russell, B., 73
Rutherford, Lord, 9, 33
Rutherford, W. E., 89–90, 105
Ruthroff, H., 107

Sacks, H., 41
Sacks, O., 100
Sapir, E., 33, 43, 48, 167
Sapir-Whorf hypothesis
　correctness of, 185
　EL and relationships in, 45*t*, 47–49
　pro-drop languages v., 48
Sartre, J. P., 44
　on authenticity, 115
Saussure, F. de, 34–35, 42, 45, 53, 57, 73, 74, 76, 125
　contributions to linguistics/semiotics by, 58–60, 77, 77n13
　Durkheim and, 34
Scaffolding, 147
　anticipation of, 147n6
　in educational software, 151–52, 151*f*
　essential characteristics in, 150
　language class conditions for use of, 150–51
　in language learning, 15, 133, 147–52, 162, 223–24
　in SCT, 148
　in SLA, 148
　in ZPD, 146–52, 151*f*
Schank, R., 124
Schiller, Johann von, 107
Schmidt, R., 100
Schutz, N., 167
Science. *See also* Social sciences
　in definition of semiotics, 55
　Descartes and development of, 9, 39, 165
　development of, 9, 165
　linguistics as, 33–37, 165
　reductionism in, 9–12, 38
　relationship of social sciences with, 9
　religion split from, 9
　revolutions in, 166–67
　Rutherford and place of physics in, 9, 34
　of values v. language education, 6, 168n2, 192
Scollon, R., 148

SCT. *See* Sociocultural theory
Sebeok, T., 57, 77
Second language acquisition (SLA)
　affective filter hypothesis of, 140
　affordance view of, 137*f*, 142–43
　comprehensible input theory/grammaticalization in, 89, 139
　input hypothesis of, 139–40
　input view of, 136–40, 137*f*
　Krashen's hypotheses of, 136–40, 198
　mediated by first language use, 222
　monitor hypothesis of, 140
　natural order hypothesis of, 139
　negotiation of meaning view of, 137*f*, 141–42
　relevance of chaos/complexity theory to, 196–99
　restructuring as process of, 89
　scaffolding in, 148
　SCT sources in, 14
　trigger view of, 136, 137*f*
　views of, 136–43, 137*f*
Self. *See also* Identity; Proto-self
　culture and notion of, 119
　development of, 114–22, 117*f*, 118*t*
　discursive construction of, 119
　ecological, 107, 118*t*, 121
　and identity in learning process, 21, 107–32
　identity v., 124–28, 131–32
　Neisser's theory of, 21
　perception of, 115
　private speech and mediation by, 12
　in Vygotsky's developmental method, 14*f*
Self-knowledge, 115–19, 117*f*, 118*t*
Semiology. *See* Semiotics
Semiosis. *See also* Engenderment
　dialogic cycle of, 113
　in language learning, 62–68, 71–73, 130
　sign relationships in, 113
　triadic system of signs and, 61, 68–73, 68*f*, 70*f*
Semiotics, 14, 55–57, 55–77, 58, 76–77, 223
　C. S. Peirce's, 16, 61–71, 102, 203*t*
　ecological worldview and theory of, 21
　ecology and, 55
　language relationships in, 76–77
　Saussure's definition of, 60
　ubiquity of signs in, 57–58
Shallow ecology. *See* Ecology
Sherwood, V., 147
Shotter, J., 94, 100, 119
Signs. *See also* Engenderment

affordance and use of, 18, 63n6, 95–96, 112–14
affordances and mediated, 96
decalogue of, 63–68, 64f, 71
in definition of semiotics, 55
dialogical nature of, 109–14, 114f, 127, 130
evolution of idea of, 58
general form of, 58
interpretations created from, 43, 58, 61, 110–14, 114f
linguistic, 110
meanings of, 58
mediation by, 12
Peirce, C. S., theory of, 61–71, 68f, 94
referents of, 58, 61
in Saussure's semiotics, 60
semiosis and relationships between, 113
semiotics and ubiquity of, 57–58
theory clarifying, 21
thought inseparable from, 110
triadic system of, 61, 61n4, 68–73, 68f, 70f, 109, 113
Skutnabb-Kangas, T., 51
on linguistic human rights, 172–73, 191
SLA. *See* Second language acquisition
Social sciences
ecology in, 8–12
qualitative v. quantitative approaches in, 10–12
standard scientific models v., 9
Socialization, 45t
Sociocultural theory (SCT), 12
approach expanded by Cole, 12
current state of, 16
ecology and, 12–22, 50
ecology compared to, 17–20
future application of, 17
Leontiev and, 14
Luria's work in, 14
mediation in, 12–13, 96
past perspectives on, 15–16
scaffolding in, 148
SCT approach expanded by, 12
socio-cultural-historical approach to, 12
various approaches to, 12
Sociolinguistics
EL and relationships in, 45t, 49–50
v. Chomsky, 167–68, 168n1
Soft-Systems Methodology (SSM), 214–18, 215f–216f
illustration of, 216–17
Sperber, D., 95

Spinoza, B., 123, 205
SSM. *See* Soft-Systems Methodology
Stenhouse, L., 62
Steps to an Ecology of Mind (Bateson), 169
Structures
patterns/systems v. rules and, 5
Sullivan, P. N., 145, 222
Swain, M.
on output and language learning, 141
pushed output of, 157
Symbolicity
in language learning, 71–73
in semiosis, 63–68, 64f
Symbols
EL view of emergence from tools, 5
Systems
rules/structures v. patterns and, 5
in SCT/ecology, 18
Systems theory
cybernetics in, 213
deep ecology linked to, 4
in ecological research, 213–18
implementing change and, 217
revived by chaos/complexity theory, 214

Terralingua
as counterpart to deep ecology, 170–72, 191
principles of, 172
Thatcher, M., 51
Theories of language, 23–53
componential assumption in, 26t, 29–30, 30f
computational assumption in, 26t, 27–28
context in, 24–25
contradictions between, 40
correctness assumption in, 26t, 30–31
ecological v. generative or abstract, 24
either-or assumption in, 26t, 28–29
EL in, 42–53
implicit, 25
linguistics in, 33–37
separateness assumption in, 26t, 32
storage assumption in, 26t, 28
teaching practices and assumptions about, 25–32, 26t
warring languages assumption in, 26t, 31–32
Thinking and Speech (Vygotsky), 146, 146n5
Thompson, E., 107
Thorne, S. L., 17, 25
phenotypic v. genotypic analysis by, 213, 218

prolepsis developed by, 152
Thought and Language (Vygotsky), 134, 146n5
Tinbergen, N., 208
Tomlin, L., 25
Toulmin, S., 122–23
Trevarthen, C., 65, 72, 131
   implicit other argued by, 144
Trim, J. L. M., 43, 167
Tudge, J., 154
Turner, J., 202–3

Valsiner, J., 17
Value
   in language use, 185–86, 192
   in Saussure's semiology, 60
   in SCT/ecology, 19
van Dam, J., 145
van der Veer, R., 17
van Manen, M., 115, 206
Varela, F. J., 107, 108, 122, 144
Variability
   in EL, 6–7
   "no child left behind" v., 11–12
   in SCT/ecology, 19, 21
Vico, 123, 127n4
Voegelin, Carl, 167
Voegelin, Frances, 167
Voice
   critical language studies and student, 189
   and identity in curriculum, 163, 191
   in language learning, 119–22, 128
   Language use and developing, 128–30
   ZPD's support for, 156
Volosinov, V. N., 111, 113, 117, 130
von Bertalanffy, L., 213
von Humboldt, W., 18, 86, 157
Vonnegut, Kurt, Jr., 170
Vygotsky, L. S., 16n8, 33, 36, 57, 58, 67n9, 75, 79n1, 86, 86n4, 101, 102, 104t, 112, 150, 159, 167, 199, 217
   on consciousness, 122–24
   on conversation, 143
   depth approach used by, 13
   developmental method of, 13, 14f, 63, 66, 82
   dialogic perspective on self of, 125
   ecology and, 17–20
   influences on, 16
   internalization of, 133
   intersection of mediation with theory of, 12–15, 96
   on language learning, 134–35, 142, 157
   on natural v. normative language, 160–61
   Neisser's theory of self v., 116
   on prolepsis, 153
   scaffolding alignment with, 148, 148n7
   SCT debt to, 14–16, 165
   ZPD of, 141, 145–47, 154, 156–57, 158f, 162

Wacquant, L., 66
Warschauer, M., 188
Weinreich, Max, 38n7
Wells, G.
   on ZPD in different contexts, 146
Wenger, E.
   legitimate peripheral participation of, 154
Werker, J., 81
Werner, H., 89n6
Wertsch, J. V.
   SCT and, 14
Whitehead, A. N., 138, 139, 159, 223
Whorf, B., 43, 48, 167
Wiener, N., 213
Wiley, N.
   on self v. identity, 124–26, 131
William of Occam, 9
Wilson, D., 95
Winnips, J. C., 151–52, 151f
Wittgenstein, L., 11, 73, 75, 90, 123, 145n4, 147n6
   on consciousness, 123–24
   on conversation, 143
   and theory of language as use, 14, 15, 16, 25n1, 33, 40, 63, 129, 129n6
Wood, D., 147, 149–50
Wordsworth, William, 33, 34
Wortham, S., 145
Wundt, W., 33, 124, 165

Zone of proximal development (ZPD)
   applied to different contexts, 146
   controversies regarding, 146
   in language learning, 133, 145–47, 146n5, 154–58, 158f
   peer interaction v., 101
   prolepsis in, 147, 152–54
   proximal processes in, 156–57
   scaffolding in, 146–52, 151f, 162, 202
   similarity of prolepsis to, 154
   v. comprehensible input theory, 154–56, 155t
   Vygotsky's extension of, 15, 148
ZPD. *See* Zone of proximal development

EDUCATIONAL LINGUISTICS

1. J. Leather and J. van Dam (eds.): *Ecology of Language Acquisition.* 2003   ISBN 1-4020-1017-6
2. P. Kalaja and A.M. Ferreira Barcelos (eds.): *Beliefs about SLA. New Research Approaches.* 2003   ISBN 1-4020-1785-5
3. L. van Lier: *The Ecology and Semiotics of Language Learning: A Sociocultural Perspective.* 2004   ISBN 1-4020-7904-4

KLUWER ACADEMIC PUBLISHERS
BOSTON / DORDRECHT / NEW YORK / LONDON

1400927R0

Printed in Great Britain by
Amazon.co.uk, Ltd.,
Marston Gate.